Nitaawichige

selected poetry and prose
by four Anishinaabe writers

Poetry Harbor Publications

Nitaawichige
(nee-tao-wih'-che-gay)
"To do something skillfully"

$ 22.95 US

ISBN: 1-886895-28-7

Poetry Harbor
P.O. Box 103
Duluth MN 55801-0103
www.poetryharbor.com
Cover photo by Vaughn Sweet-Panek

Acknowledgements:
Marcie R. Rendon: Futures, Rising Dawn, Every Woman Has A Story, The Runner Magazine, The Colour of Resistance, Eye of the Storm Theater, Speaking in Tongues, Neighborhood SafeArt Project, and Patrick's Cabaret.

This book was made possible, in part, by a grant from the Arrowhead Regional Arts Council through an appropriation from the Minnesota State Legislature; and by Poetry Harbor Members.

Table of Contents

my own grandmothers
have no names
their heroic actions
erased from history's page

In their first 400 years on this continent, the "others" attempted to either eliminate us or to subjugate us. When that didn't work, they tried denial -- denial of our existence. Although we surely continued to be, we were obliterated from their daily presence. To successfully deny our presence; our faces, images, thoughts, creative works had to be censored. We were kept in their mindset as "vanished peoples." Or as workers, not creators. And what does this erasing of individual identity do to us? Can you believe you exist if you look in a mirror and see no reflection? And what happens when one group controls the mirror market? As Native people, we have known that in order to survive we had to create, re-create, produce, re-produce. The effect of the denial of our existence is that many of us have become invisible. The systematic disruption of our families by the removal of our children was effective for silencing our voices. However, not everyone can still that desire, that up-welling inside that says sing, write, draw, move, be. We can sing our hearts out, tell our stories, paint our visions. We are in a position to create a more human reality. In order to live we have to make our own mirrors.

-- Marcie R. Rendon

JIM

NORTHRUP

Shinnob Jep

CAST:
Al Treebark, the host of the game show from the Fond du Lac Reservation. He wears a sport coat made from camouflage material called Treebark. His necktie is made from red headband material.

Franklin Lake, a contestant on the show who wears his hair in long braids, has a cowboy hat with mirror sunglasses, an AIM tee shirt, black leather vest, skinny leg Levis and cowboy boots. He has a huge beaded watchband and a drum stick hanging out of his pocket.

Tradish Ikwe, a contestant on the show who lives with the seasons on the Fond du Lac Reservation. She wears her hair in a single braid with a quill hair tie. She is wearing a ribbon shirt, ribbon skirt, dreamcatcher earrings and white tennis shoes, no laces.

John Johnson, Jr, a contestant on the show who was adopted out. He has TV anchor-styled hair, a blue blazer, grey turtleneck and slacks, shiny tassel loafers.

SETTING:
The stage contains a folding Bingo table. It is covered with a tablecloth that has Ojibwe floral beaded design stencils around the edge. On the table are three podiums with major hotel logos: Holiday Inn, Radisson, and Motel 6. Each podium has a microphone.

The host has a stand-alone podium with a hotel logo. It has a microphone and is decorated with the same stenciled beadwork designs.

There are three green pow wow toilets used as a "green room" for contestants.

There is a stand-alone chalkboard that is used to list the categories and dollar amounts.

Behind everything is a large stretched hide tied to a log frame. SHINNOB JEP is painted in the center with stenciled beadwork designs around the edge.

As the audience enters they see a dimly lit set and hear singers and a drum. It is a pow wow song, a 49 song. As the lights come up, the singers and drum fade. The announcer walks in from the back of the audience seats, greeting the crowd. When he gets to the stage he turns and says, "Biindigen! Come in. Welcome to Shinnob Jep, the show that tests your knowledge on being a Shinnob. We didn't make our casino connection yet so we're still a low-budget show. Here is your host, Alllllll Treeeeeeebark."

The announcer now becomes Al as he walks around the podium, taking off one headband and putting on another that is hanging on the podium.

AL: (Now facing the audience) Boozhoo, boozhoo. Good to see you here today. Are there any of my relatives here? (Hand shading eyes so he can see the audience, sees a relative and waves) Ever wonder how these contestants for Shinnob Jep are picked? Nepotism, pure nepotism. What good is nepotism if you can't nepet? I picked these people to take part. I am always looking for contestants for the show.

Remember that blackjack dealer that was here last time? How about if we get a tribal politician next time? Yup, always looking for contestants. Well, let's play Shinnob Jep. Our first contestant comes to us from the mean streets of Minneapolis. He is enrolled at White Earth and spends his time at the Peacemaker Center making war on racism. Help me welcome Franklin Lake to Shinnob Jep! (Tucks microphone under arm and leads applause.)

FRANKLIN: (Comes out of the pow wow toilet zipping up, pulls out his drumstick to wave to the crowd.) Boozhoo, brother. I knew I could make it up here. I was just telling Vern and Clyde about this show. (Gives the audience a clenched fist salute. The drums make a welcoming sound like at a pow wow, drum applause...)

AL: Our next contestant is from the Fond du Lac Reservation where she makes syrup in the spring, dances at pow wows all summer, goes ricing every fall, and does beadwork all winter. Welcome Tradish Ikwe to Shinnob Jep! (The drums make a welcoming sound, drum applause.)

TRADISH: (Comes out of her pow wow toilet and walks directly to the podium, waving at relatives and friends on both sides of the crowd, then nods at Al.) Boozhoo, Al. Good to see you again. How is your ma and dad?

AL: They're good. Our parents went to boarding school together. Last time I saw you was at that pow wow in Bena, wasn't it?

TRADISH: (Cupping a giggle) Yah, you were there with that blonde woman with the big, I mean really big...cameras.

AL: (Mumbling to the podium) I remember, I was helping her with a research project.

TRADISH: Oh, is that what they call it nowadays?

AL: (Trying to silence Tradish using just his eyes, fails) Daga Bizaan. Let's move on. Our next contestant comes to us from Edina, Minnesota. He is an engineer at Control Data. He just learned that he was adopted by a white couple. He is in the process of enrolling at Leech Lake and finding his real family. Welcome John Johnson, Jr. to Shinnob Jep! (The drum is tapped softly three times. Tradish and Franklin switch name plates so John isn't standing between them because he looks like a Chimook. John sees it; Al doesn't.)

JOHN: Hello, Al. I mean, Boozhoo. I hope I do well on your show.

AL: I hope so, too. We all know how the game is played. Unlike TV's Jeopardy! which does it backwards, here we ask the questions, you give the answers. There is one daily double in this round. Here are the categories in the first round of Shinnob Jep. (Al points to each category on the chalkboard.) Ricing, Pow Wows, Tribal Councils, Higher Education, Casinos and Gambling, and Race Relations. John, you lost the toss, you have to go first. Pick a category.

JOHN: I'd like Higher Education for one dollar, Al.

AL: Here's the question. What is the first fiction-writing course taken by students?

JOHN: The Financial Aid forms.

AL: That's right for a dollar. Your choice for categories.

JOHN: Higher Education for two dollars, Al.

AL: Okay, why go to summer school?

FRANKLIN: Financial Aid all year 'round.

AL: Correct for two bucks. Pick a category, Franklin.

FRANKLIN: I'd like Race Relations for five dollars, Al.

AL: For five dollars in Race Relations, who invented deodorant because they needed to?

JOHN: The BIA?

AL: Wrong, you're in the hole for four dollars. Who invented deodorant?

FRANKLIN: The white man.

AL: That's right for five. Pick again.

FRANKLIN: Tribal Councils for three.

AL: The question for three dollars in Tribal Councils is, when do the dead come to life?

TRADISH: Just before the election.

AL: Right, the dead come to life long enough to vote. That's three dollars for Tradish. Your turn to choose.

TRADISH: I'd like Ricing for four hundred, oops, I mean four dollars, Al.

AL: Here's the question. What does milky rice mean?

TRADISH: It means you're ricing too early. Jeez, I thought everyone knew that.

AL: Right again, every year some clown sets the opening of the ricing season too early. Pick a category.

TRADISH: Race Relations for three dollars.

AL: For three dollars in Race Relations, respond to the following statement: My grandmother was a Cherokee Princess.

TRADISH: Yah, right.

AL: That's wrong. Anyone else?

JOHN: Oh, that's nice.

AL: Correct for three dollars. You now have four. Pick again.

JOHN: I'd like Race Relations for four, please.

AL: In Race Relations for four, respond to the following statement: My grandmother was a REAL Cherokee Princess.

JOHN: Oh, that's nice.

AL: Incorrect, you're back to zero. Anyone else want to

respond to: My grandmother was a REAL Cherokee Princess?

FRANKLIN: Who gives a fuck?

AL: "Who gives a fuck" is the right response to: My grandmother was a REAL Cherokee Princess. Your turn.

FRANKLIN: Bekaa, am I supposed to use that F word on your program?

AL: Sure, we'll just pretend this is satellite TV or cable. Still your turn.

FRANKLIN: Pow Wows for five, Al.

AL: Okay, for five, what is the difference between a contest and a traditional pow wow?

FRANKLIN: About a thousand bucks for first place.

AL: Wrong, although we'll check. Nope, the judges say it might be true of some contest pow wows but not at all of them. Anyone else want to try? What's the difference between a contest and a traditional pow wow?

TRADISH: One is for the money and one is for the people.

AL: Right for five bucks, pick again.

TRADISH: I'll try Ricing for five, Al.

AL: In the category for Ricing, what can you use if you don't have a cast iron parching kettle?

TRADISH: Your neighbor's kettle or a galvanized tub.

AL: Correct. Your turn to pick again, Tradish.

TRADISH: Give me Casinos and Gambling for two dollars.

AL: I was betting we'd never get to this category. Okay, for two dollars, what is a good gambling tip?

JOHN: Gas up the car before you get to the casino.

AL: Right. Give that man a roll of nickels. Pick again, John.

JOHN: Casinos and Gambling for three dollars.

AL: For three dollars, what is the player's responsibility at the casino?

FRANKLIN: To get as much money as possible.

AL: Hai', wrong, although it is a nice wish. Anyone else?

TRADISH: To move the coins from one slot machine to another.

AL: That's right for three dollars.

TRADISH: Let's have Race Relations for two.

AL: The question is, why don't the Chimooks understand the Shinnobs?

TRADISH: They haven't been here long enough.

AL: Sad but true. What has it been, only 500 years? Your turn Tradish.

TRADISH: Casinos and Gambling for four dollars, please.

AL: Okay, for two rolls of nickels, what are the odds you'll meet someone you owe money to at the casino?

FRANKLIN: Even money. I know, it happens to me all the time.

AL: Correct for four dollars. Your turn again right after these commercial messages. We got to pay the bills so we can keep playing Shinnob Jep. Want to help me, Tradish? C'mon, it's easy. Hey gamblers, having trouble getting to the casino? Maybe your car was repossessed in a dispute over the payment plan. Maybe your lawyer says to wait before you try driving again. Whatever the problem, War Pony Tours is the solution. We can make the circuit of Minnesota Casinos quicker and better than anyone. One hour stops at the following casinos: Black Bear, Firefly Creek, Fond du Luth, Fortune Bay, Grand and Grand Again, Grand Portage, Jackpot Junction, Lake of the Woods, Little Six, Mystic Lake, Red Lake, River Road, Shooting Star, Treasure Island, and White Oak. We have other rez cars strategically placed so you can continue the trip when the first car dies. Wake up any driver from War Pony Tours for the death of your life. Have your kids been taken away by the county, again? Have you set the state record for DWI arrests, again? Holdem, Robbem, and Leavem can help. We've been helping Shinnobs since we found out they can pay their legal bills. Get one of our Get out of Jail Free cards. Call today for an appointment. Call 1-800-SHYSTER. Holdem, Robbem, and Leavem is an equal opportunity exploiter since 1999.

Holdem, Robbem, and Leavem is here to help.

FRANKLIN: I'll try Tribal Councils for four dollars.

AL: For four dollars, why don't incumbents get 100% of the vote?

FRANKLIN: It costs too much to buy that many votes.

AL: Correct, it just costs too much. Pick again.

FRANKLIN: I'd like Higher Education for three dollars.

AL: Okay, in that category, how long does it take to get a four-year degree?

JOHN: Four years?

AL: Wrong. Anyone else know how long it takes to get a four-year degree?

TRADISH: Six to twelve years.

AL: Absolutely right. Another category?

TRADISH: I'll try Ricing for three dollars.

AL: Ricing for three is a Daily Double. You can risk up to twenty bucks. This is an audio Daily Double.

TRADISH: Shoot the works. I'll try twenty.

AL: For twenty bucks, identify the following song. (A drum, then the sound of the AIM song is heard. Franklin whips out his drumstick and begins to sing along. Tradish is nodding her head in time to the drum. John just looks confused.) Do you have an answer, Tradish?

TRADISH: Eya', that's the AIM song.

AL: Right again, pick a category.

TRADISH: Give me Higher Education for four dollars, Al.

AL: Okay, for four dollars, what is better than a computer for studying?

JOHN: A really smart room mate.

AL: Right. I used to have one. Your turn.

JOHN: Tribal Councils for five dollars, Al.

AL: For five, how many relatives of the Tribal Council does it take to cut the grass?

TRADISH: Two or three.

AL: Gaawiin, anyone else want to try? How many relatives of the Tribal Council does it take to cut the grass?

JOHN: All of them.

AL: Eya', it takes all of the relatives to cut the grass. Next category, please.

JOHN: I'd like Tribal Councils for two bucks.

AL: What is Plan B to ensure the outcome of the election?

JOHN: Election Boards appointed by the Tribal Councils.

AL: That's right for two bucks. Give that man another roll of nickels. Another category?

JOHN: I want Casinos and Gambling for five, Al.

AL: How do you start a fight in a casino?

JOHN: Sit next to a non-smoker.

AL: Correct, just sit next to a non-smoker. Your turn.

JOHN: Higher Education for five, Al.

AL: What's better, a grant or a loan for college?

JOHN: A grant. At least that's what worked for me.

AL: Right you are. Pick again, please.

JOHN: Race Relations for a dollar, Al.

AL: The last question in Race Relations is, do you mind if I ask what ah tribe, ah band, ah group you belong to?

TRADISH: No.

AL: Incorrect, a good answer but not the one we're looking for. Anyone? Do you mind if I ask what ah tribe, ah band, ah group you belong to?

JOHN: Yes, I do mind.

AL: Correct for one dollar. Pick again.

JOHN: I'd like Pow Wows for four dollars, please.

AL: In that category, name four things that contribute to a good pow wow.

JOHN: Good dancers, good drums, a lot of giveaways, and honor songs.

AL: Good answer but not the one we're looking for. Anyone else?

FRANKLIN: Good water, good food stands, a quiet place to camp, and freshly pumped pow wow toilets.

AL: Close enough. Your turn, Franklin.

FRANKLIN: Ho wah! I'll try pow wows for three, Al.

AL: Okay, for three bucks, who comes after the traditional men dancers at most grand entries?

FRANKLIN: The grass dancers.

AL: Keereckt for three. Pick again.

FRANKLIN: Give me Tribal Councils for one dollar, Al.

AL: You can't buy a Tribal Council for one dollar. It takes much more than that. Seriously, for one dollar in that category, who gave us Tribal Councils?

JOHN: The federal government.

AL: Right, the 1934 Indian Reorganization Act. Your turn to choose.

JOHN: Casinos and Gambling for one dollar.

AL: For one dollar, should you hate someone who wins on a slot machine you just left?

JOHN: No, it's never right to hate someone.

AL: Gaawiin, haven't played the slot machines much, have you? That'll cost you a dollar. Does anyone else want to try? Should you hate someone who wins on a slot machine you just left?

FRANKLIN: Eya', for a little while anyway.

AL: Correctemundo. Give that man a half roll of nickels. Okay, before we get started on Shinnob Double Jep, let's chat with the contestants and recap the scores. Tradish is leading with thirty-six dollars; John is second with twenty dollars; and Franklin is sucking hind tit with fourteen bucks. Franklin, on your card it says you're enrolled at White Earth. Tell us an election story.

FRANKLIN: An election story, eh? Well, one time my cousin and I were guarding the cemetery but the dead got by us and voted the same dictator into office again. I like voting. Last election I voted sixteen times. My cousin was greedier and voted twenty-three times. At a hundred bucks a vote, we both made money on that election. I like getting Ben Franklins for Franklin during elections.

AL: Thank you for sharing that with us but shouldn't you be telling that story to the Inspector General of the Interior Department?

FRANKLIN: I already did. They interviewed me several times and I may get called to testify in federal court.

Al: Thanks, we'll be looking for you in the newspapers. John, your card says that you just found out that you were once a Shinnob, but were raised white. Did that make it hard for you?

JOHN: Sometimes. Now I understand why I wanted to choke my sister's rabbit. It wasn't violence, it was hereditary. I never got sunburnt like the rest of the family either. In the family photo album, I stick out like a blueberry in a glass of milk. I'm looking to find what was taken from me. I'm taking day courses in Indian Studies and night courses in the language. I'll visit my adopted parents but will connect with my real family.

AL: That's great, John. Glad to have you back with us. Tradish, on your card under marital status it says unremarried. Does that mean we can try again?

TRADISH: Nah, you had your chance. Where is your blonde with the big cameras?

AL: I ended before the project did. We don't see each other anymore. Enough about her, what are you doing this weekend?

TRADISH: I'll be washing my hare, my snowshoe hare. Seriously, what did you have in mind for the weekend? I might be around.

AL: Well Rabbit Choker, they have bingo at the Black Bear Casino. Want to join me? They gave me some packages for mentioning their name on the show. You still like bingo, don't you?

TRADISH: Yah, I like bingo at the Black Bear. I can join you there Friday night, Saturday afternoon and evening, Sunday afternoon and evening.

FRANKLIN: Hey, this is Shinnob Jep, not The Dating Game. Aaniin dina?

AL: Gaawiin gegoo. Now that we got that squared away, let's go back to the game. The categories in this round are: U.S. History, Trick or Treaties, Trick or Treatment, Body Language, Sugar Bush, and Rez Cars. Franklin, you gave me the last correct answer so it's your turn again. Pick one.

FRANKLIN: I'll try U.S. History for one dollar, Al.

AL: For one dollar, who defeated General George Armstrong Custer at the Battle of the Little Big Horn?

FRANKLIN: That's an easy one, Crazy Horse, a Lakota.

AL: That's right. Pick again.

FRANKLIN: Give me Rez Cars for a dollar.

AL: Here we go. Who never drove a Rez Car?

FRANKLIN: Crazy Horse, a Lakota.

AL: Correct, your turn again.

FRANKLIN: I'd like Trick or Treatment for a buck.

AL: For one dollar, Who never went to treatment?

FRANKLIN: Crazy Horse, a Lakota.

AL: Boy, you really know these subjects, don't you? Go ahead, pick another one.

FRANKLIN: I want Trick or Treaties for a dollar.

AL: Name a famous Indian who fought during treaty signing times.

FRANKLIN: This is too easy, Crazy Horse, a Lakota.

AL: Once again, that is the answer we were looking for. It's still your turn, Franklin.

FRANKLIN: Give me Rez Cars for two dollars.

AL: For two bucks, what is the payment plan for a rez car?

FRANKLIN: Everything down and nothing a month for the life of the car.

AL: Are you going to let anyone else play? But speaking of a payment plan, I have to take another commercial break here. (Tradish comes over without being asked to help with the commercials. John goes to his green room. Tradish holds up the Niiwin placard while Al reads from a card.) Got a big giveaway coming up? Talk to Niiwin from Niiwin's Tipi Poles.

He makes balsam and tamarack poles for tipis. They are handmade up to forty foot in length, and are smooth as a politician's promise. Niiwin likes bartering so he'll trade poles for damn near anything: money, wild rice, money, traditional dance regalia, money, bingo packages, money. He has rentals and loaners. Tipi poles do make an ideal gift for those relatives who get gambling per capita, and have everything. When you need something to hold all that canvas up, try Niiwin's Tipi Poles. Remember, our poles are biodegradable and will not harm the environment. (A toilet flushing noise is heard. John comes out and returns to his podium. Al holds up the Boogid placard as Tradish reads the next commercial.)

TRADISH: Have the kids been playing sword fighter with your knockers again? Has your old pole seen one too many seasons? Boogid's Wild Rice Tools is the answer. We're always ready for ricing because we make professional grade tools at mud-bottom prices. At Boogid's we use straight-grain white cedar for the knockers and measure them to fit. Our spruce/diamond willow poles can be used to push a Lake Superior ore boat. At Boogid's we make ricing tools your grandchildren will fight over. As my grandpa used to say, ricing is never more than eleven months away.

AL: Go ahead, Franklin. It's still your turn.

FRANKLIN: I'm on a roll here...Rez Cars for three, please.

AL: Will a Chevy wheel fit on a Ford car?

FRANKLIN: No, it will not.

AL: Hay', wrong answer. Anyone else want to try? Will a Chevy wheel fit a Ford car?

TRADISH: I suppose, if your hammer is big enough.

AL: Eya', Tradish, pick your category.

TRADISH: Rez Cars for four dollars, Al.

AL: In that category, what do you use to replace a broken radio antenna?

TRADISH: A wire coat hanger.

AL: Good answer, your turn again.

TRADISH: U.S. History for two, please.

AL: For two dollars, who invented the BIA?

FRANKLIN: Someone who was really mad at us.

AL: Right, your turn to choose.

FRANKLIN: We haven't done Body Language yet. I'll try that one for two bucks.

AL: Demonstrate someone giving directions. How would you say, "That way, around the corner to the right?"

TRADISH: Like this. (Her lips and chin pointing straight ahead, then lips turning to the right)

AL: That's right. You could get a job as a tour guide or at a ricing booth. Your turn.

TRADISH: I'll try Trick or Treatment for two dollars, Al.

AL: Here's the question. Why go to treatment?

FRANKLIN: Job security for my cousin, Wiinug, the counselor.

AL: We'll accept that. Choose again.

FRANKLIN: Trick or Treaties for three, Al.

AL: Okay. How can we improve the treaty making process?

JOHN: We write them in our language, then tell the President what it says after he signs it.

FRANKLIN: Ho wah, good answer niij.

AL: That's right. I wish we could have done that with all of them. Pick again, John.

JOHN: Trick or Treatment for three.

AL: In that category, what is the thirteenth AA step?

JOHN: To quit bragging about the previous twelve steps.

AL: Correct. Your turn to choose.

JOHN: I'd like U.S. History for three dollars.

AL: Okay, for three bucks in U.S. History, who did you cheer for during the Civil War?

FRANKLIN: Both sides.

AL: Right again. Your category, please.

FRANKLIN: U.S. History for four bucks.

AL: For four bucks, who invented canoes?

FRANKLIN: We did. Ho wah, nitaawichige.

AL: That's a good answer. Pick another one.

FRANKLIN: Trick or Treaties for two frog skins.

AL: How long does the grass grow and the river flow?

FRANKLIN: Until the white man needs the land and water.

AL: Eya', that's right. Your turn to choose.

FRANKLIN: That was a good one. Trick or Treaties for four, please.

AL: That's one of the two Daily Doubles. You have thirty-two dollars. You can wager the entire amount, if you like.

FRANKLIN: Do it all. We didn't come in here half-stepping.

AL: Okay, the category this time is Commods Spanish. Provide the English translation: "Degermed harina de maize."

FRANKLIN: The answer is enriched yellow corn meal.

AL: Eya', that's correct. You now have sixty-four dollars. Pick again.

FRANKLIN: We haven't tried Sugar Bush. Give me that one for a dollar, please.

AL: For one dollar, how did you know he was new at the Sugar Bush?

JOHN: He was tapping a basswood tree.

AL: Eya', your pick.

JOHN: Sugar Bush for two.

AL: In that category, how did you know he was new at the Sugar Bush?

JOHN: He kept looking for a bush made of sugar.

AL: Eya', pick again.

JOHN: Sugar Bush for three, please.

AL: For three bucks, how did you know he was new at the Sugar Bush?

JOHN: He kept saying, "Why do you do this? You can buy syrup at the store."

AL: Eya', we like that answer. Try again.

JOHN: I like this category. Four dollars in Sugar Bush.

AL: Okay, the question this time is, how did you know he was new at the Sugar Bush?

JOHN: He burnt himself while playing with the fire.

AL: Eya', how do you know these things? I thought you were from Edina and worked at Control Data?

JOHN: I am from Edina but I went to the Sugar Bush for the first time this year and I made all those mistakes. Can I have the last question in that category?

AL: Okay. For five bucks, how did you know he was new at the Sugar Bush?

JOHN: He went home before noon.

AL: Eya', that's right. You cleaned up in this category. Pick another.

JOHN: I'll try Body Language for three, please.

AL: For three bucks, how did you know she was mad at him?

FRANKLIN: She was staring daggers and making fists at him with her hands in her pockets.

AL: That's right, Franklin. I thought you went to sleep over there. Glad to see you back in the game. Okay, your turn to choose a category.

FRANKLIN: Trick or Treatment for four, Al.

AL: The question is, quote the source: "He was taking my inventory."

TRADISH: That's from AA's fourth step, Al.

AL: Eya', absolutely right, way to go. Your turn, Tradish.

TRADISH: I'd like Trick or Treaties for five, Al.

AL: That is the other Daily Double. You have forty-two dollars. You can risk the entire amount.

TRADISH: Nah. Since I was eighteen when we first went out, I'll bet eighteen dollars.

AL: Now that is a good reason. The category is Commods Spanish. Provide the English translation for, "Jarabe de maiz."

TRADISH: Easy beans, that's corn syrup.

AL: Right again. You're really smart. You're now tied with Franklin at sixty-four dollars. Pick again, we have a few questions left.

FRANKLIN: Still trying to snag, Al?

AL: Maybe a little bit. Pick me. I mean, pick a category, Tradish.

TRADISH: U.S. History for five, you old rat hide.

AL: I didn't think you cared enough to call me a rat hide. Thanks. Oh yah, we're in the middle of a game here. For five bucks in U.S. History, say one swear word.

JOHN: Manifest Destiny.

AL: Correct. Your turn, John.

JOHN: I'd like Rez Cars for five, Al.

AL: Here we go. Tell me a rez car story.

JOHN: I'm at a little bit of a handicap here because I drive a Volvo station wagon, the 340 DL model, but I heard one last week. Let's see if I got this right...I knocked a hole in one of the pistons and every time I cranked it, the dipstick would come shooting out of the engine. It was fun until the dipstick hit a Highway Patrolman's car.

AL: Wow, not bad, told just like the owner of a rez car. We'll give you five bucks for that story. Pick again.

JOHN: Body Language for five.

AL: Demonstrate one way Shinnobs greet each other in a crowd.

JOHN: I saw two Shinnobs doing this yesterday at the Mall of America. (Makes eye contact with Al, then tilts his head back and forth a half inch.)

AL: Close enough. I'd nod back at you. That answer is good for five bucks. It's still your turn.

JOHN: Trick or Treaties for four, Al.

AL: All right. Who owns the rights guaranteed in the treaties?

JOHN: Not the tribal governments, but the generations of Anishinaabe to come, the ones not born yet.

AL: Great answer. I want to give you four dollars of my own money for that answer.

TRADISH: I'll chip in three myself.

FRANKLIN: Me, too. Here's my three bucks.

AL: All right, that leaves both of you with sixty-four dollars. John, you now have sixty-one bucks. We're running out of time here. Pick a question.

JOHN: I'd like Body Language for three, please.

AL: Demonstrate the stroke used to knock wild rice.

JOHN: I saw this in one of the movies at the university. (Reaches out for rice with his left hand, then strokes the rice with his right hand which then reaches out for the rice which is stroked twice. He repeats until stopped by Al.)

AL: Bekaa, bekaa. Are you sure you haven't been ricing before? It looks like you were on your way to half a sack, at least. That brings your total to sixty-four dollars. That's the end of this round. We have the Shinnob Final Jep question in this category, Commods Spanish. Write down your wagers and answers for this question. Ready? Translate this into English: "Leche instantanea en polvo sin grasa." (Tradish and Franklin write down their wagers and answers to the question. They both show their answers to John who then writes his answer.)

AL: Time's up. John, show us your answer.

JOHN: I wrote down "Instant Non-fat Dry Milk" and

wagered it all.

AL: That gives you one hundred and twenty-eight dollars. Franklin, show us your answer and the amount you wagered.

FRANKLIN: I did the same thing as he did. I bet it all. Here is my answer. (Holds up a paper showing the words "Instant Non-fat Dry Milk.") Ho wah!

AL: You're tied with John at one hundred and twenty-eight dollars. Tradish, don't tell me you did the same thing, too.

TRADISH: Sure, that was an easy one because I use it all the time in my fry bread. I bet sixty-four dollars, too. (Shows her wager and answer that says "Instant Non-fat Dry Milk.")

AL: It looks like we have a tie game here. Nobody loses, you're all winners. Thank you for playing our game. Thank you all for coming to Shinnob Jep. Mii gwech. Tradish, can I have your phone number?

TRADISH: Sure, bekaa. (She takes a piece of birchbark out of her pocket, folds it, bites it, looks at it, refolds it and bites it again. When she is done, she hands her phone number to Al.)

FRANKLIN: Hey, John, we're starting a new drum group at the Peacemaker Center. Want to join us and learn how to sing? Maybe we can hit a few pow wows this summer.

JOHN: That'd be great. Here is my card with all my numbers: home, office, beeper, fax, and my email address. Will we see you there, Tradish?

TRADISH: Maybe. Why don't you stop by the house next fall. We can show you how to make rice, you know, finish it the old time way. (Gives Al the nod, the nod that means let's get away from all these people so we can talk alone.)

AL: I've never seen a three-way tie before. I wonder why it happened?

JOHN: Maybe when we share information and wisdom, we all win.

Mii sa iw

Jim Northrup

Photo © Cheryl Walsh Bellville

MARCIE

R.

RENDON

a common misconception

a common misconception
is the assumption
that god
created
flowers on a
higher
plane
than
dirt

or say...
tornados

my mother
never rode on
horses
she ran
with
mustangs

one time
a
tornado
touched
down
saw her
and
retreated
back
from

where
it
came

another
time
a man
decided
to drink
his fill
of
her
she
washed his eyes
out
with
bleach

they
left
her lying
naked
on the
bar room
floor
her
laughter
drove
them
crazy

my father
couldn't
hold

her
she
pinned
him
to
the
sky

while
she
hitch
hiked
cross
the
country
he
let them
take
his
pride

her body
ravaged,
alcohol
t.b.
-- they
say --,
she
jumped
the prison
wall

the
wind

never
blessed
her
back
she passed
salmon
on their
way
to spawn
it was
always
too hot

so
she
never
did
come in
from
the
cold

her
final
blanket
a
Montana
snowfall

yes
god
created
man
in

his
own
image

woman
made
her
own

dancing into being

lightness
into
dark
darkness
into
light

she danced
across the arctic sky
danced darkness
into
light
lightness
into
dark
the
midnight sun
called her name
she danced

midnight darkness
fed her soul
she danced
her image into being
sapphire
emerald
ruby
opal

from the caverns of the earth

she danced
mirrored prisms
she danced
the darkness
into
being

she soared
the day
into being
soaring
higher
higher
leading sun
out of dawn
into being
she soared
east to west
and back around
leading sun
she chased the midnight
out of dawn

she rumbled
waddled
sleek and sure
past the sagebrush
tiny seeds
caught in
massive paws
eating
berries
farther north
the seeds are dropped

she rumbled
waddled
sleek and sure
past tobacco leaves
seeds carried
north
in shaggy fur
she rumbled
waddled
with the healing
healing earth
as farther north
she goes

she stomped
stomped
herself
into being
striking fast
and leaving slow
she burst upon the prairie
heard them call her name
thunder
Thunder
Thunder Woman
she heard them
call her name
she stomped herself
into being
destruction reigns
and
lightning
heals
she stomped across

the sky
sun &
moon &
stars
go running
she stomps herself
into being

i am the world

i am the world
i am shape
        and form
                and revolution
i am the world

my tits are
  Mount Saint Helens and Vesuvius
    spewing forth the ash and fire
    like a first-time mother's
        letdown milk

the San Andreas fault
is an orgasm waiting to be fucked into existence

i am the world

i am the soil
of the third world countries
    waiting
    anticipating
    the next onslaught
    in my cycle of pms

i want you to stop
romanticizing
politicizing
intellectualizing
my existence

i am the world
i am shape
and form
and revolution

i am the soil

i am the soil from which all things grow
the seeds of all the nations
are carried in my womb
my children are the seventh
generation of the treaties
        and the trees are too precious
        to be made into paper
        and ink fades in the
        winds and water of time
my promises to them will be
etched into grandfather rock
with the venom of the snake
it will be a living promise
carried by the winds of
the four directions to the
sacred songs and dreams
of the next seven generations

jesus christ wasn't born a woman

jesus christ
wasn't born a woman
menstruation
would have kept him out of the
temple
at age 12
he would have been
raped
hitchhiking from bethlehem to jerusalem
his nursing children
would have screamed
and starved
without milk for
40 days and 40 nites
the loaves and fish
would have been made
into hotdish
to serve a few more
nope
jesus christ
wasn't born a woman
he wouldn't have had
time to be crucified

joe

joe spent his early adulthood
from the ages of 0 to 18
        first, in and out of bars up on the rez with his ma
        then in and out of foster homes until he was 18

he acquired a lot of skills in those years
how to be quicker, smarter, faster, quieter
self-sufficient
        he learned to hide his love deep inside
        and fire his rage out his fists

in one foster home he learned to hold his breath under water
for long periods of time
courtesy of the wife of the president of the local chamber
                                                        of commerce
        she thought she'd invented a new way to break his spirit
                in spite of her best intentions
                it only served him well

joe spent his middle age
18 to 21
in viet nam
all the skills he learned in early adulthood
fulfilled their purpose in the war zone
        in fact
it was only a continuation of the war he was already in
the only exception
was that this time
he was given a weapon
and permission to kill

joe returned home at 21
an old man
spirit finally broken
a dull glaze over his eyes that even the dope he snorted
couldn't fire

evenings he spent playing the war game Risk
conquering country after country
snorting line after line
in search of the childhood
he never had

urban rez

generational memories
passed from body to body
womb to womb
to all the future
generations
sorrow and joy
joy and sorrow

criss-cross
hip-hop
it's a brand new game of hopscotch
everyone is playing
jump and turn
turn and jump
twist and shout
the whole yard is their playground
fuck
they took over the whole damn 'hood
jumpin, twistin, screamin
and when your turn is over
don't count on getting up

generational memories
passed from body to body

in my alley
X marks the spot
where santiago's dreams
joined
the neighbor lady's hollyhock roots

he was a good-looking young man
my daughter had her eyes on
they used to go under the 16th ave railway bridge
and tag the concrete
the O's on that same lady's garage
mark the bullet entrance holes
my indian-born daughter tried to tell that young man
his snoop-doggy-dog t-shirt
was NOT some modern day ghost dance shirt
if you dare to happen under that bridge
and see her sniffin instead of taggin
(think she does a lot of that these days)
would you tell her to please come home
or at least tag the neighbor lady's garage
she can sign it with XXXX's and OOO's
and i'll get the message

carried in my womb
inside my mother's womb
inside my grandmother's womb
and my daughter's daughters
nestled inside of them
inside of me
generational memories
passed from body to body
womb to womb
to all the future
generations
sorrow and joy
joy and sorrow

the guy had john written over his left pocket
it really read asshole
but he couldn't read

shirley's floral hieroglyphics said
slut
and that was one everyone could understand
even john
as he cruised lake street
in his newly waxed 4x4
he'd just dropped his own daughter off
at the minnetonka high school prom
and had a couple of dreams to kill
with the time to do it in
fourteen-year-old shirley's dreams
had long ago
turned into nightmares
daymares
"god! don't let me go to sleep" mares
holding up her corner of lake street
she knew
what pages john wanted to read
shit
she didn't need no college degree
to read him like
a book

generational memories
passed from body to body
womb to womb
to all the future
generations
sorrow and joy
joy and sorrow

dancing blue

dancing blue
i dance across rainbows
rain falls
tears rise to heaven
blue surrounds ashes on the plain
dancing on rainbows
i escort
the warriors home

Lucky Jack
fed his children well
walleye pike
mahnomen
rabbit stew

quiet man
Lucky Jack
jackpines spoke louder than he
his presence was the loudest sound he made

warriors keen
the rainbow calls

cold
northwinds blow
dressed in ermine
flanked by giant snowy owls
i challenge Windigo
he waits silent
behind the kitchen door

Lucky Jack
quiet man
feeds his children well
frozen creek
frozen trapline

wind in jackpines
speaks louder than he

Windigo
behind the kitchen door
didn't even bother to knock the snow off his shoes
snow melts slowly across the
patched linoleum floor

Mary Jane feels the chill
warriors keen
rainbows call

i, dancing blue
dressed in ermine
flanked by giant snowy owls
couldn't fight Windigo
behind the kitchen door
dressed in ermine
i danced the warrior home

silence
silence

january thawed
the winter river floor
Windigo took his time
silent by the kitchen door

Lucky Jack crossed the trapline
one last time
water crashed in on him
while his children starved

sometimes the wind isn't lonely
it's a cover for the bodies on the rise
Dancing Blue
i dance the warriors home
rainbow of the arctic sky

dressed in ermine
i dance the warriors home
gourds rattle
death sounds
wailers keen

river rise
river rise
scaffolds to the sky

Mary Jane
blessed by saints
three continents away
couldn't find the river
Jack called
Windigo waited

patient
behind
the kitchen door

gourds rattle
death sounds

wailers keen

Dancing Blue
i dance
across rainbows
racing storms
the winds of death
i dance the warriors home

Mary Jane died
heart just couldn't feed
children all alone
the loneliness closed in

Windigo
behind the kitchen door
laughed
the dry crackle
of dead fall leaves

sometimes the wind isn't lonely
it's a cover for the bodies
on the rise
Windigo took his time

children call
children wail

Mary Jane died
seven children cried
Lucky Jack crossed the river
one last time

Dancing Blue

i dance the warriors home
dancing across rainbows
rain falls
tears rise to heaven
blue surrounds ashes on the plain

dancing on rainbows
i escort the warriors home
rain falls
tears rise to heaven
dancing blue
warriors rise
dancing blue
i dance across rainbows

racing storms
the winds of death subside
across the plains
i dance the warriors home

dancing blue
i breathe the scaffolds
in the east
out the west
i breathe the warriors home

gourds rattle
death sounds
wailers keen
dancing blue
i dance the warriors home

wounded knee
red lake

sand creek
wounded knee

i dance the warriors home
sometimes the wind isn't lonely
it's a cover for the bodies on the rise
river rise
river rise
scaffolds to the sky

death waits patiently
behind the kitchen door

children call
children wail

silence in the river
dancing blue

Marcie R. Rendon

Photo © Rebecca Dallinger

LINDA
LEGARDE
GROVER

The Refugees

To the dirging of "The Way We Were"
sung by some sweet girl nobody knows
six pallbearers
two in sweatshirts with washed-away logos
three in second-hand dress shirts
one in a borrowed sport coat
carry above their crooked lock step mince
the flocked vinyl coffin out the side door.
Inside, our beloved mother, grandma and aunt
has left has arrived,
megis shell on a black string
wound over her hard brown fingers.

Six pallbearers worn as their boot heels
ground to an unassuming humility
by the rounds of looking for work
and sometimes finding it
wear their bodies as a single suit of clothes,
fraying fast and thin at the knees.
Innocent faces first tanned by outside labor
then sun creases filled by grime and hard living
search then escape what they've found,
spending night after numb night on a stool at Mr. Z's
thinking, maybe after one more
I'll ask that blonde or her friend to dance;
no, guess I'll just go home, after all.

This is what really happened to the other Indians,
not the buff beauties you watch on made-for-TV movies,
running in clean, freshly ironed loincloths

through a pristine forest full of friendly animals
with an important message for the Chief
from his daughter, the Princess,
the ones who dazzle you today with their mystical ways
("Oh, wow, these people are just so close to nature,
so SPEARitual," I've heard you say)
that you can buy at a pow-wow stand
along with some traditional turquoise and silver
jewelry so you can be an Indian, too.

No, we're the other Indians,
the ones who did our time in boarding school,
learned to take a beating,
never quite mastered English
learned the work ethic
and learned what it meant for us,
and chose to survive in spite of it.
Off the reservation, we're refugees,
displaced persons sometimes scorned by our own people.
Our daughters married white men,
learned to take a beating,
never quite mastered Anglo housekeeping,
lived the work ethic and for them it meant
they would grow old early our daughters
beloved and revered the bearers of life
and generations to come how could we protect them,
our daughters, whose spirits tired and whose

blue-eyed children went to public school
and learned to take a beating
or sometimes give one
and never quite mastered schoolwork,
leaving when they turned sixteen,
having learned the work ethic

so they too could live hard
and grow old early.

And today we're at another funeral,
and since it's the bargain package deal
we have to hustle outside The Chapel of the Sunset
once our hour is done. We're grateful though;
it's warm out today, with room on the sidewalk
for cousins to meet and talk
("haven't seen you since our last funeral")
till the chapel needs the sidewalk back
and we head for Mr. Z's.
The corpse, beloved mother, aunt and grandma
waits, now that she's arrived west,
in the chapel's garage for a ride to the cemetery,
megis shell in black cord
wound over her hard brown fingers.

Leaving

Old enough now to walk to the depot ourselves,
we waved to Ma and she smiled back from the porch
waving goodbye! see you in the summer!
        take care of your little sister!

I looked back just before we turned the corner
and saw her wipe her eyes on her sleeve.
I almost felt that sleeve wipe my eyes, too
but it was the wind blowing cold tracks
that dried to a stiff salt soreness
from the corners of my eyes to my ears
as I blinked in the bright cold sun.
Brud the oldest carried our little sister
Angeline wrapped in her new coat a warm brown
        cut down from her own
        by Ma, for school.
On the train
Angeline cried herself a hundred miles,
her tears a spring of misery deep as China
while our own tears dripped down our throats
to our stomachs, sour puddles
that in briny darkness would never dry.
Late in the day, lulled by the rumble of the train
Angeline slept, her face hot her thin cheeks shiny
from salty runoff, then in her dreams
gasping arrhythmic short intakes of breath
that kept me awake. I looked out the window
at the progression of small towns, reversed
from our trip home last June, and familiar to me
in the reversal of their order in my heart

and when it got too dark to see outside
I stayed turned to the window, watching
reflected in the glass and now reversed
too in my senses and in the glass
in rehearsal for our destination
that life backwards from all we knew at home.
Angeline Brud Mitchell and Waboos
sleeping in the glare of the overhead light,
a tangle of children smelling home in dreams
as their heads rested on Ma's cut-down coat,
and then my own staring face blank and tearless,
smooth as stone, reflected in the window
reversed too in the glass and in my senses
in rehearsal for our destination,
that life backwards from all we knew at home.

left hand to right daylight to darkness
yes ma'am yes sir raise your hand
stand at attention take your beating
remember remember remember

Ma at Home

After they turned the corner, that huddle of children
carrying bread to eat on the train, my children
with their dark coats still faces resigned feet
that had walked down the porch stairs
moving, moving, a catch of breath seen and felt

walking forward, a catch, then pause,
but then forward, forward to the corner
in one breath looking smaller, in another out of sight,
I lowered my arm and placed into its crook my smile
        (Goodbye! See you in the summer!
        Take care of your little sister!)
and my tears, the full-blown bloom of my heart
damp on a dark cotton dress sleeve.
Back in the house my hands did their own work
without the summer help of my heart
whose season had changed in two beats:
picked up the quilts from the floor, folding
gray and black wool, old skirts and trousers
        bits of red, a man's wool shirt
        faded maroon and brown, my wedding quilt
        the lightest a summer dress, flowers blurred in fog
tucking batting where patches frayed and threads broke
smoothing soothing mothering the prints of my children's bodies
to squares that I placed under my bed, until spring.
Then I walked to work, warm without my coat,
cut down for Angeline, the smallest and today the warmest
walking to the train station in her huddle of brothers
in my cut-down coat, my arms around her arms

my shoulders on her shoulders
my cut-down coat warming her in my absence
my smile and wave the last she saw
my starving eyes the last she felt,
on the back of her small head
on the straight part between her tiny braids.
With her brothers she walked, without them I waited,
back to my old hangnail existence, three seasons deadened
but living for the day they would return.

Bemidji Wait

With my feet under the bench my legs ended at the
knees;
no brown high top shoes no black wool stockings
just legs that ended where my pants ended.
If I pushed out my stomach to a hard air-filled paunch
my hunger ended at my ribs
no growl no sorrow no emptiness
just an ache in the hollow of nothing to eat.

Passing time, passing time waiting for the priest,
strangers in a strange land waiting in the bus depot
sitting straight and quiet, as though he watched us,
passing time, three days two nights
passing time, my brothers and me watching for the car
lethargic homesick patient heartsick
then fatigued with the wait and restless,
swinging our feet from the bench, wandering the block
begging bread from a bakery,
standing on the sidewalk watching the street
for the priest in his black car. It's funny,
nobody noticed us
but the man at the ticket window minding his own
business
and we were afraid to ask him for help.
He let us sleep there in the waiting room
on wooden benches slippery as church pews.
Awake in the dark depot that first night
I sat up, then kneeled on the seat of the bench,
my mouth resting on the curved back, tasting
and smelling church, sour smell and salt taste

of damp change, soft bills, chewing gum, matchbooks,
a tackiness from other people's hands on my lips
as I passed time, awake in the dark depot,
waiting for the priest.

Funny, nobody noticed us or missed us.
The bakery lady fed us twice and we became nearly tamed,
small town wildlife, shy gray squirrels timid small birds
bringing that leftover bread back
to our den our nest our chapel the depot
past the eyes of the passive ticket seller
in our new life, brick and concrete purgatory
a waiting room between home and boarding school.

Then, uneasy as we were
the dread of returning to Indian school lessened
ever so slightly, and we began to think, maybe
we would shine shoes, wash dishes,
find lost change on the sidewalk
and we'd buy tickets home from the ticket seller
who wouldn't say, aren't you boys from the Indian school?
and we'd ride home on the bus, walk in the door
and surprise our mother. The second night we dreamed that,
moving and turning easily on our varnished pews,
turning in our dreams, turning to see out the bus windows
towns reversed from our trip north, time running backward,
a natural and right progression in the dreams
of temporarily misplaced boys, passing time.

Zip

My first night at boarding school
the girl next to me in the dormitory
talked in Indian to me, asked me
just like the people at home
where I was from and who my family was
which comforted me, then she said, don't wash
your stockings yet; we need the radiators.
Then all the dormitory girls took out the bread
they'd saved from supper, and a jar of syrup
and said they were having a party for me,
the new girl. I'd never had a party before.
They taught me to make zip sandwiches.
Have you ever heard of them, zip sandwiches?
You take a piece of bread and pour a little syrup
and fold it and let it heat up and dry out
flat and hard on the radiator. Zip sandwiches.

Next time there was a new girl
sitting shy and lonesome on her bed
I said after the matron was gone
"Aniin, ezhiyaa yayaan?"
and told her to save her bread from supper
for a party that night. She smiled sideways.

Those zip sandwiches? Hard, stiff, sticky
they were a little unsanitary for my taste,
drying out right where we hung our underwear.

And tasty? Well, they didn't have much taste
but we loved them, and to this day, to me
sweet, hard, dry, sticky food
makes me think of those days,
and I taste kindness, and generosity,
the goodness and comfort of my friends.

St. Bernard

When I got to mission school
my worries about my mother
and how she was doing without me
had to wait, when
the priest told me
I had a bigger worry than that.
When I died, he said,
they would never let me into heaven
when they heard my name.
With a name like mine, Barney,
not a real name of any kind at all
I couldn't float in past the eyes of God.
He'd turn me away for certain,
with a name like mine, Barney,
and send me back to mission school.
And so they named me after this big dog
who carried whiskey in a little barrel around his neck
and saved people's lives by giving them a drink.
I'd heard about that, and even saw it
with my own eyes, in a bar in the West End.
Thanks, Niijii, you saved my life,
a man told my uncle,
I was sure dying for a drink.
So I supposed it must be all right
and tried to feel the honor of my namesake.
But it didn't stick, and I reverted to my pagan ways.
See, when I got home and my mother said hello Barney

I was so happy I forgot all about heaven.
Seventy years later, I wonder if I should resume worrying,
with a name like mine, Barney.
Naw.

Everything You Need to Know in Life You'll Learn at Boarding School

Speak English. Forget the language and teachings of your grandparents. Those teachings are savage and from the past. Your grandparents are ignorant. Cleanliness is next to Godliness. Indians are not clean. Your parents did not teach you proper hygiene and sanitation. Stay in line. Hang your toothbrush on the hook with the others. Do not allow the bristles to touch. This spreads the diseases that you bring to school from your families. Make your bed with mitered corners. A bed not properly made will be torn apart. Start over. Remember and be grateful that the government feeds and clothes you. Always say grace before meals. In English. Don't cry. Crying never solved anything. Write home once every month. In English. Let your parents know that you are doing very well. You'll never amount to anything. Make the most of your opportunities. You'll never amount to anything. Answer when the teacher or matron addresses you. In English. If your family insists on and can provide transportation for you to visit home in the summer, report to the matron's office immediately upon your return. You will be allowed into the dormitory after you have been sanitized and de-loused. Busy hands are happy hands. Keep yourself occupied. You'll never amount to anything. In the evenings you may read a book from the library shelf. In English. Books are our friends. Forget the language of your parents and grandparents. It is dead. If you are heard speaking it you will kneel on a navy bean for one hour. We will ask if you have learned your lesson. You will answer. In English. Students who are discipline problems will be identified by their shorn hair. Learn from the day you spent in solitary confinement. Spare the rod and spoil the child. Speak English. You'll never amount to anything.

Grandmother at Indian School

Left on scrubbed wooden steps to think
about disobedience, and forgetfulness
she feels warm sun on the back of her neck
as she kneels on the pale spot worn
by other little girls' tender sore knees,
a hundred black wool stockings
grinding skin and stairs,
beneath one knee a hard white navy bean.

Small distant lightning flickers pale
flashes down her shins, felt by other
uniformed girls marching to sewing class
waiting for their own inevitable return
to the stair, to think and remember what happens
to girls who speak a pagan tongue.

Try to forget this pagan tongue.

Disobedient and forgetful she almost hears
beyond the school yard
beyond the train ride
beyond little girls crying in white iron beds

her mother far away
singing to herself as she cooks,
and speaking quietly to Grandma as they sew
the quilt for the new baby,
and laughing with her sisters
as she washes clothes

        the little bean,
        does it hurt?

Bizaan, gego mawi ken, don't cry
she thinks, moving her knee so the little bean
feels only the soft part, and not the bone
        how long can I stay here?
And when Matron returns to ask if she's thought
she says yes,
I won't talk like a pagan again
and she stands and picks up the little bean
and carries it in her lonesome lying hand
until lights out,
when the baby bean
sleeps under her pillow.

Escape

There were certain things you could do to leave school.

Finish. Graduate. Once you finished school you were free to go home, and most did. Some went on to another boarding school for further studies or to learn a trade. A few stayed on at school and worked there awhile because they didn't know what else to do.

Run away. Runaways and boarding schools always went together, and you hear them mentioned together. A lot of kids tried to run away. A lot were caught. Runaways were easy to find, because they all ran the same place, home. Some were allowed to run without pursuit. When they got home they were met at the door by someone from school, saving everyone a lot of work. Some kids, though a few, ran home and never went back to school, either because home was too far away for retrieval to be worth the trouble, or because they ran so many times the school got tired of it.

Get sick. There was sickness at boarding school, that's for sure, and at every school. Measles, whooping, impetigo all went through the schools, and everybody caught them. Influenza. Influenza closed whole schools down in 1918. Trachoma wouldn't get you home, though you might get a transfer to a trachoma school. It blinded you, eventually. You'd walk around with sore eyes, red and runny, couldn't see straight. T.B., tuberculosis, would get you out of school, but you'd go to a sanitarium where your lungs could dry out and scar over, if you were lucky. If you weren't, you could go home to cough and hemorrhage yourself to death, and give it to your family.

Die. You could die from getting sick, or you could die from getting hurt. Runaways died from exposure. One boy died after the disciplinarian kicked him down the stairs, another from pneumonia after he had to sleep outside for punishment. Another drowned swimming in the lake. Some died from broken hearts, they were just too homesick to eat and couldn't live without their mothers.

Chi-Ko-ko-koho and the Boarding School Prefect

From my owl's nest home, unsteady greasy oak
covered by cowhide long oblivious
to claws tough and curving as old tree roots
I breathe the night breeze, starry broken glass.

I am Chi-Ko-ko-koho. My black-centered
unblinking owl eyes see past the dark
growl of this old bear den of a bar,
through stinging fog of unintended
blasphemy, tobacco's tarry prayers
stuck and dusty on a hammered tin ceiling,
to grieving spirits mirrored by my own.
I am Chi-Ko-ko-koho, young among owls
as young among lush crimson blooms of death
is the embryonic seedling in my chest,
the rooting zygote corkscrew in my chest,
these days all but unseen, a pink sea spray
sunset on the rim of a thick white coffee cup.
My grieving spirit hardly notices
though, in this old bear den of a bar.

My owl head turns clear round when I see him.

I am Chi-Ko-ko-koho, I blink away
smoke and fog, my head swivels back
and he's still there, the prefect. He's still there
and real, not some ghost back to grab my throat
again with those heavy old no-hands of his
or crack my brother's homesick skinny bones

on cold concrete tattooed by miseries
of other Indian boys who crossed his path.

To the darkness of this bear den of a bar
he's brought his own sad spirit for a drink.

I am Chi-Ko-ko-koho, but who he sees
is Kwiiwizens, a boy bent and kneeling
beneath the prefect's doubled leather strap,
and Kwiiwizens I am. My belly feels
a tiny worm the color of the moon
writhe in laughter at my cowardice
as that reeking, ruined wreck, the old prefect
step-drags, step-drags his dampened moccasins
to my end of the bar. The flowers and vines
weep beaded tears in mourning for us all.

He asks me for a nickel for a beer.
With closed eyes Kwiiwizens waits for the strap.

Chi-Ko-ko-koho dives from his grimy perch
to yank the apparition by the hair,
then flies him past the blind face of the moon
to drop him in the alley back behind
the dark growl of this old bear den of a bar.

Indizhinikaaz Kwiiwizens,
gaye indizhinikaaz Chi-Ko-ko-koho.
Ni maajaa. Mi-iw. I leave him there.

I am Chi-Ko-ko-koho. I leave him there
under the stars of broken glass. I leave him there.

Mary Susan

My sister is named after an aunt who died before we were born. The story in our family is that she survived the Wounded Knee Massacre in 1890, when she was a boarding school student. She was just a young girl then, and the nuns took them out to a ditch where they spent the night. The nuns knew something bad was going on, and they wanted to take care of the children.

Left a young widow with five children to support, our aunt took a job as a cook at a boarding school, then spent many years working with boarding school children. My dad remembers her as a generous woman, only as tall as a child, who spoke softly and kindly. He honored her memory by naming my sister after her.

My sister is the only blonde in our family. As children, we were fascinated by her coloring, her hair that lightened to an icy frost in the summer, her cheeks that bloomed with a red fire in the winter. Winters, she became the sun; summers, the moon. We masked our anger and humiliation at the neighbors' stupid jokes about the stork, the wrong baby, the milkman by pretending we didn't understand. She was our sister, we could see that. We were photo negatives, reversals of the same black and white image, a bone structure interchangeable under skin, eyes and hair.

In the early 1970s an Indian Club was started at our high school. What an event that was, an organization to acknowledge and reinforce Indian ways in an institution that had stood for the annihilation of our people through education/assimilation. Our sister went to Indian Club until the day the other Indian students asked her to leave because she wouldn't match the group in the yearbook picture.

Years later she told my husband that she always felt that she stood out in pictures.

Bruneau

It was a good job.
Close to town. Regular pay.
Room and board. A good job.

Don't look at me, I wasn't the first one;
other Shinnobs had done it before me
and all things considered I didn't mind it
even if it was a goddam Indian school.

The boys? They were all right, the boys,
and we all got along when they kept their noses clean.
And when they didn't there wasn't anything new,
nothing I didn't see before, those hellish days
I was at Indian school myself.
Runaways, fighters, blanket-ass Indians sneaking around
like their ceremonies were a big secret from me,
talking Indian under their breaths. I took care of all that
and when I caught six of them having a little Indian dance
out in the woods I took care of that, too.
Every one I beat, the ones who cried, the silent ones
they all acted like I didn't know what a beating was.
What did they think, that I was born knowing how?
I went to a goddam Indian school, too.

Miss Shawn

I am afraid of that deceptive face
        (handsome, dark-eyed, intelligent
        in structure, a sheep's face, or a camel's,
        with an animal's acceptance and dignity,
        that masks a cruel soul I have seen before)
but even more of that melodic voice,
a deep and long-voweled cello song oozing
through a beige throat draped by long folds of skin
two knobs at its fearsome base, and to its
menacing and oddly tuneful hypnotic beat
"Brenda LeBrun" I rise, as learned the hard way
to stand at the right side of the desk
eyes front straight ahead face to face with Miss Shawn
chilled by the meter of that voice
left hand touching home, my desk
fixed and stable, warm wood with floral iron grillwork
a trellised passage to the tranquility and safety
of sitting behind the boy who blocks her view of me
but I have risen and now stand exposed,
eyes front straight ahead face to face with Miss Shawn.

"Your family is Indian. What tribe are you people from?"

And while above thirty-three other dark wood desks
pale faces turn to watch the glare of my misery
curious and glad it's not them
the other Indian child in class looks away,
sympathetic and sorry it's my turn. He knows,
he's had more than his share. I stand exposed,
in need of cover   <u>try not to look afraid</u>

eyes front straight ahead face to face with Miss Shawn
        and can't look down, not allowed here
as she takes two steps, and I can't help it
my eyes drop and I can see it all so clearly.

Brown leather teacher shoes, chunky heels. Two extra pairs on the shelf by her desk. Brown teacher dress, chunky pin over the left breast. More teacher dresses, gray, beige, black, in her closet at home. Teacher car in the parking lot, tan Chevy with plaid upholstery. It has a spare key and a spare tire. She's never had a flat. Never run out of gas. Her house is large and everybody sleeps in beds. Her garden is for decoration with no pit for burning trash. When she gets bored she talks about all these things and sometimes her college days, spent on the moon for all I understand what she's talking about.

My uncle, who went to Indian school awhile, and got left behind. My uncle, kinder, more decent, certainly smarter and more interesting than Miss Shawn. My brothers and sisters, who would have to have Miss Shawn for sixth grade after me. My dad, teaching my mother the most important word in the Chippewa language, migwech. Indians. Chippewas. Visiting, joking, laughing. My aunt, setting her mother's hair. "Sister, make sure you make them pincurls good and tight." "I'm making them so tight, Ma, you won't be able to shut your eyes." My cousin, who got slapped by his teacher for not speaking. Timmy, the other Indian kid in class, getting slapped by Miss Shawn for smiling during singing time. Miss Shawn.

I don't want to tell her.

Exposed, I shelter us all with a lie.

"Navajo."

"Oh. NAH vuh ho." Amazingly, she says that I may sit down. And I have survived unharmed, to take my place again behind the boy who blocks her view of what I see.

It's not such a bad day at school after all.

For Asin

Eyes down sitting alone he is
below the salt outside the pale beyond the tracks
he is a twelfth-grade Indian boy eating his lunch
on the steps outside the school.
His parents are proud, his cousins envious
of the accomplishments of this young man
this invisible warrior. Alone he is
an apparition unseen in silence unheard
by other students horsing around
and flirting on the steps after lunch,
white girls in imported peasant chic
white boys in jeans and chambray shirts,
the proletarian kitsch of 1973.
Eyes down he eats two vapor sandwiches
and folds the brown paper bag into his pocket
for tomorrow, and walks into school unnoticed,
a ghost floating past the guidance counselor's office.
This morning the ghost took a human form
for the counselor, who with blind blue eyes saw
an Indian boy, head down, too shy, unappealing,
frayed shirt, bad complexion, a C student.
"I was wondering about college," said the warrior.
"It isn't for everyone," said the counselor.

Below the salt outside the pale beyond the tracks
unseen, in silence our invisible warrior walks point.
He is a woodland warrior in a foreign jungle,
camouflaged in wash pants and frayed shirt,
a C student with bad teeth and downcast eyes,
the pride of his parents the envy of his cousins

the hope of his brothers and sisters, walking
leaving tracks impossibly shimmering tracks
tracing the shade of the sky the hue of tomorrow
through the foreign jungle, across cracked concrete
up the stairs through the Age of Aquarius crowd
to school to college. Asin, you walked before us.
Asin, we will rise to our feet and walk,
step after step, visible now we will walk
filling your tracks with our own.

The Class of 1968

Ten little, nine little, eight little Indians,
seven little, six little, five little Indians,
four little, three little, two little Indians,
one little Indian...

And that left me, the last one
of the bunch, kindergartners of 1955,
our teachers, the shade of our skin, our histories
those random chances silent banshees chasing children
one by one out of our parents' dreams, till I was
the only one left, and the one perceived as leaving,
leaving Vicky, pregnant in the eight grade
        who never came back
    Vernon and George, nomads between rez and town
        till they were forgotten
    Wanda, always sick and agonizingly shy,
        who disappeared
    Birdeen, who went to work after her father died
    Percy and John, expelled for fighting
    Susan, for skipping school
        to take care of the younger kids at home
    Jim, who studied incorrigibility at Juvenile Hall
    Pete, who furthered those studies at Red Wing
    Eliza, who never learned to read,
        and waited for her sixteenth birthday
    Bonita, who almost made it but "had to" get married
        as we said in 1968

and that left me, the last one
the forgotten the untouched the protected
the bookish the lucky the lonely
the pride of my family
the last one.

Linda LeGarde Grover

DENISE

SWEET

Palominos near Tuba City

-- for David

In the desert of burning dreams, of armadillo and centipede,
I would call this night pitch dark back home
I would watch for any star to pass into a dream song

or point of light called planet to whirl and twist like
a tiny pinwheel swallowing me into its vanishing point.
Here, under pewter sky with words out of breath

I chase poems down like wild mares into fenced corrals
watching close calls with wisdom
rear and kick against the fence of bad judgement.

I used to think the skies brought them home,
thundering hooves and swollen bellies ready
to spill arrowheads on the dry bony floor
ready to spark and fire
the sulfuric aroma real as rain;

but now the horses of white lightning gallop
towards me, afraid of nothing,
they rush with an eye for hesitation, ready to twist and brush
up against my heart with their horse-madness

here, the rider stands in the wavering heat, erect
and indisputable as a lightning rod, braced in the open.
I stand my ground and wait, ready to hold on for dear life.

Love Song of Lac Courte Oreilles: What Saxon Told Us

Where they go
has been a long mystery
much like the ikwe
in the windigo winters
of lac du flambeau

To come
to him she melt invisible
In cedar she laugh
like otters on slick ice

The voyageurs grinned
to find
her moccasins stirred into soup
over cold twig fire
pale broth to feed her
the last two nights of walk under
Grandmother Moon
towards Lake of the Short Ears

But the Odawa man
so far off his course to odanah
he lay weeping
in his own gravehouse
that long day
So sad

Even the grandfathers weeped
at the quarry

they
crack and peel and
rockslide
into wet red piles
for the pipes
of our condolence

    <u>Like the sweet moon and stars, she said</u>
    <u>Like a love song, she said.</u>

I cry too, only
singing is the same
at these
lonely times.

This is Not a Foreign Exchange: To All the Students Who Have Named Themselves

-- Leadership Conference for Students of Color, Spring '94

Then, it was the deepest azure of spring nights
when 100 of us had gathered
as strangers will, we were new in this skin
in the midst of an American university
we spied from a distance
the wise and the learned

now, as I read my speech
brittle and driven
I hardly know what I could do now
that you were finally alive
in your bodies, beautiful
and dangerous to the world

you sat looking miles down your histories
ground into the ground
at your feet, I lost my place
several times while I watched you gaze
directly into my eyes expecting something
dropping your raised hands like angel wings
as I fumbled for new words to the songs
back then we used to sing:

We shall overcome,
We shall overcome.

This has happened before, she said
to herself and to them
all of it, she said,
with grace and abundance,
all of it she said with grace
and abundance.

The Pedophile on Day Street

Every morning of the world
the children move darkness into day
and he watches from his flat close to the park

There, the children squat like guinea hens
on the ground near the teeter-totter
chewing Oreos like bars of soap

Their teeth sooted with black corrosion
for a moment they look frightening
to him; as he walks toward them in sadness

It's a familiar kind that he cannot place
from memory, but usual and often, sadness
coming by surprise. He can only remember

The hard slap of leather against the sink
the goose feathers floating like snowflakes
against the pane, the mucous stain on his

Shirt sleeve, the boy burying his eyes in
the crook of his arm; the sad
mixes with terror as he carries wet

Sheets to the dark basement, not
tall enough to reach the lightcord
but old enough to know enough

<u>To push aside fear of death and get on with it</u>
<u>moving weakness out of his body</u>
<u>and mind forever.</u> Now he wants

The little boy to call him "Daddy"
and say, "I love you, I love you,"
over and over, in a voice raw and hungry

His own disappearing into flasks of
fine brandy; he throws them
back one by one, and crouches eye level

Before the small boy, whispering
I would stop if I knew how; if I knew how
I'd bottle it and then I'd be rich, so filthy rich.

Veteran's Dance, 1995

-- after Oklahoma City

During this round
I wanted to think of you
then, when each step
meant something
and you would
be out of
the mirrored building
and in front
of me
dancing too,

instead I danced alone
under the stars
and the wild sadness
of Oklahoma City
spoors of light
burnish
the newborn darkness
there is a blank moon
tonight
and no one to sing to.
This is the worst war
we've ever seen:
surrounded and unarmed,
shadows
unraveling everywhere.

The Origin of Only

-- for Damon

Once there was a young man
whose hands held laughter
for him while he waited
for rain while he walked
night into day,
a young man whose body
was remarkably alive with lightning,
whose shoulder gave off sparks
when he walked through doors,
a young man with stallion hair
whose eyes followed rain
back into green clouds
at dusk -- a young man whose
unpleasant disposition
liked the world
with nobody in it

And so the Grandmothers said
be that way.

Right of Way

At Porkchop Road you enter
the jagged res world

with staggered pull-offs
and long stretches
of nothing and
no turn-arounds

once in awhile
a raccoon will argue
right of way down
an aspen corridor
and you come to a complete stop
he makes his point
and saunters off.

Although distance does not
matter, it's a long way
into the flat pine forest
wild turkeys with their mangled
voices chortle and wave crimson
waddles at you and you can grin
at the spectacle if you like
but they see no humor
in any of this.

Two-Step at Keweenaw Bay: Injun Joe Remembers

> "Did you think I'd forget? The injun blood ain't in me for nothing."
>
> -- Injun Joe in Adventures of Huckleberry Finn.

If I could make it rain I would
make it rain all over these hills

I'd ride that horizon not thru valley
or city but between you and me

little ikwe -- no faithful companion --
be the posse of fire behind me

we'll wear our famous smiles
and dance the dance of fire this time

where hearts rise on hope alone we'll
put words into words like watercolor

prairies tender and mute and forget
the kimosabe who waves me back beside

him, when I forget my lines -- forget that cowboy!
He's gulped the blues and it's stuck in his throat

he could never see why the sky's on fire this time
pouring light in circles and just dancing
just dancing around you and me.

How the Heart Breaks

The normal heart bears
a simple function:
lungs pull in oxygen
passing blood through
membrane,
freshly filtered
the liquid red velvet
enters the aorta
coursing its way
through the body's
blue tributaries to
replenish and cleanse.

A wounded heart drains
to the mottled scar
accumulates around
the blue-black bruise
with each surge of blood
with every drawn breath
it pulls away oxygen
in vigilance towards
the deadened muscle;

then tissue turns to
knotted stone clogged corridors
of coagulated blood and then
dwindles to thin black threads
and one day everything stops
like this -- it stops --

the scar in faint stillness
lifts like a dark star
while the heart and body
fall to earth
as if death itself
were a joyous release
as if dying
became the heart's
splendid and final wisdom.

Center of Gravity

All things moved from place to place
in San Pedro are balanced on the head
tubs of tortillas, fold upon fold of fabric
stiff bundles of firewood, jugs of water
walking in grace, sometimes running
women and children at times with
an infant slung at their waist or on
their backs; they just go.

No "walk don't walk" prodding the
pedestrian nor moments of hesitancy
to cause a tilt in the center of gravity
they just go, upright and forward, eyes
even with the horizon with a trust
that people will see the difficulty
of your burden and naturally
stop for you.

Maya men more often carry their
bundles in slings, using an arc to
balance the weight, bent at the waist
the sling anchored by the head,
again firewood or textile bundles
sometimes tables and dressers
once I saw a man moving a
black angus cow, nearly equal
to his own weight I estimate.

I worry about my posture, a flypaper
recollection of the sisters of the Sacred
Heart who demanded a straight back
and lifted the chin of a small child
with a single crooked index finger
pointing is rude, but would we know
grace otherwise, my mother asks
you'll not see this in America.

The burdens are different and require
different centers to avoid the shifting
of weight or a teetering forward; neither
will you see the grace among those on foot,
nor the trust. Mostly the trust.

Sixteen Candles

-- for my son, Damon -- September 13, 2000

This one is for the 4½ hours of labor that no one could
prepare for;
this one for Friday the 13th, this one for Van Morrison
and one for the color green
this one burns at the edge of darkness around your temples
this one burns bright like a ravenwing birthmark
this candle spits and sparks like a distempered farm cat
it never goes out
this is the candle I carried for 17 years before saying
no more
this candle, beeswax and citron, is the opiate heat
of seared neuron fibers I can never reclaim

This candle lights the way,
red and narrow with unspoken tributaries
this one comes from nowhere; I am grateful for its invention

This candle burns in spite of dying
burning like love burns
this candle has no wick, firing from octane
and the silver bullets of manic Coltrane

And the two candles before us:
the candle of knowledge
a pillar of dense paraffin, half aglow
with adisokan light; the other the
candle of wisdom, a mound of powder
and wick, dynamite,
waiting for ignition

And this candle
is molded by the bones of Taygaasha
and of George Washington Sweet,
of Basile Hudon Beaulieu, and Charles Oakes,
of Bittie Van Wert, and Odinigun,
of Chi Ogemakwenokomiss, and Cagaag,
of Buddy Sweet, and of William
and Honey Sweet Warren,
of Julia Spears, of Carrie Owen,
of Sophie Fairbanks, of Augustus Brown, of Julia Beaulieu,
of Buddy and Raymond
of Phillip Parker and
of Himhim, all at White Earth

And by the bones of Tumahdee,
daughter of Coonie Monroe
stillborn infant born
without a cranium
who lived six hours to see
the light of day,
who saw the eclipse and
laughed into her tiny fist
at the thought of darkness
at moningwanekoning, our home,
in an august summer sky.

A Young Woman's Coming of Age

-- for Melonee Montano

Part of my survival
is in your eyes, Nia
amber light, a persistence
of vision that takes you to
Lac LaCroixe, Manitou Island
Winnipeg, even Mexico where
visions go unexplained,
where condors are the messengers,
armadillos listen for your breath
and follow each step, lumbering
across the desert floor.

At Squaw Bay that February, a hard
wind shuddered through maple leaves
while you prayed with asema
your song, delicate and comforting
rises like the mist from the Big Lake
awakening the ancestors at Madeline
we know they're glad to hear us
call their names.

Part of who I am rests with
your becoming who you are;
the songs you learn bring
strength to weakened blooms
and roots eroded by neglect
by women and men who have
lost the language of prayer
who don't know prayers of

gratitude or even pity
which is what we need
the most.

It happens first in a dream:
your aging into elder is a
journey long and unmapped
and one you will make for
more than one traveler
a woman hands you her baby
ill and dying, a small boy
rests his starfish hands
on your knee, the old man --
the last to make
lacrosse sticks at Red Cliff --
nods into a deep sleep while
you gently move pillows and tuck
a ragged wool blanket across
his shrunken chest.
Your manifest is my hope, Nia.

When you come home
you'll see how many arms
extend to you
how many winter counts
were made in your name
how many women and children
call you to their birth --
your healing hands
our medicine come back.

Behind Bars

barren saturday and the cop shop
boys, my students talk over comp
about the death investigation
and the myth of doughnuts they insist
they're just doing their job
but most wives hate their
sensitivity while loser husbands
lose it and shake the baby
way too much.

I'm not surprised that they tell
me way too much. The words
break away from their mouths
before they know it. One
officer whispers "that piece
of shit will walk -- all of Dykesville
knows it!" We know it too. The
doughnuts crumble in our hands.

There are a million stories in the
Naked City. Twenty years ago,
I'd listen to that voice on the TV
while in bed. Either way
it still seems incredible --
that many stories
or a town without its clothes.

Eagle in Flight: A Word Spoken Softly

Once evening falls from the sky
and you stare across the water
to the trees -- a small animal
may hide within these hills
but through some remarkable sense
or dream, you can tumble through
light years and seize the borrowed breath of terror, arching
against
the ground with a grace
that is abundant with life.

A word softly spoken can influence
a distant being and can be heard
at a point vastly remote in space:
an eagle knows full well the speed of sound --

He has listened to the sun
move closer, heard the earth carry
our weight, listened for the surge of
blood into hearts awakened for
the first time by hunger.

A messenger must know how to listen:
the sound of a descending star or
the passage of blue sky into storm
the eagle waits for words spoken softly
guiding them towards the stem of light
mapping pathways for the journey home.

Denise Sweet

About the Authors:

Jim Northrup (Sawyer, Minnesota) is the author of Walking the Rez Road, and Rez Road Follies. He has performed his poetry and plays around the world. Since 1989, his renowned newspaper column, "The Fond du Lac Follies," has been syndicated throughout the Midwest.

Marcie R. Rendon (Minneapolis, Minnesota) is the author of Pow-wow Summer. She has received many awards for her writing, including a Jerome Fellowship, and a St. Paul Company's Leadership in Neighborhoods (LIN) Award.

Linda LeGarde Grover (Duluth, Minnesota) co-authored a children's book entitled, A Childhood in Minnesota, which compares native to immigrant experiences in Duluth, Minnesota in the early 1900's.

Denise Sweet (Green Bay, Wisconsin) is the author of Songs for Discharming, which won the Diane Decora First Book Award from the Native Writers Circle of the Americas. She was one of three finalists considered for Wisconsin's first Poet Laureate award.

THE DRAMATISTS GUILD RESOURCE DIRECTORY™

2008

The Writer's Guide
to the Theatrical Marketplace™

ISBN 13: 978-1-58510-306-5
ISBN 10: 1-58510-306-3

10 9 8 7 6 5 4 3 2 1

This book is published with permission by Focus Publishing/R. Pullins Company, 311 Merrimac, Newburyport MA 01950 www.pullins.com, with the expertise of Joshua Faigen of Folio Publishing Services.

Printed in Canada.

0108TC

Table of Contents

Preface

Welcome to the NEW, IMPROVED print edition of *The Dramatists Guild Resource Directory*, 14th edition. Each year we'll add features that we think our members will find important to their lives as dramatists. This year, in addition to the standard submission opportunities and resources, you'll notice that we've offered templates for formatting plays and musicals, we've posted a Dramatist Bill of Rights so you'll always know your rights and protections in whatever situation you find yourself in; we've published our statement of submission fees and offered you a variety of resources when you travel out and about or are looking for an avenue for education.

A strong word of advice about this *Resource Directory*: by the time we go to press, a number of the opportunities listed within these pages will no longer exist, will not have the same staff listed, will not have the same deadline date as printed. It is essential that you verify the information we provide, either by going to the Member's Lounge at www.dramatistsguild.com and double-checking the information on our website, or by going directly to the website of the theatre, contest, festival, etc. To repeat, we have confirmed these listings with as much accuracy as possible before going to press.

When looking for a listing in the index, please know that we have alphabetized entries by the first letter of the opportunity this year (next year, we'll begin listing opportunities by their dates). Individuals (primarily agents, attorneys, and producers) and opportunities named for individuals (primarily contests) are listed by the first letter of the individual's surname. For easier reference, we have also indicated any deadlines and fees in boldface next to the title of those opportunities that released them.

The organizations listed in the *Resource Directory* receive hundreds of inquiries, so please be considerate and responsible with your submissions.

1. Name the specific program you're interested in, since many groups sponsor multiple programs.
2. Include a self-addressed stamped envelope (SASE) with sufficient postage. Most organizations won't return material without one, while some organizations don't return material at all. You may also include a self-addressed stamped postcard (SASP) to be notified when the organization has received your material – or if they are interested in reading your script.
3. Include your contact information in a query letter, since some organizations prefer blind submissions, with no identification on the script itself.

Please review each organization's policies carefully to ensure that all authorial rights are upheld. If you find a listing you believe is inaccurate or misleading, or if you have questions about any listing, write to the Dramatists Guild. Remember, though, listings by their nature are never complete, and any listing or omission doesn't necessarily constitute approval or disapproval by the Guild, its Council, officers, employees, agents, or affiliates.

Finally, much thanks to Madelena Ryerson, Tari Stratton, Angela Gant, Antoinette Nwandu, Tina Lear, Brandon Kalbaugh and Chris Massimine for helping push this rock up the hill.

Gary Garrison
Executive Director, Creative Affairs

The Dramatist Bill of Rights

The Dramatists Guild is America's professional association of playwrights, librettists, lyricists and composers, with over 6000 members around the world. The Guild is governed by our country's leading dramatists, with a fifty-five member Council that includes such dramatists as Edward Albee, Stephen Sondheim, John Patrick Shanley, Tony Kushner, Marsha Norman, Lynn Nottage, Emily Mann and Christopher Durang.

Long before playwrights or musical theatre writers join the Dramatists Guild, they often struggle professionally in small-to-medium-sized theatres throughout the country. It is essential, therefore, that dramatists know their rights, which the Dramatists Guild has defended for nearly 100 years. In order to protect the dramatist's unique vision, which has always been the strength of the theatre, s/he needs to understand this fundamental principle: dramatists own and control their work.

The Guild recommends that any production involving a dramatist incorporate a written agreement in which both theatres/producers and writers acknowledge certain key rights with each other.

In Process and Production

1. ARTISTIC INTEGRITY. No one (e.g., directors, actors, dramaturgs) can make changes, alterations, and/or omissions to your script—including the text, title, and stage directions—without your consent. This is called "script approval."
2. APPROVAL OF PRODUCTION ELEMENTS. You have the right to approve the cast, director, and designers (and, for a musical, the choreographer, orchestrator, arranger, and musical director, as well), including their replacements. This is called "artistic approval."
3. RIGHT TO BE PRESENT. You always have the right to attend casting, rehearsals, previews and performances.

Compensations

4. ROYALTIES. You are generally entitled to receive a royalty. While it is possible that the amount an author receives may be minimal for a small- to medium-sized production, *some* compensation should always be paid if *any* other artistic collaborator in the production is being paid, or if any admission is being charged. If you are a member of the Guild, you can always call our business office to discuss the standard industry royalties for various levels of production.

5. BILLING CREDIT. You should receive billing (typographical credit) on all publicity, programs, and advertising distributed or authorized by the theatre. Billing is part of your compensation and the failure to provide it properly is a breach of your rights.

Ownership

6. OWNERSHIP OF INTELLECTUAL PROPERTY. You own the copyright of your dramatic work. Authors in the theatre business do not assign (i.e., give away or sell in entirety) their copyrights, nor do they ever engage in "work-for-hire." When a university, producer or theatre wants to mount a production of your play, you actually license (or lease) the public performance rights to your dramatic property to that entity for a finite period of time.
7. OWNERSHIP OF INCIDENTAL CONTRIBUTIONS. You own all approved revisions, suggestions, and contributions to the script made by other collaborators in the production, including actors, directors, and dramaturgs. You do not owe anyone any money for these contributions.

   If a theatre uses *dramaturgs*, you are not obligated to make use of any ideas the dramaturg might have. Even when the input of a dramaturg or director is helpful to the playwright, dramaturgs and directors are still employees of the theatre, not the author, and they are paid for their work *by the theatre/producer.* It has been well-established in case law, beginning with "the Rent Case" (*Thompson v. Larson*) that neither dramaturgs nor directors (nor any other contributors) may be considered a co-author of a play, unless (i) they've collaborated with you from the play's inception, (ii) they've made a copyrightable contribution to the play, and (iii) you have agreed in writing that they are a co-author.
8. SUBSIDIARY RIGHTS. After the small or medium-sized production, you not only own your script, but also the rights to market and sell it to all different media (e.g., television, radio, film, internet) in any commercial market in the world. You are not obligated to sign over any portion of your project's future revenues to any third party (fellow artist, advisor, director, producer) as a result of a production, unless that production is a professional (i.e., Actor's Equity) premiere production (including sets, costumes and lighting), of no less than 21 consecutive paid public performances for which the author has received appropriate billing, compensation, and artistic approvals.
9. FUTURE OPTIONS. Rather than granting the theatre the right to share in future proceeds, you may choose to grant a non-exclusive option to present another production of your work within six months or one year of the close of the initial production. No option should be assignable without your prior written consent.

10. AUTHOR'S CONTRACT: The only way to ensure that you get the benefit of the rights listed above is through a written contract with the producer, no matter how large or small the entity. The Guild's Department of Business Affairs offers a model "production contract" and is available to review any contracts offered to you, and advise as to how those contracts compare to industry standards.

We realize that making demands of a small theatre is a difficult task. However, you should feel confident in presenting this Bill of Rights to the Artistic Director, Producer, Literary Manager, or university administrator as a starting point for discussion. At the very least, any professional in the dramatic arts should realize that it is important for writers to understand the nature of their work—not just the artistic aspects, but the business side, as well—and that they stand together as a community, for their mutual benefit and survival, and for the survival of theatre as a viable art form in the 21st century.

Suggested Formatting for Plays and Musicals

Included in this document are suggested formats for plays and musicals drawn from suggestions of distinguished dramatists, literary managers, teachers of dramatic writing, producers, professional theatres and publishers. It is the Guild's belief that these formats present a standard that will work for most professional opportunities. A few additional elements to consider:

1. Formatting works towards two purposes: easy reading and the ability to approximate the performance time of the written story. For plays, we've given you a traditional and a more modern format to choose from. Admittedly, not all stories or styles of writing will work within a standard format. Therefore, use your better judgment in deciding the architecture of the page.
2. There is an industry standard (though some may say old-fashioned) of using the 12-point Courier-New font; we've also noted that Times New Roman is used in more modern formatting. With the proliferation of computers and word-processing programs, there are literally hundreds of fonts to choose from. Whatever your choice, we recommend that you maintain a font size of 12 points – thereby assuring some reliable approximation of performance time.
3. Though you wrote the story, someone has to read it before anyone sees it. Therefore, make your manuscript easy to read by employing a standard format with clearly delineated page numbers, scene citations and act citations. Headers and footers are optional.
4. If you're using a software program, such as Final Draft, to format your work, be aware that you have the ability to create your own format in these programs that can be uniquely named, saved and applied to all of your manuscripts.
5. Usually between the title page and the first page of the story and/or dialogue, there is a page devoted to a character break-down. What's important to note on this page is the age, gender and name of each character. Some dramatists write brief character descriptions beside each name.
6. While it is cost-effective for both xeroxing and mailing, realize that some institutions prefer that you don't send double-sided documents. We recommend that you inquire about preference.

7. There is no right or wrong way to signify the end of a scene or act. Some writers do nothing but end the scene; others write "black out", "lights fade down", "End Act 1" or some other signifier that the scene or act has concluded.
8. The binding margin should be 1.5 inches from the edge. All other margins (top, bottom, right) should be 1.0 inch from the edge.

Sample Title Page

Text is centered in the page and includes the title, genre and author.

A Dog's Life

A full-length play

By Rachel Thompson

Include as much information as needed for someone to contact you.

Contact:
Rachel Thompson
3255 Temple Drive
Lake Charles, LA 32782
rthompson@yahoo.com

If you have an agent, you won't need to provide the personal information above.

Represented by:
David Stark
The Stark Agency
250 W. 47th, Ste. 310
New York, NY 10036

DG Member

© All rights reserved. 2007

Traditional Play Format

From Tennessee Williams' *Not About Nightingales*

Essential page numbering**

16.

```
                              BOSS
                         (removes cover from basket)
Speak of biscuits and what turns up but a nice batch of
homemade cookies! Have one young lady - Jim boy!

                    (Jim takes two.)

                              BOSS
Uh-huh, you've got an awful big paw, Jimmy!
                         (laughs)
Show the new Arky-what's-it to Miss Daily news - or is it
the Morning Star? Have a chair! I'll be right with you -
                         (vanishes for a moment)
Sweat, sweat, sweat's all I do these hot breezy days!

                              JIM
                         (sotto voce)
He thinks you're a newspaper woman.

                              BOSS
Turn on that fan.
                         (emerging)
Well, now, let's see -

                              EVA
To begin with I'm not -

                              BOSS
You've probably come here to question me about that ex-
convicts story in that damned yellow sheet down there in
Wilkes county - That stuff about getting Pellagra in here
 - Jimmy, hand me that sample menu!

                              JIM
She's not a reporter.

                              BOSS
Aw. - What is your business, young lady?

                    (She opens her purse and spills
                     contents on floor.)
```

Dialogue begins 1.5 inches from left side to account for binding. Dialogue is single-spaced.

Stage action is indented 3 inches from left; put in parenthesis. A blank line is inserted before and after.

Dialogue extends to 1.0 inch from right margin

Stage action reliant on the proceeding dialogue is indented to the left of the character name.

Character name in all caps; in the center of the page.

Standard font for this formatting is 12.0 point, Courier New.

Stage action is indented 3.0 inches from left margin and enclosed in parentheses.

****There are many ways to paginate your play, from the straightforward numerical sequence of 1, 2, 3 to an older format of I-2-16, (meaning Act 1, Scene 2, Page 16).**

Modern Play Format

From Tennessee Williams' *Not About Nightingales*

Essential page numbering

16.

BOSS

You've probably come here to question me about that ex-convicts story in that damned yellow sheet down there in Wilkes county – That stuff about getting Pellagra in here – Jimmy, hand me that sample menu!

Dialogue begins 1.5 inches from left side to account for binding. Dialogue is single-spaced.

JIM

Character name in all caps; in the center of the page.

She's not a reporter.

BOSS

Aw. – What is your business, young lady?

EVA

I understand there's a vacancy here. Mr. McBurney, my landlady's brother-in-law, told her that you were needing a new stenographer and I'm sure that I can qualify for the position. I'm a college graduate, Mr. Whalen, I've had three years of business experience – references with me – but, oh – I've – I've had such abominable luck these last six months. – the last place I worked – the business recession set in they had to cut down on their sales-force – they gave me a wonderful letter – I've got in with me.

Dialogue extends to 1.0 inch from right margin

She opens her purse and spills contents on floor.

Stage action begins in the center of the page and scans to the right margin. A blank line is inserted before and after.

BOSS

Anybody outside?

EVA

Yes. That woman.

BOSS

What woman?

Standard font for this formatting is 12.0 point, New Times Roman.

EVA

The one from Wisconsin. She's still waiting –

BOSS

I told you I don't want to see her.

(talking into phone)

How's the track, Bert? Fast? Okay.

Stage action reliant on the proceeding dialogue is indented to the left of the character name.

Sailor Jack's mother, MRS. BRISTOL, has quietly entered. She carries a blanket.

MRS. BRISTOL

I beg your pardon, I – You see I'm Jack Bristol's mother, and I've been wanting to have a talk with you so long about – about my boy!

Musical Format

From *APPLAUSE*, Book by Betty Comden, Adolph Green.
Music by Charles Strouse, Lyrics by Lee Adams

Essential page numbering**
56.

KAREN
(to Margo)
Margo, you've been kicking us all around long enough. Someone ought to give *you* a good swift one for a change!

(She leaves.)

EVE
Miss Channing . . . if I ever dreamed that anything I did could possibly cause you any unhappiness, or come between you and your friends . . . please believe me.

MARGO
(in a low, weary voice)
Oh, I do. And I'm full of admiration for you.
(stands, approaches Eve)
If you can handle yourself on the stage with the same artistry you display off the stage . . . well, my dear, you are in the right place.

(She speaks the following lines as the music of WELCOME TO THE THEATRE begins.)

Welcome to the theater, to the magic, to the fun!

(She sings.)

WHERE PAINTED TREES AND FLOWERS GROW
AND LAUGHTER RINGS FORTISSIMO,
AND TREACHERY'S SWEETLY DONE!

NOW YOU'VE ENTERED THE ASYLUM,
THIS PROFESSION UNIQUE
ACTORS ARE CHILDREN
PLAYING HIDE-AND-EGO-SEEK . . .

SO WELCOME, MISS EVE HARRINGTON,
TO THIS BUSINESS WE CALL SHOW,
YOU'RE ON YOUR WAY
TO WEALTH AND FAME,
UNSHEATH YOUR CLAWS,
ENJOY THE GAME!
YOU'LL BE A BITCH
BUT THEY'LL KNOW YOUR NAME
FROM NEW YORK . . . TO KOKOMO

WELCOME TO THEATRE,
MY DEAR, YOU'LL LOVE IT SO!

Dialogue begins 1.5 inches from left side to account for binding. Dialogue is single-spaced.

Character name in all caps; in the center of the page.

Stanzas are separated by a blank line and distinguish themselves by dramatic thought and/or changes from verse to chorus to bridges, etc.

Stage action is indented 3 inches from left; put in parentheses. A blank line is inserted before and after.

Dialogue extends to 1.0 inch from right margin

Stage action reliant on the proceeding dialogue is indented to the left of the character name.

Lyric are in all CAPS, separated line to line by either musical phrasing and/or the rhyming scheme and clearly indented from the left margin.

For duets, or characters singing counter-point, create two columns side by side, following the same format here.

****There are many ways to paginate your play, from the straight forward numerical sequence of 1, 2, 3 to an older format of I-2-16, (meaning Act 1, Scene 2, Page 16).**

The DG Statement on Submission Fees

The Dramatists Guild of America denounces the practice by festivals, play contests and educational events of charging excessive fees to dramatists who submit their work. Any request for submission fees should be accompanied by a complete explanation of how those fees are to be spent. The Guild also insists that contests and festivals announce the names of all finalists and winners to all participants.

It is important that members understand that submission fees are not the norm and, when required, the festival should offer something significant in return for the writer's investment, such as a large cash prize, a residency or a production. Reading fees are in no case acceptable, as most festivals receive that money from other grant sources. In no case should playwrights have to pay to simply have their work read.

The Guild also strongly disapproves of a festival's placing any encumbrances on the work as a result of the play being chosen a finalist or a participant. Any future participation in the life of the play must be earned by the festival by producing the work, and should never be granted by the writer without consultation with the Guild. If the festival expects any subsidiary income from the plays, that information should be stated clearly in all of the organization's printed and electronic materials related to the event.

The Council of the Guild feels that its members should be made aware of all legitimate opportunities available to them, and so we have listed in this section those particular contests and festivals that charge fees and have provided explanations regarding how their submission fees are spent, as well as full disclosure of any encumbrances they place on a selected writer's work, when offered by the sponsor.

Career Development Professionals

ACCOUNTANTS

This list isn't an endorsement, indication an accountant is taking new clients, nor obviously comprehensive. Many good accountants are not listed. Unless indicated otherwise, it is acceptable to contact accountants by phone.

Marks Paneth & Shron LLP
Marks Paneth & Shron LLP, 622 3rd Ave., New York, NY, 10017
David R. Marcus, Partner
dmarcus@markspaneth.com

Est. 1907. David R. Marcus, CPA, MBA, JD

Spielman, Koenigsberg and Parker (SKP)
Spielman, Koenigsberg and Parker (SKP), 888 7th Ave., Fl. 35, New York, NY, 10106
Richard Koenigsberg

Est. 1955. Partners: Melvin Spielman, Richard Koenigsberg, Gary Parker.

AGENTS

This list isn't an endorsement, indication an agent is taking new clients, nor comprehensive. Many good agents may not be listed. Unless indicated otherwise, send a query and synopsis with SASE to ONE agent at a time.

Abrams Artists Agency
275 7th Ave., Fl. 26, New York, NY, 10001
Sarah L. Douglas, Charles Kopelman, Co-Dirs., Literary Division
Tel: 646-486-4600
literary@abramsart.com; www.abramsartists.com/literary.html

Agents: Sarah L. Douglas, Charles Kopelman, Beth Blickers, Morgan Jenness, Maura Teitelbaum, Kate Navin, Ron Gwiazda. **Application.** Best Way: professional recommendation. Best Material: query, synopsis, SASE.

Alan Brodie Representation Ltd.
Fairgate House, 78 New Oxford St., FL. 6, London, WC1A 1HB England
Alan Brodie, Managing Dir
Tel: 44-20-7079-7990, Fax: 44-20-7079-7999
info@alanbrodie.com; www.alanbrodie.com

Staff: Alan Brodie, Sarah McNair, Lisa Foster **Preference.** Author Must Be: resident of UK preferred. Material Must Be: unoptioned. **Application.** Best Way: professional recommendation. Best Material: query, resume, SASE. Response: 3 mos.

Ann Elmo Agency
60 E. 42nd St., New York, NY, 10165
Letti Lee, Dir
Tel: 212-661-2880, Fax: 212-661-2883

Staff: Mari Cronin, Letti Lee. **Application.** Best Material: query, SASE. Response: 2 mos.

Ann Wright Representatives
165 W. 46th St.,#1105, New York, NY, 10036
Dan Wright, Head of Literary Dept.
Tel: 212-764-6770, Fax: 212-764-5125

Est. 1961. **Preference.** Length: all lengths. Style: all styles. Subject: all subjects. Material Must Be: unoptioned, unpublished, unproduced. **Application.** Best Way: invitation only. Best Material: query letter (note theme addressed), submissions returned with SASE. Response: 5/15/2004.

Barbara Hogenson Agency, Inc.
165 West End Ave., #19-C, New York, NY, 10023
Barbara Hogenson, Owner
Tel: 212-874-8084, Fax: 212-362-3011

Est. 1994. Staff: Nicole Verity. **Application.** Best Way: professional recommendation. Best Material: query, synopsis, SASE. Response: 2 mos.

Beacon Artists Agency
120 E. 56th St., #504, New York, NY, 10022
Patricia McLaughlin, President
Tel: 212-736-6630

Preference. Length: full-length. Style: all styles. Subject: all subjects. **Application.** Best Way: professional recommendation. Best Material: query letter, synopsis, 30-pg writing sample. Deadline: ongoing.

Bohrman Agency
8899 Beverly Blvd., #811, Los Angeles, CA, 90048
Tel: 310-550-5444

Agents: Caren Bohrman. **Preference.** Length: full length (over 90 min). Style: all styles. Subject: all subjects. **Application.** Best Way: professional recommendation. Best Material: query, No phone queries, SASP.

Bret Adams Ltd.
448 W. 44th St., New York, NY, 10036
Bruce Ostler, Co-Owner/President
Tel: 212-765-5630
www.bretadamsltd.net

Est. 1953 Staff: Antje Oegel (theatrical); Mark Orsini; Ilguna Becker, Marie Darden (literary) Margi Rountree, Ken Melamed, Michael Golden (acting). **Preference.** Style: all styles, comedy, drama, musical. **Application.** Best Way: professional recommendation. Best Material: query.

Epstein, Wyckoff, Corsa, Ross & Associates
Gary Epstein
Tel: 212-586-9110

Eric Glass Ltd.
25 Ladbroke Crescent, London, W11 1PS England
Tel: 44-20-7229-9500, Fax: 44-20-7229-6220

Preference. Length: full-length. Style: all styles. Subject: all subjects. **Application.** Best Way: professional recommendation. Best Material: synopsis, 30-pg writing sample, submissions returned with SASE.

Farber Literary Agency Inc.
14 E. 75th St., #2-E, New York, NY, 10021
Ann Farber, President
Tel: 212-861-7075, Fax: 212-861-7076
farberlit@aol.com; www.donaldfarber.com

Est.1990. Staff: Ann Farber, Donald C. Farber, Seth Farber. **Preference.** Length: full length (over 90 min). Material Must Be: unproduced. **Application.** Best Material: query, synopsis, full script, SASE. Response: 1 mo.

Fifi Oscard Agency, Inc.
110 W. 40th St., Fl. 21, New York, NY, 10018
Peter Sawyer, President
Tel: 212-764-1100, Fax: 212-840-5019
agency@fifioscard.com; www.fifioscard.com

Est. 1956. Literary Staff: Carolyn French, Carmen LaVia, Kevin McShane, Peter Sawyer.

Gage Group Inc.
14724 Ventura Blvd., #505, Sherman Oaks, CA, 91403
Jonathan Westover
Tel: 818-905-3800, Fax: 818-905-3322
literary-gagegroupla@gmail.com

Est. 1975. Agents: Martin Gage, Olivia Bowe **Preference.** Material Must Be: unoptioned, unpublished. **Application.** Best Way: professional recommendation. Best Material: query, submissions not returned. Response: 3 mos.

Gersh Agency Inc. [NY]
41 Madison Ave., Fl. 33, New York, NY, 10010
Peter Hagan, Head, Theater Dept.
Tel: 212-997-1818, Fax: 212-391-8459

Agents: John Buzzetti, Seth Glewen, Peter Hagan, Joyce Ketay, Carl Mulert, Sonia Pabley, Phyllis Wender, Scott Yoselow. **Application.** Best Way: professional recommendation. Best Material: query, SASE.

Graham Agency
311 W. 43rd St., New York, NY, 10036
Earl Graham, Agent
Tel: 212-489-7730

Preference. Length: full length (over 90 min). Style: no adaptation, no translation. Author Must Be: resident of US. **Application.** Best Material: query, SASE.

GSK Talent (Grant, Savic, Kopaloff)
6399 Wilshire Blvd., #414, Los Angeles, CA, 90048
Tel: 323-782-1854
www.gsktalent.com

Agents: Susan Grant, Ivana Savic, Don Kopaloff.

Harden Curtis Associates
850 7th Ave, #903, New York, NY, 10019
Mary Harden, President
Tel: 212-977-8502
hcrssc@hardencurtis.com; www.hardencurtis.com

Est. 1995. Staff: Mary Harden (Pres.), Diane Riley (Agent), Scott Ewards (Agent), Diana Glazer (Assistant) **Preference.** Length: full length (over 90 min). Style: all styles. Subject: all subjects. **Application.** Best Way: professional recommendation. Best Material: query. Best Time: May-August. Response: 2 mos.

International Creative Management (ICM) [CA]
10250 Constellation Blvd., Los Angeles, CA, 90067
Tel: 310-550-4000
books@icmtalent.com; www.icmtalent.com/lit/lit.html

Talent & lit agency. **Application.** Best Way: invitation.

International Creative Management (ICM) [NY]
825 8th Ave., New York, NY, 10019
Tel: 212-556-5600
books@icmtalent.com

Talent & lit agency. Staff: Patrick Herold, Buddy Thomas. **Application.** Best Way: invite.

International Creative Management (ICM) [UK]
4-6 Soho Sq., London, W1D 3PZ England
Tel: 44-20-7432-0800
books@icmtalent.com; www.icmtalent.com/lit/lit.html

Talent & lit agency.

Jim Flynn Agency
307 W. 38th St., #801, New York, NY, 10018
Tel: 212-868-1068

Judy Boals Inc.
307 W. 38th St., #812, New York, NY, 10018
info@judyboals.com; www.judyboals.com

Agents: Judy Boals **Application.** Best Way: invitation. Best Material: query, SASE. Response: 1 mo.

Kerin-Goldberg Associates
155 E. 55th St., #5-D, New York, NY, 10022
Charles Kerin, President
Tel: 212-838-7373, Fax: 212-838-0774
kgatalent@nyc.rr.com

Est. 1989. Staff: Ron Ross, Ellison Goldberg, Chris Nichols. **Preference.** Material Must Be: unproduced. **Application.** Best Way: invite. Best Material: query, SASE.

Lantz Office

200 W. 57th St., #503, New York, NY, 10019
Robert Lantz, Owner
Tel: 212-586-0200, Fax: 212-262-6659

Staff: Robert Lantz, Dennis Aspland. **Application.** Best Way: invite.

Mark Christian Subias Agency

331 W. 57th St, #462, New York, NY, 10019
Mark Christian Subias, Owner
marksubias@earthlink.net

Est. 2002. **Application.** Best Way: professional recommendation. Best Material: query.

Marton Agency, Inc.

1 Union Sq. W., #815, New York, NY, 10003
Tonda Marton, Agent
Tel: 212-255-1908, Fax: 212-691-9061
info@martonagency.com

Staff: Tonda Marton, Anne Reingold. Specializes in brokering foreign-language rights to US theater works. Promotes plays to associates abroad, generally after a production has been mounted in the US.

Paradigm

19 W. 44th St, #1410, New York, NY, 10036
Literary Dept.
Tel: 212-391-1112

Est. 1971. Agents: William Craver, Chris Till. **Preference.** Material Must Be: unoptioned, unpublished, unproduced. **Application.** Best Way: professional recommendation. Best Material: query, SASE. Response: 6 mos.

Peregrine Whittlesey Agency

279 Central Park West, New York, NY, 10024
Peregrine Whittlesey, Agent
Tel: 212-787-1802, Fax: 212-787-4985
pwwagy@aol.com

Preference. Length: full length (over 90 min). Material Must Be: unoptioned. **Application.** Best Way: invitation. Best Material: query, SASE.

Phoenix Artists, Inc.

321 West 44th Street, Ste 401, New York, NY, 10036
Tel: 212-586-9110

Agents: Gary Epstein and Randi Ross. Former partner of Epstein, Wyckoff & Associates. Reperesents Playwrights, Actors, composers and lyricists for stage and tv. **Application.** Best Material: synopsis, full script.

Robert A. Freedman Dramatic Agency Inc.

1501 Broadway, #2310, New York, NY, 10036
Marta Praeger, Agent

Est. 1917. **Preference.** Length: full length (over 90 min), mid-length (60-90 min). **Application.** Best Way: invite. Best Material: query, SASE. Response: 4 mos.

Soiree Fair Inc.

133 Midland Ave., #10, Montclair, NJ, 07042
Karen Gunn, Pres.
Soireefair@yahoo.com; www.soireefair.com

Est. 1995. **Preference.** Length: full length (over 90 min). Style: comedy, drama. Subject: GLBT, women. Author Must Be: resident of US. Material Must Be: unoptioned, unpublished, unproduced. **Application.** Best Way: professional recommendation. Best Material: query, synopsis.

Stephen Pevner, Inc.
382 Lafayette St., Fl. 8, New York, NY, 10003
Stephen Pevner, Producer
Tel: 212-674-8403

Susan Gurman Agency, LLC
865 West End Ave., #15-A, New York, NY, 10025
Tel: 212-749-4618
www.gurmanagency.com

Est. 1993. **Application.** Best Way: professional recommendation. Best Material: query, submissions not returned. Response: 2 wks.

Talent Representatives Inc.
307 E. 44th St., New York, NY, 10017
Tel: 212-752-1835

Application. Best Way: professional recommendation. Best Material: submissions returned with SASE.

William Morris Agency
1325 6th Ave., New York, NY, 10019
Tel: 212-586-5100

Staff: Val Day, Peter Franklin, Biff Liff, Roland Scahill, Jack Tantleff, Susan Weaving.

ATTORNEYS

This list isn't an endorsement, indication an attorney is taking new clients, nor comprehensive. Many good attorneys may not be listed. Unless indicated otherwise, it is acceptable to contact attorneys by phone.

Brooks & Distler
Brooks & Distler, 110 E. 59th St., Fl. 23, New York, NY, 10022
Marsha Brooks, Esq., Partner
Tel: 212-486-1400, Fax: 212-486-2266

Christensen, Glaser, Fink, Jacobs, Weil & Shapiro, LLP
10250 Constellation Blvd., Fl. 19, Los Angeles, CA, 90067
Joan Vento-Hall
Tel: 310-556-7840, Fax: 310-553-5336
jvento@chrisglase.com; www.chrisglase.com

Est. 1988.

Coblence & Associates
Coblence & Associates, 200 Park Ave. S., #910, New York, NY, 10003
Patricia Crown, Esq.
Tel: 212-593-8389, Fax: 212-358-9058
pcrown@coblence.com; www.coblence.com

Est. 1981. Formerly Coblence & Warner.

Cohen & Grossberg
Cohen & Grossberg, 770 Lexington Ave., New York, NY, 10065
David Grossberg, Partner
Tel: 212-688-6940

Est. 1955.

Cowan, DeBaets, Abrahams & Sheppard LLP
41 Madison Ave., Fl. 34, New York, NY, 10010
Frederick P. Bimbler, Esq., Partner
Tel: 212-974-7474, Fax: 212-974-8474
fbimbler@cdas.com; www.cdas.com

David H. Friedlander, Esq.
David H. Friedlander, Esq., 81 Park Dr., Mount Kisco, NY, 10549
David H. Friedlander, Esq.
Tel: 914-241-1277, Fax: 914-470-2244
david@dfriedlander.com; www.dfriedlander.com

Dumler & Giroux
488 Madison Ave., #1703, New York, NY, 10022
Leigh A. Giroux, Esq.
Tel: 212-759-4580, Fax: 212-751-1839
lgiroux@dumlerandgiroux.com

Firemark. Law Offices of Gordon P. Firemark
10940 Wilshire Blvd., Fl. 16, Los Angeles, CA, 90024
Gordon P. Firemark, Attorney at Law, Partner
Tel: 310-443-4185, Fax: 310-477-7676
gfiremark@theatrelawyer.com, gfiremark@firemark.com; www.theatrelawyer.com; www.firemark.com

Our practice is devoted exclusively to Theatre and Entertainment Law. We represent artists, directors, designers and producers of live, filmed, and recorded entertainment.

Fish & Richardson PC
Fish & Richardson PC, 225 Franklin St., Boston, MA, 02110
Elaine M. Rogers
Tel: 617 521-7886
elaine.rogers@fr.com; www.fr.com

Fitelson, Lasky, Aslan & Couture
Fitelson, Lasky, Aslan & Couture, 551 5th Ave., #605, New York, NY, 10176
Jerold Couture
Tel: 212-586-4700, Fax: 212-949-6746
dramalex@aol.com

Frankfurt, Kurnit, Klein & Selz
488 Madison Ave., New York, NY, 10022
S. Jean Ward, Esq.
Tel: 212-826-5584, Fax: 212-593-9175
sjward@fkkslaw.com; www.fkkslaw.com

Franklin, Weinrib, Rudell & Vassallo PC
Franklin, Weinrib, Rudell & Vassallo PC, 488 Madison Ave., New York, NY, 10022
Elliot H. Brown, Partner
Tel: 212-935-5500, Fax: 212-308-0642
www.fwrv.com

Graubart. Law Offices of Jeffrey L. Graubart
350 W. Colorado Blvd., #200, Pasadena, CA, 91105
Tel: 626-304-2800, Fax: 626-3042807
info@jlgraubart.com; www.lawyers.com/entertainmentlaw

Est. 1970.

Jassin. Law Offices of Lloyd J. Jassin
Jassin Law, 1560 Broadway, #400, New York, NY, 10036
Lloyd J. Jassin, Attorney
Tel: 212-354-4442, Fax: 212-840-4124
jassin@copylaw.com; www.copylaw.com

Est. 1991.

Jay Julien, Esq.
Jay Julien, Esq., 1501 Broadway, #1609, New York, NY, 10036
Jay Julien, President
Tel: 212-221-7575, Fax: 212-221-7386

Kaufmann, Feiner, Yamin, Gildin & Robbins LLP
777 3rd Ave., New York, NY, 10017
Ronald Feiner, Esq., Sr. Partner
Tel: 212-755-3174, Fax: 212-755-0431
rfeiner@kaufmannfeiner.com

Lazarus & Harris LLP
561 7th Ave., Fl. 11, New York, NY, 10018
Tel: 212-302-5252, Fax: 212-302-8181
www.lazhar.com

McLaughlin & Stern
260 Madison Ave., New York, NY, 10016
Alvin Deutsch, Esq., Partner
Tel: 212-448-1100, Fax: 212-448-0066
adeutsch@mclaughlinstern.com; www.mclaughlinstern.com

Est. 1898.

Paul, Weiss, Rifkind, Wharton & Garrison LLP
1285 6th Ave., New York, NY, 10019
John Breglio, Esq., Partner
Tel: 212-373-3391, Fax: 212-373-2092
jbreglio@paulweiss.com; www.paulweiss.com

Peter S. Cane, Esq.
410 W. 24th St., New York, NY, 10011
Tel: 212-922-9800
peter@canelaw.com

Robinson, Brog, Leinwand, Greene, Genovese & Gluck
1345 6th Ave., New York, NY, 10105
Richard M. Ticktin, Partner
Tel: 212-603-6308, Fax: 212-581-5981

Application. Best Way: professional recommendation. Best Material: query, SASE.

Sendroff & Baruch, LLP
Sendroff & Baruch, LLP, 1500 Broadway, #2001, New York, NY, 10036
Mark D. Sendroff, Esq., Partner
Tel: 212-840-6400, Fax: 212-840-6401
msendruff@sendroffbaruch.com; www.sendroffbaruch.com

Staff: Mark Sendroff, Jason Baruch, Eric S. Goldman.

Steiger. Law Office of Susan J. Steiger, Esq.
Susan J. Steiger, Esq., 11 E. 44th St., Fl. 9, New York, NY, 10017
Tel: 212-880-0865, Fax: 212-983-0415

Est. 1982.

Stern. Law Office of Miriam Stern
Miriam Stern, Esq., 303 E. 83rd St., Fl. 20, New York, NY, 10028
Miriam Stern, Esq., Attorney
Tel: 212-794-1289

Preference. Length: full length (over 90 min). **Application.** Best Way: recommendation, Telephone call. Best Material: query, SASE.

Volunteer Lawyers for the Arts (VLA)
Volunteer Lawyers for the Arts (VLA), 1 E. 53rd St., Fl. 6, New York, NY, 10022
Elena M. Paul, Esq., Exec Dir
Tel: 212-319-2787 x1, Fax: 212-752-6575
vlany@vlany.org; www.vlany.org

Est. 1969. Leading provider of pro bono legal and mediation services, educational programs and publications, and advocacy to the arts community in NYC area. Thru public advocacy, VLA frequently acts on issues vitally important to the arts community in NYC and beyond. **Consideration.** Fees: based on client's finances. **Preference.** Author Must Be: under certain income ceiling.

COMMERCIAL PRODUCERS

Some producers list a phone number. However, as a general rule, DO NOT call any producer. It is best to first inquire by mail, unless indicated otherwise.

Araca Group
260 W. 44th St., #501, New York, NY, 10036
Kirsten Berkman, Development Assoc
Tel: 212-869-0070, Fax: 212-869-0210
www.araca.com

Est. 1997. Matthew Rego, Michael Rego and Hank Unger are principals. Wicked, The Wedding Singer, 'night Mother, The Good Body, Urinetown, Frankie and Johnny in the Clair de Lune, Match, Debbie Does Dallas, The Vagina Monologues, The Laramie Project. **Application.** Best Way: agent. Best Material: full script, audio, SASE.

Cameron Mackintosh Inc.
Cameron Mackintosh Inc., 1650 Broadway, #800, New York, NY, 10019
Shidan Majidi, Production Assoc.
Tel: 212-921-9290, Fax: 212-921-9271

Mary Poppins, Les Miserables, The Phantom of the Opera, Oliver!, Oklahoma!, My Fair Lady, The Witches of Eastwick. **Application.** Best Way: agent.

Carole Shorenstein Hays Prods. (CSHP)
95 Fifth Ave, Fl 5, New York, NY, 10003
Michael Hurst, Exec Producer

Est. 2006.

Dodger Properties
311 W. 43rd St., #603, New York, NY, 10036
info@dodger.com; www.dodger.com

Est. 1978. The Farnsworth Invention, Jersey Boys. **Application.** Best Way: agent.

Frankel-Baruch-Viertel-Routh Group
729 7th Ave., Fl. 12, New York, NY, 10019
Richard Frankel, President
www.rfpny.com

Est. 1985. Principals: Richard Frankel, Tom Viertel, Steven Baruch, Marc Routh. Young Frankenstein, Hairspray, The Producers, The Fantasticks, Sweeney Todd Tour

Harold Prince
10 Rockefeller Plaza, #1004, New York, NY, 10020

Jane Harmon Associates
One Lincoln Plaza, #280, New York, NY, 10023
Jane Harmon

Est. 1979. Staff: Valentina Fratti, Jill Alexander. **Preference.** Length: full length (90 min and over). Style: no musical. Production: no orchestra size. Material Must Be: unoptioned, unpublished. **Application.** Best Way: unsolicited, professional recommendation, agent. Best Material: query, synopsis, SASE. Best Time: all year. Response: 4-6 wks..

Margery Klain

2107 Locust St., Philadelphia, PA, 19103
Margery Klain, Producer
Tel: 215-567-1512, Fax: 215-567-2049
mklain1011@aol.com

Est. 1985. A Shanya Maidel, Mountain, Das Barbecu, Broadway Opus. Staff: Matthew Klein. **Preference.** Length: full length (over 90 min). Material Must Be: unoptioned. **Application.** Best Way: professional recommendation. Best Material: query, SASE. Response: 2 mos.

Margo Lion Ltd.

Margo Lion Ltd., 246 W. 44th St., Fl. 8, New York, NY, 10036
Katie Marie Zouhary, Assoc Producer
Tel: 212-869-1112, Fax: 212-730-0381
office@margolionltd.com; www.margolionltd.com

Hairspray, The Cryptogram, Angels in America, Jelly's Last Jam. **Preference.** Length: full length (over 90 min). **Application.** Best Way: agent. Best Material: synopsis, 10-pg sample, audio, SASE. Response: 1 yr.

Nederlander Organization

The Nederlander Organization, 1450 Broadway, Fl. 6, New York, NY, 10018
Charlene Nederlander, VP, Corporate Development
Tel: 212-840-5577
www.nederlander.com

Est. 1912. **Application.** Best Way: agent.

New Time Productions

New Time Productions, 311 W. 43rd St., #305, New York, NY, 10036
Lauren Doll, Producer
Tel: 212-265-9659, Fax: 212-956-0498
www.newtimeproductions.com

Est. 1998. Equity Broadway, Off-Broadway, MSUA., Radio Golf, Faith Healer, Brooklyn, Squonk, Electra, On the Waterfront. **Preference.** Length: full length (over 90 min), mid-length (60-90 min). **Application.** Best Way: agent. Best Material: query, SASE.

Rick Hobard

Rick Hobard, 234 W. 44th St., New York, NY, 10036

Rodger Hess Productions Inc.

Rodger Hess Productions Inc., 1501 Broadway, New York, NY, 10036
Tel: 212-719-2233

Est. 1973.

Shubert Organization

234 W. 44th St., New York, NY, 10036
D.S. Moynihan, VP, Creaive Projects
www.shubertorganization.com

Est. 1900. Amour, The Blue Room, Closer, Amy's View, The Ride Down Mt. Morgan, Dirty Blonde, Dance of Death. **Application.** Best Way: agent.

Stewart F. Lane

Stewart F. Lane, 200 W. 57th St., #801, New York, NY, 10019
Stewart F. Lane
www.mrbroadway.com

Formerly Stellar Productions.

Susan Gallin Productions Inc.

Susan Gallin Productions Inc., 1501 Broadway, #1614, New York, NY, 10036
Susan Gallin, Producer
Tel: 212-840-1725, Fax: 212-768-4614
sgallin@aol.com

Spamalot, Woman Before a Glass, The Retreat From Moscow, Man of La Mancha, Hedda Gabler, The Shape of Things, Fully Committed, Burn This, The Rothschilds, Cowgirls, Other People's Money, From the Mississippi Delta, Angels in America, Stomp, The Cryptogram (London). **Preference.** Material Must Be: unoptioned, unproduced. **Application.** Best Way: agent. Best Material: full script.

Weissberger Theater Group

Weissberger Theater Group, 240 W. 44th St., New York, NY, 10036
Richard Garmise
Tel: 212-644-3335, Fax: 212-644-3343
jayharrisnyc@aol.com

Est. 1992. Want scripts with plot line and edge. Past productions: Dirty Rotten Scoundrels, Never Gonna Dance, Side Man, Down the Road, Freefall, Dates and Nuts, Where the Truth Lies, Enter the Guardsman, Tamicanfly. **Preference.** Length: full length (over 90 min). Style: comedy, drama. Subject: topical, issue-oriented. Production: cast limit 7. Material Must Be: unoptioned, unproduced. **Application.** Best Material: query, synopsis. Response: 1 mo query, 2 mos script.

PUBLISHERS

Many publishers also license performances; that is, they grant permission to perform your work and collect royalties for you. To the best of our knowledge, the author retains copyright with all the publishers we list.

Alaska Quarterly Review (AQR)
Univ. of Alaska, Anchorage (UAA), 3211 Providence Dr., Anchorage, AK, 99508
Ronald Spatz, Editor
Tel: 907-786-6916, Fax: 907-786-6916
ayaur@uaa.alaska.edu; www.uaa.alaska.edu/aqr

Est. 1982. Fiction, short plays, poetry and literary nonfiction in traditional and experimental styles. **Consideration.** Remuneration: 1 contributor's copy and a 1-year subscription. Frequency: semiannual. **Preference.** Length: one-act (up to 60 min), short (up to 30 min). Style: open to all styles. Subject: open to a full range of literary subject matter for adult audiences. **Application.** Best Material: application, full script. Response: 6 mos.

Alfreda's Reader's Theater
Box 480443, Denver, CO, 80248
A. Doyle, Founder
www.alfredasreaderstheater.com

Est. 1999. **Preference.** Length: short (under 30 min). Material Must Be: under copyright. **Application.** Best Way: invite. Best Material: SASE. Best Time: when advertised.

Anchorage Press Plays Inc.
Anchorage Press Plays Inc., 617 Baxter Ave., Louisville, KY, 40204
Marilee Hebert Miller, Publisher
Tel: 502-583-2288, Fax: 502-583-2288
applays@bellsouth.net; www.applays.com

Est. 1935. Performances licensed. Educational, professional and amateur venues. **Consideration.** Remuneration: royalty. **Preference.** Length: full length (over 90 min), one-act (30-60 min). Style: adaptation, musical, translation. Subject: children's, teen, young adult. **Application.** Best Material: full script. Response: 6 -9 mos.

Arte Publico Press
Univ. of Houston, 452 Cullen Performance Hall, Houston, TX, 77204
Nicolas Kanellos, Publisher
Tel: 713-743-2988, Fax: 713-743-2847
www.arte.uh.edu

Est. 1979. Contemporary and recovered lit by US Hispanic authors. **Consideration.** Remuneration: royalty, copies. **Preference.** Length: full length (over 90 min), one-act (30-60 min). Subject: Hispanic. Material Must Be: unpublished, in English or Spanish. **Application.** Best Material: full script, SASE. Response: 6 mos.

Asian American Writers Workshop
Asian American Writers Workshop, 16 W. 32nd St. #10-A, New York, NY, 10001
Quang Bao, Executive Director
Tel: 212-494-0061, Fax: 212-494-0062
desk@aaww.org; www.aaww.org

Est. 1991. Semiannual paperback incl short fiction, poems, essays, stage scripts, translations and artwork. **Consideration.** Remuneration: 2 copies. Frequency: semiannual. **Preference.** Length: one-act (30-60 min). **Application.** Best Material: full script (4 copies). Response: 8 mos.

Asian Theatre Journal

Univ. of Hawai'i Press, 2840 Kolowalu St., Honolulu, HI, 96822
Journals Dept.
Tel: 808-956-8255, Fax: 800-650-7811
uhpjourn@hawaii.edu; www.uhpress.hawaii.edu/journals

Dedicated to performing arts of Asia, traditional and modern, incl. original and translated plays. **Preference.** Subject: Asian. **Application.** Best Material: query, submissions not returned.

Audience

303 Park Ave. S., #1440, New York, NY, 10010
M. Stefan Strozier, Editor
Tel: 646-620-7406
stozier@worldaudience.org; www.worldaudience.org

Quarterly literary journal of short stories, poetry, plays, interviews, essays, and more. **Consideration.** Remuneration: royalties. Frequency: quarterly. **Preference.** Length: all length. Style: all styles. Subject: all subjects. **Application.** Best Way: unsolicited, professional recommendation, agent. Best Material: query, synopsis, 10-page sample. Best Time: September. Response: 2-4 wks..

Baker's Plays

45 W. 25th Street, New York, NY, 10010
Assoc. Editor
Tel: 212-255-8085, Fax: 212-627-7753
publications@bakersplays.com; www.bakersplays.com

Consideration. Remuneration: royalty. **Preference.** Length: full length (over 90 min), one-act (30-60 min). Subject: high school, junior high school, religious. Material Must Be: produced. **Application.** Best Way: web submissions. Best Material: full script, audio, resume, SASE. Response: 8 mos.

Big Dog Publishing

Box 1400, Tallevast, FL, 34270
Dawn Remsing, Editor
info@bigdogplays.com; www.bigdogplays.com

Est. 2005. Plays for family and school audiences (K-12). Publishes 25-40 plays/year. **Consideration.** Remuneration: 50\% royalty, 10\% book, complimentary copies (50\% discount on additional copies). **Preference.** Length: full length, one-act, short play collections, adaptations, plays for young audiences, children's plays, musicals, skit collections, monologue collections, Halloween, Christmas (no religious plays). Material Must Be: unpublished, prefers produced works. **Application.** Best Material: send entire script, production history, music, no email submissions accepted, SASE. Response: 2-3 mos.

Broadway Play Publishing Inc. (BPPI)

56 E. 81st St., New York, NY, 10028
Christopher Gould, President
Tel: 212-772-8334, Fax: 212-772-8358
sara@broadwayplaypubl.com; www.broadwayplaypubl.com

Est. 1982. **Consideration.** Remuneration: 10\% book, 80\% amateur, 90\% stock royalty; 10 complimentary copies. **Preference.** Length: full length (over 90 min). Style: comedy, drama. Material Must Be: produced, original. **Application.** Best Material: query. Response: 2 mos query, 4 mos script.

Brooklyn Publishers

Brooklyn Publishers, 1841 Cord St., Odessa, TX, 79762
David LeMaster, Sr Editor
Tel: 432-550-5532, Fax: 432-368-0340
info@brookpub.com; www.brookpub.com

Est. 1996. **Consideration.** Remuneration: royalty, 10 copies. **Preference.** Length: full length (over 90 min), one-act (30-60 min), monologue. Style: adaptation, comedy, drama, mystery. Subject: children's. Production: performers grades 6-12. **Application.** Best Material: full script. Response: 2 mos.

Callaloo

Texas A&M Univ. (TAMU), 4227 TAMU, College Station, TX, 77843
Charles H. Rowell, Editor
Tel: 979-458-3108, Fax: 979-458-3275
callaloo@tamu.edu; callaloo.tamu.edu

Quarterly journal by/about African-Americans and the African Diaspora, incl. original, unpublished essays, interviews, short fiction, poetry, drama, and visual art. **Consideration.** Remuneration: complimentary copies. Frequency: quarterly. **Preference.** Length: short (under 30 min). Style: no musical. **Application.** Best Material: query, full script (3 copies), SASE. Response: 6 mos.

Capilano Review (TCR)

Capilano Coll., 2055 Purcell Way, N. Vancouver, BC, V7J 3H5 Canada
Carol Hamshaw, Managing Editor
Tel: 604-984-1712
contact@thecapilanoreview.ca; www.thecapilanoreview.ca

Est. 1972. **Consideration.** Remuneration: publication, pay. **Preference.** Length: short (under 20 pages). Style: drama. Material Must Be: unpublished. **Application.** Best Material: SASE (Canadian postage). Response: 4 mos.

Contemporary Drama Service

Meriwether Publishing Ltd., 885 Elkton Dr., Colorado Springs, CO, 80907
Arthur Zapel
Fax: 719-594-9916
merpcds@aol.com; www.contemporarydrama.com

Est. 1970. School, college, church and amateur venues. **Consideration.** Remuneration: 10\% royalty. **Preference.** Length: mid-length (60-90 min), one-act (30-60 min), short (under 30 min). Style: no translation. Subject: Asian, Black, children's, religious, women. Production: age 12-30, cast limit 20. Author Must Be: age 16 or older, resident or citizen of US. Material Must Be: unoptioned, unpublished, unproduced. **Application.** Best Material: query, SASE. Response: 1 mo.

Drama Source

1588 E. 361 N., St. Anthony, ID, 83445
Daris Howard, President
Tel: 208-624-4726
info@dramasource.com; www.dramasource.com

Est. 1997. **Consideration.** Remuneration: 70\% royalty, 10\% sales, 50\% video. **Preference.** Subject: no profanity, family friendly. **Application.** Best Way: email. Best Material: query, synopsis, audio. Best Time: Aug. Response: 3 mos.

Dramatic Publishing Company

Dramatic Publishing Company, 311 Washington St., #129, Woodstock, IL, 60098
Linda Habjan, Submissions Editor
Tel: 800-448-7469, Fax: 800-334-5302
plays@dramaticpublishing.com; www.dramaticpublishing.com

Est. 1885. Performances licensed, all venues but 1st Class. **Application.** Best Material: full script, SASE. Response: 8 mos.

Dramatics Magazine

Educational Theatre Assn., 2343 Auburn Ave., Cincinnati, OH, 45219
Don Corathers, Editor
Tel: 513-421-3900, Fax: 513-421-7077
dcorathers@edta.org; www.edta.org/publications/dramatics.asp

Est. 1929. Natl. monthly magazine for HS theater students & teachers, printing 7 one-acts and full-lengths/yr. **Consideration.** Remuneration: $100-$500 honorarium, 5 copies. **Preference.** Length: full length (over 90 min), one-act (30-60 min). Style: comedy, drama. Subject: suitable for HS. Material Must Be: unpublished. **Application.** Best Material: full script. Response: 5 mos.

Dramatists Play Service Inc.
440 Park Ave. S., New York, NY, 10016
Michael Q. Fellmeth, VP, Publications
Tel: 212-683-8960, Fax: 212-213-1539
fellmeth@dramatists.com; www.dramatists.com

Performances licensed. All venues except commercial. **Consideration.** Remuneration: 10\% book, 80\% amateur, 90\% stock; 10 copies. **Preference.** Length: full length (over 90 min). Style: comedy, drama, musical. **Application.** Best Material: query, synopsis. Response: 6 mos.

Eldridge Publishing Company Inc.
Box 14367, Tallahassee, FL, 32317
Nancy S. Vorhis, Sr Editor
Tel: 800-447-8243, Fax: 850-385-2463
editorial@histage.com; www.histage.com

Est. 1906. Performances licensed, all venues. **Consideration.** Remuneration: 10\% book, 50\% amateur/educational. **Preference.** Material Must Be: email (MS Word, PDF) to newworks@histage.com. **Application.** Best Material: query, full script, audio, SASE. Response: 2 mos.

Empire Publishing Service
Box 1344, Studio City, CA, 91614

Est. 1960. Publishes performing arts books, incl. sheet music. Distributes for Players Press, Java Publications, Arte Publico Press, D-Books Intl., and others. Also distributes performing arts cassettes through direct mail and trade sales. **Consideration.** Remuneration: royalty. **Preference.** Material Must Be: produced. **Application.** Best Material: query, SASE.

Freelance Press
Box 548, Dover, MA, 02030
Narcissa Campion, Managing Editor
Tel: 508-785-8250, Fax: 508-785-8291
www.freelancepress.org

Est. 1979 **Consideration.** Remuneration: 10\% sales, 70\% performance royalty. **Preference.** Length: one-act (30-60 min). Style: musical. Subject: children's. Material Must Be: unpublished. **Application.** Response: 3 mos.

Green Integer
6022 Wilshire Blvd., #200-A, Los Angeles, CA, 90036
Per Bregne, Editor
Tel: 323-857-1115
info@greeninteger.com; www.greeninteger.com

Works published to date incl. essays, interviews, poems, plays, speeches and novels. **Consideration.** Remuneration: royalty, 10 copies. **Preference.** Length: full length (over 90 min). Style: comedy, drama, translation. Material Must Be: unpublished. **Application.** Best Material: query. Response: 1 mo.

Gumbo Media
Box 480443, Denver, CO, 80248
A. Doyle, Founder
www.gumbomedia.com

Markets comedy scripts, e-books, stories, lyrics, film, etc. Licenses lyrics, scripts, music, content, stories, educational products, etc.

HaveScripts.com
Tidewater Dramatists Guild (TDG), 204 Oakengate Turn, Virginia Beach, VA, 23462
Jean Klein, President
www.havescripts.com

Est. 2003. Online catalog of new plays. **Preference.** Length: full length (over 90 min), mid-length (60-90 min), one-act (30-60 min). Material Must Be: unpublished. **Application.** Best Material: query, submissions not returned. Best Time: Jun. Response: 1 mo.

Heuer Publishing LLC

Box 248, Cedar Rapids, IA, 52406
Steven S. Michalicek, Publisher
Tel: 800-950-7529, Fax: 319-368-8011
editor@hitplays.com; www.hitplays.com

Est. 1928. Serves educational & community markets. Publish plays, musicals, anthologies, resource books. Performances licensed, amateur & professional venues. Staff: Geri Albrecht (Editor). **Consideration.** Remuneration: outright purchase or royalty. **Preference.** Style: musical, light opera, serial, interactive, dinner theater, radio; no translation. Subject: education-based, multicultural, social awareness; no disabled. Production: age 13 and older. Material Must Be: unpublished. **Application.** Best Material: query, synopsis, full script, SASE. Best Time: Oct-May. Response: 2 mos.

Kalliope: A Journal of Women's Literature & Art

Florida Community College, 11901 Beach Blvd., Jacksonville, FL, 32246
Margaret Clark, Editor
www.fccj.org/kalliope

Kalliope publishes poetry, short fiction, interviews, reviews, and visual art by women. Copyright reverts to the author upon request. **Consideration.** Remuneration: 2 copies. Frequency: semiannual. **Preference.** Length: one-act (30-60 min). Author Must Be: female. Material Must Be: unpublished. **Application.** Best Material: query, full script, SASE. Response: 6 mos.

1/31/08. Kenyon Review

Walton House, 104 College Dr., Gambier, OH, 43022
Daniel Kramer, Drama Editor
Tel: 740-427-5208, Fax: 740-427-5417
kenyonreview@kenyon.edu; www.kenyonreview.org

Est. 1939. **Consideration.** Remuneration: cash payment; 2 copies. **Preference.** Length: one-act (30-60 min), or excerpt or translation. Style: comedy, drama. Material Must Be: unpublished. **Application.** Best Way: online. Best Material: query. Best Time: Sep-Jan. Deadline: 31-Jan-08. Response: 4 mos.

Lazy Bee Scripts

2 Wood Rd., Ashurst, Southampton, SO40 7BD England
Stuart Ardern

Consideration. Remuneration: royalties. **Preference.** Length: all length. Style: all styles. Subject: all subjects. Material Must Be: unpublished. **Application.** Best Way: unsolicited. Best Material: query, SASE overseas postage. Response: query response within 7 days.

Lillenas Drama Resources

Box 419527, Kansas City, MO, 64141
Kimberly R. Messer, Drama Resources Editor
Tel: 816-931-1900, Fax: 816-412-8390
drama@lillenas.com; www.lillenasdrama.com

Perfs licensed (school, church, dinner & community). **Consideration.** Remuneration: outright purchase or royalty. **Preference.** Length: full length (over 90 min), one-act (30-60 min). Style: comedy, drama. Subject: Christian. Material Must Be: unpublished, produced. **Application.** Best Material: full script, SASE. Response: 4 mos.

Limelight Scripts

152 Southey Hill, Sheffield, S5 8BN England
Dewey Willis, Jacqueline Willis

est. 2005 **Preference.** Length: all length. Style: comedy, drama, musical. Subject: all subjects. Author Must Be: over 18. **Application.** Best Way: invitation only, make inquiry. Best Material: query, synopsis, SASE. Response: 24 hours.

Moose Hide Books
Moose Enterprise Book & Theatre Play Publishing, 684 Walls Rd., Sault Ste. Marie, ON, P6A 5K6 Canada
Richard Mousseau, Publisher
Tel: 705-779-3331, Fax: 705-779-3331
www.moosehidebooks.com

Application. Best Way: unsolicited. Best Material: query, SASE. Response: 1 month.

Music Theatre International (MTI)
421 W. 54th St., New York, NY, 10019
Russell Ochocki, Assoc Dir, Professional Licensing
Tel: 212-541-4684
www.mtishows.com

Est. 1952. Performances licensed, all venues. MTI is a secondary licensing agency and prefers musicals that have been produced. **Preference.** Length: full length (over 90 min). Style: musical. Material Must Be: produced. **Application.** Best Material: query.

New Plays Inc.
Box 5074, Charlottesville, VA, 22905
Patricia Forrest, Editor/Publisher
Tel: 434-823-7555
pat@newplaysforchildren.com; www.newplaysforchildren.com

Est. 1963. Publishing house representing plays for young audiences. **Consideration.** Remuneration: 10\% sales, 50\% performance royalty. **Preference.** Length: mid-length (60-90 min), one-act (30-60 min). Subject: children's. Material Must Be: produced. **Application.** Best Material: query, full script, SASE. Response: 2 mos.

Norman Maine Publishing
Box 1400, Tallevast, FL, 34270
Dawn Remsing, Editor
info@normanmaineplays.com; www.normanmaineplays.com

Est. 2005. Plays for community, professsional, and university theatre. **Consideration.** Remuneration: 50\% royalty, 10\% book, complimentary copies (50\% discount on additional copies). **Preference.** Length: full length (over 90 min), one-act (30-60 min.), adaptations, musicals, short play collections, Halloween, Christmas (no religious plays). Material Must Be: unpublished, prefers produced and/or award-winning works. **Application.** Best Material: full script, production history, music, no email submissions accepted, SASE. Response: 2-3 mos.

Original Works Publishing
4611 Ambrose Ave., Los Angeles, CA, 90027
Jason Aaron Goldberg, President
info@originalworksonline.com; www.originalworksonline.com

Est. 2000. **Consideration.** Fees: never. Remuneration: 80\% production royalty, 15\% sales; 2 copies. **Preference.** Length: all length. Style: comedy, drama, musical, truly original works. Subject: all subjects. Author Must Be: over 18. Material Must Be: produced. **Application.** Best Material: check website for specific submission guidelines. Response: 1-2 months.

PAJ: A Journal of Performance and Art
Box 532, Village Sta., New York, NY, 10014
Bonnie Marranca, Editor
Tel: 212-243-3885, Fax: 212-243-2885
pajpub@mac.com; mitpress.mit.edu/paj

Est. 1976. **Preference.** Length: one-act (30-60 min). Style: translation, solo. **Application.** Best Material: query, synopsis. Response: 2 mos query, 2 mos script.

Players Press Inc.
Box 1132, Studio City, CA, 91614
Robert W. Gordon, VP Editor
Tel: 818-789-4980

Est. 1960. **Consideration.** Remuneration: royalties. **Preference.** Length: all length. Style: all styles. Subject: all subjects. Material Must Be: unpublished, produced. **Application.** Best Material: query, SASE. Response: 2 wks query, 6 mos script.

Playscripts, Inc.
325 W. 38th St, #305, New York, NY, 10018
Publications Director
Tel: 866-639-7529
submissions@playscripts.com; www.playscripts.com

Est. 1998. Acting editions sold and performances licensed to amateur/professional venues worldwide. **Preference.** Length: all length. Style: no musical. Subject: all subjects. Material Must Be: unpublished by another exclusive publisher. **Application.** Best Way: see website for latest submission preferences and guidelines; electronic submissions preferred.

11/30/2008. Poems & Plays
Middle Tennessee State Univ. (MTSU), MTSU English Dept., Murfreesboro, TN, 37132
Gaylord Brewer, Editor
Tel: 615-898-2712
gbrewer@mtsu.edu; www.mtsu.edu/~english2/Journals/poemsandplays/index.html

Est. 1993. **Consideration.** Remuneration: 1 copy. Frequency: annual. **Preference.** Length: short (under 30 min). Material Must Be: unpublished. **Application.** Best Material: full script, SASE. Best Time: Oct-Nov. Deadline: 30-Nov-08. Response: 3 mos.

Popular Play Service
Box 3365, Bluffton, SC, 29910
Editor
Tel: 843-705-7981
popplays@hargray.com; www.popplays.com

Performances licensed. All venues, particularly community. **Consideration.** Remuneration: feedback. **Preference.** Length: full-length. Style: comedy, farce. Subject: all subjects. Material Must Be: unoptioned, unpublished, unproduced, still in development. **Application.** Best Way: professional recommendation. Best Material: query letter (note theme addressed), synopsis, cast 26 scene list, SASE.

Prism International
Univ. of British Columbia, Buchanan E462, 1866 Main Mall, Vancouver, BC, V6T 1Z1 Canada
Kellee Ngan, Exec Editor
Tel: 604-822-2514, Fax: 604-822-3616
prism@intercharge.ubc.ca; prism.arts.ubc.ca

Est. 1959 **Consideration.** Remuneration: $20/printed pg. Frequency: quarterly. **Preference.** Length: short (under 30 min). Material Must Be: unpublished. **Application.** Best Way: no email submissions. Best Material: query, full script, resume, SASE (Canadian). Response: 6 mos, email.

Resource Publications, Inc.
160 E. Virginia St., #290, San Jose, CA, 95112
Wiliam Burns, Editor
Tel: 408-286-8505, Fax: 408-287-8748
editor@rpinet.com; www.resourcepublications.com

Consideration. Remuneration: royalty. **Preference.** Length: short (10-30 min.). Subject: suitable for middle or high school students. **Application.** Best Material: full script. Response: 2 mos.

Rockford Review
Rockford Writers' Guild, Box 858, Rockford, IL, 61105
David Ross, Editor
daveconnieross@aol.com; writersguild1.tripod.com

Est. 1947. Semiannual (winter, summer) 100-pg literary arts journal. Summer issue is devoted to RWG members. **Consideration.** Remuneration: publication, 1 copy. Frequency: semiannual. **Preference.** Length: short (under 30 min). Material Must Be: unpublished. **Application.** Best Material: query, full script, SASE. Response: 2 mos.

Samuel French Inc.
45 W. 25th St., New York, NY, 10010
Roxane Heinze-Bradshaw, Managing Editor
Tel: 212-206-8990, Fax: 212-206-1429
publications@samuelfrench.com; www.samuelfrench.com

Est. 1830. Performances licensed for amateur, stock, professional and foreign venues in all media. **Consideration.** Remuneration: 10\% sales, performance royalty. **Application.** Best Material: full script, SASE. Response: 2 mos.

Sinister Wisdom Journal
Box 1180, Sebastopol, CA, 95473
Fran Day, Editor
fran@sonic.net; www.sinisterwisdom.org

Est. 1976. Lesbian-feminist triannual literary journal. **Consideration.** Remuneration: 2 copies. **Preference.** Length: short (under 30 min). Style: drama. Subject: lesbian, multiethnic. Author Must Be: age 21 or older. Material Must Be: unoptioned, unproduced. **Application.** Best Material: synopsis, SASE. Response: 6 mos.

Slavic and East European Performance
Martin E. Segal Theatre Center, Graduate Center, 365 5th Ave., New York, NY, 10016
Daniel Gerould, Editor
Tel: 212-817-1866
seep@gc.cuny.edu; web.gc.cuny.edu

Preference. Material Must Be: unpublished. **Application.** Best Way: unsolicited.

Smith and Kraus
Box 127, Lyme, NH, 03768
Marisa Smith, Publisher
Tel: 603-643-6431, Fax: 603-643-1831
sandk@sover.net; www.smithkraus.com

Consideration. Remuneration: payment or royalty. **Preference.** Length: full length (over 90 min), one-act (30-60 min), monologues. Style: no musical. Subject: children's. **Application.** Best Material: query, synopsis. Response: 3 wks query; 4 mos script.

Speert Publishing
New York, NY
Eleanore Speert, President
Tel: 212-979-7656
espeert@speertpublishing.com; www.speertpublishing.com

Self-publishing services for acting editions of original plays. **Preference.** Length: full length (over 90 min), one-act (30-60 min). Style: no musical. **Application.** Best Way: email. Best Material: query. Response: 1 wk.

Story Time Stories That Rhyme

Box 416, Denver, CO, 80201
A. Doyle, Founder
Tel: 303-575-5676
mail@storytimestoriesthatrhyme.net; www.storytimestoriesthatrhyme.net

Est. 1989. Educational partnership with literacy, entertainment, storytelling, bibliotherapy and poetry therapy. **Preference.** Length: short (under 30 min). Subject: children's. **Application.** Best Material: query.

Tams-Witmark Music Library Inc.

560 Lexington Ave., New York, NY, 10022
Tel: 212-688-2525, Fax: 212-688-3232

Classic broadway musicals for stage performance around the world.

Theater Magazine

Yale Univ. School of Drama, Box 208244, New Haven, CT, 06520
Tom Sellar, Editor
www.theatermagazine.org

Est. 1968. Tri-quaterly journal of criticism, reports, interviews and plays. **Preference.** Length: full length (over 90 min). Material Must Be: unpublished. **Application.** Best Material: query. Response: 6 mos.

Theatre Communications Group (TCG)

520 8th Ave., Fl. 24, New York, NY, 10018
Terence Nemeth, Publisher
Tel: 212-609-5900 x239, Fax: 212-609-5901
tnemeth@tcg.org; www.tcg.org

Consideration. Remuneration: 7\%-10\% royalty.

Theatrefolk

P.O. Box 1064, Crystal Beach, ON, M6P 1Y9 Canada
Craig Mason, Publisher
Tel: 866-245-9138, Fax: 1-877-245-9138
tfolk@theatrefolk.com; www.theatrefolk.com

We publish plays specifically for student performers **Consideration.** Remuneration: royalties. **Preference.** Style: all styles. Subject: youth issues 26 themes. Production: simple. **Application.** Best Way: unsolicited. Best Material: full script. Response: 6-8 wks..

TheatreForum

Univ. of California, San Diego, 9500 Gilman Dr., 0344, La Jolla, CA, 92093
Summer Moshy, Business Mgr
Tel: 858-822-2719, Fax: 858-534-1080
theatreforum@ucsd.edu; www.theatreforum.org

Published twice/yr. Editors: Jim Carmody, John Rouse, Adele Edling Shank, Theodore Shank. **Consideration.** Remuneration: $200 , 10 copies. Frequency: semiannual. **Preference.** Length: full length (over 90 min). Material Must Be: produced professionally. **Application.** Best Way: professional recommendation. Best Material: query, submissions not returned. Response: 3 mos.

Theatrical Rights Worldwide

1359 Broadway, #914, New York, NY, 10018
Steve Spiegel, President & CEO
Tel: 866-378-9758, Fax: 212-643-1322
licensing@theatricalrights.com; www.theatricalrights.com

Est. 2006. Staff: Steve Spiegel (Pres/CEO). **Consideration.** Remuneration: royalties. **Preference.** Length: full length (over 90 min), mid-length (60-90 min.), one-act (30-60 min.). Style: musical. Subject: all subjects. Material Must Be: unpublished. **Application.** Best Way: professional recommendation, agent. Best Material: query, full script, audio. Response: 3-6 mos.

Career Development Opportunities

COLONIES & RESIDENCIES

12/31/08. $10. Alden B. Dow Creativity Center

Northwood Univ., 4000 Whiting Dr., Midland, MI, 48640
Grover B. Procter Jr., Exec Dir
Tel: 989-837-4478, Fax: 989-837-4468
creativity@northwood.edu; www.northwood.edu/abd

Residency of 10 wks (Jun-Aug) on campus. Residents housed in furnished apts that double as workspace. **Consideration.** Fees: $10 application. Assistance: $750 stipend, $500 travel, $1,750 per diem limit. Frequency: annual. **Application.** Best Material: application, sample, resume, SASE. Deadline: 31-Dec-08.

Altos de Chavon

Parsons School of Design, 66 5th Ave., #604-A, New York, NY, 10011
Carmen Lorente, Program Coord.
Tel: 212-229-5370, Fax: 212-229-8988
altos@earthlink.net; www.altosdechavon.com

Est. 1981. 3-mo residencies in La Romana, Dominican Rep, for visual artists, writers, musicians, and architects.

Artward Bound Residency Program

The Field, 161 6th Ave., Fl. 14, New York, NY, 10013
Jennifer Wright Cook, Executive Dir.
Tel: 212-691-6969, Fax: 212-255-2053
jennifer@thefield.org; www.thefield.org

Residencies of 10-14 days (Jun-Sep) at rural facilities outside NYC. **Consideration.** Fees: free ($100 refundable deposit). Assistance: room/board, travel. **Preference.** Length: short (under 30 min). Author Must Be: resident of NYC area, 3-yr professional. **Application.** Best Material: application. Best Time: after 3/1/08. Response: 1 mo.

$25+$850. Atlantic Center for the Arts

1414 Art Center Ave., New Smyrna Beach, FL, 32168
James Frost, Program Mgr.
Tel: 386-427-6975, Fax: 386-427-5669
program@atlanticcenterforthearts.org; www.atlanticcenterforthearts.org

Est. 1982. Residencies of 3 wks with master artists on FL's east coast. Workspace incl black box theater, music/recording studio, dance studio, art & sculpture studios, digital lab, and resource library. **Consideration.** Fees: $25 application, $850 program. Assistance: $800 limit stipend, $800 limit room/board. **Application.** Best Material: application, SASE.

2/1/08. $20. Blue Mountain Center

Box 109, Blue Mt. Lake, NY, 12812
Ben Strader
Tel: 518-352-7391
bmc@bluemountaincenter.org; www.bluemountaincenter.org

Residencies of 4 wks (Jun-Oct) in Adirondack Mts. Workspace incl music studio. Cell phones are not allowed on the property. **Consideration.** Fees: $20 application. **Application.** Best Material: query, application, 30-pg sample, bio. Deadline: 1-Feb-08.

3/3/08. $35 + $300. Byrdcliffe Arts Colony Artist-in-Residence (AIR)

Woodstock Byrdcliffe Guild (WBG), 34 Tinker St., Woodstock, NY, 12498
Katherine Burger, Dir, Artist in Residence
Tel: 845-679-2079, Fax: 845-679-4529
wguild@ulster.net; www.woodstockguild.org

Est. 1980. located in the Catskill Mountains, Woodstock, NY USA. Founded as an Arts & Crafts community in 1903, it has been a haven for visual artists, potters, writers, cafts people, musicians and theatre artists for almost a century. The Residency Program offers writers, visual artists and composers one-month residencies from June-September. **Consideration.** Fees: $35 application, $300 . Assistance: $100 stipend (writers under 35) and Handel Playwright Fellowship, and Handel Playwright Fellowship. **Application.** Best Material: application, SASE. Deadline: 3-Mar-08. Response: 3 wks.

1/12/2008. Camargo Foundation

1 ave Jermini, Cassis, 13260 France
Jean-Pierre Dautricourt, Dir
Tel: 011-334-4201-1157, Fax: 011-334-4201-3657
apply@camargofoundation.org; www.camargofoundation.org

Est. 1967. Residency of 1 semester (Sep-Dec, Jan-May) in Cassis, France, for scholars, visual artists, composers and writers. Workspace incl. ref library and music studio. **Consideration.** Assistance: $3,500 stipend. Frequency: annual. **Preference.** Material Must Be: specific creative project. **Application.** Best Way: online. Best Material: application, 40-pg sample, audio, SASE. Deadline: 12-Jan-08.

Centauri Arts

Centauri Summer Arts Camp, 85 Humbercrest Blvd, Toronto, ON, M6S 4L2 Canada

Est. 1995. A specialist arts training camp for youth ages 9 to 18 which offers courses in creative writing and playwriting. **Consideration.** Fees: Session fee plus $200 deposit. Frequency: 4 summer sessions. **Preference.** Author Must Be: age.

$300/wk. Centrum Creative Residencies Program

Box 1158, Port Townsend, WA, 98368
Sally Rodgers, Residency Program Facil.
Tel: 360-385-3102 x128, Fax: 360-385-2470
sally@centrum.org; www.centrum.org

Est. 1980. Residencies of 1 wk to 1 mo (Jan-May, Sep-Dec) in Ft. Worden State Park. Residents housed in private cabins or apts. **Consideration.** Fees: $300/wk. **Application.** Best Material: application, sample, SASE.

2/15/08 $30. Djerassi Resident Artists Program

2325 Bear Gulch Rd., Woodside, CA, 94062
Judy Freeland, Residency Coord.
Tel: 650-747-1250
drap@djerassi.org; www.djerassi.org

Est. 1979. 4-5 wk residence, Mar-Nov, for writers and artists on 580-acre ranch nr San Francisco. Living space, studio space and meals provided. **Consideration.** Fees: $30 application. **Application.** Best Material: application, full script, SASE. Deadline: 15-Feb-08.

3/31/2008. Envision Retreat

Voice & Vision, 520 8th Ave., #308, New York, NY, 10018
Jean Wagner, Artistic Dir.
Tel: 212-268-3717, Fax: 212-268-5462
vandv@vandv.org; www.vandv.org

Projects initiated by women in summer workshop development on Bard Coll. campus. **Consideration.** Fees: $15 reading. **Application.** Best Material: query, 1-pg synopsis, full script (2 copies), resume. Deadline: 31-Mar-08.

$50/night. Gell Center of the Finger Lakes
Writers & Books, 740 University Ave., Rochester, NY, 14607
Kathy Pottetti, Dir, Operations/Programming
Tel: 585-473-2590 x103, Fax: 585-442-9333
Kathyp@wab.org; www.wab.org

Consideration. Fees: $50/night. **Application.** Best Material: sample.

2/1/08. $20. Hall Farm Center for Arts and Education
392 Hall Dr., Townshend, VT, 05353
Scott Browning, Dir.
Tel: 802-365-4483
info@hallfarm.org; www.hallfarm.org

Est. 1999. Up to 4-wk residency, with private room, studio, and meals provided, in Jun-Jul or Aug-Sep. **Consideration.** Fees: $20 application. Assistance: room/board. Frequency: annual. **Preference.** Author Must Be: age 18 or older. **Application.** Best Material: application, 30-pg sample (4 copies), SASE. Best Time: Jun-Sep. Deadline: 1-Feb-08. Response: 2 mos.

1/15, 4/15, 9/15. $150/wk. Hambidge Center
Box 339, Rabun Gap, GA, 30568
Bob Thomas, Residency Dir.
Tel: 706-746-5718, Fax: 706-746-9933
center@hambidge.org; www.hambidge.org

Residencies of 2-8 wks (Feb-Dec) on 650 acres in Blue Ridge Mts. Residents housed in private cottage-studios for emerging or professional writers, performers, and visual artists. **Consideration.** Fees: $30 application, $150/wk. Frequency: annual. **Application.** Best Material: application, 30-pg sample (3 copies), audio, resume, SASE. Deadline: 15-Jan-08, 15-Apr-08, 15-Sep-08.

9/30/2008. Hawthornden Castle International Retreat for Writers
Hawthornden Castle, Lasswade, Midlothian, Scotland, EH18 1EG
Daniel Farrell, Admin.
Tel: 44-131-440-2180

Est. 1982. Residencies of 4 wks (Feb-Jul, Sep-Dec) in 17th-century castle, 40-min bus to Edinburgh. Residents housed in study bedrooms. **Consideration.** Assistance: room/board. Frequency: annual. **Preference.** Author Must Be: produced or published. **Application.** Best Material: application, 30-pg sample. Deadline: 30-Sep-08.

6/2/2008. Headlands Center for the Arts
944 Fort Barry, Sausalito, CA, 94965
Holly Blake, Residency Mgr
Tel: 415-331-2787 x24
info@headlands.org; www.headlands.org

Est. 1987. Headlands Center for the Arts hosts an internationally recognized Artists in Residence Program, interdisciplinary public programs, and subsidezed studio rentals for artists of all disciplines. **Consideration.** Assistance: grant or stipend, room and board, travel. Frequency: 30 residencies per year, 1-3 mos. **Application.** Best Way: unsolicited. Best Material: application, SASE. Best Time: Spring. Deadline: 2-Jun-08. Response: 4-5 mos.

10/15/08 $15. Hedgebrook
2197 Millman Rd., Langley, WA, 98260
Amy Wheeler, Exec Dir
Tel: 360-321-4786, Fax: 360-321-2171
www.hedgebrook.org

Est. 1988. Residencies of 2 wks-2 mos in 48-acre retreat on Whidbey Island. Residents housed in private cottages with electricity and wood stoves. 1 bathhouse serves all 6 cottages. Writers eat in farmhouse each night; meals by staff chef using local organic produce. **Consideration.** Fees: $15 application. Assistance: travel, stipend (low-income women w/o college degree or older than 55). Frequency: annual. **Preference.** Author Must Be: female. **Application.** Best Material: application. Deadline: 15-Oct-08.

1/18/08. Helene Wurlitzer Foundation of New Mexico
Box 1891, Taos, NM, 87571
Michael Knight, Dir.
Tel: 505-758-2413, Fax: 505-758-2559
HWF@taosnet.com; www.artistcommunities.org/wurlitzer.html

Est. 1956. Residences of 2-3 mos (Apr-Oct) for visual artists, writers and composers. Individual single-floor dwellings accessible for walkers but not wheel chairs; composer studios each have a grand piano. Artists must provide for their own meals. **Application.** Best Way: send SASE in fall for application. Best Material: application. Deadline: 1/18/08.

Institute of Gunnar Gunnarsson - Klaustrid
Institute of Gunnar Gunnarsson - Klaustrid, Skriduklaustur, 701 Egilsstadir, Egilsstadir, N-MUL, IS-707 Iceland
Halladora Tomasdohir, Centre Manager

Est. 1989 **Consideration.** Assistance: room / board. **Preference.** Style: all styles. Subject: all subjects. **Application.** Best Material: application. Deadline: 15-Jun. Response: 2-3 mos..

International Writing Program (IWP)
Univ. of Iowa, 100 Shambaugh House, 430 N. Clinton St., #100, Iowa City, IA, 52242

Est. 1967. For writers of fiction, poetry, drama, or screenplays who are not US residents. **Consideration.** Frequency: Aug.-Nov.. **Preference.** Author Must Be: published author, proficient in English.

2/16/2008. Isle Royale National Park Artist-in-Residence
800 E. Lakeshore Dr., Houghton, MI, 49931
Greg Blust, Supervisory Park Ranger
Tel: 906-482-0984, Fax: 906-482-8753
gregblust@nps.gov

Est. 1991. 2-3 wk residency (Jun-Sep) in primitive cabin supplied with propane light, stove, fridge, and canoe. Artist conducts 1 program/wk and donates a finished piece. **Preference.** Length: short (under 30 min). **Application.** Best Material: application, sample, audio, SASE. Best Time: Jun-Jan. Deadline: 16-Feb-08.

$408-$1605/wk. Kalani Oceanside Retreat
RR2, Box 4500, Pahoa, HI, 96778
Richard Koob, Founder/Dir.
Tel: 808-965-7828, Fax: 808-965-0527
artists@kalani.com; www.kalani.com

Artist residencies of 2 wks to 3 mos in 4 lodge and 22 cottage rooms on 120 acres of secluded coast forest. Fee incl. meals and use of facilities. Work space limited to shared multipurpose studios in lodges. **Consideration.** Fees: $408-$1605/wk. Assistance: stipend (May-Dec). **Application.** Best Way: email. Best Material: application.

Kimmel Harding Nelson (KHN) Center for the Arts
801 3rd Corso, Nebraska City, NE, 68410
Denise Brady, Exec. Dir.
Tel: 402-874-9600, Fax: 402-874-9600
info@khncenterforthearts.org

Est. 2001. 2-8 week residencies for visual artists, writers, music composers. **Consideration.** Fees: $25 . Assistance: $100/wk, room/board. Frequency: biennial. **Preference.** Subject: all subjects. **Application.** Best Way: see guidelines on website. Best Material: SASE. Deadline: 1-Mar, 1-Sep. Response: approx. 2 mos..

6/15/2008. Lanesboro Residency Program Fellowships
Cornucopia Arts Center, 103 Parkway Ave. N., Box 152, Lanesboro, MN, 55949
Tel: 507-467-2446, Fax: 507-467-4446
Info@lanesboroarts.org; www.lanesboroarts.org

Consideration. Assistance: $1,250/wk. **Application.** Best Material: application. Deadline: 15-Jun-08.

11/30/2008. Ledig House Writers Residency Program
Art Omi Intl. Arts Center, 55 5th Ave., Fl. 15, New York, NY, 10003
Ruth Adams, Admin Dir
Tel: 212-206-6060, Fax: 212-206-6114
writers@artomi.org; www.artomi.org

Est. 1992. Residencies of 1 wk-2 mos (Mar-Jun, Sep-Nov) in Catskill Mts. Residents provided with separate or combined work/bedroom areas. All meals included. **Consideration.** Frequency: annual. **Application.** Best Material: query, 10-pg sample, bio, SASE. Deadline: 30-Nov-08.

$55/day. Leighton Studies for Independent Residencies
The Banff Centre, Box 1020, Banff, AB, T1L 1H5 Canada
Office of the Registrar
Tel: 800-565-9989, Fax: 403-762-6345
artsinfo@banffcentre.ca; www.banffcentre.ca

Residencies for writers, composers and visual artists housed in private rooms w/bath, phone, and cleaning service. Workspace incl kitchenette, washroom, phone, CD/tape player, piano (3 of 8 studios), and G4 Mac (w/printer & Internet). Residents have access to library, fitness/rec center, dining room, and small store. **Consideration.** Fees: $55/day (studio), $53/day (room). **Preference.** Author Must Be: professional level. **Application.** Best Material: application, 30-pg sample.

1/15, 4/15, 9/15. $20. MacDowell Colony
100 High St., Peterborough, NH, 03458
Courtney Bethel, Admissions Dir.
Tel: 603-924-3886, Fax: 603-924-9142
admissions@macdowellcolony.org; www.macdowellcolony.org

Est. 1907. Residencies up to 8 wks (Jun-Sep, Oct-Jan, Feb-May) for uninterrupted time and seclusion to work and enjoy a community of creative artists. Workspace incl. studios. **Consideration.** Fees: $20 application. Assistance: $1,000 stipend limit, travel. Frequency: triannual. **Application.** Best Material: project proposal, application, synopsis, full script (3 copies of all docs), SASE. Deadline: 15-Jan-08, 15-Apr-08, 15-Sep-08. Response: 10 wks.

$10.00 . Mary Anderson Center for the Arts
Box 12, 101 St. Francis Dr., Mt. Saint Francis, IN, 47146
Lisa Angell, Exec Dir
Tel: 812-923-8602, Fax: 888-785-3911
macarts@onebox.com; www.maryandersoncenter.org

Est. 1989. Residencies of 1 wk to 1 mo. Staff: Ardis Moonlight (Communications Dir). **Consideration.** Fees: $10 application, $60/night incl. all meals; $40/night, no meals. Assistance: work exchange fellowships. Frequency: annual. **Preference.** Author Must Be: age 21 or older. **Application.** Best Material: application, 5-pg sample, SASE. Response: 3 wks.

10/1/08. $30. Millay Colony for the Arts
The Millay Colony for the Arts, 454 East Hill Rd, Box 3, Austerlitz, NY, 12017
Calliope Nicholas, Residency Dir
Tel: 518-392-3103, Fax: 518-392-4944
apply@millaycolony.org; www.millaycolony.org

Est. 1973. Month-long residencies (Apr-Nov) for writers, visual artists and composers. **Consideration.** Fees: $30 application. Assistance: room/board. Frequency: annual. **Application.** Best Way: download application on website. Best Material: application, 30-pg sample (6 copies), audio (4 copies), score (4 copies), SASE. Deadline: 10/1/2008. Response: by 2/1/08.

4/15, 5/15, 6/15. $750/mo. Montana Artists Residency
Box 8, Basin, MT, 59631
Debbie Sheehan, Residency Coord.
Tel: 406-225-3500
mar@mt.net; www.montanarefuge.org

Est. 1993. Residencies of 1-9 mos in Nov-Jul (6/15 deadline). Fully funded residencies for Writers in Oct (5/15 deadline) and American Indian Artists in Sep (4/15 deadline). Facilities incl. 2 apts. w/large studios, 1 soundproof apt., and 1 small studio apt.; all incl. kitchen, double bed, private phone, and wireless internet. **Consideration.** Fees: $300-550/mo. **Application.** Best Material: application, 15-pg sample (3 copies), audio, resume. Deadline: Apr 15, 2008 (American Indians), May 15, 2008 (writers), Jun 15, 2008(others).

New York Mills Arts Retreat
24 N. Main Ave., Box 246, New York Mills, MN, 56567
Tel: 218-385-3339
nymills@kulcher.org; www.kulcher.org

Application. Best Material: query, synopsis, 12-pg sample, resume, letters of recommendation, SASE. Deadline: Apr 1, 2008 (Jul-Dec), Oct 1, 2008 (Jan-Jun).

1/15/08, 6/1/08. $30. Ragdale Foundation
1260 N. Green Bay Rd., Lake Forest, IL, 60045
Regin Igloria, Dir, Artists in Residence
Tel: 847-234-1063 x206, Fax: 847-234-1063
admissions@ragdale.org; www.ragdale.org

Est. 1976. Residenceies of 2 wks-2 mos (Jun-Dec, Jan-Apr) for composers, artists, and writers in private rooms with meals included. Workspace incl. 1 composing studio, 3 visual arts studios, and 8 writing rooms. Public workshops also offered. **Consideration.** Fees: $30 application, $25/day. Assistance: financial aid w/demonstrated need. **Application.** Best Material: query, application, synopsis, sample, SASE. Deadline: Jan 15, 2008 (summer-fall), Jun 1, 2008 (winter-spring). Response: 3 mos.

12/1/08. $35. Rocky Mountain National Park Artist-in-Residence Program
1000 Hwy. 36, Estes Park, CO, 80517
Tel: 970-586-1206
www.nps.gov/romo

Consideration. Fees: $35 application. **Application.** Best Material: query, application, 6-pg sample (writers), audio (composers), resume (6 copies of all above), submissions not returned. Deadline: 1-Dec-08.

Studio for Creative Inquiry
Carnegie Mellon Univ. (CMU), College of Fine Arts, #111, Pittsburgh, PA, 15213
Marge Myers, Assoc Dir.
Tel: 412-268-3454, Fax: 412-268-2829
mmbm@andrew.cmu.edu; www.cmu.edu/studio

Est. 1989. Currently accepting proposals for experimental and interdisciplinary arts projects that don't require full funding by CMU. Proposals should be submitted at least 6 mos in advance of the desired residency. **Application.** Best Material: query, sample, resume.

Sundance Institute Playwrights Retreat
8530 Wilshire Blvd., Fl. 3, Beverly Hills, CA, 90211
Christopher Hibma, Associate Dir.
Tel: 310-360-1981, Fax: 310-360-1975
theatre@sundance.org; www.sundance.org

Est. 2001. 18-day retreat for 5 playwrights and 1 theater composer at Ucross Foundation, Clearmont, WY. **Consideration.** Assistance: $500 stipend, room/board, travel. Frequency: annual. **Preference.** Material Must Be: unproduced. **Application.** Best Way: invite. Best Time: Feb.

650 euro/wk. Tyrone Guthrie Centre, Newliss, Co. Monaghan, Ireland

The Tyrone Guthrie Centre, Annaghmakerrig, Newbliss, Co., Ireland
Dr. Pat Donlon, Resident Dir.
Tel: 353-47-54003, Fax: 353-47-54380
info@tyroneguthrie.ie, director@tyroneguthrie.ie; www.tyroneguthrie.ie

Est. 1981. Year-round residencies of varying duration. Residents housed in private rooms and artists' studios in country house or self-catering farmyard cottages. Workspace incl. music room and darkroom. **Consideration.** Fees: 600 euro/wk Big House, 300 euro/wk (self-catering). **Preference.** Author Must Be: produced or published. **Application.** Best Material: application. Response: 1 mo.

2/1/08. U.S./Japan Creative Artists' Program

Japan-US Friendship Commission (JUSFC), 1201 15th St. NW, #330, Washington, DC, 20005
Eric J. Gangloff, Exec Dir
Tel: 202-653-9800, Fax: 202-418-9802
jusfc@jusfc.gov; www.jusfc.gov

Est. 1979. 5-mo residency in Japan for produced professional US artists. **Consideration.** Assistance: up to $6,000 stipend, room/board, travel, language training and storage, 400,000 yen/mo stipend, 100,000 yen/mo housing supplement, 100,000 yen for professional services. Frequency: annual. **Preference.** Author Must Be: citizen or resident of US. **Application.** Best Material: application. Deadline: 1-Feb-08.

3/1/08 10/1/08. $20. Ucross Foundation Residency Program

30 Big Red Ln., Clearmont, WY, 82835
Sharon Dynak, Exec Dir.
Tel: 307-737-2291, Fax: 307-737-2322
ucross@wyoming.com; www.ucrossfoundation.org

Est. 1991. Residencies of 2 weeks to 2 months (Feb-Jun, Aug-Dec) near Big Horn Mts. Residents are provided living & studio space. **Consideration.** Fees: $20 application. Frequency: semiannual. **Application.** Best Material: application, SASE. Deadline: Mar 1, 2008 (fall), Oct 1, 2008 (spring).

1/15, 5/15, 9/15. $25. Virginia Center for the Creative Arts (VCCA)

154 San Angelo Dr., Amherst, VA, 24521
Suny Monk, Exec Dir
Tel: 434-946-7236, Fax: 434-946-7239
vcca@vcca.com; www.vcca.com

Est. 1971. Residencies of 2 wks-2 mos on 12-acre hilltop in foothills of Blue Ridge Mts near Sweet Briar Coll. **Consideration.** Fees: $25 aplication, $30-$60/day. Assistance: room/board. **Application.** Best Material: application, full script, submissions not returned. Deadline: Jan 15, 2008 (Jun-Sep), May 15, 2008 (Oct-Jan), Sep 15, 2008 (Feb-May). Response: 2 mos.

3/1/2008. William Flanagan Memorial Creative Persons Center

Edward F. Albee Foundation, 14 Harrison St., New York, NY, 10013
Jakob Holder, Secy.
Tel: 212-226-2020, Fax: 212-226-5551
info@albeefoundation.org; www.albeefoundation.org

Est. 1966. Residencies of 1 mo (Jun-Sep) in Montauk, NY, for writers and composers. **Consideration.** Frequency: annual. **Application.** Best Material: application, full script, SASE. Best Time: Jan-Mar. Deadline: 1-Mar-08. Response: by 4/15/07.

William Inge Center for the Arts

Box 708, Independence, KS, 67301
Peter Ellenstein, Artistic Dir
Tel: 620-331-7768
info@ingecenter.org; www.ingecenter.org

3 artists at a time on 50 acre wh 1-wk Actors' Equity Reading workshop of new play, and some teaching. **Consideration.** Assistance: $4,000 stipend, room/board, travel. Remuneration: reading. Frequency: semiannual. **Preference.** Length: full length (over 90 min). Author Must Be: produced with three Equity productions.. Material Must Be: unproduced. **Application.** Best Material: query, SASE. Response: ongoing.

12/15/2008. Women's Work Project

New Perspectives Theatre Company, 456 W. 37th St., New York, NY, 10018
Melody Brooks, Artistic Dir
Tel: 212-630-9945
www.newperspectivestheatre.org

Residencies of 9-18 mos, incl. in-house readings and directorial-dramaturgical sessions, culminating in public presentation. **Consideration.** Remuneration: reading. Frequency: annual. **Preference.** Length: full length (over 90 min). Style: comedy, drama. Author Must Be: female, women of color encouraged. Material Must Be: unoptioned, unpublished, unproduced. **Application.** Best Material: query, application, full script, bio, SASE. Deadline: 15-Dec-08.

$130/mo. Writers' Studio

Mercantile Library Center for Fiction, 17 E. 47th St., New York, NY, 10017
Tel: 212-755-6710
info@mercantilelibrary.org; www.mercantilelibrary.org

Desk on which to work, locker, ref materials, electrical outlets for computers, plus comp library membership. Open Mon-Fri, 9am-midnight, and Sat-Sun, 9am-6pm. Fiction writers given priority. **Consideration.** Fees: $75 administrative, $130/mo (full), $110/mo (basic: Mon-Fri), $100/mo (eve/weekend). **Application.** Best Material: application.

1/1/08, 8/1/08 $20. Yaddo

Box 395, Saratoga Springs, NY, 12866
Candace Wait, Program Dir.
Tel: 518-584-0746, Fax: 518-584-1312
yaddo@yaddo.org; www.yaddo.org

Est. 1900. Residencies of 2 wks-2 mos on 400-acre turn-of-century estate in Saratoga Springs, NY. Room/board, and private studio space free of charge. **Consideration.** Fees: $20 application. Assistance: room/board, travel (limited). Frequency: semiannual. **Application.** Best Way: professional recommendation. Best Material: application, synopsis, sample, SASE. Deadline: 1-Jan-08, 1-Aug-08.

CONFERENCES & FESTIVALS

12/31/2008. 6 Women Playwriting Festival

Pikes Peak Arts Council (PPAC), Box 1073, Colorado Springs, CO, 80901
Donna Guthrie, Festival Dir
www.sixwomenplayfestival.com

Est. 2007. **Consideration.** Remuneration: $75 . Frequency: annual. **Preference.** Length: 10-min. Production: age 16 and older, cast of 2-4. Author Must Be: age 16 or older, female. Material Must Be: unproduced. **Application.** Best Material: full script, SASE. Deadline: 31-Dec-08. Response: 2 mos.

Alabama Shakespeare Festival

1 Festival Dr., Montgomery, AL, 36117
Nancy Rominger, Artistic Assoc.
Tel: 334-271-5300, Fax: 334-271-5348
www.asf.net

est. 1972. Souther Writers' Project develops new plays with Southern or African-American themes by Southern or African-American writers. **Preference.** Subject: African-American; Southern. **Application.** Best Way: unsolicited for Southern Writers Project only, all else agent.

12/1/08. $350. American College Theater Festival (ACTF)

Kennedy Center, Kennedy Center, Washington, DC, 20566
Susan Shaffer, Co-Mgr, Admin.
www.KCACTF.org

Est. 1969. National fest of student productions, selected from regional college fests. Regional deadlines vary. Michael Kanin (1910-93) arranged for awards for the national fest (see website). **Consideration.** Fees: $350 . **Preference.** Author Must Be: college student. Material Must Be: original. **Application.** Best Material: application, 1-pg synopsis, full script. Deadline: 1-Dec-08.

Annual Black Theatre Festival

Cincinnatti Black Theatre Company, 5919 Hamilton Ave, Cincinnatti, OH, 45224
Don Sherman, Artistic Director
Tel: 513-241-6060, Fax: 513-241-6671
dsherman@cincyblacktheatre.com; www.ciincyblacktheatre.com

Preference. Subject: African-American. **Application.** Best Way: unsolicited, year-round open submissions.

3/31/2008. Appalachian Festival of Plays and Playwrights

Barter Theatre, Box 867, Abingdon, VA, 24212
Nicholas Piper, Dir.
Tel: 276-619-3316, Fax: 276-619-3335
apfestival@bartertheatre.com; www.bartertheatre.com/season/festival.html

Est. 2001. Plays must be written by Appalacian playwright or must contain Applacian settings & themes. Stagings of 2 plays from previous AFPP, and readings of 6 new scripts in 2-wk fest, judged by panel. Staff: Richard Rose (Artistic Dir), Mary Lucy Bivins (New Plays Coord.) **Consideration.** Remuneration: $250-$500, 5\% royalty. Frequency: annual. **Preference.** Length: full length (preferred). Subject: Appalachia. Author Must Be: Appalachian. Material Must Be: unoptioned, unpublished, unproduced. **Application.** Best Material: full script, SASE. Deadline: 31-Mar-08. Response: by 6/30/08.

3/15/2008. Backdoor Theatre New Play Project

Box 896, Wichita Falls, TX, 76307
Artistic Dir
Tel: 940-322-5000, Fax: 940-322-8167
need-info@backdoortheatre.org; www.backdoortheatre.org

Est. 1985. Selected plays receive 6 mainstage performances (170-seat theater). **Consideration.** Remuneration: $500 . **Preference.** Length: full length (over 90 min). Style: comedy, drama. Material Must Be: unproduced. **Application.** Best Material: synopsis, full script, resume, SASE. Deadline: 15-Mar-08.

1/30/2008. Baldwin New Play Festival

Univ. of California, San Diego (UCSD), 9500 Gilman Dr., MC0509, La Jolla, CA, 92093
Allan Havis, Provost/Head, MFA Playwriting
Tel: 858-534-3791, Fax: 858-534-8931
ahavis@ucsd.edu; theatre.ucsd.edu

Est. 2006. **Consideration.** Assistance: room/board, room/board. Remuneration: $1,000 , reading. Frequency: annual. **Preference.** Length: full length (over 90 min), mid-length (60-90 min). Style: comedy, drama. Subject: Black. Author Must Be: college undergrad. Material Must Be: unpublished, unproduced. **Application.** Best Material: application, synopsis, full script, SASE. Best Time: Sep-Dec. Deadline: 1/30/2008. Response: by 2/28/08.

3/15/2008. Barnstormers Theatre

Box 434, Tamworth, NH, 03886
Clayton Phillips, Producing Artistic Dir.
www.barnstormerstheatre.org

Evening of original one-acts in Oct. **Consideration.** Remuneration: $100 honorarium. Frequency: annual. **Preference.** Length: one-act (30-60 min), short (under 30 min). Production: cast limit 6. Material Must Be: unoptioned, unpublished, unproduced. **Application.** Best Material: full script. Deadline: 15-Mar-08.

Bilingual Foundation of the Arts (BFA)

Bilingual Foundation, 421 N. Ave. 19, Los Angeles, CA, 90031
Margarita Galban, Artistic Dir.
Tel: 323-225-4044, Fax: 323-225-1250
www.bfatheatre.org

Est. 1973. Summer reading fest of new works. **Consideration.** Assistance: TBA. Remuneration: TBA. Frequency: annual. **Preference.** Length: full length (over 90 min). Style: no musical. Subject: Latino. Production: cast limit 10, simple set. **Application.** Best Way: unsolicited. Best Material: query, full script, SASE. Best Time: Jan. Response: 6 mos-1 yr.

Black Playwrights Festival

Black Ensemble Theatre, 4520 N. Beacon, Chicago, IL, 60640
Jackie Taylor, Artistic Director
blackensemble@aol.com; www.blackensemble.org

Year-round open submissions. Clearly note script is for festival. See website for details.

3/15/2008. Blank Theatre Company Young Playwrights Festival

Blank Theatre Company, 1301 Lucile Ave., Los Angeles, CA, 90026
Stacy Reed, Festival Producer
www.youngplaywrights.com

Est. 1990. Winning plays assigned mentors and given professional workshop. Staff: Noah Wylie (Artistic Producer), Daniel Henning (Artistic Dir/Producer). **Consideration.** Frequency: annual. **Preference.** Length: all lengths. Author Must Be: age 19 or younger. Material Must Be: unoptioned, unpublished. **Application.** Best Material: query, full script, submissions not returned. Best Time: Jan. Deadline: 15-Mar-08. Response: by mid-May.

11/15/2008. Boston Theater Marathon

Boston Playwrights' Theatre, 949 Commonwealth Ave., Boston, MA, 02215
Kate Snodgrass, Artistic Director
Tel: 617-353-5443
newplays@bu.edu; www.bu.edu/btm

Est. 1999. 50 10-min plays by New England playwrights by 50 New England theaters over 10 hrs in 1 day. Staff: Bill Lattanzi (Consultant), Jacob Strautmann (Managing Dir). **Consideration.** Frequency: annual. **Preference.** Length: 10 min. Style: comedy, drama, musical. Production: small orchestra, minimal set. Author Must Be: resident of New England. **Application.** Best Material: full script, SASE. Deadline: 15-Nov-08. Response: 4 mos.

Breaking Ground Festival

Huntington Theatre Company, 281 Huntington Ave, Boston, MA, 02115
Ilana Brownstein, Literary Mgr.
ibrownstein@huntingtontheatre.bu.edu; www.huntingtontheatre.org

Est. 2001. **Preference.** Length: full length (over 90 min), mid-length (60-90 min). **Application.** Best Way: (unsolicited: MA 26 RI writers only), agent (US, Canada, UK). Best Material: full script, SASE. Response: 1 yr.

3/1/2008. Centre Stage South Carolina New Play Festival

Centre Stage South Carolina, Box 8451, Greenville, SC, 29604
Brian Haimbach, New Play Fesitval Director
Tel: 864-233-6733
haimbach@hotmail.com; www.centrestage.org

Est. 2002. 5 finalists in reader's theatre during 1-week fest. Audience selects winner for full production next season. **Consideration.** Frequency: annual. **Preference.** Length: full length (over 90 min). Style: adaptation, comedy, drama. Production: age 16 or older, cast limit 6, minimal set. Material Must Be: unpublished, unproduced. **Application.** Best Material: synopsis, full script, scripts will not be returned. Best Time: Oct-Feb. Deadline: 3/1/2008. Response: by 6/1/08.

Children's Festival

Annenberg Center for the Performing Arts, 3680 Walnut St, Philadelphia, PA, 19104

Circle Theatre of Forest Park [IL]

7300 W. Madison St., Forest Park, IL, 60130
Jim Wall, Literary Mgr.
Tel: 708-771-0700
www.circle-theatre.org

Est. 1985. Opportunities incl new play fest of shorts and full-lengths. **Preference.** Material Must Be: unproduced. **Application.** Best Material: full script, SASE. Best Time: Mar-Sep.

11/1/08. Coe College Playwriting Festival & Symposia

Coe College, 1220 1st Ave. NE, Cedar Rapids, IA, 52402
Susan Wolverton, Chair, Theater Arts Dept.
Tel: 319-399-8624, Fax: 319-399-8557
swolvert@coe.edu; www.public.coe.edu/departments/theatre

Est. 1993. Biennial spring fest. Winner of New Works for the Stage Competition receives weeklong residency, workshop with students, and staged reading. **Consideration.** Assistance: room/board, room/board. Remuneration: $500 , reading. Frequency: biennial. **Preference.** Length: full length (over 90 min), mid-length (60-90 min). Style: comedy, drama. Subject: all subjects. Production: age 16-50, cast of 3-8. Author Must Be: citizen of US. Material Must Be: unpublished, unproduced, in development stage. **Application.** Best Way: unsolicited. Best Material: 1-pg synopsis, full script, SASE. Best Time: Begin 10/1/08. Deadline: Postmarked 11/1/08. Response: 8 wks.

10/1/08. Cultural Conversations

Penn State University, 103 Arts Bldg., University Park, PA, 16801
Susan Russell, Artistic Dir.
sbr13@psu.edu; www.theatre.psu.edu

Est. 2007. Readings of 3 new plays about local and global topics on diversity. One week rehearsal, One week festival. Playwright residency 2-3 days. Staff: Prof. Susan Russel (Artistic Dir.), Prof. Steve Broadnax **Consideration.** Assistance: room/board, room/board. Remuneration: reading. Frequency: annual. **Preference.** Length: full-length (over 90 min), mid-length (60-90 min). Style: comedy, drama. Subject: all subjects. Material Must Be: unoptioned, unpublished, unproduced. **Application.** Best Way: unsolicited. Best Material: full script, SASE. Deadline: Postmarked by 10/1/08. Response: by 1/15/09.

6/30/2008. Festival of New American Plays

Firehouse Theatre Project, 1609 W. Broad St., Richmond, VA, 23220
Carol Piersol, Artistic Dir
Tel: 804-355-2001, Fax: 804-355-0999
info@firehousetheatre.org; www.firehousetheatre.org

Est. 2003. **Consideration.** Remuneration: $1,000 1st, $500 2nd, reading. Frequency: annual. **Preference.** Length: full length (over 90 min). Style: comedy, drama, musical, no translation. Subject: all subjects. Author Must Be: resident or citizen of USA. Material Must Be: unproduced. **Application.** Best Way: professional recommendation. Best Material: full script, submissions not returned. Best Time: Jan-Jun. Deadline: 30-Jun-08. Response: 7 mos.

9/1/2008. Festival of New Plays

Jewish Ensemble Theatre, 6600 W. Maple Rd., West Bloomfield, MI, 48322
Evelyn Orbach, Artistic Dir.
Tel: 248-788-2900
e.orbach@jettheatre.org; www.jettheatre.org

Est. 1989. Staff: Pearl Orbach (Lit Desk Asst), Chris Bremer (Managing Dir). **Consideration.** Remuneration: $100 , reading. Frequency: annual. **Preference.** Length: full length (over 90 min), mid-length (60-90 min). Style: no musical, no translation. Subject: Jewish. Production: cast limit 8. Material Must Be: unpublished, unproduced. **Application.** Best Material: full script, SASE. Deadline: 1-Sep-08.

First Flight

Boomerang Theatre Company, Box 237166, Ansonia Sta., New York, NY, 10023
Attn: Literary Mgr.
Tel: 212-501-4069
info@boomerangtheatre.org; www.boomerangtheatre.org

Est. 1999. Nov reading series of new plays. **Consideration.** Frequency: annual. **Preference.** Length: full length (over 90 min). Style: no musical. Material Must Be: unproduced. **Application.** Best Material: query, synopsis, 10-pg sample, resume, SASE.

2/1/08. Fresh Fruit Festival

New Village Productions, 145 E. 27th St., #1-A, New York, NY, 10016
Carol Polcovar, Artistic Dir.
artisticdirector@freshfruitfestival.com; www.freshfruitfestival.com

Est. 2003. **Consideration.** Frequency: annual. **Preference.** Subject: GLBT. Material Must Be: unoptioned. **Application.** Best Way: Details and Application can be downloaded on-line.. Best Material: SASE. Deadline: 2/15/2008. Response: 2 mos..

Fringe of Toronto Theatre Festival

344 Bloor St., #208, Toronto, ON, M5S 3A7 Canada
www.fringetoronto.com

FusionFest

Cleveland Play House, 8500 Euclid Ave., Cleveland, OH, 44106
Seth Gordon, Assoc Artistic Dir
Tel: 216-795-7000, Fax: 216-795-7007
www.clevelandplayhouse.com

Est. 1995. Reading series of new plays. **Consideration.** Assistance: $1,000 stipend, room/board, room/board. **Preference.** Material Must Be: unoptioned, unproduced. **Application.** Best Way: agent. Best Material: query, synopsis, 10-pg sample, SASE. Response: 6 mos.

10/31/08. FutureFest

Dayton Playhouse, 1301 E. Siebenthaler Ave., Dayton, OH, 45414
Amy Brown, Exec Dir
Tel: 937-424-8477, Fax: 937-424-0062
amy@daytonplayhouse.com; www.daytonplayhouse.org

Est. 1990. Adjudicated July fest of new work with 3 full productions and 3 staged readings. **Consideration.** Remuneration: $1,000 , production, reading. Frequency: annual. **Preference.** Length: full length (over 75 min.). Style: no musical. Material Must Be: unoptioned, unpublished, unproduced. **Application.** Best Material: synopsis, full script, submissions not returned. Best Time: Jul-Oct. Deadline: 31-Oct-08. Response: by 4/20/09.

Genesis Festival

Crossroads Theatre Company [NJ], P.O. Box 238, 7 Livingston Ave., New Brunswick, NJ, 08901
Marshall Jones, Executive Dir.
Tel: 732-545-8100, Fax: 732-907-1864
info@crossroadstheatrecompany.org; www.crossroadstheatrecompany.org

Consideration. Remuneration: reading. Frequency: annual. **Preference.** Subject: African-American. **Application.** Best Way: unsolicited. Best Material: query letter (note theme addressed), synopsis, 30-pg writing sample, bio. Deadline: 12/31/2008.

7/1/2008. Global Age Project (GAP)

Aurora Theatre Company [CA], 2081 Addison St., Berkeley, CA, 94704
Tom Bentley, Coord.
Tel: 510-843-4042, Fax: 510-843-4826
tbentley@auroratheatre.org; www.auroratheatre.org

5 plays given staged readings in fest of forward-looking works on issues of the 21st century. **Consideration.** Remuneration: $1,000 1st, reading (finalists). Frequency: annual. **Preference.** Material Must Be: unproduced. **Application.** Best Way: online. Best Material: full script. Deadline: 7/1/2008. Response: 5 mos.

Humana Festival of New American Plays

Actors Theatre of Louisville [KY], 316 W. Main St., Louisville, KY, 40202
Adrien-Alice Hansel, Literary Mgr.
Tel: 502-584-1265, Fax: 502-561-3300
awegener@actorstheatre.org; www.actorstheatre.org/humanasubmission.htm

Est. 1976. Fest of 10-15 produced plays in Mar-Apr, incl. premieres and second productions. **Consideration.** Assistance: room/board, room/board, per diem. Remuneration: production consideration, publication. Frequency: annual. **Preference.** Length: full length (over 90 min). **Application.** Best Way: agent. Best Material: query, synopsis, 10-pg sample, SASE for return of materials; email address otherwise.

International Mystery Writers' Festival

Discovering New Mysteries, 101 Daviess St., Owensboro, KY, 42303
Kimberly Johnson, Fest Coord.
Tel: 270-687-2770
kjohnson@riverparkcenter.org; www.newmysteries.org

Est. 2007. Accepts sumbissions of original plays, screenplays, and teleplays for June Festival. Staff: Kimberly Johnson, Zev Buffman, Roxi Wiff **Consideration.** Assistance:. Remuneration: $1,000-$10,000. Frequency: annual. **Preference.** Length: all length. Style: adaptation, drama, Mystery. Subject: all subjects. Material Must Be: unproduced. **Application.** Best Way: unsolicited. Best Material: full script, submission not returned. Deadline: 11/30/2008. Response: 3 months.

3/1/2008. Kitchen Dog Theater (KDT) New Works Festival

3120 McKinney Ave., #100, Dallas, TX, 75204
Tina Parker, Co-Artistic Dir
Tel: 214-953-2258, Fax: 214-953-1873
tina@kitchendogtheater.org; www.kitchendogtheater.org

Est. 1990. Winner receives production, travel stipend, and royalty; 7 finalists receive reading. Staff: Christopher Carlos (Co-Artistic Dir). **Consideration.** Frequency: annual. **Preference.** Length: full length (over 90 min). Production: cast limit 5. **Application.** Best Material: full script, submissions not returned. Deadline: 1-Mar-08. Response: 8 mos.

3/1/08. Last Frontier Theatre Conference

Prince William Sound Community Coll. (PWSCC), Box 97, Valdez, AK, 99686
Dawson Moore, Coord.
Tel: 907-834-1614, Fax: 907-834-1611
dmoore@pwscc.edu; www.pwscc.edu/conference

Est. 2003. Application free. See website for conference fees. **Consideration.** Remuneration: reading. **Preference.** Length: 20 mins to 2 hrs. Style: comedy, drama. Subject: all subjects. Material Must Be: unproduced. **Application.** Best Way: unsolicited. Best Material: synopsis, full script. Deadline: 2/1/2008. Response: 3 mos.

12/31/2008. Lavender Footlights Festival

Creative Arts Enterprises (CAE), 59 NE 46th St., Miami, FL, 33137
Doug Williford, Aristic Dir.
Tel: 305-672-7818, Fax: 305-672-7818
mdougwill@mac.com; www.caemia.org

Est. 2000. Fest of readings with gay and lesbian themes. Staff: Ellen Wedner (Exec Dir). **Consideration.** Remuneration: reading. Frequency: annual. **Preference.** Style: comedy, drama, musical. Subject: gay. Material Must Be: unproduced in FL. **Application.** Best Material: synopsis, full script, SASE. Deadline: 12/31/2008. Response: 3/1/2009.

12/31/2008. Little Festival of the Unexpected

Portland Stage Company (ME), Box 1458, Portland, ME, 04104
Daniel Burson, Literary Mgr.
Tel: 207-774-1043, Fax: 207-774-0576
dburson@portlandstage.com; www.portlandstage.com

Est. 1989. 1-wk fest of new plays with writers developing work thru staged readings. **Consideration.** Assistance: $300 stipend. Frequency: annual. **Preference.** Length: full length (over 90 min), mid-length (60-90 min). Style: adaptation, comedy, drama. Production: cast limit 8. Material Must Be: unoptioned, unpublished, unproduced. **Application.** Best Material: query, synopsis, 10-pg sample. Best Time: Sep-Dec. Deadline: 31-Dec-08.

12/1/2008. New American Playwrights Project (NAPP)

Utah Shakespearean Festival, 351 W. Center St., Cedar City, UT, 84720
Charles Metten, Dir, NAPP
Tel: 435-586-7880, Fax: 435-865-8003
metten@bard.org; www.bard.org

Equity LORT B+. 2000 Regional Theater Tony winner. Aug fest of 4 play readings, with writers in residence. **Consideration.** Assistance: room/board, room/board, tickets to USF summer season. Remuneration: reading. Frequency: annual. **Preference.** Length: full length, 90 page script limit. Style: no musical. Subject: US West; no children's. Production: cast of 8-10, set limit 2, flexible stage. Author Must Be: resident or citizen of US. Material Must Be: unproduced. **Application.** Best Material: full script, submissions not returned. Best Time: Jul-Nov. Deadline: 1-Dec-08.

New Jersey Playwrights Festival of New Plays

12 Miles West Theatre Company, Box 1663, Bloomfield, NJ, 07003
Lenny Bart, Artistic Dir.
Tel: 973-259-9187, Fax: 973-259-9188
info@12mileswest.org; www.12mileswest.org

Annual fest of plays by NJ playwrights. **Consideration.** Remuneration: $500 . **Preference.** Length: full length (over 90 min), one-act (30-60 min). Production: cast of 2-7, unit set. Author Must Be: resident of NJ. **Application.** Best Material: synopsis, full script (3 copies), cast breakdown, SASE. Response: 1 yr.

New Musical Theatre Festival

Penn State University, 103 Arts Bldg., University Park, PA, 16801
Raymond Sage, Artistic Dir.
www.psunewmusicals.org

Est. 2006. Two week festival, 2 or more musical in 29 hour equity format. **Preference.** Style: musical. Production: ages 18-25.

6/1/08. New Professional Theatre Writers Festival

229 W. 42nd St., #501, New York, NY, 10036
Mark D. Wood, Literary Mgr.
Tel: 212-398-2666
newprof@aol.com; www.newprofessionaltheatre.com

Est. 1991. Annual fest of work by African-Americans. Also business seminars, mentoring, and 2-wk residencies. NPT takes 1-yr option on works. **Consideration.** Assistance: $1,000 . Frequency: annual. **Preference.** Length: full length (over 90 min). Subject: minorities. Author Must Be: African-American. Material Must Be: unoptioned, unpublished, unproduced, original. **Application.** Best Material: full script, submissions not returned. Best Time: Apr-May. Deadline: 1-Jun-08.

New South Play Festival

Horizon Theatre Company [GA], Box 5376, Atlanta, GA, 31107
J. Caleb Boyd, Literary Mgr
Tel: 404-523-1477
literary@horizontheatre.com; www.horizontheatre.com

Est. 1997. Summer fest of developmental workshops, readings and productions. **Consideration.** Remuneration: production, reading. Frequency: annual. **Preference.** Length: full length (over 90 min). Subject: contemporary South. Production: cast limit 8. **Application.** Best Material: query, full script, SASE. Response: 6 mos.

New Voice Play Festival

Old Opera House Theatre Company (OOH), 204 N. George St., Charles Town, WV, 25414
Tel: 304-752-4420
ooh@oldoperahouse.org; www.oldoperahouse.org

Est. 2001. Call or email for application and deadlines. One act play festival- plays 10 to 40 minutes in length.

12/15/08. New York City 15-Minute Play Fest

American Globe Theatre/Turnip Theatre Company, 145 W. 46th St., Fl. 3, New York, NY, 10036
Elizabeth Keefe, Exec Dir
Tel: 212-869-9809
liz@americanglobe.org; www.americanglobe.org

Est. 1993. 2-wk fest in late Apr of 4-5 new plays each night under Equity Showcase. Staff: John Basil (Artistic Dir, AGT), Gloria Falzer (Artistic Dir, Turnip). **Consideration.** Remuneration: $100 award, $25 royalty. Frequency: annual. **Preference.** Length: short (under 15 min). Production: cast of 2-10, no set. Material Must Be: unpublished. **Application.** Best Material: full script, SASE. Best Time: Oct. Deadline: 15-Dec-08. Response: 2 mos.

Off-Off-Broadway Original Short-Play Festival

Samuel French, Inc., 45 W. 25 St., New York, NY, 10010
Kenneth Dingledine, Festival Coord.
Tel: 212-206-8990, Fax: 202-206-1429
oobfestival@samuelfrench.com; www.samuelfrench.com

Est. 1976. Summer 2-wk fest in NYC of approx 100 shows. 6 finalists chosen for publication and representation by Samuel French. **Consideration.** Remuneration: publication. Frequency: annual. **Preference.** Length: short (under 30 min). Material Must Be: unpublished. **Application.** Best Way: thru producing sponsor. Best Material: application, SASE. Deadline: website.

2/14/2008. Penobscot Theatre

131 Main Street, Bangor, ME, 04401
Tel: 207-947-6618
info@penobscottheatre.org; www.penobscottheatre.org

2 wk. New Play Fest. featuring readings & workshops. **Preference.** Material Must Be: unpublished, unproduced. **Application.** Deadline: 2/14/2008. Response: works selected notified by 5/1/08.

8/1/2008. Playfest! Harriett Lake Festival of New Plays

Orlando Shakespeare Theater in partnership with UCF, 812 E. Rollins St., #100, Orlando, FL, 32803
Patrick Flick, Dir., New Play Development & Casting
Fax: 407-447-1701
patrickf@shakespearefest.org; www.orlandoshakes.org

Est. 1989. 10 new plays receive readings, 2-3 developmental in Feb-Mar Festival of new plays. **Consideration.** Assistance: stipend, room/board, room/board, actors, directors 26 rehearsal time, access to copiers, email, etc., while on site.. **Preference.** Length: (75-120 min) An intermission is required after 100 min. Production: cast prefer 6 at most, but will consider more for musicals or other special circumstances. Material Must Be: unpublished, suitable to our mission. Please see website.. **Application.** Best Material: 1-pg synopsis (no longer than 200 words), 10-pg sample, bio of writer, casting including doubling, name, address, email on the cover page of the submission. Please see our website for exact, or additional submission requirements after 4/1/08., submissions not returned. Best Time: Apr-Aug. Deadline: 1-Aug-08.

8/1/2008. Political Theatre Festival

Teatro del Pueblo, 209 W. Page St., #208, St. Paul, MN, 55107
Christina Akers, Co. Mgr.
Tel: 651-224-8806
teatrom@bitstream.net; www.teatrodelpueblo.org

Est. 2001. One-acts about political issues of Latino identity. **Consideration.** Assistance: stipend. Remuneration: production, reading. **Preference.** Length: one-act (30-50 min), short (15-30 min). Style: interactive encouraged. Subject: Latino, political. Production: cast limit 3, up to 3 set pieces. Material Must Be: in English or Spanish. **Application.** Best Material: synopsis, full script, resume/bio, submissions not returned. Deadline: 1-Aug-08.

1/15/08. Premiere Stages Play Festival

Kean Univ., Hutchinson Hall, 1000 Morris Ave., Fl. 2, Union, NJ, 07083
John Wooten, Producing Artistic Dir.
www.kean.edu/premierestages

Est. 2004. Annual fest for playwrights born or living in NJ, CT, NY, PA. Three public readings in Apr, full Equity production of winner in Jul. **Consideration.** Remuneration: $2,000 1st, $750 2nd, $500 3rd, reading. Frequency: annual. **Preference.** Length: full length (over 90 min). Style: comedy, drama. Production: cast limit 8. Author Must Be: resident of NY, NJ, CT, or PA. Material Must Be: unoptioned, unpublished, unproduced. **Application.** Best Material: synopsis, 8-pg sample, cast list, production history, bio, SASE. Best Time: winter. Deadline: 15-Jan-08.

3/1/2008. ReOrient

Golden Thread Productions, 131 10th St., San Francisco, CA, 94103
Torange Yeghiazarian, Artistic Dir
Tel: 415-626-4061, Fax: 415-626-1138
www.goldenthread.org

Est. 1996. **Consideration.** Assistance: $100 stipend. Frequency: annual. **Preference.** Length: short (under 40 min). Subject: Middle East. **Application.** Best Material: full script, submisssions not returned. Deadline: 3/1/2008.

5/1/2008. Richard & Betty Burdick New Play Reading Series

Florida Studio Theatre, 1241 N. Palm Ave., Sarasota, FL, 34236
Cristin Kelly, Literary Manager
Tel: 941-366-9017, Fax: 941-955-4137
ckelly@floridastudiotheatre.org; www.floridastudiotheatre.org

May workshop readings of 3 new full-length plays or musicals by contemporary US writers. **Consideration.** Assistance: stipend, room/board, room/board. Frequency: annual. **Preference.** Length: full length (over 90 min). **Application.** Best Material: query, synopsis, sample, SASE.

Scratch Pad Festival

Centenary College of Louisiana, 2911 Centenary Blvd., Shreveport, LA, 71134
Don Hooper, Chair
www.centenary.edu/theatre

Est. 2006. **Consideration.** Remuneration: production, reading. Frequency: annual. **Preference.** Length: full length (over 90 min). Production: age 12-40, cast of 2-20. Material Must Be: unoptioned, unproduced. **Application.** Best Material: synopsis, 10-pg sample, submissions not returned. Best Time: early spring. Response: by early fall.

3/15/2008. Short Attention Span PlayFEST

Atlantis Playmakers, 4611 Monroe St., Hollywood, FL, 33021
Kimberly Davis Basso, Artistic Dir.
kdb@atlantisplaymakers.com; www.atlantisplaymakers.com

Est. 1998. **Consideration.** Remuneration: honorarium. Frequency: annual. **Preference.** Length: short (under 30 min). Style: comedy, drama, musical. Material Must Be: unpublished, unproduced. **Application.** Best Material: full script, submissions not returned. Deadline: 3/15/2008. Response: 4/30/2008.

9/30/08. Southern Appalachian Playwrights' Conference

Southern Appalachian Repertory Theatre (SART), Box 1720, Mars Hill, NC, 28754
Rob Miller, Managing Dir.
Tel: 828-689-1384, Fax: 828-689-1272
sart@mhc.edu; www.sartheatre.com

Est. 1981. Readings & critique of 5 plays in 3-day conference at Mars Hilll Coll. Staff: William Gregg (Artistic Dir). **Consideration.** Assistance: N/C, N/C. Remuneration: $1,000 award, possible future production. Frequency: Annually, one-time award. **Preference.** Length: full-length. Style: no adaptation, Comedy, Drama, Musical, no translation. Subject: All Subjects, Appalachian culture. Production: cast, orchestra, full. Material Must Be: Not Published, unproduced, amatuer produced scripts are eligible. **Application.** Best Way: unsolicited, Professional Recommendation, Agent. Best Material: query letter (note theme addressed), full script, audio, submissions returned with SASE. Best Time: Jan 1-Sept. 30. Deadline: 9/30/2008. Response: Feb. or March announcement.

11/1/2008. Stages

Theatre Building Chicago (TBC), 1225 W. Belmont Ave., Chicago, IL, 60657
John Sparks, Artistic Dir.
Tel: 773-929-7367 x222, Fax: 773-327-1404
jsparks@theatrebuildingchicago.org; www.theatrebuildingchicago.org

Est. 1984. 2-day Aug fest with Equity and non-Equity actors in readings of 8 full-length musicals. Works not ready for fest are considered for development series. **Consideration.** Remuneration: reading. Frequency: annual. **Preference.** Length: full length (over 90 min). Style: musical. Production: cast limit 16, piano only, no set. Material Must Be: considered work-in-progress. **Application.** Best Way: professional recommendation. Best Material: application, submissions not returned. Best Time: fall. Deadline: 1-Oct-08. Response: 3 mos.

Summer Writing Workshops

Center for Continuing Education and Professional Advancement Hofstra Univ., 7200 Hofstra Univ., Hempstead, NY, 11549
Kenneth Henwood, Managing Director, Univ. College
Tel: 516-463-5737, Fax: 516-463-4833
kenneth.a.henwood@hofstra.edu; www.ccepa.hofstra.edu/univcollege

Opportunity to teach a 2-week workshop in Dramatic Writing at conference in July. **Consideration.** Remuneration: feedback. Frequency: annual. **Application.** Best Way: unsolicited. Best Material: query letter (note theme addressed), synopsis, submissions returned with SASE.

Theater 150 Ten-Minute Play Festival

Box 925, Ojai, CA, 93024
Gai Jones, Producer, New Play Series
Tel: 805-646-4300
theater150@ojai.net; www.theater150.org

Est. 1996. **Preference.** Production: cast limit 8, small set. Author Must Be: resident of Ventura/Santa Barbara cos. Material Must Be: unpublished. **Application.** Best Material: full script, SASE. Response: 6 mos.

9/30/08. Theatre Three [NY] One-Act Play Festival

Box 512, 412 Main St., Port Jefferson, NY, 11777
Jeffrey Sanzel, Exec Artistic Dir
Tel: 631-928-9202, Fax: 631-928-9120
www.theatrethree.com

Est. 1969. Festival of one-act plays in Mar. **Consideration.** Remuneration: $70 . Frequency: annual. **Preference.** Length: one-act (10-40 min). Style: comedy, drama, experimental. Production: 8-Feb, minimal set. Material Must Be: unproduced. **Application.** Best Material: full script, visit website for detailed guidelines, SASE. Deadline: 9/30/2008. Response: 8 mos.

Woodstock Fringe

Box 157, Lake Hill, NY, 12448
Wallace Norman, Producing Artistic Dir.
Tel: 845-810-0123, Fax: 212-602-0061
wnorman@woodstockfringe.org; www.woodstockfringe.org

Est. 2003. Monthlong fest of theater and song at Byrdcliffe Arts Colony. **Consideration.** Assistance: $250 stipend. Remuneration: 6\% royalty. Frequency: annual. **Preference.** Production: cast of 2-5. **Application.** Best Material: query, synopsis, 15-pg sample, SASE. Best Time: autumn. Response: 6 mos.

CONFERENCES & FESTIVALS (Fee Charged)

5/1/08. $10. Actors' Playhouse National Children's Theatre Festival

Actors' Playhouse, 280 Miracle Mile, Coral Gables, FL, 33134
Earl Maulding, Dir, TYA
Tel: 305-444-9293 x615, Fax: 305-444-4181
maulding@actorsplayhouse.org; www.actorsplayhouse.org

Est. 1994. Annual 4-day fest. Winning show runs 4-6 wks. Non-Equity. **Consideration.** Fees: $10 reading. Assistance:. Remuneration: $500 , production. Frequency: annual. **Preference.** Length: one-act (45-60 min). Style: musical. Subject: children's. Production: cast limit 8, touring set. Material Must Be: unpublished. **Application.** Best Material: application, script, audio, SASE. Deadline: 1-May-08. Response: by 10/1/08.

1/15/08. $15. Ashland New Plays Festival

ArtWork Enterprises Inc., Box 453, Ashland, OR, 97520-0453
Janet Rodkey, President
Tel: 541-482-4357
www.ashlandnewplays.org

Est. 1992. Fest in Oct. with 12 hrs rehearsal for 2 unstaged readings with professional director and actors (often from Ore Shakespeare Fest). Workshops offered during fest. **Consideration.** Fees: $15 entry. Assistance: $500 stipend, room (1 wk), room (1 wk). Remuneration: reading. Frequency: annual. **Preference.** Length: full length (over 90 min). Style: comedy, drama. Subject: no children's. Production: cast limit 8. Author Must Be: resident of US. Material Must Be: unpublished, unproduced. **Application.** Best Material: query, application, synopsis, full script, bio, SASE. Best Time: Oct-Dec. Deadline: 15-Jan-08. Response: by 8/31/08.

12/31/08. $15. Attic Theatre One-Act Marathon

Attic Theatre, 5429 W. Washington Blvd., Los Angeles, CA, 90016
Laura Carson, Literary Mgr
Tel: 323-525-0600, Fax: 323-525-0661
litmanager@attictheatre.org; www.attictheatre.org

Entries read by ensemble, finalists read by staff, with 3-10 selected for production or reading in marathon. Panel from L.A. theater community chooses 2 winners. **Consideration.** Fees: $15 entry. Remuneration: $300 1st, $150 2nd, publication. Frequency: annual. **Preference.** Length: one-act (up to 40 min). Style: comedy, drama. Production: cast limit 8, no orchestra, unit set. Material Must Be: unproduced. **Application.** Best Material: query, application, synopsis, full script (2 copies), character breakdown, bio, SASE. Deadline: 31-Dec-08. Response: 3 mos.

9/30/08. $10. Baltimore Playwrights Festival

Baltimore Playwrights Festival, Box 38537, Baltimore, MD, 21231
Rich Espey, Chair
Tel: 410-276-2153
chairman@baltimoreplaywrightsfestival.org; www.baltimoreplaywrightsfestival.org

Est. 1981. Plays chosen by 1 of 6 companies for 3-wk summer production. Selected public readings given thru year. **Consideration.** Fees: $10 entry. Remuneration: up to $250, honoraria up to $100. Frequency: annual. **Preference.** Author Must Be: current or former resident or employee in MD. Material Must Be: unpublished, unproduced. **Application.** Best Material: synopsis, full script (3 copies), SASE. Best Time: after 4/1/08. Deadline: 30-Sep-08.

12/15/08. $20. Bay Area Playwrights Festival (BAPF)

Playwrights Foundation, 131 10th St, Third Floor, San Francisco, CA, 94103
Jonathan Spector, Literary Mgr
literary@playwrightsfoundation.org; www.playwrightsfoundation.org

Est. 1976. BAPF is 2-wk Jul fest of 5-6 full-length plays by US writers, given rehearsal and 2 readings (1 wk apart for rewrites) before production. **Consideration.** Fees: $20 entry. Assistance: stipend, room/board, room/board. Remuneration: reading. Frequency: annual. **Preference.** Length: full length (over 90 min), mid-length (60-90 min). Style: comedy, drama. Author Must Be: US resident. Material Must Be: unproduced, original, in English. **Application.** Best Material: query, full script, submissions not returned. Best Time: after 10/1/08. Deadline: 15-Dec-08. Response: 4 mos.

11/1/08. $10. Black Box New Play Festival

The Gallery Players, 199 14th St., Brooklyn, NY, 11215
Heather S. Curran, New Play Development
info@galleryplayers.com; www.galleryplayers.com

Est. 1996. AEA/Non-AEA showcase. 3 week run of show plus workshop. Staff: Heather Siobhan Curran (Pres/Artistic Dir), Matt Schicker (VP). Cathy Bencivenga (Dir. of Prod.) **Consideration.** Fees: $10 entry (Admin costs). Remuneration: production. Frequency: annual. **Preference.** Length: full length (over 90 min). Style: comedy, drama, no musical, no translation. Subject: all subjects. Production: ages 20-40's, cast 5-10, unit set. Author Must Be: resident of CT, NJ, NY. Material Must Be: unproduced, readings ok. **Application.** Best Way: unsolicited. Best Material: synopsis, full script, resume, submissions not returned. Best Time: Begin 9/7/08. Deadline: 11/1/2008. Response: 1/1/2009.

1/4/08. $15. Boston Theatre Works Unbound

Boston Theatre Works Unbound, 31 St. James Ave., #360, Boston, MA, 02116
Bridget Frey, Literary Mgr.
Tel: 617-728-4321, Fax: 617-262-8633
litmanager@bostontheatreworks.com; www.bostontheatreworks.com

Est. 1999. Annual fest of 3-6 new works over 1 weekend. Staff: Jason Southerland (Artistic Dir). **Consideration.** Fees: $15 reading. Remuneration: $500 1st, $250 2nd. Frequency: annual. **Preference.** Subject: unbound by convention, driven toward discovery, engaging new audiences. Material Must Be: unproduced. **Application.** Best Material: full script (1/author). Deadline: 4-Jan-08. Response: by 6/15/08.

12/31/2008. Cincinnati Fringe Festival

Know Theatre of Cincinnati, 1120 Jackson Street, Cincinnati, OH, 45202
Jason Bruffy, Artistic Dir.
Tel: 513-300-5669
www.knowtheatre.com; www.cincyfringe.com

Est. 2003. Fringe Festival occurs annually late May/early June. See applications online at cincyfringe.com for specifics. **Consideration.** Fees: $25 . Remuneration: split box offc. Frequency: annual. **Preference.** Length: all length. Style: all styles. Subject: all subjects. **Application.** Best Way: unsolicited. Best Material: application, materials will not be returned. Best Time: Generally after 9/1. Deadline: 12/31/2008. Response: 3 mos..

3/31/08. $5. Fire Rose Prods. 10-Min. Play Festival

coe college, 11246 Magnolia Blvd., N. Hollywood, CA, 91601
Kaz Mata-Mura, Artistic Dir
Tel: 818-766-3691
info@fireroseproductions.com; www.fireroseproductions.com

Est. 2000. Equity 99-seat. **Consideration.** Fees: $5 entry. Frequency: annual. **Preference.** Length: 10-min. **Application.** Best Material: full script, submissions not returned. Best Time: Nov-Mar. Deadline: 31-Mar-08. Response: 3 mos.

3/15/08. $15. Juneteenth Jamboree of New Plays

Juneteenth Legacy Theatre (JLT), 323 W. Broadway, #505, Louisville, KY, 40202
Lorna Littleway, Founder/Producing Dir.
juneteenthlegacy@aol.com; www.juneteenthlegacytheatre.com

Est. 1999. Staged readings on African-American experience in 19th-20th centuries, incl. Harlem Renaissance, Caribbean/Native American influences, contemporary youth, and new images of women. Send 3 copies of submissions to KY address above, send 1 copy w/entry fee to JLT, 605 Water St., #21-B, New York, NY 10002. **Consideration.** Fees: $15 entry (send to NY). Remuneration: reading. **Preference.** Style: adaptation, comedy, drama. Subject: African-American, GLBT, women. **Application.** Best Material: query, full script (4 copies: send 3 to KY, 1 to NY), SASE. Best Time: Nov-Feb. Deadline: 15-Mar-08.

3/15/08. $2. Lamia Ink! Intl. One-Page Play Competition

Box 202, Prince St. Sta., New York, NY, 10012
Ms. Cortland Jessup, Artistic Dir.
www.lamiaink.org

Est. 1989. Annual. **Consideration.** Fees: $2 entry ($5 for 3). Remuneration: $200 , publication, reading. Frequency: annual. **Preference.** Length: 1-pg.. **Application.** Best Material: full script, 50-word bio, SASE. Deadline: 15-Mar-08.

$10.00 . Long Beach Playhouse New Works Festival

Long Beach Playhouse, 5021 East Anaheim Street, Long Beach, CA, 90804
Jo Black-Jacob, New Works Literary Mgr.
Tel: 562-494-1014 x507, Fax: 562-961-8616
LBPH75@aol.com; www.lbph.com

Est. 1989. Fest of 4 new plays in staged readings (Spring) plus possible consideration of one world premiere prod. of previous year's winner. Staff: Gigi Fusco Meese (Exec Producer/Dir). **Consideration.** Fees: $10 entry. Remuneration: $100 reading $300 full production. Frequency: annual. **Preference.** Length: full length (over 90 min). Style: no musical. Production: cast limit 10, limited set. Material Must Be: unproduced. **Application.** Best Material: application, synopsis, full script, cast list, SASE. Best Time: Jan-Nov. Response: 3 mos after festival concludes.

12/1/08. $35. National Music Theater Conference (OMTC)

Eugene O'Neill Theater Center, 305 Great Neck Rd., Waterford, CT, 06385
Paulette Haupt, Artistic Dir.
Tel: 860-443-5378 x301
musictheater@theONEILL.org; www.oneilltheatercenter.org

Est. 1978. 2-3 wk residency (Jul-Aug), with rehearsal and in-hand public readings. **Consideration.** Fees: $35 entry. Assistance: $1,000 stipend, room/board, room/board. Remuneration: reading. Frequency: annual. **Preference.** Style: musical. Production: no orchestra, no set. Author Must Be: resident or citizen of US. Material Must Be: unproduced. **Application.** Best Material: application, synopsis, 30-pg sample, audio. Deadline: 1-Dec-08.

10/15/08. $35. National Playwrights Conference (OPC)

Eugene O'Neill Theater Center, 305 Great Neck Rd., Waterford, CT, 06385
Martin Kettling, Literary Manager
Tel: 860-443-5378 x227
litoffice@theoneill.org; www.oneill.org

Est. 1964. Month residency (Jun-Jul), incl. 4-day workshop and 2 in-hand readings with professional actors and directors. **Consideration.** Fees: $35 entry. Assistance: $1,000 stipend, room/board, room/board. Remuneration: reading. Frequency: annual. **Preference.** Length: full length (over 90 min). Material Must Be: unproduced. **Application.** Best Material: application, full script (3 copies). Deadline: 15-Oct-08.

1/15/2008. Perishable Theatre Women's Playwriting Festival

Box 23132, Providence, RI, 02903
WPF Festival Coord.
Tel: 401-331-2695, Fax: 401-331-7811
wpf@perishable.org; www.perishable.org

Fall festival. Up to 3 winners produced in mainstage season. Publication in anthology. **Consideration.** Fees: $10 by post/$12.50 by internet. Assistance:. Remuneration: $500 award, possible future production, publication. Frequency: biennial. **Preference.** Length: one-act (10-45 mins.). Style: all styles. Subject: all subjects. Author Must Be: female. Material Must Be: unoptioned, unproduced. **Application.** Best Way: unsolicited. Best Material: full script (up to 2 entries), cast and scene breakdown, submissions returned with SASE. Deadline: 1/15/2004. Response: 5/15/2004.

4/1/08. $10. Pittsburgh New Works Festival (PNWF)

Box 42419, Pittsburgh, PA, 15203
Play Selection Mgr
Tel: 412-881-6888
info@pittsburghnewworks.org; www.pittsburghnewworks.org

Est. 1991. Non-Equity 6-wk fest after Labor Day, 6 seated readings, 12 staged productions, 3 young-playwright staged productions, 18 production companies under fest umbrella. **Consideration.** Fees: $10 entry. Frequency: annual. **Preference.** Length: short (under 30 min). Style: no musical. Production: age 12 and up, cast limit 8, simple set, limited props. Material Must Be: unproduced. **Application.** Best Material: query, full script (3 copies), SASE. Best Time: Jan-Mar. Deadline: 4/1/2008. Response: 3 mos.

2/15/08. $20. Playwrights' Week

Lark Play Development Center, 939 8th Ave., #301, New York, NY, 10019
Andrea Hiebler, Literary Assoc.
Tel: 212-246-2676
andreah@larktheatre.org; www.larktheatre.org

The first step in development at Lark is Playwrights' Week, a Sep fest of 8 public readings with script in-hand. Staff: John Eisner (Producing Dir), Daniella Topol (Managing Dir). **Consideration.** Fees: $20 application. Frequency: annual. **Preference.** Length: full length (over 90 min). Author Must Be: age 18 or older. **Application.** Best Material: application, full script (1 entry/author), SASE. Deadline: 11/15/2008. Response: 9 mos.

11/30/08. $5. Raymond J. Flores Short Play Festival

Around the Block, 5 E. 22nd St., #9-K, New York, NY, 10010
Carlos Jerome, President
Tel: 212-673-9187
info@aroundtheblock.org; www.aroundtheblock.org

Est. 2004. Part of annual Urban Arts Fest is its Raymond J. Flores Short Play Competition & Reading Series. Staff: Gloria Zelaya, Louis Vuolo (Co-dir, Theater Arts). **Consideration.** Fees: $5 entry (free for ATB members). Remuneration: $50 , reading. Frequency: annual. **Preference.** Length: short (limit 15 min). Style: no musical. Subject: life and aspirations of NYC; no children's. Author Must Be: owner of all production and publishing rights. Material Must Be: in English, Spanish or Chinese. **Application.** Best Way: email. Best Material: application, full script (2 copies, unless e-mailed), 1-paragraph bio. Deadline: 30-Nov-08.

12/31/08. $5. Seven Devils Playwrights Conference

id Theatre Company, 343 E. 30th St., #19-K, New York, NY, 10016
Jeni Mahoney, co-Artistic Dir
jeni@sevendevils.org; www.sevendevils.org

Est. 2001. Equity 2-wk play development conference in McCall, ID, ending w/fully staged readings of new plays. **Preference.** Length: full length (over 90 min), mid-length (60-90 min.). **Application.** Deadline: 12/31/08.

10/15/08. $10. ShowOff! Playwriting Festival

Camino Real Playhouse, 31776 El Camino Real, San Juan Capistrano, CA, 92675
Tom Scott, President
www.caminorealplayhouse.org

Est. 1993. **Consideration.** Fees: $10 entry. Frequency: annual. **Preference.** Length: 10 min. Material Must Be: unpublished. **Application.** Best Material: full script, submissions not returned. Deadline: 10/15/2008. Response: 3 mos.

$10. Sketchbook Festival

Collaboraction, 437 N. Wolcott, #201, Attn: SKBK06, Chicago, IL, 60622
Becky Perlman, Lit. Manager
becky@collaboraction.org; http://collaboraction.typepad.com/sketchbook/2007/01/post.html

Collaboraction is accepting short play submissions (seven minutes or less in length) to be performed in May and June of 2008 in the Garage Theater at Steppenwolf Theatre Company. **Consideration.** Fees: $10 (if not submitted online). **Preference.** Length: sketch (1 min. or 6 min.). Style: audience participation. Material Must Be: unproduced. **Application.** Best Way: email (rtf or doc only). Best Material: application, full script. Deadline: 12/15/2008.

5/15/08. $10. Stage 3 Theatre Festival of New Plays

208 S. Green St., Sonora, CA, 95370
Don Bilotti, Artistic Dir
Tel: 209-536-1778, Fax: 209-536-1778
info@stage3.org; www.stage3.org

Est. 1994. 3-day fest of 3 rehearsed readings, with winner. Winner may have full production following year. **Consideration.** Fees: $10 entry. Assistance: room/board, room/board. Frequency: annual. **Preference.** Length: full length (over 90 min). Production: cast limit 10. Material Must Be: unpublished, unproduced. **Application.** Best Material: full script, SASE. Best Time: Mar-Apr. Deadline: 5/15/2008. Response: 4 mos.

$25. 11/25/08. Tennessee Williams/New Orleans Literary Festival

938 Lafayette St., #514, New Orleans, LA, 70113
Laura Miller, Contest Coord.
Tel: 504-581-1144, Fax: 504-581-3270
info@tennesseewilliams.net; www.tennesseewilliams.net

Includes Saints and Sinners Annual Playwrighting Festival. **Consideration.** Fees: $25 entry. Remuneration: $1,000 . Frequency: annual. **Preference.** Production: small, minimal. **Application.** Deadline: 11/25/2008.

$25. Theater League Festival of New Musicals

Box 140206, Kansas City, MO, 64114
Chris McCoy, Artistic Dir
Tel: 913-652-7407
chris@kcmusicals.org; www.theaterleague.com/newmusicals

Est. 2006. Incl. Kansas City Fest of New Musicals (formerly KC Crossroads Musical Theater Fest) and Thousand Oaks Fest of New Musicals. **Consideration.** Fees: $25 entry. Remuneration: reading. **Application.** Best Material: full script, audio, score, bio, SASE. Deadline: 5-Jan-08 (see website).

1/13/08, 8/15/08. $25. TRU Voices

Players Theater, 115 MacDougal St., New York, NY, 10002
Bob Ost, Pres.
Tel: 212-714-7628, Fax: 212-864-6301
trunltd@aol.com; www.truonline.org

Winter musical series (est. 1999) and spring play series (est. 1997) of 2-3 readings each. Prefer submissions from producers, but writers may submit and TRU will try to find a sponsoring producer. **Consideration.** Fees: $25 entry. Frequency: annual. **Preference.** Length: full length (over 90 min). Production: cast limit 12. Material Must Be: unpublished, unproduced. **Application.** Best Material: application, synopsis, full script, audio, SASE. Best Time: Jun (musicals), Sep (plays). Deadline: Jan 13, 2008 (plays), Aug 15, 2008 (musicals). Response: 6 mos.

CONTESTS

10/1/08. $15. Actors' Theatre [CA] Full-Length Play Contest

1001 Center St., #12, Santa Cruz, CA, 95060
Wendy Adler, Office Mgr
Tel: 831-425-1003, Fax: 831-425-7560
actors@sbcglobal.net; www.sccat.org

Est. 1985. **Consideration.** Fees: $15 entry. Remuneration: $200 , reading. Frequency: annual. **Preference.** Length: full length (over 90 min). Material Must Be: unpublished, unproduced, original. **Application.** Best Material: full script (2 copies), submissions not returned. Deadline: 10/1/2008.

7/1/08. $10. Actors' Theatre [CA] Ten-Minute Play Contest

1001 Center St., #12, Santa Cruz, CA, 95060
Wendy Adler, Office Mgr
Tel: 831-425-1003, Fax: 831-425-7560
actors@sbcglobal.net; www.sccat.org

Est. 1985. **Consideration.** Fees: $10 entry, goes to costs of festival specifically judges honorarium, festival prize and photocopying costs. Remuneration: $50, production, reading. Frequency: annual. **Preference.** Length: 10-min. Material Must Be: unpublished, unproduced, original. **Application.** Best Material: full script (5 copies), cover letter, submissions not returned. Deadline: 7/1/2008.

6/1/08. American Scandinavian Foundation Translation Prize

American Scandinavian Foundation, 58 Park Ave., New York, NY, 10016
grants@amscan.org; www.amscan.org

Est. 1979. Prize for best translation of drama written after 1800 by a Scandinavian author (Danish, Finnish, Icelandic, Norwegian, Swedish). **Consideration.** Remuneration: $2,000; $1,000, publication of exerpt in Scandinavian Review. **Preference.** Length: full length (over 90 min), mid-length (60-90 min.). Style: translation. Material Must Be: unpublished. **Application.** Best Way: translation (4 copies), original (1 copy). Best Material: resume/bio. Deadline: 1-Jun-08.

3/3/08. Anna Zornio Memorial Children's Theatre Playwriting Award

Univ. of New Hampshire, UNH Theatre/Dance Dept., PCAC, 30 College Rd., Durham, NH, 03824
Michael Wood
Tel: 603-862-3038, Fax: 603-862-0298
www.unh.edu/theatre-dance

Est. 1979. Quadrennial award for original children's script, selected by UNH Youth Drama Program. Students and faculty produce premiere. **Preference.** Length: one-act (30-60 min). Subject: children's. Author Must Be: resident of US or Canada. Material Must Be: unoptioned, unpublished, unproduced, original. **Application.** Best Way: email. Best Material: application, full script, audio, cast/tech list, SASE. Deadline: 3/3/2008.

3/1/2008. Arthur W. Stone New Play Award

The School of Performing Arts, Box 8608,, Ruston, LA, 71272
Louisiana Tech University
Tel: 318-257-2711, Fax: 318-257-4571
stoneplaywritingaward@yahoo.com; http://performingarts/latech.edu

Est. 2006. **Consideration.** Assistance: room/board, room/board. Remuneration: $500 , plus production. Frequency: biennial. **Preference.** Length: full length (over 90 min). Style: no musical. Production: college age. Material Must Be: unpublished, produced no more than twice, original. **Application.** Best Way: email (DOC, FDR, RTF). Best Material: full script, bio, SASE. Best Time: Begin 10/1. Deadline: 3/1/2008.

5/31/08. Award Blue

Buntville Crew, Box 445, Buckley, IL, 60918
Steven Packard, Artistic Dir.
buntville@yahoo.fr

Est. 1999. **Consideration.** Remuneration: $200 . Frequency: annual. **Preference.** Length: short (under 15 min.). Author Must Be: IL high school student. **Application.** Best Material: full script, bio. Deadline: 31-May-08.

Baker's Plays High School Playwriting Contest

45 W. 25th Street, New York, NY, 10010
Tel: 212-255-8085, Fax: 212-627-7753
www.bakersplays.com

Est. 1989. For student plays, preferably about HS experience. Plays must be accompanied by signature of HS English or drama teacher. **Consideration.** Remuneration: $500 1st, $250 2nd, $100 3rd, publication, royalty. **Preference.** Author Must Be: HS student. Material Must Be: produced. **Application.** Best Material: full script, SASE. Deadline: TBA. Response: TBA.

6/30/2008. Brevard Little Theatre New-Play Competition

Box 426, Brevard, NC, 28712
Al Edick, Coord.
Tel: 828-890-1495
aedick@bellsouth.net; www.brevardlittletheatre.com

Consideration. Remuneration: public production. **Preference.** Length: full length (over 90 min), one-act (30-60 min). Production: cast limit 20, simple set. Material Must Be: unproduced, original. **Application.** Best Material: query, full script, SASE. Deadline: 30-Jun-08. Response: by 9/30/08.

11/15/2008. California Musical Theatre Award

Beverly Hills Theatre Guild, Box 148, Beverly Hills, CA, 90213
Patricia Mock
Tel: 310-273-3390
www.beverlyhillstheatreguild.org

Consideration. Remuneration: $4,000 . **Preference.** Style: musical. Author Must Be: resident of CA, citizen of US. Material Must Be: unproduced, original, in English. **Application.** Best Material: query, application, full script, audio. Best Time: May-Oct. Deadline: 15-Nov-08.

6/1/08. California Young Playwrights Contest

Playwrights Project, Playwrights Project, 2356 Moore St., #204, San Diego, CA, 92110
Deborah Salzer, Exec Dir
Tel: 619-239-8222, Fax: 619-239-8225
write@playwrightsproject.com; www.playwrightsproject.com

Est. 1984. All entrants receive evaluation. Winners work with a dramaturg and receive 4 performances at Old Globe. **Consideration.** Assistance: room/board, room/board. Remuneration: $100 , production. Frequency: annual. **Preference.** Style: comedy, drama. Author Must Be: age 18 or younger, resident of CA. Material Must Be: unoptioned, unpublished, original. **Application.** Best Material: query, full script (2 copies). Deadline: 1-Jun-08.

Canadian Jewish Playwriting Contest

Miles Nadal Jewish Community Centre, 750 Spadina Ave., Fl. 2, Toronto, ON, M5S 2J2 Canada
Esther Arbeid, Miles Nadal Jewish Community Centre
Tel: 416-924-6211 x 606
esthera@mnjcc.org; www.mnjcc.org

Consideration. Remuneration: 4 hour workshop with public reading, professional artists only. Frequency: annual. **Preference.** Length: mid-length (60-90 min.), one-act (30-60 min.). Subject: Jewish Culture. Author Must Be: Canada or strong Canadian ties. Material Must Be: unpublished, unproduced. **Application.** Deadline: May-08. Response: no reponse unless playis chosen as winner, no feedback from jury.

6/1/2008. Charles M. Getchell Award
Clemson University, 221 Brooks Center, Dept. of Performing Arts, Clemson, SC, 29634
Mark Charney
Tel: 864-656-5415
cmark@clemson.edu

Consideration. Remuneration: $1,000 . **Preference.** Length: full length (over 90 min). Author Must Be: resident or student in AL, FL, GA, KY, MS, NC, SC, TN, VA or WV. Material Must Be: unpublished, unproduced. **Application.** Best Way: email or CD. Best Material: application, full script (2 copies), SASE. Best Time: Mar-May. Deadline: 1-Jun-08.

6/1/08. Christopher Brian Wolk Award
Abingdon Theatre Company, 312 W. 36th St., 6th floor, New York, NY, 10018
Kim T. Sharp, Literary Mgr
Tel: 212-868-2055, Fax: 212-868-2056
ksharp@abingdontheatre.org; www.abingdontheatre.org

Est. 2001. **Consideration.** Remuneration: $1,000 , reading. Frequency: annual. **Preference.** Length: full length (over 90 min). Style: comedy, drama. Production: cast limit 8. Author Must Be: resident or citizen of US. Material Must Be: unoptioned, unproduced in NYC. **Application.** Best Material: full script, SASE. Deadline: 1-Jun-08. Response: 3 mos.

2/1/2008. City Attic Theatre Playwriting Contest
19-25 Ditmars Blvd., 3rd Floor, Astoria, NY, 10032
Melissa Gawlowski, Literary Mgr.
mgawlowski@gmail.com; www.freewebs.com/visualfields

Est. 2004. **Consideration.** Frequency: biennial. **Preference.** Length: full length (over 90 min), no children's. Production: cast limit 6. Material Must Be: unpublished. **Application.** Best Material: query, full script. Deadline: 1-Feb-09. Response: 4 mos.

12/1/2008. Cunningham Commission for Youth Theatre
DePaul Univ., 2135 N. Kenmore Ave., Chicago, IL, 60614
Anna Ables, Dir., Marketing & PR
Tel: 773-325-7938
aables@depaul.edu; theatreschool.depaul.edu/specialprogramscunninghamcommission.php

Est. 1991. Commission to write theater for youth that affirms the centrality of religion, broadly defined, and the human quest for meaning, truth and community. **Consideration.** Remuneration: $5,000 commission. Frequency: annual. **Preference.** Subject: children's, religious. Author Must Be: resident of Chicago (100 miles of Loop), not Cunningham winner in last 5 yrs. **Application.** Best Material: 20-pg sample, resume. Deadline: 1-Dec-08.

12/31/2008. Dorothy Silver Playwriting Competition
The Mandel Jewish Community Center of Cleveland, 26001 S. Woodland Ave., Beachwood, OH, 44122
Deborah Bobrow, Coord.
Tel: 216-831-0700, Fax: 216-831-7796
dbobrow@clevejcc.org; www.clevejcc.org

Award for original works of significant, fresh perspective on Jewish experience. **Consideration.** Remuneration: $1,000 , reading. Frequency: annual. **Preference.** Length: full length (over 90 min). Subject: Jewish. Material Must Be: unoptioned, unpublished, unproduced. **Application.** Best Material: full script, audio, SASE. Deadline: 31-Dec-08. Response: 4 mos.

1/30/2008. Dr. Floyd Gaffney PLaywriting Award on the African-American Experience
UCSD, 9500 Gilman Drive, MC 0344, La Jolla, CA, 92093
Tel: 858-534-4791
theatre.ucsd.edu/playwritingcontest

est. 2007. Contest seeking scripts highlighting the African-American experience in comtemporary or historical terms. No adaptations. **Consideration.** Remuneration: $1,000 . **Preference.** Author Must Be: undergraduate, enrolled student. **Application.** Best Way: unsolicited. Best Material: application, full script. Response: announced by 2/28/08.

11/30/2008. Edgar Allan Poe Award for Best Play

Mystery Writers of America, 17 E. 47th St., Fl. 6, New York, NY, 10017
Margery Flax, Admin Dir
Tel: 212-888-8171
mwa@mysterywriters.org; www.mysterywriters.org

Est. 1945. **Consideration.** Frequency: annual. **Preference.** Length: full length (over 90 min), mid-length (60-90 min). Style: comedy, drama, musical. Subject: crime, mystery. Material Must Be: produced. **Application.** Best Material: application, full script (5 copies), submissions not returned. Best Time: Jan-Nov. Deadline: 30-Nov-08.

Eileen Heckart Drama For Seniors Competition

Jerome Laurence & Robert E. Lee Theatre Research Institute, Ohio State University, 1430 Lincoln Tower,, 1800 Cannon Drive, Columbus, OH, 43210
Alan Wood, Director
Tel: 614-292-6614
woods.1@osu.edu; www.heckartdrama.blogspot.com

est. 2003. Biennial.

4/23/2008. Essential Theatre Playwriting Award

Box 8172, Atlanta, GA, 30306
Peter Hardy, Producing Art. Dir.
Tel: 404-212-0815
pmhardy@aol.com; www.essentialtheatre.com

Consideration. Remuneration: $500 , production. **Preference.** Author Must Be: resident of GA. Material Must Be: unproduced. **Application.** Best Way: email. Best Material: full script. Deadline: 23-Apr-08.

6/29/2008. Fred Ebb Award

Roundabout Theater, 231 W. 39th St., #1200, New York, NY, 10018
info@fredebbfoundation.org; www.fredebbfoundation.org

Est. 2005. Named for lyricist Fred Ebb (1928-2004), award recognizes excellence by a songwriter or songwriting team that hasn't yet achieved significant commercial success. **Consideration.** Remuneration: $50,000 . Frequency: annual. **Preference.** Style: musical. Author Must Be: produced, published, or professional workshop member. **Application.** Best Material: application, audio (up to 4 songs), lyrics and context for songs. Best Time: after 6/1/08. Deadline: 29-Jun-08. Response: by 11/30/08.

4/30/08. $15. Fremont Centre Theatre New Playwright Contest

California Performing Arts Centre (CPAC), 1000 Fremont Ave., S. Pasadena, CA, 91030
Carol Doehring, Literary Mgr.
Tel: 626-441-5977, Fax: 626-441-5976
fct@fremontcentretheatre.com; www.fremontcentretheatre.com

Consideration. Fees: $15 entry. Remuneration: $350 1st, $250 2nd, $100 3rd, reading. Frequency: annual. **Preference.** Length: full length (over 90 min), one-act (30-60 min). Subject: all subjects, Black, historical themes. Production: cast limit 10. Material Must Be: unpublished, unproduced professionally. **Application.** Best Material: 1-pg synopsis, full script, cast list, resume. Deadline: 30-Apr-08.

12/31/2008. Goshen College Peace Playwriting Contest

1700 S. Main St., Goshen, IN, 46526
Douglas Caskey, Dir. of Theatre
Tel: 574-535-7393, Fax: 574-535-7660
douglc@goshen.edu; www.goshen.edu

Consideration. Remuneration: $500 1st; $100 2nd, production. Frequency: biennial. **Preference.** Length: short (under 30 min). Subject: peace or justice theme. Material Must Be: unproduced. **Application.** Best Material: 1-paragraph synopsis, full script, resume. Deadline: 31-Dec-08.

12/31/2008. Harold Morton Landon Translation Award

The Academy of American Poets, 584 Broadway, #604, New York, NY, 10012
Ryan Murphy, Awards Coord.
Tel: 212-274-0343 x17, Fax: 212-274-9427
rmurphy@poets.org; www.poets.org

Est. 1976. Recognizes translation of poetry (incl. verse drama) from any language into English. A noted translator chooses the winning book published that year. **Consideration.** Remuneration: $1,000 . Frequency: annual. **Preference.** Length: full length (over 90 min). Style: translation. Author Must Be: citizen of US. Material Must Be: published in US. **Application.** Best Way: unsolicited. Best Material: full script (3 copies). Deadline: 31-Dec-08.

1/2/2008. Hawai'i Prize

Kumu Kahua Theatre, 46 Merchant St., Honolulu, HI, 96813
Harry Wong III, Artistic Dir.
Tel: 808-536-4222, Fax: 808-536-4226
kumukahuatheatre@hawaiiantel.net; www.kumukahua.org

Consideration. Remuneration: $600 . Frequency: annual. **Preference.** Length: full length (over 90 min). Subject: Hawaii. **Application.** Best Material: full script (3 copies). Deadline: 2-Jan-08.

7/1/08. Henrico Theatre Company One-Act Playwriting Competition

Henrico Co. Recreation & Parks, Box 27032, Richmond, VA, 23273
Amy Perdue, Cultural Arts Coord.
Tel: 804-501-5138
per22@co.henrico.va.us; www.co.henrico.va.us/rec

Est. 1984. **Consideration.** Remuneration: $300 , production. Frequency: annual. **Preference.** Length: one-act (30-60 min). Subject: nothing controversial, no excessive language. Material Must Be: unpublished, unproduced, original. **Application.** Best Material: full script (2 copies), SASE. Deadline: 1-Jul-08.

4/30/2008. International Radio Playwriting Competition

BBC World Service Drama, Rm 118 East Wing, Bush House, London, WC2B 4PH England
intradioplaycomp@bbc.co.uk; http://www.bbc.co.uk/worldservice/specials/1521intplaycomp

Consideration. Assistance:. Remuneration: 2,500. Frequency: biennial. **Preference.** Length: mid-length (50-75 pgs). Production: cast limit 6. Author Must Be: resident outside UK. Material Must Be: unoptioned, unpublished, unproduced professionally, original, in English. **Application.** Best Material: application, full script. Deadline: 30-Apr-08.

5/15/2008. Jacksonville Univ. Helford Prize

2800 University Blvd. N., Jacksonville, FL, 32211
Laura Porter, Fine Arts Coord.
lporter1@ju.edu; arts.ju.edu/CFA/helford/prize.html

Consideration. Remuneration: $10,000 . **Preference.** Length: full length (90-120 min). Production: cast of 5-10. Author Must Be: resident of US. Material Must Be: unpublished, unproduced, original, in English. **Application.** Best Material: query, full script (3 blind copies), audio, score, submissions nor returned. Deadline: 15-May-08.

3/31/2008. James D. Phelan Literary Award

Intersection for the Arts, 446 Valencia St., San Francisco, CA, 94103
Awards Coord.
Tel: 415-626-2787
www.theintersection.org/resourceawards.php

Est. 1937. Named for James Duval Phelan (1861-1930). **Consideration.** Remuneration: $2,000 . Frequency: annual. **Preference.** Length: one-act (30-60 min). Author Must Be: age 20-35, mar. Material Must Be: unpublished. **Application.** Best Material: application, full script (3 copies). Best Time: Jan-Mar. Deadline: 31-Mar-08.

4/1/2008. Joining Sword and Pen

Babes With Blades, 1903 W. Addison, #3, Chicago, IL, 60613

Contest est. 2005; company est. 1997. **Application.** Deadline: 1-Apr-08.

11/1/2008. Julie Harris Playwright Awards

Beverly Hills Theatre Guild, Box 148, Beverly Hills, CA, 90213
Candace Coster, Coordinator
Tel: 310-273-3390
www.beverlyhillstheatreguild.org

Consideration. Remuneration: $3,500 1st, $2,500 2nd, $1,500 3rd. Frequency: annual. **Preference.** Length: full length (over 90 min). Style: comedy, drama. Author Must Be: citizen or resident of US. Material Must Be: unoptioned, unpublished, unproduced, original, in English. **Application.** Best Material: query, application, full script. Best Time: Aug-Oct. Deadline: 1-Nov-08.

6/15/2008. L. Arnold Weissberger Award

Williamstown Theatre Festival, Box 428, Williamstown, MA, 01267
Suzanne Agins, Artistic Assoc, New Plays
Tel: 413-458-3200, Fax: 413-458-3147
sagins@wtfestival.org; www.wtfestival.org

Est. 1988. Honors theater attorney and supporter L. Arnold Weissberger (1907-81). **Consideration.** Remuneration: $10,000 , publication. Frequency: annual. **Preference.** Length: full length (over 90 min). Style: drama, no musical, no screenplay. Subject: no children's. Material Must Be: unpublished, professionally unproduced. **Application.** Best Way: invite. Best Material: query, SASE. Deadline: 15-Jun-08.

5/1/08. Lewis Galantiere Award

American Translators Assn., 225 Reinekers Ln., #590, Alexandria, VA, 22314
Chair, Honors and Awards
Tel: 703-683-6100, Fax: 703-683-6122
ata@atanet.org; www.atanet.org

Est. 1982. Biennial award (even yrs) for outstanding published translation from language other than German into English. **Consideration.** Assistance:. Remuneration: $1,000 . Frequency: biennial (even yrs). **Preference.** Length: full length (over 90 min). Style: translation. Material Must Be: published, from language other than German. **Application.** Best Material: query, 10-pg sample of original and translation (2 copies), full script of translation (2 copies), bio. Deadline: 5/1/2008.

Macy's New Play Prize for Young Audiences

Cincinnati Playhouse in the Park, Box 6537, Cincinnati, OH, 45206
Literary Dept.
Tel: 513-345-2242, Fax: 513-345-2254
www.cincyplay.com

Est. 1999. **Consideration.** Remuneration: $5,000 commission. Frequency: annual. **Preference.** Length: one-act (50-55 min). Style: no musical. Subject: youth. Production: cast of 3-5, touring set. Material Must Be: unproduced. **Application.** Best Material: synopsis, 3-pg sample, full script (of another TYA), resume, SASE.

2/28/2008. Marilyn Hall Awards

Beverly Hills Theatre Guild, Box 148, Beverly Hills, CA, 90213
Candace Coster
www.beverlyhillstheatreguild.org

Consideration. Remuneration: $700 1st, $300 2nd. Frequency: annual. **Preference.** Length: one-act (30-60 min). Subject: children (grades 6-8, 9-12). Author Must Be: citizen or resident of US. Material Must Be: unoptioned, unpublished, unproduced, in English. **Application.** Best Material: query, application, full script. Deadline: 28-Feb-08.

6/1/08. Met Life Nuestras Voces Playwriting Competition

Repertorio Espanol, 138 E. 27th St., New York, NY, 10016
Allison Astor-Vargas, Special Project Mgr.
Tel: 212-225-9950
aav@repertorio.org; www.repertorio.org

Est. 1999. **Consideration.** Remuneration: production, reading. Frequency: annual. **Preference.** Length: full length (over 90 min). Style: comedy, drama. Subject: Latino. Author Must Be: age 18 or older, resident or citizen of US. Material Must Be: unpublished. **Application.** Best Material: application, full script, submissions not returned. Deadline: 1-Jun-08. Response: 6 mos.

12/31/08. Mickey Kaplan New American Play Prize

Cincinnati Playhouse in the Park, Box 6537, Cincinnati, OH, 45206
Literary Dept.
Tel: 513-345-2242, Fax: 513-345-2254
www.cincyplay.com

Est. 2004. **Consideration.** Remuneration: $15,000 , production. Frequency: annual. **Preference.** Length: full length (over 90 min). Style: adaptation, comedy, drama, musical, no translation. Author Must Be: citizen of US. Material Must Be: unoptioned, unpublished, unproduced. **Application.** Best Way: agent submission of full script. Best Material: query, synopsis, 10-pg sample, audio. Best Time: Jun-Dec. Deadline: 31-Dec-08.

Mildred & Albert Panowski Playwriting Award

Northern Michigan Univ., 701 W. College Ave., Marquette, MI, 49855
Matthew W. Hudson, Playwriting Coord
Tel: 906-227-2559, Fax: 906-227-2567
www.nmu.edu/theatre

Est. 1977. Winning playwright expected to participate in script development workshop during summer. **Consideration.** Assistance: room/board, room/board. Remuneration: $2,000 , production. Frequency: annual. **Preference.** Length: full length (over 90 min). Style: comedy, drama. Material Must Be: unoptioned, unpublished, unproduced. **Application.** Best Material: 1-pg synopsis, full script, SASE. Deadline: 31-Oct-08.

2/1/2008. Morton R. Sarett National Playwriting Competition

Univ. of Nevada Las Vegas (UNLV), Nevada Conservatory Theatre (NCT), 4505 Maryland Pkwy., Box 455036, Las Vegas, NV, 89154
Stacey Jansen, Coord
Tel: 702-895-3663
www.unlv.edu/programs/nct

A memorial to Morton R. Sarett, the award is funded by Gwynneth and Robert C. Weiss. **Consideration.** Assistance: room, room. Remuneration: $3,000 , production. Frequency: biennial. **Preference.** Length: full length (over 90 min). Material Must Be: unpublished, unproduced, original, in English. **Application.** Best Material: application, 50-word synopsis, full script (2 copies), audio. Deadline: 1-Feb-08.

12/31/08. Mountain Playhouse Playwriting Contest

7690 Somerset Pike, Box 205, Jennerstown, PA, 15547
Teresa Stoughton Marafino, Producer
Tel: 814-629-9201, Fax: 814-629-9201
erica@mountainplayhouse.com; www.mountainplayhouse.org

Consideration. Remuneration: $3,000 , reading. Frequency: annual. **Preference.** Length: full length (over 90 min). Style: comedy. Production: cast limit 8. Material Must Be: unproduced, not previously submitted for this award unless revised 70\% or more. **Application.** Best Material: full script. Deadline: 31-Dec-08.

Nathan Miller History Play Contest

Sprenger-Lang Foundation, 1614 20th St. NW, Washington, DC, 20009
Laura VanDruff
Tel: 202-518-5357 x2

Consideration. Remuneration: $2,000 . Frequency: annual. **Preference.** Length: full length (over 90 min). Subject: History. Material Must Be: unproduced. **Application.** Best Way: Contact Sprenger Land Foundation for sumbission guidelines. Deadline: 12/31/2008.

12/31/2008. National Latino Playwriting Award

Arizona Theatre Company, 343 S. Scott Ave., Tucson, AZ, 85701
Elaine Romero, Playwright-in-Residence
Tel: 520-884-8210 x5510, Fax: 520-628-9129
eromero@arizonatheatre.org; www.aztheatreco.org

Consideration. Remuneration: $1,000 . Frequency: annual. **Preference.** Length: full length (over 90 min), mid-length (60-90 min). Author Must Be: resident of US, its territories, or Mexico, Latino. Material Must Be: unpublished, unproduced, English, Spanish (with English translation), or bilingual. **Application.** Best Material: synopsis, full script, bio. Best Time: Aug-Dec. Deadline: 31-Dec-08.

1/2/2008. National Playwriting Competition

Young Playwrights Inc (YPI), Box 5134, New York, NY, 10185
Sheri Goldhirsch, Artistic Dir.
Tel: 212-594-5440, Fax: 212-684-4902
admin@youngplaywrights.org; www.youngplaywrights.org

Winning playwrights receive full Off-Broadway productions in Young Playwrights Festival. **Consideration.** Frequency: annual. **Preference.** Style: drama, musical. Author Must Be: age 18 or younger. Material Must Be: original. **Application.** Best Material: full script. Deadline: 1/2/2008.

11/1/08. National Ten-Minute Play Contest

Actors Theatre of Louisville [KY], 316 W. Main St., , Louisville, KY, 40202
Amy Wegenen, Literary Mgr.
Tel: 502-561-3300, Fax: 502-561-3300
ahansel@actorstheatre.org; www.actorstheatre.org/humanacontest.htm

Est. 1989. **Consideration.** Remuneration: $1,000 , production consideration. Frequency: annual. **Preference.** Length: 10-min. Subject: no children's. Author Must Be: citizen or resident of US. Material Must Be: unproduced. **Application.** Best Way: unsolicited. Best Material: full script (1 entry/author), SASE. Deadline: 1-Nov-08.

9/1/08. New Playwrights Competition

Santa Fe Performing Arts (SFPA), Box 22372, Santa Fe, NM, 87502
N. Sabato, Exec. Artistic Dir.
Tel: 505-582-7992, Fax: 505-982-7993
www.sfperformingarts.org

Consideration. Frequency: annual. **Preference.** Length: full length (over 90 min), one-act (30-60 min). Style: comedy, drama. Author Must Be: citizen of US. Material Must Be: unproduced. **Application.** Best Material: synopsis, cast list. Deadline: 1-Sep-08.

2/5/2008. New Works for Young Women

Univ. of Tulsa (TU), Kendall Hall, 600 S. College Ave., Tulsa, OK, 74104
Michael Wright, Dir., Creative Writing
Tel: 918-631-2566, Fax: 918-631-5155
michael-wright@utulsa.edu; www.cas.utulsa.edu/writing

Est. 2002. **Consideration.** Assistance: room/board, room/board. Remuneration: $1,000 1st, $500 2nd, $250 3rd/4th. **Preference.** Length: full length (over 90 min), mid-length (60-90 min). Style: comedy, drama, musical. Production: ages 18-30, medium cast, medium orchestra. Author Must Be: graduate student of any age. Material Must Be: unpublished, unproduced. **Application.** Best Material: full script (3 copies). Best Time: Oct-Jan. Deadline: 5-Feb-08. Response: see website for submission details.

8/31/08. None of the Above Playwriting Contest

Box 2373, Astoria, NY, 11102
Robert Liebowitz
liebo12360@yahoo.com

Est. 1981. New short plays using the last words of Dutch Schultz. **Consideration.** Remuneration: $100 . **Preference.** Length: short (under 30 min.). **Application.** Best Material: full script, SASE. Deadline: 8/31/2008. Response: 1 mo.

North Carolina New Play Project (NCNPP)

Greensboro Playwrights' Forum, 200 N. Davie St., Box 2, Greensboro, NC, 27401
Stephen Hyers, Dir.
Tel: 336-335-6426, Fax: 336-373-2659
drama@greensboro-nc.gov; www.playwrightsforum.org

Consideration. Remuneration: $500 . Frequency: annual. **Preference.** Subject: no nudity. Production: small cast, simple set. Author Must Be: resident of NC. Material Must Be: unpublished, unproduced professionally, original. **Application.** Best Way: email (DOC, PDF, RTF). Best Material: application, synopsis, full script, cast/scene list, submissions not returned. Best Time: Jun-Jul. Deadline: 15-Aug-08. Response: 6 mos.

12/31/2008. Ohioana Career Award

Ohioana Library Assn., 274 E. 1st Ave., #300, Columbus, OH, 43201
Linda Hengst, Exec Dir
Tel: 614-466-3831, Fax: 614-728-6974
ohioana@sloma.state.oh.us; www.ohioana.org

Est. 1943. Award to native Ohioan for outstanding professional accomplishments in arts and humanities. Recipient is honored guest at Ohioana Day and must be present to receive award. **Consideration.** Assistance: room/board, room/board. Frequency: annual. **Preference.** Author Must Be: native of OH **Application.** Best Material: query, application, 10-pg sample, 2-pg resume, submissions not returned. Best Time: Jul. Deadline: 31-Dec-08.

12/31/2008. Ohioana Citations

Ohioana Library Assn., 274 E. 1st Ave., #300, Columbus, OH, 43201
Linda Hengst, Exec Dir
Tel: 614-466-3831, Fax: 614-728-6974
ohioana@sloma.state.oh.us; www.ohioana.org

Est. 1945. Award for outstanding contributions and accomplishments in specific area of arts and humanities. Four citations may be given each year. **Consideration.** Assistance: room/board, room/board. Frequency: annual. **Preference.** Author Must Be: native or 5-yr resident of OH. **Application.** Best Way: professional recommendation. Best Material: query, application, 10-pg sample, 2-pg resume, submissions not returned. Best Time: Jul. Deadline: 31-Dec-08.

12/31/2008. Ohioana Pegasus Award

Ohioana Library Assn., 274 E. 1st Ave., #300, Columbus, OH, 43201
Linda Hengst, Exec Dir
Tel: 614-466-3831, Fax: 614-728-6974
ohioana@sloma.state.oh.us; www.ohioana.org

Est. 1964. Award for unique or outstanding contributions or achievements in arts and humanities, given at discretion of trustees. **Consideration.** Assistance: room/board, room/board. Frequency: annual. **Preference.** Author Must Be: native or 5-yr resident of OH. **Application.** Best Way: professional recommendation. Best Material: query, application, 10-pg sample, 2-pg resume, submissions not returned. Best Time: Jul. Deadline: 31-Dec-08. Response: by 5/31/08.

12/1/08. One-Act Playwriting Competition

Drury Univ., 900 N. Benton Ave., Springfield, MO, 65802
Dr. Mick Sokol, Asst Prof, Theatre
Tel: 417-873-6821
msokol@drury.edu; www.drury.edu

Est. 1984. **Consideration.** Remuneration: $300 1st, $150 2nd, $150 3rd. Frequency: biennial. **Preference.** Length: one-act (30-60 min.). Material Must Be: unpublished, unproduced. **Application.** Best Material: full script, SASE. Best Time: May-Dec. Deadline: 12/1/2008. Response: by 4/1/09.

1/2/2008. Pacific Rim Prize

Kumu Kahua Theatre, 46 Merchant St., Honolulu, HI, 96813
Harry Wong III, Artistic Dir.
Tel: 808-536-4222, Fax: 808-536-4226
kumukahuatheatre@hawaiiantel.net; www.kumukahua.org

Consideration. Remuneration: $450 . Frequency: annual. **Preference.** Length: full length (over 90 min). Subject: Pacific Rim, Pacific Asian-American. **Application.** Best Material: full script (3 copies). Deadline: 2-Jan-08.

1/14/2008. PEN/Laura Pels Foundation Awards for Drama

PEN American Center, 588 Broadway, #303, New York, NY, 10012
Nick Burd, Coord
Tel: 212-334-1660 x108
awards@pen.org; www.pen.org

Est. 1998. Award to US playwright in mid-career writing in English with professional productions of at least 2 full-lengths (excl. musicals, translations) in theaters of at least 299 seats. Playwrights don't apply on their behalf but are nominated by peers. **Consideration.** Remuneration: $7,500 . Frequency: annual. **Application.** Best Way: professional recommendation. Best Time: Sep-Dec. Deadline: 16-Jan-08.

Playhouse on the Square New Play Competition

51 S. Cooper St., Memphis, TN, 38104
Jackie Nichols, Exec Dir
Tel: 901-725-0776, Fax: 901-272-7530
www.playhouseonthesquare.org

Est. 1980. Formerly Mid-South Playwright Contest. **Consideration.** Assistance: $1,000 stipend. Remuneration: $500 . Frequency: annual. **Preference.** Length: full length (over 90 min). Material Must Be: unproduced. **Application.** Best Material: full script, SASE.

10/15/2008. Playwrights First Award

Playwrights First - National Arts Club, 15 Gramercy Park S., New York, NY, 10003
Emily Andrew
Tel: 212-744-1312
www.playwrightsfirst.com

Est. 1993. **Consideration.** Remuneration: $1,000 award, reading. Frequency: annual. **Preference.** Length: full length (over 90 min). Style: comedy, drama. Production: in English. Material Must Be: unproduced, in English, by 1 author. **Application.** Best Material: full script, resume, submissions not returned. Best Time: after July 1. Deadline: 10/15/2008. Response: by 5/01/08.

1/2/078. Resident Prize

Kumu Kahua Theatre, 46 Merchant St., Honolulu, HI, 96813
Harry Wong III, Artistic Dir.
Tel: 808-536-4222, Fax: 808-536-4226
kumukahuatheatre@hawaiiantel.net; www.kumukahua.org

Consideration. Remuneration: $250 . Frequency: annual. **Preference.** Author Must Be: resident of HI. **Application.** Best Material: full script (3 copies). Deadline: 2-Jan-08.

11/1/2008. Richard Rodgers Awards for Musical Theater

American Academy of Arts & Letters, 633 W. 155th St., New York, NY, 10032
Jane E. Bolster, Richard Rodgers Awards Coord.
Tel: 212-368-5900, Fax: 212-491-4615
www.artsandletters.org

Est. 1978. Awards for musicals by writers and composers not already established in this field. Staff: Virginia Dajani (Exec. Dir.), Ezra Laderman (Pres.) **Consideration.** Frequency: annual. **Preference.** Length: full length (over 90 min). Style: musical. Author Must Be: citizen or resident of US. **Application.** Best Material: application, synopsis, full script, audio, SASE. Deadline: 1-Nov-08. Response: 3/1/2009.

Robert Chesley Award

828 N. Laurel Ave., Los Angeles, CA, 90046
Victor Bumbalo, President

Est. 1991. In honor of Robert Chesley (1943-90) to recognize gay and lesbian themed work. Nominations open in early fall. **Consideration.** Remuneration: $2,000 . Frequency: annual. **Preference.** Subject: gay. **Application.** Best Material: full script, SASE. Best Time: Nov.

12/31/2008. Robert J. Pickering Award for Playwriting Excellence

Coldwater Community Theater, 89 Division St., Coldwater, MI, 49036
J. Richard Colbeck, Award Chair
Tel: 517-279-7963

Est. 1984. Award for unproduced plays and musicals. **Consideration.** Remuneration: $200 1st, $50 2nd, $25 3rd. Frequency: annual. **Preference.** Length: full length (over 90 min). Material Must Be: unproduced. **Application.** Best Material: full script, SASE. Best Time: Nov-Dec. Deadline: 31-Dec-08.

12/5/08. Ruby Lloyd Apsey Award

Univ. of Alabama, Birmingham, ASC 255, 1530 3rd Ave. S., Birmingham, AL, 35294
Lee Shackleford, Resident Playwright
Tel: 205-934-3236, Fax: 205-934-8076
leeshack@uab.edu; theatre.hum.uab.edu

In even-number years, UAB seeks new, original full-lengths on racial or ethnic issues, with ethnically diverse casting. **Consideration.** Remuneration: $1,000 , possible production, reading. Frequency: biennial (even yrs). **Preference.** Length: full length (over 90 min). Style: comedy, drama. Production: college age. **Application.** Best Material: query, synopsis, full script, cast and scene list. Best Time: after Sep 1, 2008. Deadline: 5-Dec-08.

Scholastic Art & Writing Awards

Alliance for Young Artists & Writers, 557 Broadway, New York, NY, 10012
Bryan Doerries, Sr Mgr, National Programs
Tel: 212-343-7783, Fax: 212-389-3939
A&WGeneralInfo@scholastic.com; www.artandwriting.org

Est. 1923. National awards in 2 categories (grades 7-8; grades 9-12), selected from regional contests. Regional deadlines vary. Regional Gold Key works are considered for national awards. **Preference.** Length: one-act (30-60 min), short (under 30 min). Style: comedy, drama. Author Must Be: student (grades 7-12) in US or Canada. Material Must Be: by 1 author. **Application.** Best Material: application (2 copies), full script. Best Time: check on-line for local deadlines and guidelines.

1/15/08. Southern Playwrights Competition

Jacksonville State Univ. English Dept., 700 Pelham Rd. N, Jacksonville, AL, 36265
Joy Maloney, Coord.
Tel: 256-782-5469
jmaloney@jsu.edu; www.jsu.edu/depart/english/southpla.htm

Est. 1991. **Consideration.** Remuneration: $1,000 , production. Frequency: annual. **Preference.** Length: full length (over 90 min). Style: no musical. Subject: South. Author Must Be: native or resident of South. Material Must Be: unoptioned, unproduced professionally. **Application.** Best Material: application, synopsis, full script, SASE. Best Time: Sep-Dec. Deadline: 15-Jan-08.

1/15/08. STAGE International Script Competition

Univ. of California, Santa Barbara, CNSI, MC 6105, 3241 Elings Hall -Bldg. 226, UCSB, Santa Barbara, CA, 93106-6105
Nancy Kawalek, Professional Artists Lab Dir.
stage@csni.ucsb.edu; www.cnsi.ucsb.edu/stage

Est. 2005. The Professional Artists Lab and California NanoSystems Institute (CNSI) at UCSB collaborate on Scientists, Technologists and Artists Generating Exploration (STAGE), Competition for best new play about science and technology. **Consideration.** Remuneration: $10,000 , reading. Frequency: annual. **Preference.** Length: full length (over 90 min), mid-length (60-90 min.). Style: adaptation, comedy, drama, nontraditional, multimedia; no musicals or translations. Subject: science and technology, in content and/or form. Material Must Be: unoptioned, unpublished, unproduced, not reviewed, in English. **Application.** Best Material: query, application, synopsis, full script (3 copies), cover letter, written statement, bio/resume, submissions not returned. Deadline: 15-Dec-08. Response: 8-Jul.

1/15/2008. Summerfield G. Roberts Award

Sons of the Republic of Texas (SRT), 1717 8th St., Bay City, TX, 77414
Janet Hickl, Admin. Asst.
Tel: 979-245-6644, Fax: 979-244-3819
www.srttexas.org

Award for creative writing about the Republic of Texas, to encourage literature & research about the events and personalities of 1836-46. **Consideration.** Remuneration: $2,500 . Frequency: annual. **Application.** Best Material: full script (5 copies), SASE. Deadline: 15-Jan-08.

9/20/08. Susan Smith Blackburn Prize

3239 Avalon Pl., Houston, TX, 77019
Emilie Kilgore, Founder/President
www.blackburnprize.org

Est. 1978. Plays accepted only from specified source theaters in US, UK and Ireland. Writers should bring their work to the attention of those listed on website. **Consideration.** Remuneration: $20,000 winner; $5,000 special commendation; $1,000 finalists. Frequency: annual. **Preference.** Length: full length (over 75 min). Style: comedy, drama, musical. Author Must Be: female. Material Must Be: unproduced or produced within a year of deadling submission, in English. **Application.** Best Material: full script (2 copies), SASE. Deadline: 20-Sep-08. Response: by 1/30/09 see www.blackburnprize.org.

4/23/08. TADA! One-Act Playwriting Competition

15 W. 28th St., Fl. 3, New York, NY, 10001
Joanna Greer, Assoc. Artistic Dir.
Tel: 212-252-1619 x17, Fax: 212-252-8763
jgreer@tadatheater.com; www.tadatheater.com

Est. 1990. **Consideration.** Remuneration: $150 , reading. Frequency: annual. **Preference.** Length: one-act (30-60 min). Subject: youth. Production: youth/teen cast (limit 2 adults). Author Must Be: age 19 or younger (Young Writer), age 20 or older (General). Material Must Be: unpublished, unproduced. **Application.** Best Material: application, full script, submissions not returned. Deadline: 23-Apr-08. Response: by 9/24/08.

8/31/2008. Ten-Minute Musicals Project

Box 461194, West Hollywood, CA, 90046
Michael Koppy, Producer
info@tenminutemusicals.org; www.tenminutemusicals.org

Est. 1989. **Consideration.** Remuneration: $250 . Frequency: annual. **Preference.** Length: short (7-20 min). Style: musical. Production: cast limit 10. **Application.** Best Material: full script, audio, lead sheets/score, SASE. Deadline: 31-Aug-08.

7/1/2008. Theodore Ward Prize

Columbia College [IL], 72 E. 11th St., #413, Chicago, IL, 60605
Chuck Smith, Facilitator
Tel: 312-344-6136
csmith@colum.edu; www.colum.edu/undergraduate/theater/workshops.php

Consideration. Remuneration: $2,000 1st, $500 2nd, production. Frequency: annual. **Preference.** Length: full length (over 90 min). Subject: African-American. Author Must Be: resident of US, African-American. Material Must Be: unproduced. **Application.** Best Material: full script, SASE. Best Time: Apr-Jun. Deadline: 1-Jul-08.

1/1/2008. Towngate Theatre Playwriting Contest

Oglebay Institute, Stifel FAC, 1330 National Rd., Wheeling, WV, 26003
Kate H. Crosbie, Dir., Performing Arts
Tel: 304-242-7700, Fax: 304-242-7747
kcrosbie@oionline.com; www.oionline.com

Est. 1976. check website for programs and contest details. **Consideration.** Assistance: $500 room/board limit, $500 room/board limit. Remuneration: $300 , production. Frequency: annual. **Preference.** Length: full length (over 90 min). Style: comedy, drama. Material Must Be: unpublished, unproduced. **Application.** Best Material: full script, SASE. Deadline: 1-Jan-08. Response: by 5/15/08.

6/15/2008. Towson Univ. Prize for Literature

8000 York Rd., Towson, MD, 21252
Edwin Duncan, Chair, English Dept.
Tel: 410-704-2871, Fax: 410-704-3999
drjohnson@towson.edu; www.towson.edu/english

Est. 1979. **Consideration.** Remuneration: $1,000 . Frequency: annual. **Preference.** Length: full length (over 90 min). Author Must Be: resident of MD. Material Must Be: published. **Application.** Best Material: application, full script (5 copies). Deadline: 15-Jun-08.

5/1/2008. Ungar German Translation Award

American Translators Assn., 225 Reinekers Ln., #590, Alexandria, VA, 22314
Marilyn Gaddis Rose, Chair, Honors and Awards
Tel: 703-683-6100, Fax: 703-683-6122
ata@atanet.org; www.atanet.org

Biennial award (odd yrs) for outstanding published translation from German into English. **Consideration.** Assistance:. Remuneration: $1,000 . Frequency: biennial (odd yrs). **Preference.** Length: full length (over 90 min). Style: translation. Material Must Be: published, from German original. **Application.** Best Material: query, 10-pg sample of original and translation (2 copies), full script of translation (2 copies), bio. Deadline: 5/1/2008.

10/15/08. Valencia Character Company

Valencia Community College, Box 3028, Orlando, FL, 32802
Julia Gagne, Artistic Dir.
Tel: 407-582-2296
jgagne@valenciacc.edu; valenciacharacterco.com

Est. 1991. Winning script receives development and full production by college. **Consideration.** Assistance: $800 stipend. Frequency: annual. **Preference.** Length: full length (over 90 min). Style: comedy, drama. Production: some college age. Author Must Be: resident of FL. **Application.** Best Material: 15-pg sample, sample willnot be returned. electronic transmission prefered.. Best Time: Jun-Sep. Deadline: 15-Oct-08. Response: 2 mos.

2/1/08. Vermont Playwrights Award

The Valley Players, Box 441, Waitsfield, VT, 05673
Sharon Kellermann, Coord
valleyplayers@madriver.com; www.valleyplayers.com

Est. 1982. **Consideration.** Remuneration: $1,000 , production or reading. Frequency: annual. **Preference.** Length: full length (over 90 min). Style: comedy, drama. Author Must Be: resident of ME, NH, VT. Material Must Be: unoptioned, unpublished, unproduced. **Application.** Best Material: application, full script, SASE. Deadline: 1-Feb-08.

4/15/08. VSA arts Playwright Discovery Program

VSA arts, 818 Connecticut Ave. NW, #600, Washington, DC, 20006
Elena Widder, Director, Performing Arts
Tel: 202-628-2800
www.vsarts.org

Est. 1984. Annual contest for one-acts by students grades 6-12 on how disability affects a person's life. **Consideration.** Remuneration: $1,500 , production, trip to Washington DC. Frequency: annual. **Preference.** Length: one-act (30-60 min). Subject: disability. Author Must Be: Resident or Citizen of US, grades 6-12. Material Must Be: unoptioned, unpublished, unproduced. **Application.** Best Way: online. Best Material: application, full script. Best Time: Fall. Deadline: 4/15/2008. Response: 2 mos.

Whiting Writers' Awards

Mrs. Giles Whiting Foundation, 1133 6th Ave., Fl. 22, New York, NY, 10036
www.whitingfoundation.org

Est. 1985. Annual awards of $50,000 each to 10 emerging writers in fiction, nonfiction, poetry and drama, based on accomplishment and promise. Writers cannot apply for the awards. **Consideration.** Remuneration: $50,000 .

1/15/08. Wichita State Univ. (WSU) New Play Competition

1845 Fairmount, Campus Box 153, Wichita, KS, 67260
Steve Peders, Director, School of Performing Arts
Tel: 316-978-3360, Fax: 316-978-3202
finearts.wichita.edu/performing

Contest for original plays of at least 90 min. by undergrad or graduate students enrolled in any US college. ACTF production of new, unproduced script. **Consideration.** Frequency: annual. **Preference.** Length: full length (over 90 min), one-act (30-60 min). Style: comedy, drama. Author Must Be: US college student. Material Must Be: unpublished, unproduced, original. **Application.** Best Material: query, full script, SASE. Deadline: 15-Jan-08. Response: by 3/15/08.

4/11/2008. Write a Play! NYC Contest

Young Playwrights Inc (YPI), Box 5134, New York, NY, 10185
Sheri Goldhirsch, Artistic Dir.
Tel: 212-594-5440
admin@youngplaywrights.org; www.youngplaywrights.org

Open to all NYC students in 3 categories: elementary, middle, and high school. All receive certificate of merit, written evaluation, and invitation to awards ceremony. **Consideration.** Frequency: annual. **Preference.** Style: comedy, drama. Author Must Be: resident of NYC, student in school. Material Must Be: original. **Application.** Best Material: full script, submissions not returned. Deadline: 4/11/2008.

CONTESTS (Fee Charged)

3/15/08. $15. Arts & Letters Prize in Drama

Georgia College & State Univ., GCSU Campus Box 89, Milledgeville, GA, 31061
David Muschell, Assoc Prof
Tel: 478-445-1289, Fax: 478-445-5961
al@gcsu.edu

Est. 1999. **Consideration.** Fees: $15 entry. Remuneration: $1,000 , production, publication, 1-yr subscription (2 issues). **Preference.** Length: one-act (30-60 min). Material Must Be: unpublished, original, in English. **Application.** Best Material: query, full script. Best Time: Jan-Feb. Deadline: 15-Mar-08. Response: 3 mos.

5/1/08. $10. Aurand Harris Memorial Playwriting Award

New England Theater Conference, 215 Knob Hill Dr., Hamden, CT, 06518
Joseph Juliano, Mgr, Operations
Tel: 617-851-8535
mail@netconline.org; www.netconline.org

Est. 1997. Honors Aurand Harris for his lifetime dedication to all aspects of professional theater for young audiences. **Consideration.** Fees: $10 entry (NETC non-members). Remuneration: $1,000 1st, $500 2nd. Frequency: annual. **Preference.** Length: full length (over 90 min). Style: comedy, drama. Subject: children's. Material Must Be: unpublished, unproduced. **Application.** Best Material: application, full script. Deadline: 1-May-08. Response: by 11/1/08.

5/15/08. $20. CTAM Playwriting Contest

Community Theatre Assn. of Michigan, 22323 Cedar St., St. Clair Shores, MI, 48081
Mary Lou Britton
mellbee@earthlink.net; www.communitytheatre.org

Consideration. Fees: $20 entry. Remuneration: $500 . Frequency: annual. **Preference.** Length: full length (over 90 min). Style: comedy, drama. Author Must Be: resident of AACT Region 3 (IL, IN, OH, MI, WI). **Application.** Best Material: full script, SASE. Deadline: 15-May-08.

5/31/08. $8. Das Goldkiel

Buntville Crew, Box 445, Buckley, IL, 60918
Steven Packard, Artistic Dir.
buntville@yahoo.fr

Est. 1999. **Consideration.** Fees: $8 entry. Remuneration: $250 . Frequency: annual. **Preference.** Length: full length (over 90 min). Material Must Be: unpublished, unproduced, original; in English, French, German, Italian, Portuguese or Spanish. **Application.** Best Material: full script, resume. Deadline: 31-May-08.

8/15/08. $25. David C. Horn Prize

Yale Univ. Press Drama Series, Box 209040, New Haven, CT, 06520
Keith Condon, Associate Editor
www.yalebooks.com

Est. 2006. **Consideration.** Fees: $25 entry (c/o Yale U Press). Remuneration: $10,000 , publication by Yale Press, staged reading at Yale Rep. **Preference.** Length: full length (over 90 min). Style: no musical. Subject: no children's. Author Must Be: citizen of US, Canada, UK or Ireland, not published in full-length. Material Must Be: unpublished, unproduced professionally, original, in English. **Application.** Best Material: full script (unbound), cover pg (w/title, contact info, pg count), cast/scene list, submissions not returned. Best Time: after 7/15/08. Deadline: 15-Aug-08.

5/1/08. $25. Eric Bentley New Play Competition

New Phoenix Theatre [NY], 95 Johnson Park, Buffalo, NY, 14201
Richard Lambert, Exec Dir
Tel: 716-853-1334, Fax: 716-853-1334
newphnxtheatre@aol.com; www.newphoenixtheatre.com

Consideration. Fees: $25 entry. Remuneration: production. Frequency: annual. **Preference.** Subject: GLBT. Author Must Be: any. Material Must Be: unproduced. **Application.** Best Material: full script, SASE. Deadline: 5/1/08.

11/15/08. $10. FirstStage One-Act Play Contest

FirstStage [CA], Box 38280, Los Angeles, CA, 90038
Dennis Safren, Literary Mgr.
Tel: 323-350-6271
firststagela@aol.com; www.firststagela.org

Est. 1983. Staged readings of 3 finalists. **Consideration.** Fees: $10 entry. Remuneration: $300 1st, $100 2nd/3rd, reading. Frequency: annual. **Preference.** Length: short (under 30 min). Material Must Be: unproduced. **Application.** Best Material: full script, submissions not returned. Deadline: 15-Nov-08. Response: 3 wks.

2/15/08. $25. Francesca Primus Prize

American Theatre Critics Association (ATCA), 773 Nebraska Ave. W., St. Paul, MN, 55117
Katie Burger
Tel: 651-261-7804
www.americantheatrecritics.org/awards.html

In memory of Francesca Primus (d.1992). **Consideration.** Fees: $25 application. Remuneration: $10,000 . Frequency: annual. **Preference.** Length: full length (over 90 min). Style: comedy, drama. Author Must Be: female. Material Must Be: professionally produced in previous yr. **Application.** Best Way: professional recommendation. Best Material: query, full script (6 copies). Deadline: 15-Feb-08.

1/21/08. Grawemeyer Award for Music Composition

Univ. of Louisville, Univ. of Louisville School of Music, Louisville, KY, 40292
Marc Satterwhite
GrawemeyerMusic@louisville.edu; www.grawemeyer.org

Est. 1984. **Consideration.** Fees: $40 application. Remuneration: $200,000 . **Preference.** Material Must Be: produced in the past 4 yrs. **Application.** Best Way: professional recommendation. Best Material: application, full score, audio, bio. Deadline: 21-Jan-08.

12/1/08. $10. High School New Play Award

Southeastern Theatre Conference (SETC) High School New Play Project, 700 Cobb Pkwy. N., Marietta, GA, 30062
Katie Watts, The Walker School
wattsk@thewalkerschool.org; www.setc.org/scholarship

Consideration. Fees: $10 entry. Remuneration: $250 , reading. **Preference.** Length: one-act (30-60 min). Author Must Be: student in AL, FL, GA, KY, MS, NC, SC, TN, VA or WV. Material Must Be: unpublished, unproduced. **Application.** Best Material: full script, SASE. Best Time: Oct-Nov. Deadline: 1-Dec-08.

6/1/08. $20. Jackie White Memorial 's Play Writing Contest

Columbia Entertainment Co (CEC), 1400 Forum Blvd., #38, Box 214, Columbia, MO, 65203
Betsy Phillips, Dir.
Tel: 573-874-5628
bybetsy@yahoo.com; www.cectheatre.org

Est. 1988. In memory of Jackie Pettit White (1947-91). All scripts read by at least 3, finalists by at least 12. All receive written evaluation. **Consideration.** Fees: $20 entry. Remuneration: $500 . Frequency: annual. **Preference.** Length: full length (over 90 min), mid-length (60-90 min). Subject: family-oriented but no cute animal stories. Production: at least 7 speaking roles, sets appropriate for community theaters. Material Must Be: unpublished. **Application.** Best Material: application, full script, SASE. Deadline: 1-Jun-08. Response: by 8/31/08.

2/15/08 $15. Jane Chambers Playwriting Award

ATHE Women & Theatre Program (WTP), Georgetown Univ., 108 Davis Center, Box 571063, Washington, DC, 20057
Maya Roth
www.athe.org/wtp/html/chambers.html

Award for plays and texts by women that reflect a feminist perspective and contain a majority of opportunities for women performers. **Consideration.** Fees: $15 entry, $10 entry (low income). Remuneration: $1,000 , reading. Frequency: annual. **Preference.** Subject: women. Author Must Be: female. Material Must Be: original. **Application.** Best Material: application, synopsis, full script (3 copies), resume, submissions not returned. Deadline: 15-Feb-08.

2/15/08. $10. Jane Chambers Student Playwriting Award

ATHE Women & Theatre Program (WTP), 230 W. 56th St., #65-A, New York, NY, 10019
Jen-Scott Mobley
www.athe.org/wtp/html/chambers.html

Award for plays and texts by female students that reflect a feminist perspective and contain a majority of opportunities for women performers. **Consideration.** Fees: $10 entry. Remuneration: $250 , reading. Frequency: annual. **Preference.** Subject: women. Author Must Be: female student. Material Must Be: original. **Application.** Best Material: application, synopsis, full script (3 copies), resume, submissions not returned. Deadline: 15-Feb-08.

1/14/08. $10. Jewel Box Theatre Playwriting Award

3700 N. Walker Ave., Oklahoma City, OK, 73118
Chuck Tweed, Production Dir.
Tel: 405-521-1786
www.jewelboxtheatre.org

Est. 1986. **Consideration.** Fees: $10 aplication. Remuneration: $500 . Frequency: annual. **Preference.** Length: full length (over 90 min). Style: adaptation, comedy, drama. Material Must Be: unoptioned, unpublished, unproduced. **Application.** Best Material: application, full script, SASE. Best Time: Oct-Dec. Deadline: 14-Jan-08. Response: by 5/30/08.

4/15/08. $10. John Gassner Memorial Playwriting Award

New England Theater Conference, 215 Knob Hill Dr., Hamden, CT, 06518
Joseph Juliano, Mgr, Operations
Tel: 617-851-8535
mail@NETConline.org; www.NETConline.org

Est. 1967. Honors theater historian John Gassner for his lifetime dedication to all aspects of professional and academic theater. **Consideration.** Fees: $10 entry (NETC non-members). Remuneration: $1,000 1st, $500 2nd. Frequency: annual. **Preference.** Length: full length (over 90 min). Style: comedy, drama. Material Must Be: unpublished, unproduced. **Application.** Best Way: submissions not returned. Best Material: application, full script. Deadline: 15-Apr-08. Response: by 11/01/08.

10/31/08. $20. Little Theatre of Alexandria National One-Act Playwriting Competition

The Little Theatre of Alexandria, 600 Wolfe St., Alexandria, VA, 22314
Tel: 703-683-5778, Fax: 703-683-1378
asklta@thelittletheatre.com; www.thelittletheatre.com

LTA reserves the right to produce selected script without payment of royalties. **Consideration.** Fees: $20 . Remuneration: $350 1st; $250 2nd; $150 3rd, reading. Frequency: annual. **Preference.** Length: one-act (30-60 min.). Style: comedy, drama. Subject: all subjects. Production: unit set. Material Must Be: unpublished, unproduced, original. **Application.** Best Way: unsolicited. Best Material: synopsis, full script, character breakdown, SASE. Best Time: Jan-Oct. Deadline: 10/31/08..

7/1/08. $25. Maxim Mazumdar New Play Competition

Alleyway Theatre, 1 Curtain Up Alley, Buffalo, NY, 14202
Joyce Stilson, Literary Mgr.
www.alleyway.com

Est. 1990. Named for Maxim Mazumdar **Consideration.** Fees: $25 entry. Remuneration: $400 (full-length), $100 (one-act). Frequency: annual. **Preference.** Length: full length (over 90 min), short (under 20 min). Material Must Be: unoptioned, unproduced. **Application.** Best Material: full script, SASE. Deadline: 1-Jul-08. Response: 5 mos.

2/28/08. $15. McLaren Memorial Comedy Playwriting Competition

Midland Community Theater (MCT), 2000 W. Wadley Ave., Midland, TX, 79705
William Payne, Chair
www.mctmidland.org

Est. 1989. Staff: Marla Cooper, Brenda Tumlin. **Consideration.** Fees: $15 entry. Remuneration: $400 (full-length), $200 (one-act). Frequency: annual. **Preference.** Length: full length (over 90 min), one-act (30-60 min). Style: comedy, no musical. Subject: suitable for conservative Texas city. Material Must Be: unoptioned, unpublished, unproduced. **Application.** Best Material: full script, SASE. Deadline: 28-Feb-08.

1/31/2008. Moving Arts Premiere One-Act Competition

Box 481145, Los Angeles, CA, 90048
Trey Nichols, Literary Dir.
www.movingarts.org

Consideration. Fees: first entry free additional scripts $10 fee. Remuneration: $200 , production. Frequency: annual. **Preference.** Length: one-act 50 page limit. Style: comedy, drama. Production: cast limit 8, unit set. Material Must Be: unproduced in L.A.. **Application.** Best Material: query, full script, SASE. Best Time: Nov-Jan. Deadline: 31-Jan-08.

$10. National Children's Theatre Festival

Actors' Playhouse, Miracle Theatre, 280 Miracle Mile, Coral Gables, FL, 33134
Earl Maulding, Director of Theatre for Young Audiences
Tel: 305-444-9293 x615
www.actorsplayhouse.org

Consideration. Fees: $10 reading. Assistance:. Remuneration: $500 first place, production, publication. **Application.** Deadline: 1-Apr-08. Response: 10/1/2008.

1/31/08. $10. National One-Act Playwriting Contest

Dubuque Fine Arts Players, 1686 Lawndale St., Dubuque, IA, 52001
Gary Arms, Contest Coord.
gary.arms@clarke.edu

Est. 1977. **Consideration.** Fees: $10 entry. Remuneration: $600 1st, $300 2nd, $200 3rd. Frequency: annual. **Preference.** Length: one-act (30-60 min.). Production: cast of 2-5, unit set. Material Must Be: unpublished, unproduced. **Application.** Best Material: application, full script (2 copies), SASE. Best Time: Dec-Jan. Deadline: 31-Jan-08. Response: 6 mos.

$10. New Play Festival

Yellow Taxi Productions, Box 1515, Nashua, NH, 03060
Suzanne Delle, Artistic Dir.
sdelle@yellowtaxiproductions.org; www.yellowtaxiproductions.org

Est. 2002. Multi-day new-play fest of readings and productions with talkbacks. **Consideration.** Fees: $10 for reading, venue rental, director stipend. Remuneration: production, reading. **Preference.** Length: 10 min. Production: cast limit 6. Material Must Be: unpublished, unproduced. **Application.** Best Material: SASE. Deadline: 12/30/08.

4/15/08. $5. New Rocky Mountain Voices
Westcliffe CPA/Jones Theater, Box 790, Westcliffe, CO, 81252
Steve Miller, Chair
wcpa@ris.net; www.westcliffecenter.org

Est. 1999. Winning plays staged at Jones Theater in Westcliffe, CO. Authors asked to speak afterward. Staff: Anne Kimbell Relph (Artistic Dir). **Consideration.** Fees: $5 entry. Remuneration: $200 , production. Frequency: annual. **Preference.** Length: one-act (30-60 min). Style: comedy, drama. Production: cast of 6-8, unit set. Author Must Be: resident of Rocky Mts (AZ, CO, ID, MT, NM, UT). Material Must Be: unproduced professionally. **Application.** Best Material: query, synopsis, full script, no author on title page. On letter only., SASE. Best Time: Jan-Apr. Deadline: 4/15/2008. Response: 2 mos.

12/15/08. $15. Next Generation Playwriting Contest
Reverie Productions, 520 8th Ave, #317, New York, NY, 10018
Kimberly Wadsworth, Literary Mgr.
Tel: 212-244-7803, Fax: 212-244-7813
info@ReverieProductions.org; www.ReverieProductions.org

Est. 2004. New work from emerging wrietrs on sociopolitical issuses in highly theatrical contexts. Finalists recieve public staged reading; grand prize receives workshop production. Staff: Colin D. Young (Artistic Dir). **Consideration.** Fees: $15 entry (full-length), $10 entry (one-act). Remuneration: $300 (full-length), $150 (one-act). Frequency: annual. **Preference.** Style: comedy, drama, radio. Material Must Be: unpublished, not produced in NY, NJ or CT. **Application.** Best Material: application, full script, SASE. Deadline: 15-Dec-08.

1/31/08. $35. PEN Center USA Literary Awards
c/o Antioch Univ. Los Angeles, 400 Corporate Pointe, Culver City, CA, 90230
Tel: 310-862-1555 x361, Fax: 310-862-1556
awards@penusa.org; www.penusa.org

Est. 1982. Prizes for plays, teleplays, and screenplays. **Consideration.** Fees: $35 entry. Remuneration: $1,000 . Frequency: annual. **Preference.** Author Must Be: author must reside west of the Mississippi River, or in the states of Minnesota or Louisiana. **Application.** Best Material: application, full script (4 copies), submissions not returned. Deadline: 31-Jan-08.

12/15/08 $50. PEN Translation Prize
PEN American Center, 588 Broadway, #303, New York, NY, 10012
Nick Burd, Coord
Tel: 212-334-1660 x108
awards@pen.org; www.pen.org

Est. 1963. **Consideration.** Remuneration: $3,000 . **Preference.** Length: full length (over 90 min). Style: translation. Material Must Be: published in US. **Application.** Best Material: full script (3 copies), submissions not returned. Best Time: Sep-Nov. Deadline: 15-Dec-08.

3/15/08. $20. Plays for the 21st Century
Playwrights Theater, 6732 Orangewood Dr., Dallas, TX, 75248
Jack Marshall, Artistic Dir. - Virtual Programs
www.playwrightstheater.org

Est. 1995. Staff: Alberto Rubio (Dir. of Operations), John Luis Navarro (Artistic Dir. - Theatrical Prod.) **Consideration.** Fees: $20 aplication. Remuneration: $750 1st, $500 2nd, $250 3rd (full-length); $250 (one-act). Frequency: annual. **Preference.** Length: full length (over 90 min), one-act (35-40 min.). Style: no musical. Subject: no children's. Material Must Be: unoptioned, unpublished, unproduced professionally, original, in English. **Application.** Best Way: email to 2.act.play@sbcglobalnet or 1.act.play@sbcglobal.net. Best Material: synopsis, full script (DOC, HTML, RTF). Best Time: Jan-Feb. Deadline: 15-Mar-08.

5/31/08. $8. Prix Hors Pair
Buntville Crew, Box 445, Buckley, IL, 60918
Steven Packard, Artistic Dir.
buntville@yahoo.fr

Est. 1999. **Consideration.** Fees: $8 entry. Remuneration: $200 . Frequency: annual. **Preference.** Length: short (under 15 min). Material Must Be: original; in English, French, German, Italian, Portuguese or Spanish. **Application.** Best Material: full script, resume. Deadline: 31-May-08.

10/31/08. $10. Reva Shiner Full-Length Play Contest

Bloomington Playwrights Project, 107 W. 9th St., Bloomington, IN, 47404
Literary Mgr
Tel: 812-334-1188
bpplitma@newplays.org; www.bloomingtonplays.org

BPP is a development group. Winning writers are expected to be part of development process. **Consideration.** Fees: $10 reading. Remuneration: $500 , production. Frequency: annual. **Preference.** Length: full length (75-150 min). Material Must Be: unpublished, unproduced. **Application.** Best Way: unsolicited. Best Material: query, full script, audio. Deadline: Postmarked by 10/31/08.

Reverie Productions

Reverie Productions, 520 Eighth Ave., #317, New York, NY, 10018
Colin D. Young, Artistic Dir.
Tel: 212-244-7803
kimberly@reverieproductions.org; www.reverieproductions.org

est. 2002 check website for guidelines. **Consideration.** Fees: app. and reading; $18 full script; $12 one-act. Remuneration: $500 . Frequency: annual. **Preference.** Length: all length. Style: comedy, drama. Subject: all subjects. Material Must Be: unoptioned, unpublished, unproduced. **Application.** Best Material: application, full script, SASE. Best Time: starting 9/1. Deadline: 12/15/2008. Response: April.

$10. 7/1/08. Smith Prize

National New Play Network (NNPN), c/o InterAct Theatre, 2030 Sansom St., Philadelphia, PA, 19103
Toni Press-Coffman, Contest Admin.
tpplay@cox.net; www.nnpn.org

Est. 2006. Prize for a play on issues of national or global import that examine our civic institutions. NNPN is an alliance of nonprofit professional theaters aiding the development, production and continued life of new plays for American theater. **Consideration.** Fees: $10 entry. Assistance:. Remuneration: $2,500 , reading. Frequency: annual. **Preference.** Length: full length (over 90 min). Style: comedy, drama. Subject: political. Material Must Be: unproduced in LORT or NYC Equity venue. **Application.** Best Way: unsolicited. Best Material: full script, submissions not returned. Deadline: 1-Jul-08.

12/15/08. $10. TeCo Theatrical Productions New Play Competition

215 S. Tyler St., Dallas, TX, 75208
Teresa Coleman Walsh, Exec. Dir.
Tel: 214-948-0716, Fax: 214-948-3706
teresa@tecotheater.org; www.tecotheater.org

Est. 1993. Multicultural theater promoting quality theatre through dramatic artistic expression. **Consideration.** Fees: $10 entry. Assistance:. Remuneration: $1,000 . Frequency: annual. **Preference.** Length: 15-min. Style: romantic comedy. Production: cast limit 4, minimal set. Author Must Be: resident of Dallas metro. Material Must Be: unoptioned, unpublished, unproduced. **Application.** Best Material: full script, SASE. Best Time: Nov. Deadline: 15-Dec-08. Response: 2 mos.

12/31/08 CA$25. Theatre in the Raw Play Writing Contest

Theatre in the Raw, 3521 Marshall St., Vancouver, BC, V5N 4S2 Canada
Jay Hamburger, Artistic Dir.
Tel: 604-708-5448, Fax: 604-708-1454
theatreintheraw@telus.net; www.theatreintheraw.ca

Est. 1994. **Consideration.** Fees: CA$25 entry. Remuneration: CA$150 1st, CA$75 2nd, CA$50 3rd. Frequency: biennial. **Preference.** Length: short (under 30 min). Style: comedy, drama, radio. Production: cast limit 6, set limit 2 (scene limit 3). Material Must Be: unoptioned, unpublished, unproduced. **Application.** Best Material: full script, SASE. Deadline: 10/31/2008.

2/15/08. $10. Theatre Oxford 10-Minute Play Contest
Box 1321, Oxford, MS, 38655
Dinah Swan, Dir
www.10minuteplays.com

Est. 1998. **Consideration.** Fees: $10 reading. Remuneration: $1,000 , production. Frequency: annual. **Preference.** Length: 10-min. Style: no musical. Subject: no children's. Production: casts limit 5, minimal set. Material Must Be: unoptioned, unpublished, unproduced. **Application.** Best Material: full script, submissions not returned. Best Time: fall. Deadline: Postmarked by 2/15/08. Response: 3 mos.

$10.00 . Urban Stages Emerging Playwright Award
17 E. 47th St., Fl. 6, New York, NY, 10017
Frances Hill, Artistic Dir
www.urbanstages.org

Est. 1986. **Consideration.** Fees: $10 reading. Remuneration: $500 (in lieu of royalty), production. Frequency: annual. **Preference.** Length: full length (over 90 min). Style: comedy, drama. Production: cast limit 7. Material Must Be: unoptioned, unpublished, unproduced. **Application.** Best Material: full script, SASE. Response: 3 mos.

5/1/08. $5. W. Keith Hedrick Playwriting Contest
HRC (Hudson River Classics) Showcase Theater, Box 940, Hudson, NY, 12534
Jan M. Grice, President
Tel: 518-851-7244
jangrice2002@yahoo.com; www.hrc-showcasetheatre.org

Est. 1993. 1 winner and 4 finalists receive public staged reading by professional actors. **Consideration.** Fees: $5 entry. Remuneration: $500 1st, $100 finalist, reading. Frequency: annual. **Preference.** Length: mid-length (60-90 min). Production: cast limit 8. Author Must Be: resident of Northeast. Material Must Be: unpublished. **Application.** Best Material: full script, SASE. Best Time: Feb-Apr. Deadline: 1-May-08. Response: 3 mos.

5/15/08. $15. Writer's Digest Writing Competition
4700 E. Gablbraith Rd., Cincinnati, OH, 45236
Competition Coord
Tel: 513-531-2222, Fax: 513-531-0798
writing-competition@fwpubs.com; www.writersdigest.com

Est. 1931. **Consideration.** Fees: $15 entry. Assistance:. Remuneration: $3,000 1st. Frequency: annual. **Preference.** Material Must Be: unpublished, unproduced. **Application.** Best Material: application, 1-pg synopsis, 15-pg sample. Deadline: 15-May-08.

GRANTS & FELLOWSHIPS

3/1/2008. Alabama State Council on the Arts

201 Monroe St., Montgomery, AL, 36130
Randy Shoults, Community Arts, Lit & Design Mgr.
Tel: 334-242-4076 x224, Fax: 334-240-3269
randy.shoults@arts.alabama.gov; www.arts.state.al.us

Opportunities incl. Artist Fellowships and Artist in Education Residency in performing artists (music, dance, theater), literature (fiction, creative nonfiction, poetry, screenwriting, playwriting), and visual artists. **Preference.** Author Must Be: 2-yr resident of AL. **Application.** Deadline: 1-Mar-08.

3/1, 6/1, 9/1, 12/1. Alaska State Council on the Arts (ASCA)

411 W. 4th Ave., #1-E, Anchorage, AK, 99501
Tel: 888-278-7424, Fax: 907-269-6601
akscainfo@eed.state.ak.us; www.eed.state.ak.us/aksca

Est. 1966. Opportunities incl. quarterly Career Opportunity Grants and biennial Connie Boochever Artist Fellowships (Aug 31 deadline, odd yrs). Staff: Andrea Noble (Dir, Career Grants), Charlotte Fox (Dir, Artist Fellowships). **Preference.** Author Must Be: age 18 or older, resident of AK. **Application.** Best Material: 10-pg sample, audio. Deadline: 1-Mar-08, 1-Jun-08, 1-Sep-08, 1-Dec-08.

Alfred Hodder Fellowship

Princeton Univ., Joseph Henry House, Princeton, NJ, 08544
Council of the Humanities
Tel: 609-258-4717, Fax: 609-258-2783
www.princeton.edu/~humcounc/

1-yr fellowship for individuals outside academia who've published one acclaimed book and are undertaking significant new work. Fellows teach 1 course while pursuing independent projects. **Consideration.** Assistance: $58,000 stipend. **Application.** Best Material: query, 10-pg sample, resume, SASE. Deadline: see website for deadlines.

Allen Lee Hughes Fellowship Program

Arena Stage, 1101 6th St. SW, Washington, DC, 20024
Katherine Keefe, Dir. of Human Resources

Preference. Subject: Asian, Black, latino.

11/1/08. $20. American-Scandinavian Foundation (ASF)

58 Park Ave., New York, NY, 10016
Fellowship Program
Tel: 212-879-9779, Fax: 212-249-3444
grants@amscan.org; www.amscan.org

Grants for short visits and fellowships for full year of study or research in Denmark, Finland, Iceland, Norway or Sweden. **Consideration.** Fees: $20 application. Remuneration: $20,000 fellowship limit; $4,000 grant limit. Frequency: annual. **Preference.** Author Must Be: citizen or resident of US, college graduate, proficient in host language preferred. **Application.** Best Way: online. Best Material: application. Deadline: 1-Nov-08. Response: by 3/15/08.

10/5/08. American Antiquarian Society Fellowships

American Antiquarian Society (AAS), 185 Salisbury St., Worcester, MA, 01609
Cheryl McRell, Outreach Asst.
Tel: 508-471-2149
cmcrell@mwa.org; www.americanantiquarian.org

Up to 4 fellowships to creative and performing artists and writers for 4-wk residency to research works about pre-20th century US history. **Consideration.** Assistance: $1,200/mo. **Application.** Deadline: 5-Oct-08. Response: by 12/5/07.

11/30/2008. Arch & Bruce Brown Foundation

The Arch & Bruce Brown Foundation, 2500 N. Palm Canyon Dr., Palm Springs, CA, 92262
Arch Brown, President
ArchWrite@aol.com; www.aabbfoundation.org

Formed by Arch Brown in memory of Bruce Allen Brown (d1993). Awards for gay-positive arts projects on historic subjects. Awards rotate thru short fiction & one-act plays (2010), drama (2008), novel (2009). **Consideration.** Remuneration: $1,000 . Frequency: triennial. **Preference.** Length: full length (over 90 min), one-act (30-60 min). Subject: gay-lesbian. Material Must Be: unpublished. **Application.** Best Way: unsolicited. Best Material: full script, submissions not returned. Deadline: 30-Nov-08.

Arizona Commission on the Arts (ACA)

417 W. Roosevelt St., Phoenix, AZ, 85003
Claire West, Dir, Performing Arts
Tel: 602-771-6501, Fax: 602-256-0282
cwest@azarts.gov; www.azarts.gov

Est. 1966. Artist Career Advancement Grants (ACAG) and Artist Project Grants. Check website for deadlines. **Preference.** Author Must Be: age 18 or older, resident of AZ, not a student. **Application.** Best Way: online.

Arkansas Arts Council

323 Center St., #1500, Little Rock, AR, 72201
Sally A. WIlliams, Artist Services Mgr
Tel: 501-324-9348, Fax: 501-324-9207
sally@arkansasheritage.org; www.arkansasarts.com

Est. 1971. Check website for 2008 fellowship categories **Preference.** Author Must Be: age 25 or older, resident of AR, not a student, not a former fellow. **Application.** Best Material: application, SASE. Deadline: check website.

2/22/2008. Artist Trust

1835 12th Ave., Seattle, WA, 98122
Heather Helbach-Olds, Dir, Programs
Tel: 206-467-8734, Fax: 206-467-9633
info@artisttrust.org; www.artisttrust.org

Grants for Artist Projects (GAP) program. **Consideration.** Assistance: $1,500 stipend. Frequency: annual. **Preference.** Author Must Be: age 18 or older, resident of WA, not a student. **Application.** Best Material: application, 12-pg sample, audio, SASE. Deadline: 22-Feb-08. Response: 4 mos.

10/3/2008. Artists' Fellowships

New York Foundation for the Arts (NYFA), 155 6th Ave., Fl. 14, New York, NY, 10013
Margie Lempert, Senior Officer
Tel: 212-366-6900, Fax: 212-366-1778
fellowships@nyfa.org; www.nyfa.org

Est. 1984. Artistists Fellowships are intended to fund an artists vision or voice, regardless of the level of her or his artistic development. Grants of $7000 are given to individual originating artists living in New York State. **Consideration.** Assistance: $7,000 grant. Frequency: biennial. **Preference.** Author Must Be: age 18 or older, resident of NYS, not a student. **Application.** Best Material: application. Deadline: 10/3/2008.

1/17/2008. ArtsLink Projects

National Endowment for the Arts (NEA), 435 Hudson St, Fl. 8, New York, NY, 10014
Tel: 212-643-1985 x22, Fax: 212-643-1996
al@cecartslink.org; www.cecartslink.org

Est. 1992. Grants for collaborative projects with colleagues in Central or Eastern Europe or Central Asia, alternating between visual/media arts (2007) and performing arts or literature (2008). **Consideration.** Assistance: $1,000 stipend, $2,500- $10,000 grants. Frequency: biennial. **Application.** Best Way: send SASE in fall for application. Best Material: application. Deadline: 17-Jan-08.

1/15/2008. Asian Cultural Council
6 West 48th Street, 12th Fl, New York, NY, 10036
Ralph Samuelson, Dir.
Tel: 212-812-4300, Fax: 212-812-4299
acc@accny.org; www.asianculturalcouncil.org

Est. 1963. Support for cultural exchange in performing/visual arts between US and Asia, primarily fellowships for artists from Asia to pursue projects in US, but some support for Americans for research and creative work in Asia. **Consideration.** Frequency: annual. **Preference.** Author Must Be: citizen of US or Asian country. **Application.** Deadline: 15-Jan-08.

4/30/2008. Aurand Harris Fellowship
Children's Theatre Foundation of America (CTFA), 617 Baxter Ave., Louisville, KY, 40204
Marilee Miller, Awards Committee
www.childrenstheatrefoundation.org

Est. 1958. For individuals with specific projects or with specific plans for developing excellence in children's theater. **Consideration.** Remuneration: $5,000 max. Frequency: annual. **Preference.** Subject: children's. Author Must Be: age 18 or older, resident or citizen of US. Material Must Be: unoptioned. **Application.** Best Material: application, info on websites, submissions not returned. Deadline: 30-Apr-08.

1/1/2008. Berlin Artists-in-Residence
Deutsche Akademische Austausch Dienst (DAAD), Markgrafenstrasse 37, Berlin, BE, 10117 Germany
Tel: 49-030-202-2080, Fax: 49-030-204-1267
bkp.berlin@daad.de; www.daad-berlin.de

1-yr residency for authors/composers to produce work and contribute to Berlin's cultural life. Grant incl. rent for furnished living/work area. **Application.** Best Material: application, sample. Deadline: 1-Jan-08.

10/1/2008. City of Los Angeles (COLA) Performing Arts Fellowships
Los Angeles Cultural Affairs Dept., 201 N. Figueroa St., #1400, Los Angeles, CA, 90012
Michelle Berne, Grants Mgr
Tel: 213-202-5566, Fax: 213-202-5515
dca.grants@lacity.org; www.culturela.org

COLA Fellowships allow accomplished artists to focus on creating new works. Cultural Affairs collaborates with community partners to organize exhibitions, showcases, and catalogs that promote new work by these artists. **Preference.** Author Must Be: resident of Los Angeles, 15-yr professional. **Application.** Best Material: application. Deadline: 4th Fri. in Oct..

3/15/2008. Colorado Council on the Arts
1625 Broadway, #2700, Denver, CO, 80202
Jeanette Albert, Program Admin.
Tel: 303-892-3838, Fax: 303-892-3848
coloarts@state.co.us; www.coloarts.state.co.us

Application. Deadline: 15-Mar-08.

9/1/08. Connecticut Commission on Culture & Tourism (CCT)
Connecticut Commission on Culture & Tourism (CCT), One Constitution Plaza, Hartford, CT, 06103
Tamara Dimitri, Arts Div.
Tel: 860-256-2720
tamara.dimitri@ct.gov; www.cultureandtourism.org

Artistic fellowships alternating between visual art (odd yrs) and choreography, fiction, music composition and film/video, playwriting, and poetry (even yrs). **Application.** Deadline: 9/1/2008.

8/15/2008. Delaware Division of the Arts

820 N. French St., Wilmington, DE, 19801
Paul Weagraff, Dir.
Tel: 302-577-8278, Fax: 302-577-6561
paul.weagraff@state.de.us; www.artsdel.org

Invidual artists fellowships. **Consideration.** Frequency: annual. **Preference.** Author Must Be: age 18 or older, resident of DE, not a student. **Application.** Best Material: application, 10-20 pg sample, SASE. Deadline: 15-Aug-08.

Emerging Writers Group

The Public Theatre, 425 Lafayette Street, New York, NY, 10003

Seeks to target playwrights at the earliest stages in their careers. The Public hopes to create an artisitic home for a diverse and exceptionally talented group of up-and-coming writers. See website for further details. **Consideration.** Assistance: $3,000 . **Preference.** Author Must Be: see website.

5/2/08, 11/07/08. Fiscal Sponsorship

New York Foundation for the Arts (NYFA), 155 Ave. of the Americas, New York, NY, 10013
Mary Six Rupert, Managing Officer
Tel: 212-366-6900, Fax: 212-366-1778
msrupert@nyfa.org; www.nyfa.org/fs

Est. 1971. Allows artists to apply for funds usually available only to nonprofits. **Consideration.** Fees: $100 contract fee (if accepted), 4\%-8\% admin fee. Frequency: semiannual. **Preference.** Author Must Be: not a student. **Application.** Best Material: application, SASE. Deadline: 5/2/2008, 11/7/2008. Response: 2 mos.

8/1/08. Fulbright Program for US Scholars

Institute of Intl. Education/Council for Intl. Exchange of Scholars, 3007 Tilden St. NW, #5-L, Washington, DC, 20008
Anne Clift Boris, Sr Program Officer, Recruitment
info@cies.iie.org; www.cies.org

Est. 1947. Grants for US faculty or professionals to research or lecture abroad for 2-12 mos. in 140 countries. **Consideration.** Assistance: grant / stipend varies, Room / board varies, Room / board varies. Remuneration: award varies. Frequency: annual. **Preference.** Author Must Be: citizen of US. **Application.** Best Material: application, SASE. Best Time: begin March 1st. Deadline: 1-Aug-08.

Fund for New Work

Harlem Stage at The Gatehouse, 150 Convent Avenue, New York, NY, 10030
Tel: 212-281-9240, Fax: 212-281-9318
www.harlemstage.org

Grants & funding for emerging artists. See website for application and details.

$5.00 . George Bennett Fellowship

Phillips Exeter Academy, 20 Main St., Exeter, NH, 03833
Charles Pratt, Coord.
english@exeter.edu; www.exeter.edu

Est. 1968. Fellowship for academic year to early-career writer, who will live in Exeter and be available to students but not be on faculty nor be required to teach. **Consideration.** Fees: $5 entry. Assistance: $10,000 stipend, room/board, room/board. Frequency: annual. **Preference.** Author Must Be: writing a work in process. **Application.** Best Material: application, 50-pg sample, SASE.

11/1/08. Humanities Projects in Media

National Endowment for the Humanities (NEH), 1100 Pennsylvania Ave. NW, Washington, DC, 20506
Margaret Scrymser, Lead Program Analyst
Tel: 202-606-8269
publicpgms@neh.gov; www.neh.gov

Planning, scripting, and production grants for humanities projects of broad appeal. **Consideration.** Assistance: $30,000-$500,000 grant. Frequency: annual. **Preference.** Length: full length (over 90 min), mid-length (60-90 min). Style: documentary. Subject: humanities. **Application.** Best Way: online. Best Material: application, submissions not returned. Deadline: 11/1/2008. Response: 6 mos.

Indiana Arts Commission (IAC)

150 W. Market St., #618, Indianapolis, IN, 46204
Monica R. Peterson, IAP, Theater
Tel: 317-232-1279
mpeterson@iac.in.gov; www.state.in.us/iac

Est. 1969. Individual Artist Program (IAP). See website for deadlines. **Consideration.** Assistance: $2,000 grant limit. Frequency: annual. **Preference.** Author Must Be: age 18 or older, resident of IN, not a student. **Application.** Best Material: application, 10-pg sample (10 copies). Deadline: 1-Feb-08.

4/1/08, 10/1/08. Iowa Arts Council

600 E. Locust, Des Moines, IA, 50319
Bruce Williams, Public Art & Design
Tel: 515-281-4006
bruce.williams@iowa.gov; www.iowaartscouncil.org

Consideration. Assistance: $10,000 grant/ $1,500 minor grant. **Preference.** Author Must Be: age 18 or older, resident of IA, not a student. **Application.** Deadline: Apr 1 (Jul-Jun), Oct 1 (Jan-Jun). Response: Appx. 4-6 wks..

Japan Foundation

152 W. 57th St., Fl. 17, New York, NY, 10019
Kenji Matsumoto, Program Director, Arts & Culture
Tel: 212-489-0299, Fax: 212-489-0409
info@jfny.org; www.jfny.org

Touring Grants help U.S. nonprofit organizations present Japanese performing arts in the U.S. and Canada. Collaboration Grants help American and Japanesse artists develop new works, which will further an appreciation of Japanese culture when presented to an American audience. **Consideration.** Assistance: $1,000 stipend. Frequency: annual. **Preference.** Subject: Asian. **Application.** Best Way: unsolicited. Best Material: application. Deadline: see website. Response: 3 mos..

9/14/08. Jerome Playwright-in-Residence Fellowships

The Playwrights' Center, 2301 Franklin Ave. E., Minneapolis, MN, 55406
Steve Moulds, Membership/Lit Assoc.
Tel: 612-332-7481, Fax: 612-332-6037
info@pwcenter.org; www.pwcenter.org

Fellowships to emerging playwrights for 1-yr residency (Jul-Jun) in MN using Center services. **Consideration.** Assistance: $9,000 grant. Frequency: annual. **Preference.** Author Must Be: citizen or resident of US, not produced professionally more than twice. **Application.** Best Way: online. Best Material: application. Deadline: 14-Sep-08.

9/15/2008. John Simon Guggenheim Memorial Foundation

90 Park Ave., New York, NY, 10016
Keith B. Lewis, Program Assoc
Tel: 212-687-4470, Fax: 212-697-3248
fellowships@gf.org; www.gf.org

Est. 1925. Fellowship to scholars and artists for research or creation. **Application.** Best Material: query, application, sample. Deadline: 9/15/2008.

9/14/2008. Jonathan Larson Performing Arts Foundation

Box 672, Prince St. Sta., New York, NY, 10012
Nancy Diekmann, Exec Dir
Tel: 212-529-0814, Fax: 212-253-7604
jlpaf@aol.com; www.jlpaf.org

Est. 1996. Annual grants to theater composers, lyricists, book writers and to theaters developing new musicals by former Larson award recipients. **Consideration.** Remuneration: $2,500-$15,000. Frequency: annual. **Preference.** Style: musical. **Application.** Best Material: application, SASE. Deadline: 14-Sep-08. Response: 4 mos.

9/15/2008. Kleban Award

New Dramatists, 424 W. 44th St., New York, NY, 10036
Kleban Award Coordinator
Tel: 212-757-6960, Fax: 212-265-4738
newdramatists@newdramatists.org; www.newdramatists.org/klebanaward.htm

Award to lyricists and librettists working in the American musical theater. **Consideration.** Remuneration: $100,000 each to a lyricist and a librettist. Frequency: annual. **Preference.** Style: musical. Author Must Be: produced or member of a professional musical theater workshop. **Application.** Best Material: application. Deadline: 15-Sep-08.

1/8/08. Literature Fellowships: Translation Projects

National Endowment for the Arts (NEA), 1100 Pennsylvania Ave. NW, Washington, DC, 20506
Tel: 202-682-5400
www.arts.gov

3/3/2008. Louisiana Division of the Arts

Box 44247, Baton Rouge, LA, 70804
Vanessa Ledbetter, Grant Services Asst
Tel: 225-342-8184, Fax: 225-342-8173
arts@crt.state.la.us; www.crt.state.la.us/arts

Application. Deadline: 3/3/2008.

Ludwig Vogelstein Foundation, Inc.

Ludwig Vogelstein Foundation, Inc., Box 510, Shelter Island, NY, 11964
Diana Braunschweig, Exec Dir
lvf@earthlink.net

Provides one-time grants to individuals working in playwriting, fiction/non-fiction, and the arts (paint sculpture, prints). **Consideration.** Remuneration: $1,000-$3,000. **Application.** Best Way: email inquiries.

6/27/08. Maine Arts Commission

25 State House Station, Augusta, ME, 04333
Donna McNeil, Asst Dir
Tel: 207-287-2724, Fax: 207-287-2725
donna.mcneil@maine.gov; mainearts.maine.gov

Preference. Author Must Be: age 18 or older, resident of ME, not a student. **Application.** Deadline: 6/27/2008.

Many Voices Playwriting Residency Awards

The Playwrights' Center, 2301 Franklin Ave. E., Minneapolis, MN, 55406
Steve Moulds, Membership/Lit Assoc.
Tel: 612-332-7481, Fax: 612-332-6037
info@pwcenter.org; www.pwcenter.org

Grants, education, and development opportunities to writers of color living in MN. **Consideration.** Assistance: $1,250 grant. Frequency: annual. **Preference.** Author Must Be: resident of MN. **Application.** Best Way: online. Best Material: application. Deadline: 25-Jul-08.

2/15/08. Marin Arts Council Fund for Artistis

Marin Arts Council, 555 Northgate Dr., #270, San Rafael, CA, 94903
Lance Walker, Grants Coord.
Tel: 415-499-8350, Fax: 415-499-8537
lance@marinarts.org; www.marinarts.org

Est. 1985. New Work Fellowships ($10,000) and career development grants ($1,500) to individual artists. Check website for upcoming deadlines. **Preference.** Author Must Be: age 18 or older, resident of Marin Co, not a student. **Application.** Best Material: application. Deadline: 2/15/08, 5/15/08 for Career Dev. Grants, 1/31/08 for New Work Fellowships.

Massachusetts Cultural Council (MCC)

Massachusetts Cultural Council (MCC), 10 St. James Ave., Fl. 3, Boston, MA, 02116
Dan Blask, Program Coord
Tel: 617-727-3668 x329, Fax: 617-727-0044
dan.blask@art.state.ma.us; www.massculturalcouncil.org

Grants alternating between dance, drawing, prose, painting, poetry, traditional arts (2008) and crafts, film/video, music, photography, playwriting, sculpture (2009). **Consideration.** Assistance: $7,500 grant. **Preference.** Author Must Be: age 18 or older, resident of MA. **Application.** Best Way: online. Best Material: application. Deadline: see website.

McKnight Advancement Grants

The Playwrights' Center, 2301 Franklin Ave. E., Minneapolis, MN, 55406
Steve Moulds, Membership/Lit Assoc.
Tel: 612-332-7481, Fax: 612-332-6037
info@pwcenter.org; www.pwcenter.org

Grants to advance a writer's art and career. **Consideration.** Assistance: $25,000 grant. Frequency: annual. **Preference.** Author Must Be: 2-yr resident of MN, professionally produced, not recipient of this grant in past 3 yrs. **Application.** Best Way: online. Best Material: application. Deadline: 2/1/2008.

McKnight National Playwriting Residency and Commission

The Playwrights' Center, 2301 Franklin Ave. E., Minneapolis, MN, 55406
Steve Moulds, Membership/Lit Assoc.
Tel: 612-332-7481, Fax: 612-332-6037
info@pwcenter.org; www.pwcenter.org

Commissioning and production of new works from nationally recognized playwrights. Recipient in residence at Center while play is in development. **Consideration.** Assistance: $12,500 grant. Frequency: annual. **Preference.** Author Must Be: nationally recognized playwright with 2 full professional productions. **Application.** Best Way: agent. Best Material: application. Deadline: See website for details of deadline.

3/14/08. Meet the Composer Grant Programs

75 Ninth Ave, Fl. 3R, New York, NY, 10010
Edward Ficklin, Senior Program Mgr.
Tel: 212-645-6949, Fax: 212-645-9669
eficklin@meetthecomposer.org; www.meetthecomposer.org

Est. 1988. **Consideration.** Assistance: $30,000 . Frequency: biennial. **Preference.** Length: all length. Style: all styles. Subject: all subjects. Author Must Be: U.S. citizen or permanent resident. **Application.** Best Way: unsolicited. Best Material: application, audio, submissions returned with SASE. Deadline: 3/14/2008. Response: 7/1/2008.

Michener Center for Writers

Univ. of Texas, Austin, 702 E. Dean Keeton St., Austin, TX, 78705
Tel: 512-471-1601, Fax: 512-471-9997
mcw@www.utexas.edu; www.utexas.edu/academic/mcw

Est. 1993. Financial assistance for full-time students in MFA program. **Consideration.** Assistance: $25,000 stipend, free tuition. Frequency: annual. **Preference.** Author Must Be: holder of a BA degree.

11/15/2008. Nebraska Arts Council

1004 Farnam St., Plaza Level, Omaha, NE, 68102
Suzanne Wise, Exec Dir
Tel: 402-595-2122, Fax: 402-595-2334
info@nebraskaartscouncil.org; www.nebraskaartscouncil.org

Individual Artist Fellowship (IAF). **Consideration.** Frequency: annual. **Preference.** Author Must Be: resident of NE. **Application.** Best Material: application, SASE. Deadline: 15-Nov-08.

4/6/2008. Nevada Arts Council
716 N. Carson St., Ste. A, Carson City, NV, 89701
Fran Morrow, Artist Services Coord
Tel: 775-687-7106
fkmorrow@clan.lib.nv.us; dmla.clan.lib.nv.us/docs/arts

Artist Fellowships. **Consideration.** Assistance: $5,000 grant. **Preference.** Author Must Be: age 21 or older, 1-yr resident of NV, citizen of US, not a student. **Application.** Best Material: application, full script (5 copies), resume, SASE. Deadline: 6-Apr-08.

10/1/2008. New Generations Program: Future Collaborations
Theater Communications Group (TCG), 520 8th Ave., Fl. 24, New York, NY, 10018
David Nugent, Artistic Programs Assoc.
Tel: 212-609-5900, Fax: 212-609-5901
grants@tcg.com; www.tcg.org

Early-career thatre professionals in any discipline are given 2-yr paid ($35,000/yr) mentorship at a theater. In addition, grants of $15,000 available to repay student loans. Theaters submit application. **Application.** Deadline: 10/1/2008.

4/13/2008. New Hampshire State Council on the Arts
2 Beacon St., Fl. 2, Concord, NH, 03301
Yvonne Stahr, Programs Info
Tel: 603-271-0791
yvonne.m.stahr@dcr.nh.gov; www.state.nh.us/nharts

$5,000 Fellowships awarded to 6 individual artists annually. Criteria are: Artistic excellence based on work sample, and professional commitment based on resume. **Consideration.** Assistance: $5,000 Fellowships awardrd to 6 individual artists annually.. **Preference.** Author Must Be: age 18 or older, resident of NH. **Application.** Best Way: professional commitment based on resume. Best Material: application, 20-pg sample (6 copies). Deadline: 13-Apr-08.

7/8/2008. New Jersey State Council on the Arts
Box 306, Trenton, NJ, 08625
Tom Moran, Artists' Services Sr Program Officer
Tel: 609-292-6130, Fax: 609-989-1440
tom@arts.sos.state.nj.us; www.njartscouncil.org

Artists fellowships in 14 disciplines, 7/yr (playwrights in odd yrs, composers in even yrs) thru Mid-Atlantic Arts Foundation (midatlanticarts.org). See website for details. **Preference.** Author Must Be: age 18 or older, resident of NJ, not a student. **Application.** Deadline: 8-Jul-08.

New York State Council on the Arts (NYSCA)
175 Varick St., Fl. 3, New York, NY, 10014
Heather Hitchens, Exec Dir
Tel: 212-627-4455, Fax: 212-620-5911
www.nysca.org

New York Theatre Workshop (NYTW) Playwriting Fellowship
New York Theatre Workshop (NYTW), 83 E. 4th St., New York, NY, 10003
Geoffrey Scott, Literary Assoc.
Tel: 212-780-9037, Fax: 212-460-8996
www.nytw.org

Visit Website for list of Fellowships and opportunities.

2/15/2008. North Dakota Council on the Arts

North Dakota Council on the Arts, 1600 E. Century Ave., #6, Bismarck, ND, 58503
Jan Webb, Exec Dir
Tel: 701-328-7590, Fax: 701-328-7595
www.nd.gov/arts

Est. 1984. Individual Artist Fellowship. Rotates thru literary and musical arts (2007), traditional, dance, and theater arts (2008), visual arts/crafts and media arts (2009). **Consideration.** Assistance: $2,500 grant. Frequency: triennial. **Preference.** Author Must Be: age 18 or older, resident of ND. Material Must Be: unpublished, new work. **Application.** Best Material: application, SASE. Best Time: Dec-Jan. Deadline: 15-Feb-08. Response: 3 mos.

9/1/2008. Ohio Arts Council

727 E. Main St., Columbus, OH, 43205
Ken Emerick, Dir, Individual Creativity
Tel: 614-466-2613, Fax: 614-466-4494
www.oac.state.oh.us

Individual Excellence Awards in choreography, crafts, fiction/nonfiction, poetry, play/screen writing, criticism, design/illustration, performance/interdisciplinary art, media art, music composition, photography, and visual art. **Consideration.** Assistance: $5,000-$10,000 grants. Frequency: annual. **Preference.** Length: full length, or two one-acts. Author Must Be: 1-yr resident of OH, not a student. **Application.** Best Material: application, full script (4 copies), audio. Deadline: 9/1/2008.

Oklahoma Arts Council

Box 52001-2001, Oklahoma City, OK, 73152
Betty Price, Exec Dir
Tel: 405-521-2931, Fax: 405-521-6418
okarts@arts.state.ok.us; www.oklaosf.state.ok.us/~arts

3/1/08. P73 Playwriting Fellowship

Page 73 Productions, Inc., 138 S. Oxford St. #5C, Brooklyn, NY, 11217
Liz Jones, Producing Dir.
Tel: 718-598-2099, Fax: 718-3982794
info@p73.org; www.p73.org

Est. 1997. Committed to developing and producing the work of emerging playwrights. Fellowship program applicants considered for future projects, incl. writing group, summer residency, and mainstage production. **Consideration.** Assistance: $2,000 stipend. Frequency: annual. **Preference.** Author Must Be: resident of US, have 2 full-lengths or 3 one-acts, never had production budgeted above $65k, not a student. **Application.** Best Way: unsolicited, professional recommendation. Best Material: query, application, 10-pg sample, resume, SASE. Deadline: Check Wesite for details.

8/1/2008. Pennsylvania Council on the Arts

Finance Bldg, #216, Harrisburg, PA, 17120
Lori Frush Schmelz, Program Dir.
Tel: 717-787-6883, Fax: 717-783-2538
www.pacouncilonthearts.org

Est. 1966. **Consideration.** Frequency: annual. **Preference.** Author Must Be: resident of PA. **Application.** Best Material: application. Deadline: 1-Aug-08. Response: 8 mos.

12/1/2008. Pew Fellowships in the Arts (PFA)

Philadelphia Center for Arts and Heritage, 1608 Walnut St., Fl. 18, Philadelphia, PA, 19103
Melissa Franklin, Dir.
Tel: 267-350-4920, Fax: 267-350-4997
pfa@pcah.us; www.pewarts.org

Est. 1991. Awards rotate in 4-yr cycle (3 disciplines chosen each Aug), incl. choreography, crafts, fiction/creative nonfiction, folk/traditional arts, media arts, music composition, painting, performance art, poetry, sculpture/installation, stage/screen scripts, and works on paper. **Consideration.** Assistance: $1,000 grant. **Preference.** Author Must Be: age 25 or older, 2-year resident of eastern PA (Bucks, Chester, Delaware, Montgomery, Philadelphia cos.), not a student. **Application.** Best Material: application. Deadline: 1-Dec-08.

Pilgrim Project

156 5th Ave., #400, New York, NY, 10010
Davida Goldman, Secy.
Tel: 212-627-2288, Fax: 212-627-2184
davida@firstthings.com

Est. 1987. Small grants for a reading, workshop or full production of plays that deal with questions of moral significance. Grants are for production of plays and not administrative costs. **Consideration.** Assistance: $1,000-$7,000 grant. **Preference.** Length: full length (over 90 min). **Application.** Best Material: full script, SASE. Response: 5 mos.

Princess Grace Foundation USA Playwriting Fellowship

150 E. 58th St., Fl.25, New York, NY, 10155
Kathleen Richards, Program Associate
Tel: 212-317-1470
grants@pgfusa.org; www.pgfusa.com

Est. 1982. 10-wk residency with New Dramatists; $7,500 stipend; and publication/representation by Samuel French for 1 winning playwright. **Consideration.** Assistance: $7,500 grant. Remuneration: publication, residency. Frequency: annual. **Preference.** Length: full length (over 90 min). Style: comedy, drama. Author Must Be: resident or citizen of US. Material Must Be: unpublished, unproduced, original. **Application.** Best Material: application, full script. Best Time: Jan-08. Deadline: See website after January 1, 2008.

10/1/2008. Radcliffe Institute Fellowships

Harvard Univ., 34 Concord Ave., Cambridge, MA, 02138
Application Office
Tel: 617-496-1324
fellowships@radcliffe.edu; www.radcliffe.edu/fellowships

To support scholars, scientists, artists, and writers of exceptional promise and demonstrated accomplishments to pursue work in academic and professional fields and in the creative arts.

4/1/08, 10/1/08. Rhode Island State Council on the Arts

1 Capitol Hill, Fl. 3, Providence, RI, 02908
Cristina Di Chiera, Dir, Individual Artists
Tel: 401-222-3880, Fax: 401-422-3018
cristina@arts.ri.gov; www.arts.ri.gove

Fellowships in: crafts, film/video, poetry, fiction, play/screenwriting, sculpture, and photography (Apr 1); choreography, design, painting, and music (Oct 1). **Consideration.** Assistance: $5,000 Fellowship, $500-$10,000 Project Grant. Frequency: annual. **Preference.** Author Must Be: age 18 or older, resident of RI, not a student. **Application.** Best Material: application. Deadline: Apr 1, 2008 (playwrights), Oct 1, 2008 (composers).

11/1/08. Rome Prize

American Academy in Rome Programs, 7 E. 60th St., New York, NY, 10022
Tel: 212-751-7200
www.aarome.org

Est. 1894. Annual yearlong fellowships to 15 emerging artists (literature, music, etc.) and 15 scholars (Italian studies). Literature candidates must be nominated through the American Academy of Arts and Letters. Music candidates may apply themselves. **Preference.** Author Must Be: recipient of BA in music. **Application.** Best Material: application, 2-3 orchestral scores, CDs of included scores, resume, 1-pg proposal, 3 reference letters. Deadline: 11/1/2008.

10/1/2008. South Carolina Arts Commission

1800 Gervais St., Columbia, SC, 29201
Jeanette Guinn, Performing Arts Coord.
Tel: 803-734-8677
jguinn@arts.state.sc.us; www.southcarolinaarts.com

Fellowships in three categories each yr, rotating between prose/poetry (odd yrs) and visual arts/crafts (even yrs), with third changing category, incl. music (2007), dance (2008), theater (2009). **Consideration.** Assistance: $5,000 grant. **Preference.** Author Must Be: age 18 or older, 2-yr resident of SC, not a student. **Application.** Best Material: application, support materials, SASE. Deadline: 1-Oct-08.

3/1/2008. South Dakota Arts Council

711 E. Wells Ave., Pierre, SD, 57501
Dennis Holub, Exec Dir
Tel: 605-773-3301, Fax: 605-773-5657
sdac@state.sd.us; www.artscouncil.sd.gov

Est. 1966. **Consideration.** Assistance: $3,000 grant. Frequency: annual. **Preference.** Author Must Be: resident of SD. **Application.** Best Material: application, 30-pg sample, SASE. Best Time: Jul-Feb. Deadline: 1-Mar-08. Response: 3 mos.

10/26/2008. TCG/ITI Intl. Fellowship

Theater Communications Group (TCG), 520 8th Ave., Fl. 24, New York, NY, 10018
Casey Baltes, Assistant Director
Tel: 212-609-5900, Fax: 212-609-5901
grants@tcg.org; www.tcg.org

Travel grants in fall/winter and spring/summer for travel to Russia and Eastern and Central Europe, to foster cultural exchange and artistic partnerships. **Consideration.** Assistance: $3,000 grant. Frequency: semiannual. **Application.** Best Material: application. Deadline: 26-Oct-08. Response: 2 months.

Theater Museum

The Theater Museum, 723 7th Ave., New York, NY, 10019
Helen Marie Guditis, Exec. Dir.
Tel: 212-764-4112 x201, Fax: 212-764-0458

Est. 1986. Nonprofit organizationto preserve, perpetuate and protect the legacy of live theater on Broadway. AKA Direct from Broadway.

2/15/2008. Travel & Study Grant Program

Jerome Foundation, 400 Sibley St., #125, St. Paul, MN, 55101
Cynthia Gehrig, Pres.
Tel: 651-224-9431, Fax: 651-224-3439
www.jeromefdn.org

Preference. Author Must Be: resident of MN or NYC, emerging artist. **Application.** Deadline: 15-Feb-08.

10/1/2008. U.S. Dept. of State Fulbright Program for US Students

Institute of Intl. Education, 809 United Nations Plaza, New York, NY, 10017
Tel: 212-984-5330
www.iie.org/fulbright/us

Est. 1946. Funds for graduate study, research, or teaching. Students in US colleges must apply thru campus Fulbright Advisers. Those not enrolled in US may apply directly to IIE. **Consideration.** Frequency: annual. **Application.** Best Material: application. Best Time: May. Deadline: 1-Oct-08.

1/5/2008. Utah Arts Council

617 E. South Temple, Salt Lake City, UT, 84102
Margaret Hunt, Dir.
Tel: 801-236-7555, Fax: 801-236-7556
arts.utah.gov

Application. Deadline: 5-Jan-08.

10/1/08. $20. Vermont Arts Council

136 State St., Drawer 33, Montpelier, VT, 05633
Michele Bailey, Sr Program Dir
Tel: 802-828-3293, Fax: 802-828-3363
mbailey@vermontartscouncil.org; www.vermontartscouncil.org

Est. 1994. Opportunity Grants for creation and for artist development. **Consideration.** Fees: $20 aplication. Assistance: $1,000-$5,000 grant. Frequency: annual. **Preference.** Author Must Be: age 18 or older, resident of VT, not a student. Material Must Be: original. **Application.** Best Way: online. Best Material: application, synopsis, 10-pg sample, SASE. Deadline: 1-Oct-08. Response: 2 mos.

Villar-Hauser Theatre Development Fund
188 E. 93rd St., #2-B, New York, NY, 10128
Ludovica Villar-Hauser, Artistic Dir.
Tel: 917-304-6823
lvillarhauser@aol.com

8/1/2008. Virginia Commission for the Arts
223 Governor St., Fl. 2, Richmond, VA, 23219
Peggy J. Baggett, Exec Dir
Tel: 804-225-3132, Fax: 804-225-4327
arts@arts.virginia.gov; www.arts.state.va.us

Artists Fellowships in rotating disciplines announced each Jun (photography, fiction in 2006). **Consideration.** Remuneration: $5,000 . Frequency: annual. **Preference.** Author Must Be: age 18 or older, resident of VA. **Application.** Best Material: application. Deadline: 1-Aug-08.

9/17/08. Wisconsin Arts Board
101 E. Wilson St., Fl. 1, Madison, WI, 53702
Mark Fraire, Grant Programs & Services Specialist
Tel: 608-264-8191, Fax: 608-267-9629
mark.fraire@arts.state.wi.us; arts.state.wi.us/static

Artist Fellowship Awards of unrestricted funds to professional WI artists. Rotating between Lit Arts, Music Composition, Choreography/Performance Art (even yrs), and Visual/Media Arts (odd yrs). **Consideration.** Assistance: $8,000 grant. Frequency: biennial. **Preference.** Author Must Be: 1-yr resident of WI, others. Material Must Be: not a student. **Application.** Best Material: online application, 2-pg statement, 25-pg sample, 3-track audio (composers only), 3-pg resume, SASE. Deadline: 17-Sep-08.

THEATERS

12 Miles West Theatre Company
Box 1663, Bloomfield, NJ, 07003
Lenny Bart, Artistic Dir.
Tel: 973-259-9187, Fax: 973-259-9188
info@12mileswest.org; www.12mileswest.org

Est. 1992. Equity SPT-1. **Consideration.** Remuneration: $500 or 5\% royalty. **Preference.** Length: full length (over 90 min), short comedic pieces (under 10 min). Production: cast of 2-7, simple set. **Application.** Best Material: query, synopsis, full script, SASE. Response: 1 yr.

1812 Productions
421 N. 7th St., #218, Philadelphia, PA, 19123
Jennifer Childs, Artistic Dir.
Tel: 215-592-9560, Fax: 215-592-9580
jen@1812productions.org; www.1812productions.org

Est. 1997. **Preference.** Length: full length (over 90 min). Style: comedy, musical comedy. **Application.** Best Material: full script. Best Time: summer. Response: 6 mos.

40th Street Stage
809 W. 40th St., Norfolk, VA, 23508
Frankie Little Hardin, Managing Director
frankielhardin@aol.com; www.40thstreetstage.com

Preference. Length: plays that showcase women and women's issues. Style: plays for young audiences. Production: cast limit 6, minimal set. Material Must Be: unpublished. **Application.** Best Material: query, full script, SASE. Response: 6 mo.

5th Avenue Theatre
1308 5th Ave., Seattle, WA, 98101
Bill Berry, Assoc Artistic Dir.
Tel: 206-625-1418, Fax: 206-292-9610
admin@5thavenuetheatre.org; www.5thavenuetheatre.org

Est. 1980. **Preference.** Style: musical. Production: cast of 8 or more. Material Must Be: unproduced. **Application.** Best Way: agent. Best Material: full script, audio. Response: 6 mos.

A Noise Within (ANW)
234 S. Brand Blvd., Glendale, CA, 91204
Geoff Elliot, Co-Artistic Dir.
Tel: 818-240-0910, Fax: 818-240-0826
www.anoisewithin.org

Est. 1991. Equity Special Agreement. **Preference.** Length: full length (over 90 min). Style: adaptation, translation. Subject: classics. **Application.** Best Material: full script. Best Time: fall. Response: 8 mos.

A. D. Players
2710 W. Alabama St., Houston, TX, 77098
Lee Walker, Literary Mgr.
Tel: 713-526-2721, Fax: 713-439-0905
lee@adplayers.org; www.adplayers.org

Est. 1967. **Preference.** Length: full-length (mainstage), one-act (children's). Subject: children's, religious, senior, women, family. Production: cast limit 12 (mainstage)/8 (children's), piano only, set limit 3. **Application.** Best Way: professional recommendation. Best Material: query, synopsis, 10-pg sample, SASE. Best Time: Jan. Response: 10 mos.

Abingdon Theatre Company
312 W. 36th St., Fl. 6, New York, NY, 10018
Kim T. Sharp, Literary Mgr
Tel: 212-868-2055, Fax: 212-868-2056
ksharp@abingdontheatre.org; www.abingdontheatre.org

Est. 1993. Equity readings and full productions. Staff: Jan Buttram (Artistic Dir). **Preference.** Length: full length (over 90 min). Style: comedy, drama. Production: cast limit 8. Author Must Be: permanent resident or citizen of US. Material Must Be: unoptioned, unproduced in NYC. **Application.** Best Material: full script, SASE see website for details. Response: 3 mos.

About Face Theatre (AFT)
1222 W. Wilson Ave., Fl. 2, Chicago, IL, 60640
Heather Schmucker, Producing Director
Tel: 773-784-8565, Fax: 773-784-8557
www.aboutfacetheatre.com

Est. 1995. New plays exploring gender and sexuality. Opportunities incl. production and workshop/reading. **Preference.** Length: full length (over 90 min), one-act (30-60 min). Style: performance art considered. Subject: gay-lesbian. Production: no fly space. **Application.** Best Material: query, synopsis, 10-pg sample, cast list, SASE. Response: 6 mos query, 3 mos script.

Absinthe-Minded Theatre Company
1484 Stadium Ave., Bronx, NY, 10465
Ralph Scarpato, Producing Artistic Dir.
Tel: 212-714-4696
rscarp@aol.com

Act II Playhouse
56 E. Butler Pike, Ambler, PA, 19002
Stephen D. Blumenthal, Producing Artistic Dir.
www.act2.org

Est. 1998. 130-seat SPT. Staff: Steve Blumenthal & Gene Frank. **Preference.** Length: full length (over 90 min). Style: comedy, drama, musical. Production: cast limit 5, orchestra limit 5, unit set. Material Must Be: unproduced. **Application.** Best Material: synopsis, full script, SASE. Response: 3 mos.

ACT Theater (A Contemporary Theatre)
700 Union St., Seattle, WA, 98101
Anita Montgomery, Literary Assoc.
Tel: 206-292-7660, Fax: 206-292-7670
www.acttheatre.org

Est. 1965. Equity LORT C. Special programs incl. new play award and new play development workshops. **Preference.** Length: full length (over 90 min). **Application.** Best Way: agent. Best Material: synopsis, 20-pg sample (NW writers only), SASE. Response: 6 mos.

Acting Company
Box 898, Times Sq. Sta., New York, NY, 10108
Margot Harley, Producing Dir
Tel: 212-258-3111, Fax: 212-258-3299
mail@theactingcompany.org; www.theactingcompany.org

Est. 1972. Prefer solo one-acts on US historical figures for HS tours and full-length adaptations of classic novels. **Preference.** Length: full length (over 90 min). Production: cast limit 13, touring theater. **Application.** Best Way: agent.

Actor's Express

887 W. Marietta St. NW, #J-107, Atlanta, GA, 30318
Freddy Ashley, Artistic Dir
www.actors-express.com

Est. 1988. AEA Guest Artist Contract. Opportunities incl. readings, workshops, production. **Consideration.** Assistance: room/board, room/board. Remuneration: 6\%-8\% royalty. **Preference.** Length: full length (over 90 min), mid-length (60-90 min). Style: no adaptation. Subject: Black, disabled, gay. **Application.** Best Way: agent. Best Material: full script. Response: 6 mos.

Actors' Guild of Lexington

141 E. Main St., Lexington, KY, 40507
Richard St. Peter, Artistic Dir
Tel: 859-233-7330, Fax: 859-233-3773
actorsguild@qx.net; www.actorsguildoflexington.org

Est. 1984. **Preference.** Length: full length (over 90 min). Production: cast limit 6, unit set, no fly space. **Application.** Best Way: email. Best Material: query, synopsis. Response: 1 mo query, 6 mos script.

Actors Art Theatre (AAT)

6128 Wilshire Blvd., #110, Los Angeles, CA, 90048
Jolene Adams, Artistic Dir
actorsart@actorsart.com; www.actorsart.com

Est. 1994. 32-seat theater developing plays thru workshops and labs. Produces 1 original play each year, plus one-acts and solos under Equity 99-seat. **Consideration.** Remuneration: 6\% royalty. **Preference.** Style: no musical. Production: no orchestra. Material Must Be: unoptioned, unproduced on West Coast. **Application.** Best Way: email. Best Material: query, synopsis, 10-pg sample, submissions not returned. Response: 1 yr.

Actors Collective

447 W. 48th St., # 1-W, New York, NY, 10036
Catherine Russell, Managing Dir.
Tel: 212-956-9456, Fax: 212-445-1015
postarvis@aol.com; www.perfect-crime.com

Est. 1981. Equity Off-Broadway. **Preference.** Production: cast limit 8. **Application.** Best Way: professional recommendation. Best Material: query, SASE. Response: 1 mo.

11/1/2008. Actors Theatre of Louisville [KY]

316 W. Main St., Louisville, KY, 40202
Amy Wegener, Literary Mgr.
Tel: 502-584-1265, Fax: 502-561-3300
ahansel@actorstheatre.org; www.actorstheatre.org

Est. 1964. Equity LORT B, C and D. 1980 Regional Theater Tony winner. Staff: Marc Masterson (Artistic Dir), Jennifer Bielstein (Managing Dir). **Preference.** Length: full length (over 90 min). Material Must Be: unproduced. **Application.** Best Way: agent. Best Material: query, synopsis, 10-pg sample. Best Time: Apr-Oct. Deadline: 11/1/2008. Response: 9 mos.

Actors Theatre of Phoenix

Box 1924, Phoenix, AZ, 85001
Matthew Wiener, Producing Artistic Dir.
Tel: 602-253-6701, Fax: 602-254-9577
info@actorstheatrePHX.org; www.actorstheatrephx.org

Est. 1985. **Preference.** Length: full length (over 90 min). Style: adaptation, comedy, drama. Subject: Southwest. Production: cast limit 8. **Application.** Best Way: professional recommendation. Response: 10 mos.

Adirondack Theatre Festival

Box 3203, Glens Falls, NY, 12801
Mark Fleischer, Producing Artistic Dir.
Tel: 518-798-7479, Fax: 518-793-1334
atf@ATFestival.org; www.atfestival.org

Est. 1995. **Preference.** Length: full length (over 90 min). Subject: contemporary. Production: cast limit 10, no fly space. **Application.** Best Way: professional recommendation. Best Time: Aug-Jan. Response: 6 mos query, 6 mos script.

Adventure Stage Chicago (ASC)

Northwestern University Settlement House (NUSH), 1012 N. Noble St., Chicago, IL, 60622
Tom Arvetis, Porducing Artistic Dir
Tel: 773-342-4141, Fax: 773-278-2621
info@vittumtheater.org; www.vittumtheater.org

Est. 1998. Annual TYA season. **Consideration.** Remuneration: 6\% royalty. **Preference.** Length: mid-length (60-90 min). Subject: family friendly. Production: ages 18 and older, cast limit 10. **Application.** Best Material: synopsis, 10-pg sample. Best Time: Sep. Response: 1 mo.

African Continuum Theatre Co. (ACTCo)

3523 12th St. NE, Fl. 2, Washington, DC, 20017
Jennifer L. Nelson, Producing Artistic Dir.
Tel: 202-529-5764, Fax: 202-529-5782
info@africancontinuumtheatre.com; www.africancontinuumtheatre.com

Est. 1996. Not accepting submissions of any kind in 2008 as it is a transition year. Fresh Flavas Reading Series: staged readings of three-works-in-progress per year. **Preference.** Subject: African-American. Production: small cast, unit set.

AfroSolo Theatre Company

762 Fulton St. #307, San Francisco, CA, 94102
Thomas R. Simpson, Artistic Dir.
Tel: 415-771-2376, Fax: 415-771-2312

Solo work only, usually to be performed by writer. Send up to 10pg synosis, bio, photo.

Algonkuin Theatre Company

1231 Pulaski Blvd., Bellingham, MA, 02019
Marty BlackEagle-Carl, Artistic Dir.
algonkuintheatre@comcast.net; hometown.aol.com/algonkuin

Est. 1993. **Preference.** Length: full length (over 90 min), one-act (30-60 min). Style: no musical. Subject: Native American. Production: unit set. **Application.** Best Way: email. Best Material: query. Best Time: summer. Response: 1 mo.

All Arts Matter

Box 513, Greenville, NY, 10283
Tony DeVito, Artistic Dir.
Tel: 518-966-4038
allartsmatter@juno.com; www.allartsmatter.org

Est. 2000. Producing unit of diversified arts organization. Reading series and play productions. **Consideration.** Assistance: room/board, room/board. **Preference.** Subject: children's, senior, women. **Application.** Best Way: agent. Best Material: full script, SASE. Response: 6 wks.

Allenberry Playhouse

Box 7, Boiling Springs, PA, 17007
Claude Giroux, Artistic Dir.
Tel: 717-960-5273
www.allenberry.com

Consideration. Remuneration: royalty. **Preference.** Length: full length (over 90 min), mid-length (60-90 min). Style: adaptation, comedy, musical, farce. Subject: children's, disabled, senior, women. Production: age 20-60, cast of 6-10, orchestra limit 5. **Application.** Best Material: query, 20-pg sample, submissions not returned.

Alley Theatre

615 Texas Ave., Houston, TX, 77002
Joe Luis Cedillo, LIterary Mgr
Tel: 713-228-9341
www.alleytheatre.org

Est. 1947. 1996 Regional Theater Tony winner. **Preference.** Length: full length (over 90 min). **Application.** Best Way: professional recommendation. Response: 8 mos.

Alliance Theatre

1280 Peachtree St. NE, Atlanta, GA, 30309
Freddie Ashley, Literary Mgr
Tel: 404-733-4650, Fax: 404-733-4625
ATCliterary@woodruffcenter.org; www.alliancetheatre.org

Est. 1968. Equity LORT B and D, TYA. 2007 Regional Theater Tony winner. 11 shows in 2 spaces: 800-seat proscenium, 200-seat black box. Staff: Susan Booth (Artistic Dir), Celise Kalke (Artistic Assoc/Dramaturg). **Preference.** Length: full length (over 90 min), mid-length (60-90 min). **Application.** Best Way: agent. Best Material: query, 10-pg sample, full script, SASE. Response: 1 yr.

Allied Theatre Group/Stage West

4821 West Vickery Blvd., Fort Worth, TX, 76107
Jim Covault, Artistic. Dir.
Tel: 817-735-9995, Fax: 817-735-4060
boxoffice@stagewest.org; www.stagewest.org

Equity SPT. Formerly Stage West & Fort Worth Shakespeare Festival. **Preference.** Length: full length (over 90 min). Style: adaptation, comedy, drama, musical, translation. Production: cast limit 9. **Application.** Best Material: query, synopsis. Best Time: Jan-Mar. Response: 1 mo query, 3 mos script.

Altarena Playhouse / Alameda Little Theater

1409 High St., Alameda, CA, 94501
Susan Dunn, President
www.altarena.org

Est. 1938. Non-Equity volunteer community theater offering readings, new works by local playwrights. **Preference.** Length: full length (over 90 min). Style: comedy, drama, musical, solo. Production: cast limit 16, orchestra limit 10, minimal set, in the round. Author Must Be: resident of Bay Area. **Application.** Best Way: professional recommendation. Best Material: query, full script. Response: 6 mos.

Amas Musical Theatre

115 MacDougal St., #2-B, New York, NY, 10012
Donna Trinkoff, Producing Artistic Dir.
Tel: 212-563-2565, Fax: 212-239-8332
amasevents@aol.org; www.amasmusical.org

Est. 1968. Most productions begin in Six O'Clock Musical Theater Lab, featuring 1-hr staged readings of new musicals (3 in spring, 3 in fall). **Preference.** Style: musical. Subject: ethnic encouraged. Production: small cast (multi-ethnic encouraged). **Application.** Best Material: synopsis, full script, audio, scene list, SASE. Response: 6 mos.

American Folklore Theatre (AFT)

Box 273, Fish Creek, WI, 54212
Jeffrey Herbst, Artistic Dir
Tel: 920-854-6117, Fax: 920-854-9106
aft@folkloretheatre.com; www.folkloretheatre.com

Est. 1990. Equity LOA, LORT D. Original musical works for families. **Consideration.** Remuneration: royalty. **Preference.** Length: mid-length (60-90 min). Style: musical. Subject: cultural historical. Production: cast of 3-10. **Application.** Best Way: professional recommendation. Best Material: synopsis, SASE.

American Musical Theatre of San Jose (AMT)

1717 Technology Dr., San Jose, CA, 95110
Dir, New Works
Tel: 408-453-1545, Fax: 408-453-7123
newworks@amtsj.org; www.amtsj.org

Equity WCLO. New Works program devoted to new talent in musical theater. Songwriters and librettists with production history may submit scripts and demo tapes of new projects. **Preference.** Length: full length (over 90 min). Style: musical. Author Must Be: age 21 or older. **Application.** Best Way: agent. Best Material: synopsis, audio, SASE.

American Repertory Theatre

64 Brattle St., Cambridge, MA, 02138
Arthur Holmberg, Literary Dir.
Tel: 617-495-2668
www.amrep.org

Est. 1979. 1986 Regional Theater Tony winner. **Preference.** Length: full length (over 90 min). Style: non-realistic material. **Application.** Best Way: agent. Best Material: SASE. Best Time: Sep-Jan. Response: 6 mos.

American Stage [FL]

211 3rd St. S., St. Petersburg, FL, 33731
Todd Olson, Producing Artistic Dir
Tel: 727-823-1600, Fax: 727-821-2444
www.americanstage.org

Est. 1977. **Preference.** Length: full length (over 90 min). Subject: children's. Production: cast limit 4, unit set.

American Theater Company

1909 W. Byron St., Chicago, IL, 60613
Tel: 773-929-5009, Fax: 773-929-5171
info@atcweb.org; www.atcweb.org

Est. 1985. **Preference.** Length: full length (over 90 min). Style: musical or, play. Subject: social and political. Production: cast limit 20. **Application.** Best Material: query, synopsis, 10-pg sample, SASE. Response: 4 mos query, 1 yr script.

American Theatre of Actors, Inc. (ATA)

314 W. 54th St., New York, NY, 10019
James Jennings, Artistic Dir.
Tel: 212-581-3044
www.americantheatreofactors.org

Est. 1976. New plays by new writers for 1-4 wks, both Equity and non-Equity. Plays rehearse 3-4 wks. Staff: Jane Culley. **Preference.** Length: full length (over 90 min), mid-length (60-90 min), one-act (30-60 min). Style: comedy, drama. Production: age 20-80, cast of 3-6, set limit 2. Author Must Be: age 20 or older, resident of US. Material Must Be: unoptioned, unpublished, unproduced. **Application.** Best Material: full script, SASE. Response: 3 wks.

Amherst Players/Upstage NY

56 Bright St., Lockport, NY, 14094
Debra Cole, VP, Production
Tel: 716-713-2649
colebuffalo@aol.com

Preference. Length: one-act (30-60 min). Style: comedy, musical. Author Must Be: age 21 or older, resident of US. Material Must Be: unoptioned, unpublished, unproduced. **Application.** Best Material: full script, submissions not returned.

Amphibian Productions

2429 Colonial Pkwy., Fort Worth, TX, 76109
Kathleen Culebro, Artistic Dir.
info@amphibianproductions.org; www.amphibianproductions.org

Est. 2000. Produces plays and readings in Ft. Worth and New York City. **Consideration.** Remuneration: production, reading. **Preference.** Length: full length (over 90 min), mid-length (60-90 min). Style: no musical. Subject: no children's. Production: cast limit 6, set limit 2. **Application.** Best Way: professional recommendation. Best Material: query, SASE. Best Time: Jan-Apr. Response: 8 mos.

Animated Theaterworks Inc.

240 Central Park S., #13-B, New York, NY, 10019
Elysabeth Kleinhans, President
info@animatedtheaterworks.org; www.animatedtheaterworks.org

Est. 1999. Readings and showcase productions of new and developing works. **Preference.** Length: full length (over 90 min), mid-length (60-90 min). Style: comedy, drama. Production: cast limit 6, unit set. Material Must Be: unpublished, unproduced. **Application.** Best Material: query, synopsis, 10-15 pg sample, SASE. Response: 6 mos.

Aquila Theatre Company

4 Washington Square N., #452, New York, NY, 10003
Peter Meineck, Artistic Dir.
Tel: 212-998-8017
aquila@aquilatheatre.com; www.aquilatheatre.com

Est. 1991. **Preference.** Length: full length (over 90 min), one-act (30-60 min). Style: no musical. **Application.** Best Way: professional recommendation. Response: 3 mos.

Arden Theatre Company

40 N. 2nd St., Philadelphia, PA, 19106
Dennis Smeal, Literary Mgr
dsmeal@ardentheatre.org; www.ardentheater.org

Est. 1988. Equity LORT D, TYA. 7 shows/yr in 360-seat and 175-seat house. **Preference.** Length: full length (over 90 min). Style: adaptation, drama, musical. **Application.** Best Material: synopsis, 10-pg sample, submissions not returned. Response: 10 wks.

Arena Players Repertory Theater

296 Rte. 109, E. Farmingdale, NY, 11735
Fred De Feis, Producer
Tel: 516-293-0674, Fax: 516-777-8688
arena109@aol.com; www.arenaplayers.org

Est. 1950. **Consideration.** Remuneration: $600 . **Preference.** Length: full length (over 90 min), mid-length (60-90 min). Production: cast of 2-10. Material Must Be: unoptioned, unpublished, unproduced. **Application.** Best Material: query, synopsis, full script, SASE. Response: 6 mos.

Arena Stage
1101 6th St. SW, Washington, DC, 20024
Mark Bly, Sr. Dramaturg
Tel: 202-554-9066
www.arenastage.org

Est. 1950. Equity LORT B+, B and D. 1976 Regional Theater Tony winner. Staff: Molly Smith (Artistic Dir), Stephen Richard (Exec Dir), Mark Bly (Sr Dramaturg). **Consideration.** Remuneration: royalty. **Preference.** Length: full length (over 90 min). Subject: US. Material Must Be: unproduced preferred. **Application.** Best Way: professional recommendation. Best Material: query, synopsis, 10-pg sample, SASE. Response: 3 mos.

Arizona Theatre Company
Box 1631, Tucson, AZ, 85702
Jennifer Bazzell, Literary Mgr
Tel: 520-884-8210
www.arizonatheatre.org

Est. 1966. Equity LORT B. **Preference.** Length: full length (over 90 min). **Application.** Best Material: query, synopsis, 10-pg sample, SASE. Response: 6 mos.

Arkansas Arts Center Children's Theatre
Box 2137, Little Rock, AR, 72203
Bradley Anderson, Artistic Dir.
Tel: 501-372-4000
banderson@arkarts.com; www.arkarts.com/childrenstheatre

Est. 1979. **Preference.** Length: full length (over 90 min), one-act (30-60 min). Style: adaptation, musical. Subject: children's. **Application.** Best Way: professional recommendation. Best Time: Nov-Dec. Response: 4 mos.

Arkansas Repertory Theatre
Box 110, Little Rock, AR, 72201
Brad Mooy, Literary Mgr.
Tel: 866-6THEREP, Fax: 501-378-0012
www.therep.org

Preference. Length: full length (over 90 min). Production: small cast. **Application.** Best Material: query, synopsis. Response: 3 mos query, 6 mos script.

Ars Nova
511 W. 54th St., New York, NY, 10019
Jason Eagan, Artistic Dir

Ars Nova is committed to developing and producing eclectic theater, comedy and music to feed today's popular culture. To that end, Ars Nova strives to meld disciplines and give clear voice to a new generation of artists. Ars Nova was founded in memory of Gabe Weiner. **Consideration.** Remuneration: music series, comedy series, and a playwrights' group.

ART Station
Box 1998, Stone Mountain, GA, 30086
Jon Goldstein, Literary Manager
Tel: 770-469-1105, Fax: 770-469-0355
jon@artstation.org; www.artstation.org

Est. 1986. Equity SPT. Works representing Southern experience. Staff: David Thomas (Artistic Dir.). **Consideration.** Remuneration: 7\% royalty. **Preference.** Length: full length (over 90 min), mid-length (60-90 min). Style: comedy, musical. Subject: South. Production: cast limit 6. **Application.** Best Material: synopsis, 10-pg sample, SASE. Response: 1 yr.

Artists Repertory Theatre

1516 SW Alder St., Portland, OR, 97205
Stephanie Mulligan, Literary Mgr
Tel: 503-241-9807 x110, Fax: 503-241-8268
stephanie@artistsrep.org; www.artistsrep.org

Est. 1981. Equity SPT-8, with 7 shows per season on 2 stages, plus staged readings. Staff: Alen Nause (Artistic Dir), Jon Kretzu (Assoc Artistic Dir). **Preference.** Length: full length (over 90 min). Style: no musical. **Application.** Best Material: query, synopsis, SASE. Response: 2 mos query, 6 mos script.

ArtsPower National Touring Theatre

39 S. Fullerton Ave., Montclair, NJ, 07042
Gary Blackman, Managing Dir.
gblackman@artspower.org; www.artspower.org

Tourable theater presenting one-act plays and musicals for young and family audiences. **Preference.** Length: one-act (30-60 min). Style: adaptation, drama, musical. Subject: children's. Production: cast limit 4. Material Must Be: unpublished. **Application.** Best Material: synopsis, audio, SASE.

Asian American Theater Company

690 Fifth St., #211, San Francisco, CA, 94107
Sean Lim, Artistic Dir.
Tel: 415-543-5738
www.asianamericantheater.org

Est. 1973. **Preference.** Subject: Asian, Asian-American. **Application.** Best Material: synopsis, 30-pg sample, submissions not returned.

Asolo Theatre Company

5555 N. Tamiami Tr., Sarasota, FL, 34243
Corinne Gabrielson, Asst Managing Dir.
Tel: 941-351-9010
corinnegabrielson@asolo.org; www.asolo.org

Est. 1960. **Preference.** Length: full length (over 90 min), mid-length (60-90 min). **Application.** Best Way: invite. Best Material: query.

Asylum Theatre

4441 Rockaway Beach St., Las Vegas, NV, 89129
Sarah O'Connell, Artistic Dir.
Tel: 702-604-3417, Fax: 702-650-0242
sarah@asylumtheatre.org; www.asylumtheatre.org

Est. 1997. **Consideration.** Assistance: 100-200. **Preference.** Length: all length. Style: all styles. Subject: all subjects. Material Must Be: unoptioned, prefer non-produced but not required. **Application.** Best Material: full script, SASE. Best Time: fall.

Atlantic Theater Company

76 9th Ave., #537, New York, NY, 10011
Christian Parker, Assoc Artistic Dir
Tel: 212-691-5919, Fax: 212-645-8755
www.atlantictheater.org

Est. 1985. Off-Broadway, LOA. 4-show mainstage season, 2-show second stage season. Staff: Neil Pepe (Artistic Dir). **Preference.** Length: full length (over 90 min). Style: all styles. Subject: all subjects. **Application.** Best Way: professional recommendation, agent. Best Material: query, synopsis, 20 pg sample, full script, audio, SASE. Best Time: Sep-Jan. Response: 6 mos.

Attic Ensemble
83 Wayne St., Jersey City, NJ, 07302
Tel: 201-413-9200
www.atticensemble.org

Est. 1970. **Consideration.** Fees: 10. **Preference.** Length: full-length, mid-length (60-90 min.). Style: comedy, drama, no musical. Subject: all subjects. Production: cast 4-8, unit set, or conceptual. Author Must Be: ages 15-65. Material Must Be: unpublished, unproduced. **Application.** Best Way: unsolicited. Best Material: full script, submissions returned with SASE. Best Time: after 12/15/03. Response: 5/15/2004.

Attic Theatre and Film Center
5429 W. Washington Blvd., Los Angeles, CA, 90016
Kacey Camp, Literary Mgr
Tel: 323-525-0600
litmanager@attictheatre.org; www.attictheatre.org

Est. 1987. LA 99-seat. **Preference.** Length: full length (over 90 min). Production: simple set, no fly or wing space. **Application.** Best Material: query, synopsis, sample, SASE. Response: 3 mos query, 6 mos script.

August Wilson New Play Initiative
Congo Square Theatre Company, 2936 N. Southport Avenue, # 210, Chicago, IL, 60657
Daniel Bryant, Asst. Artistic Dir.

Preference. Subject: African-American. **Application.** Best Material: query, synopsis, 10-15 pg. sample, SASE. Best Time: March.

Aurora Theatre, Inc. [GA]
128 E Pike St., Lawrenceville, GA, 30045
Anthony Rodriguez, Producing Artistic Dir.
Tel: 678-266-6222
info@auroratheatre.com; www.auroratheatre.com

Est. 1999. **Preference.** Length: full length (over 90 min). Subject: children's, Hispanic. Production: small cast, simple set, no fly. **Application.** Best Material: full script, audio, bio. Response: 3 mos.

Austin Playhouse
Larry L. King Theater, Box 50533, Austin, TX, 78763
Don Toner, Producing Artistic Dir
Tel: 512-476-0084, Fax: 512-476-3063
austinplayhouse@aol.com; www.austinplayhouse.com

Axis Theatre Company
1 Sheridan Sq., New York, NY, 10014
Randy Sharp, Artistic Dir.
Tel: 212-807-9300, Fax: 212-807-9039
www.axiscompany.org

Est. 1997. **Preference.** Length: one-act (30-60 min.). Material Must Be: unpublished. **Application.** Best Way: invite. Best Material: query.

B Street Theatre
2711 B St., Sacramento, CA, 95816
Buck Busfield, Artistic Dir.
Tel: 916-443-5391, Fax: 916-443-0874
www.bstreettheatre.org

Est. 1991. Equity SPT & TYA. 220 seat thrust. **Preference.** Length: full length (over 90 min). Style: comedy, drama. Production: cast limit 6, no fly. **Application.** Best Way: agent.

Bailiwick Repertory
1229 W. Belmont Ave., Chicago, IL, 60657
David Zak, Artistic Dir.
Tel: 773-883-1090
Bailiwick@Bailiwick.org; www.bailiwick.org

Est. 1982. Mainstage Series; Deaf Bailiwick Artists; The Lesbian Initiative; College/University Playwriting Festival. **Preference.** Length: full length (over 90 min). Subject: gay-lesbian, political, reflecting the diversity of our world. **Application.** Best Way: online.

Barksdale Theatre
1601 Willow Lawn Dr., #301-E, Richmond, VA, 23230
Bruce Miller, Artistic Dir.
Tel: 804-783-1688, Fax: 804-288-6470
www.barksdalerichmond.org

Est. 1953. **Preference.** Length: full length (over 90 min). Production: small cast, no fly or wing space. **Application.** Best Material: query, synopsis. Response: 6 mos query, 1 yr script.

Barrington Stage Company
30 Union Street, Pittsfield, MA, 01201
Attn: Literary Mgr.
Tel: 413-499-5446, Fax: 413-499-5447
bsc@berkshire.net; www.barringtonstageco.org

Est. 1995. **Preference.** Length: full length (over 90 min). Production: cast of 4-8 (plays) or 10-12 (musicals), modest set. **Application.** Best Material: query, 1-pg synopsis, 10-pg sample, audio. Best Time: fall. Response: 1 mo query, 6 mos script.

Barrow Group
312 W. 36th St., #4-W, New York, NY, 10018
K. Lorrel Manning, Literary Mgr.
Tel: 212-760-2615
www.barrowgroup.org

Est. 1986. Equity Nonprofit Tier 2. Offers 1-2 mainstage shows/yr, plus readings and workshops. **Application.** Best Material: query, synopsis. Response: 1 mo query, 4 mos script.

Barter Theatre
Box 867, Abingdon, VA, 24212
Richard Rose, Producing Artistic Dir.
Tel: 276-628-2281, Fax: 276-619-3335
barterinfo@bartertheatre.com; www.bartertheatre.com

Est. 1933. Equity LORT D. 1948 Regional Theater Tony winner. Staff: Mary Lucy Bivins (Assoc. Dir.), Nicholas Piper (Assoc. Dir.), Katy Brown (Art. Dir. of Children's Theatre). **Consideration.** Remuneration: reading, royalties. **Preference.** Length: full length (over 90 min), mid-length (60-90 min.). Style: all styles. Subject: all subjects. **Application.** Best Way: professional recommendation, agent, invite. Best Material: query, synopsis, 10-pg. sample, audio, submission returned with SASE. Best Time: January - April. Deadline: Ongoing. Response: 6-8 months.

Bay Street Theatre
Box 810, Sag Harbor, NY, 11963
Mia Grosjean, Literary Mgr.
Tel: 631-725-0818, Fax: 631-725-0906
www.baystreet.org

Est. 1991. Equity LORT C. Opportunities incl. mainstage season and play reading series. **Preference.** Length: full length (over 90 min). Production: cast limit 9, unit set, no fly or wing space. **Application.** Best Way: agent. Response: 6 mos.

bcurrent
720 Bathurst St, #402, Toronto, ON, M5S 2R4 Canada
Tel: 416-533-1500, Fax: 416-533-1560
info@bcurrent.com; www.bcurrent.ca

Toronto-based arts company that presents and supports performance works emerging from the Canadian and International Black Diaspora. bcurrent hosts annual themed festival. See website for details.

Berkeley Repertory Theatre
2025 Addison St., Berkeley, CA, 94702
Madeleine Oldham, Dramaturg/Literary Mgr
Tel: 510-647-2900
www.berkeleyrep.org

Est. 1968. 1997 Regional Theater Tony winner. Staff: Tony Taccone (Artistic Dir), Les Waters (Assoc Artistic Dir). **Preference.** Length: full length (over 90 min). **Application.** Best Way: professional recommendation. Best Material: full script, SASE. Response: 8 mos.

Berkshire Theatre Festival
Box 797, Stockbridge, MA, 01262
Kate Maguire, Artistic Dir.
Tel: 413-298-5536, Fax: 413-298-3368
www.berkshiretheatre.org

Est. 1928. Equity LORT B. Opportunities incl. student productions, new works. **Preference.** Length: full length (over 90 min), mid-length (60-90 min). Production: cast of up to 8, small orchestra. **Application.** Best Way: agent. Best Material: submissions not returned. Best Time: Oct-Dec. Response: only if interested.

Black Ensemble Theater
4520 North Beacon, Chicago, IL, 60640
Jackie Taylor, Artistic Dir.

Est. 1976 **Preference.** Length: full length (over 90 min). Style: musicals only, except for Black Playwrights Fest. Subject: African-American.

Black Rep
1717 Olive St., Fl. 4, St. Louis, MO, 63103
Ron Himes, Founder & Producing Dir.
Tel: 314-534-3807, Fax: 314-534-4035
www.theblackrep.org

est. 1976 **Preference.** Length: full length (over 90 min). Subject: African-American. **Application.** Best Material: query, synopsis, 3-5 pg. sample, resume to Ameer Harper, Assistant to Executive Director, at ameerh@theblackrep.org.

Black Spectrum Theatre
Roy Wilkins Park, 177 St. & Baisley Blvd Entrance, Mailing Only: 119-07 Merrick Blvd., Jamaica, NY, 11434
Tel: 718-723-1800, Fax: 718-723-1806
info@blackspectrum.com; www.blackspectrum.com

Application. Best Way: Mail full script and contact information.

Black Swan Theater
825-C Merrimon Ave., #318, Asheville, NC, 28804
David B. Hopes, Artistic Dir.
Fax: 828-251-6603
swanthtre@aol.com; www.blackswan.org

Est. 1988. Non-Equity theater specializing in developing new scripts or revisiting classics. **Preference.** Production: modest cast, simple set. Material Must Be: unpublished. **Application.** Best Material: full script. Response: 3 mos.

Blinn College Speech and Theatre Arts Program
Blinn College Speech and Theatre Arts Program, 902 College Ave., Brenham, TX, 77833
Bradley Nies, Theatre Arts Dir./ Speech Instructor

Bloomsburg Theatre Ensemble (BTE)

266 Center St., Bloomsburg, PA, 17815
Gerard P. Stropnicky, Dir
Tel: 570-784-5530, Fax: 570-784-4912
www.bte.org

Est. 1978. **Preference.** Length: full length (over 90 min). Style: adaptation, translation. Subject: rural themes. Production: small to mid-sized cast, unit set. **Application.** Best Way: professional recommendation. Best Material: query, synopsis, sample. Best Time: summer. Response: 3 mos query, 6 mos script.

Blowing Rock Stage Company

Box 2170, Blowing Rock, NC, 28605
Kenneth Kay, Producing Artistic Dir.
Tel: 828-295-9168
info@blowingrockstage.com; www.blowingrockstage.com

Est. 1986. Equity SPT. Opportunities incl. New Voices of the South reading series (est. 2001). **Preference.** Production: cast limit 15, orchestra limit 8. **Application.** Best Material: query, 10-pg sample, audio, submissions not returned. Response: 1 yr.

Blue Coyote Theater Group (BCTG)

Access Theater, 380 Broadway, Fl. 4, New York, NY, 10013
Stephen Speights, Producing Dir.
Tel: 212-966-1047, Fax: 212-966-1047
readings@bluecoyote.org; www.bluecoyote.org

Resident company at Access Theater. Equity Showcase productions, workshops, and readings. **Application.** Best Material: full script, SASE. Response: 2 mos.

Blue Heron Theatre Inc.

Blue Heron Arts Center, Box 20328, Park West Station, New York, NY, 10025
Ardelle Striker, Artistic Dir.
Fax: 212-979-8144
ardelle@blueheron-nyc.org; www.blueheron-nyc.org

Est. 1986. Equity Showcase, Tier V. LOA. Opportunities incl. reading, workshop, or showcase production. **Consideration.** Remuneration: possible future production, reading. **Preference.** Length: full-length. Style: adaptation, drama, translation. Subject: no children's, sociopolitical themes encouraged. **Application.** Best Way: professional recommendation. Best Material: query letter (note theme addressed), synopsis, submissions returned with SASE. Deadline: ongoing. Response: 5/15/2004.

BoarsHead Theatre: Michigan Public Theater

425 S. Grand Ave., Lansing, MI, 48933
Jonathan Courtemanche, Assoc Dir
Tel: 517-484-7800, Fax: 517-484-2564
www.boarshead.org

Est. 1966. Equity SPT-6, 250 seat house. Staff: Kristine Thatcher (Artistic Dir), Marlene Shelton (Managing Dir). **Consideration.** Remuneration: royalty. **Application.** Best Material: query, synopsis, SASE. Response: 6 mos.

Bond Street Theatre

2 Bond St., New York, NY, 10012
Joanna Sherman, Artistic Dir.
Tel: 212-254-4614, Fax: 212-460-9378
info@bondst.org; www.bondst.org

Preference. Style: nonverbal scripts (dance, masks, music, circus arts, gestural arts). **Application.** Best Material: query, synopsis, SASE. Response: 1 mo.

Borderlands Theater
Box 2791, Tucson, AZ, 85702
Toni Press-Coffman, Literary Mgr.
Tel: 520-882-8607, Fax: 520-884-4264
tpplay@cox.net; www.borderlandstheater.org

Est. 1986. **Preference.** Length: full length (over 90 min). Style: adaptation, translation. Subject: cultural diversity, race relations, border issues. Production: cast limit 12, minimal set. **Application.** Best Material: query, synopsis. Response: 1 mo query, 6 mos script.

Boston Playwrights' Theatre
Boston Univ., 949 Commonwealth Ave., Boston, MA, 02215
Michael Duncan Smith, Program Coordinator
Tel: 617-353-5443, Fax: 617-353-6196
newplays@bu.edu; www.bu.edu/bpt

Est. 1981. Equity SPT. Opportunities incl. production and workshop. **Consideration.** Remuneration: $500 honorarium. **Preference.** Production: cast limit 8, black box set. Author Must Be: student or alum of Boston Univ. Material Must Be: unoptioned, unpublished, unproduced. **Application.** Best Way: unsolicited. Best Material: query, SASE. Response: 6 mos.

Brat Productions
56 S. 2nd St., Philadelphia, PA, 19106
Tel: 215-627-2577, Fax: 215-627-4304
info@bratproductions.org; www.bratproductions.org

Est. 1996. **Preference.** Length: full length (over 90 min). Production: cast limit 7, unit set. **Application.** Best Material: query, synopsis, sample. Best Time: summer. Response: 1 mo query, 6 mos script.

Brava! for Women in the Arts
2781 24th St., San Francisco, CA, 94110
Ellen Gavin, Artistic Dir
Tel: 415-641-7657, Fax: 415-641-7684
ellen@brava.org; www.brava.org

Est. 1986. **Preference.** Length: full length (over 90 min), one-act (30-60 min). Author Must Be: lesbian or woman of color. **Application.** Best Material: query, synopsis, sample. Response: 6 mos query, 8 mos script.

Bristol Riverside Theatre [PA]
Box 1250, Bristol, PA, 19007
Edward Keith Baker, Artistic Dir
Tel: 215-785-6664, Fax: 215-785-2762
Keith@brtstage.org; www.brtstage.org

Est. 1986. **Preference.** Subject: cutting-edge works, plays that experiment with form. Production: cast limit 10 (plays) or 18 (musicals), orchestra limit 9. **Application.** Best Material: full script. Response: 18 mos.

Broken Watch Theatre Company
311 W. 43rd St., #602, New York, NY, 10036
Drew DeCorleto, Artistic Dir
Tel: 212-397-2935, Fax: 775-263-6024
contact@brokenwatch.org; www.brokenwatch.org

Est. 2001. Equity Showcase. Staff: Stephen P. Brumble Jr (Development Dir). **Preference.** Length: full length (over 90 min), mid-length (60-90 min). Style: comedy, drama. Author Must Be: resident or citizen of US. Material Must Be: unoptioned, unpublished, unproduced. **Application.** Best Way: professional recommendation. Best Material: synopsis, SASE.

Bryant-Lake Bowl Theater

810 W. Lake St., Minneapolis, MN, 55408
Kristin Van Loon, Artistic Dir.
Tel: 612-825-8949, Fax: 612-825-7109

Cabaret performance space of 90 seats that facilitates performance through active collaboration between producer and staff. **Preference.** Length: one-act (under 90 mins.). Style: all styles. Subject: all subjects. **Application.** Best Way: unsolicited. Best Material: query letter (note theme addressed), submissions returned with SASE. Deadline: ongoing. Response: 5/15/2004.

Buntville Crew

118 North Railroad, Buckley, IL, 60918
Steven Packard, Artistic Director

est. 1999 **Preference.** Material Must Be: unoptioned, unpublished. **Application.** Best Way: unsolicited. Best Material: full script.

12/16/2008. Burning Coal Theatre Company

Box 90904, Raleigh, NC, 27675
Marc Williams, Dir, New Works
Tel: 919-834-4001
burningcoal@ipass.net; www.burningcoal.org

Est. 1995. 4 staged readings/yr. **Consideration.** Remuneration: reading. **Preference.** Length: mid-length (60-90 min). Author Must Be: resident of NC. Material Must Be: unpublished, unproduced. **Application.** Best Material: full script, SASE. Deadline: 16-Dec-08. Response: 6 mos.

Caldwell Theatre Company

7873 N. Federal Hwy., Boca Raton, FL, 33487
New Plays
www.caldwelltheatre.com

Est. 1975. Equity LOA. Playsearch series reads 4 plays annually with 500-600 people in audience. **Consideration.** Assistance: Travel assistance. **Preference.** Length: full-length. Style: all styles. Subject: all subjects. Production: cast of up to 8. **Application.** Best Way: professional recommendation, agent submission. Best Material: synopsis. Best Time: spring/summer. Response: varies.

California Theatre Center

Box 2007, Sunnyvale, CA, 94087
Will Huddleston, Resident Dir.
Tel: 408-245-2979, Fax: 408-245-0235
resdir@ctcinc.org; www.ctcinc.org

Est. 1976. Nonprofit for youth. Theatre for young audiences- non- quity. Two types of scripts sought. Cast of 4-8 one hour plays performed for children. Cast of 15-30 one-hour plays performed by children. **Consideration.** Remuneration: neg. fee. **Preference.** Length: one-act (30-60 min). Subject: children's. Production: cast limit 6, touring set. **Application.** Best Way: unsolicited. Best Material: query, synopsis, SASE. Best Time: spring. Response: 4 mos.

Capital Repertory Theatre

111 N. Pearl St., Albany, NY, 12207
Elizabeth Doran, Managing Director
Tel: 518-462-4531, Fax: 518-465-0213
www.capitalrep.org

Est. 1981. LORT D.

Caribbean American Repertory Theatre

114-13 Ovid Pl., St. Albans, NY, 11412
Rudolph Shaw, Executive/Art. Dir.
Tel: 718-454-4234
shawcart@aol.com; www.offbroadwayonline.com

Est. 1975. Equity showcase contract. Plays addresing Aforcentric themes. **Preference.** Length: full length (over 90 min). Style: comedy, drama. Subject: Black. Production: cast size 6. Author Must Be: resident NY. **Application.** Best Way: unsolicited. Best Material: full script. Best Time: July. Response: 3 weeks.

Casa Manana Inc.

930 W. 1st St., #200, Ft. Worth, TX, 76102
Denton Yockey, Exec. Producer

Celebration Theatre

7985 Santa Monica Blvd., #109-1, Los Angeles, CA, 90046
John Lavin, Literary Mgr.
Tel: 323-957-1884, Fax: 323-957-1826
celebrationthtr@earthlink.net; www.celebrationtheatre.com

Est. 1982. Equity 99-seat. Accepts scripts for its mainstage season, as well as Celebrating: New Works, a monthly reading series of original, completed, and unproduced works. **Preference.** Length: full length (over 90 min). Subject: GLBT. Production: cast limit 12. Material Must Be: original. **Application.** Best Material: 1-pg synopsis, full script, bio. Response: not unless interested.

Center Stage [MD]

700 N. Calvert St., Baltimore, MD, 21202
Otis Ramsey-Zoe, Literary Mgr.
Tel: 410-986-4042
oramseyz@centerstage.org; www.centerstage.org

Est. 1963. Equity LORT B, C. **Preference.** Length: full length (over 90 min). Material Must Be: unproduced. **Application.** Best Material: query, synopsis, 10-pg sample, audio, SASE.

Center Stage Community Playhouse

Box 138, Bronx, NY, 10461
Donna Bellone, Gen Mgr
Tel: 212-823-6434
info@centerstageplayhouse.org; www.centerstageplayhouse.org

Est. 1969. Nonprofit community theater. **Preference.** Length: one-act (30-60 min), short (under 30 min). Style: adaptation, comedy, drama. Material Must Be: unoptioned, unpublished, unproduced. **Application.** Best Way: invite. Best Material: query, SASE. Best Time: Jan. Response: 2 mos.

Center Theatre Group (CTG)

601 W. Temple St., Los Angeles, CA, 90012
Pier Carlo Talenti, Literary Mgr/Resident Dramaturg
www.centertheatregroup.org

Est. 1967. Incl. Ahmanson Theatre and Mark Taper Forum (1977 Regional Theater Tony winner) at Music Center in L.A. and Kirk Douglas Theatre in Culver City. **Preference.** Length: full length (over 90 min), mid-length (60-90 min.). **Application.** Best Way: professional recommendation. Best Material: query, synopsis, 5-10 pg sample, SASE. Response: 6 wks.

Chameleon Theatre Company Ltd.

25-26 42nd St., #3-B, Astoria, NY, 11103
Robert D. Carver, Artistic Dir.
tdcarver 2526 @hotmail; robertcarver@yahoo.com

Est. 1987. Dedicated to developing new plays and musicals, primarily originated in-house or recommended by professional associates. Staff: Cash Tilton (Co-Artistic Dir). **Preference.** Material Must Be: unoptioned, unpublished, unproduced. **Application.** Best Way: professional recommendation. Best Material: query, SASE. Response: 2 mos.

Charleston Stage
Box 356, Charleston, SC, 29402
Julian Wiles, Producing Artistic Dir.
Tel: 843-577-5967, Fax: 843-577-5422
cstage@charlestonstage.com; www.charlestonstage.com

Est. 1977. In residence at the Historic Dock Street Theater. **Preference.** Length: full length (over 90 min). Production: small cast. **Application.** Best Way: professional recommendation. Response: 2 mos.

Chicago City Limits
318 W 53rd St., New York, NY, 10019
Tel: 212-888-5233
info@chicagocitylimits.com; www.chicagocitylimits.com

Children's Theatre Company (CTC) [MN]
2400 3rd Ave. S., Minneapolis, MN, 55404
Elissa Adams, Dir, New Play Dev.
Tel: 612-874-0500, Fax: 612-874-8119
www.childrenstheatre.org

Est. 1965. 2003 Regional Theater Tony winner. **Preference.** Length: full length (over 90 min). Subject: children's. **Application.** Best Way: agent.

Childsplay
Box 517, Tempe, AZ, 85280
David Saar, Artistic Dir.
Tel: 480-350-8101, Fax: 480-350-8584
info@childsplayaz.org; www.childsplayaz.org

Est. 1977. Non-Equity TYA. 6 mainstage and 3 touring productions/yr. Opportunities incl Whiteman New Plays Program. **Preference.** Length: mid-length (60-90 min), one-act (30-60 min). Subject: children's. Production: cast of 2-12. **Application.** Best Material: synopsis, 10 pg sample, SASE.

Chinese Theatre Works
34-23 Steinway St., #241, Long Island City, NY, 11101
Tel: 718-392-3493
chinesethrwks@aol.com

Cincinnati Black Theatre Company
5919 Hamilton Avenue, Cincinnati, OH, 45224
Don Sherman, Artistic Dir.
Tel: 513-241-6060, Fax: 513-241-6671
dsherman@cincyblacktheatre.com; www.cincyblacktheatre.com

Preference. Subject: African-American.

Cincinnati Playhouse in the Park
Box 6537, Cincinnati, OH, 45206
Literary Dept.
Tel: 513-345-2242, Fax: 513-345-2254
www.cincyplay.com

Est. 1960. Equity LORT B+ and D. 2004 Regional Theater Tony winner. **Preference.** Length: full length (over 90 min). **Application.** Best Way: agent. Best Material: script, audio, SASE. Response: 8 mos.

Cinnabar Theater
3333 Petaluma Blvd. N., Petaluma, CA, 94952
Elly Lichenstein, Exec/Artistic Dir
Tel: 707-763-8920, Fax: 707-763-8929
www.cinnabartheater.org

Est. 1970. Equity MBATT. **Preference.** Length: full length (over 90 min). Production: Youth Program age 8 or older, small set. Material Must Be: unproduced. **Application.** Best Material: synopsis, 10-pg sample, audio, submissions not returned. Response: 1 mo.

City Theatre [FL]
444 Brickell Ave., #229, Miami, FL, 33131
Marco Ramirez, Literary Mgr
Tel: 305-755-9401, Fax: 305-755-9404
info@citytheatre.com; www.citytheatre.com

Est. 1996. Opportunities incl. Winter Shorts and Summer Shorts fests (thru Actors Theater of Louisville), as well as Short Cuts educational tours, Festival Reading Series, and Kid Shorts Project. Summer Shorts also incl. City Dialogues guest artist residency. **Consideration.** Remuneration: royalty. **Preference.** Length: short (under 30 min). Subject: multicultural encouraged. Production: age 20-65, cast limit 10, unit set. Material Must Be: bilingual encouraged. **Application.** Best Material: full script, submissions not returned.

City Theatre Company [PA]
1300 Bingham St., Pittsburgh, PA, 15203
Carlyn Ann Aquiline, Literary Mgr./Dramaturg
Tel: 412-431-4400, Fax: 412-431-5535
caquiline@citytheatrecompany.org; www.citytheatrecompany.org

Est. 1974. Prefer innovative works from under-represented voices that engage the intellect and emotions, that challenge preconceptions about life and theater thru unconventional form, content, and language. **Preference.** Length: full length (over 90 min). Subject: plays of substance and ideas; unconventional in form, content or use of language. Production: cast limit 10. **Application.** Best Material: query, synopsis, 15-20 pg sample, audio, cast list, resume, production history, SASE.

Clarence Brown Theatre (CBT)
Univ. of Tennessee, 206 McClung Tower, Knoxville, TN, 37996
Calvin MacLean, Artistic Dir.
Tel: 865-974-6011, Fax: 865-974-4867
cbt@utk.edu; www.clarencebrowntheatre.org

Est. 1974. **Preference.** Length: full length (over 90 min). Style: comedy, drama. Subject: contemporary US. **Application.** Best Material: query, synopsis, 1-2 pg sample. Response: 1 mo.

Classical Theatre of Harlem
520 Eighth Ave., #313, New York, NY, 10018
Tel: 212-564-9983
www.classicaltheatreofharlem.com

Cleveland Play House
8500 Euclid Ave., Cleveland, OH, 44106
Seth Gordon, Dir, New Play Development
Tel: 216-795-7000, Fax: 216-795-7005
www.clevelandplayhouse.com

Est. 1916. **Preference.** Length: full length (over 90 min). **Application.** Best Material: query, synopsis, 10-pg sample, resume, SASE. Response: 2 mos query, 6 mos script.

Cleveland Public Theatre
Cleveland Public Theatre, 6415 Detroit Ave., Cleveland, OH, 44102
Raymond Bobgan, Exec Artistic Dir.
Tel: 216-631-2727, Fax: 216-631-2575
rbobgan@cptonline.org; www.cptonline.org

Est. 1983. **Consideration.** Remuneration: production. **Preference.** Style: experimental, poetic; politically, intellectually, or spiritually challenging. Subject: challenging, outside mainstream - politically, aesthetically, sociall, etc.... **Application.** Best Material: query, 1-pg synopsis, 10-pg sample, SASE. Response: 9-12 mos.

Cleveland Signstage Theater
11206 Euclid Ave., Cleveland, OH, 44106
William Morgan, Artistic Dir/Producer
Tel: 216-231-8787 x 302, Fax: 216-231-7141
www.signstage.org

Est. 1975. In-school residencies, educational performances about deaf awareness. **Application.** Best Material: synopsis, SASE. Response: only if interested.

Colony Theatre Company

555 N. Third St., Burbank, CA, 91502
Michael David Wadler, Literary Mgr.
Tel: 818-558-7000, Fax: 818-558-7110
michaelwadler@colonytheatre.org; www.colonytheatre.org

Est. 1975. Equity LOA. **Preference.** Length: full length (over 90 min). Production: cast limit 5. **Application.** Best Material: query, synopsis, 10-pg sample, breakdown, resume.

Columbus Children's Theatre (CCT)

372 W. Nationwide Blvd., Columbus, OH, 43215
William Goldsmith, Artistic Dir.
Tel: 614-224-6673, Fax: 614-224-8844
BGShows@aol.com; www.colschildrenstheatre.org

Est. 1963. **Preference.** Length: one-act (30-60 min). Subject: children's, social issues. Production: cast limit 4, touring set. **Application.** Best Material: full script. Best Time: Sep-Nov. Response: 4 mos.

Commonweal Theatre Company

Box 15, Lanesboro, MN, 55949
Hal Cropp, Exec Dir
hal@commonwealtheatre.org; www.commonwealtheatre.org

Est. 1989. Non-Equity company producing at least 1 new work/season. **Consideration.** Remuneration: 8\% royalty. **Preference.** Length: full length (over 90 min). Style: adaptation, comedy, drama. Production: cast of 3-10. Material Must Be: unproduced. **Application.** Best Material: query, synopsis, 10-pg sample, SASE. Response: 6 mos.

Company of Fools

Box 329, Hailey, ID, 83333
Denise Simone, Assoc Artistic Dir.
Tel: 208-788-6520, Fax: 208-788-1053
Denise@companyoffools.org; www.companyoffools.org

Est. 1992. **Preference.** Length: full length (over 90 min), one-act (30-60 min). Style: no musical. Subject: children's, US themes. Production: cast limit 13. **Application.** Best Material: query, synopsis. Response: 3 mos query, 4 mos script.

Conejo Players Theatre

351 S. Moorpark Rd., Thousand Oaks, CA, 91361
Dick Johnson, Exec Dir.
Tel: 805-495-3715, Fax: 805-435-8100
www.conejoplayers.org

Est. 1958. Mainstage productions run 5 wks; Afternoon series, 4 wks; Children's series, 2 wks. **Consideration.** Remuneration: royalty. **Preference.** Length: full length (over 90 min). Style: comedy, drama, musical. **Application.** Best Material: full script, SASE. Best Time: Jan-Mar. Response: 3 mos.

Coney Island, USA

1208 Surf Ave., Brooklyn, NY, 11224
Dick D. Zigun, Artistic Dir.
Tel: 718-372-5159, Fax: 718-372-5101
dzigun@coneyisland.com; www.coneyisland.com

Est. 1980. **Preference.** Style: vaudeville, Americana sideshow. **Application.** Best Material: query, synopsis, resume, reviews. Response: 1 mo query, 6 mos script.

Congo Square Theatre Company

2936 N. Southportt #210, Chicago, IL, 60657
Derrick Sanders, Artistic Dir.
Tel: 773-296-1108, Fax: 773-472-6634
atdouglas125@congosquaretheatre.org; www.congosquaretheatre.org

Preference. Subject: theatre spawned from the African..

Contemporary American Theater Festival (CATF)
Box 429, Shepherdstown, WV, 25443
Ed Herendeen, Producing Dir.
Tel: 304-876-3473, Fax: 304-876-5443
eherende@shepherd.edu; www.catf.org

Est. 1991. Equity LORT D. **Preference.** Length: full length (over 90 min). **Application.** Best Way: agent. Best Material: query, synopsis.

Contemporary American Theatre Company (CATCO)
77 S. High St., Fl. 2, Columbus, OH, 43215
Jonathan Putnam, Assoc Artistic Dir.
writers@catco.org; www.catco.org

Est. 1984. Equity SPT 6, LORT B. 5-6 plays/season. **Consideration.** Remuneration: royalty. **Preference.** Length: full length (over 90 min), mid-length (60-90 min). Subject: no children's. Production: cast limit 10, set limit 2. **Application.** Best Material: synopsis, 10-pg sample. Response: 6 mos.

Cornerstone Theater Company
708 Traction Ave., Los Angeles, CA, 90013
Michael John Garces, Artistic Dir.
Tel: 213-613-1700, Fax: 213-613-1714
mgarces@cornerstonetheater.org; www.cornerstonetheater.org

Est. 1986. Primaily interested in collaborating with playwrights to develop new work. **Preference.** Length: full length (over 90 min). **Application.** Best Material: query. Response: 2 mos.

Coterie Theatre
2450 Grand Ave., #144, Kansas City, MO, 64108
Jeff Church, Artistic Dir.
Fax: 816-474-7112
www.coterietheatre.org

Est. 1979. Equity TYA. **Preference.** Length: mid-length (60-90 min). Style: adaptation, drama, musical. Subject: TYA. Production: cast limit 10, orchestra limit 3, no fly or wing space. **Application.** Best Material: query, synopsis, 1-scene sample, audio, SASE. Response: 1 mo query, 4 mos script.

Court Theatre
Univ. of Chicago, 5535 S. Ellis Ave., Chicago, IL, 60637
Charles Newell, Artistic Dir.
Tel: 773-702-0434, Fax: 773-834-1897
www.courttheatre.org

Est. 1955. Equity LORT D. In residence at Univ. of Chicago. New adaptations and translations of classical material or new work that corresponds to a classical-based repertory. **Preference.** Length: full length (over 90 min). Style: adaptation, translation. Subject: classics. Production: cast of 8-10, thrust stage, limited fly. **Application.** Best Way: invite. Best Material: query, synopsis, 30-pg sample.

Creative Evolution
21-70 Crescent St., #A-1, Astoria, NY, 11105
Michelle Colletti, Artistic Dir.
Tel: 718-821-2682
cevolution@mindspring.com; www.creative-evolution.org

Est. 2000. Nonprofit for women to present work in development. Staff: Lisa Haas (Treasurer). **Preference.** Length: short (under 30 min). **Application.** Best Way: email. Best Material: query, 1-pg proposal, sample, resume, SASE.

Crossroads Theatre Company [NJ]

P.O. Box 238, 7 Livingston Ave., New Brunswick, NJ, 08901
Marshall Jones, Executive Dir.
Tel: 732-249-5581
info@crossroadstheatrecompany.org; www.crossroadstheatrecompany.org

est. 1978 **Preference.** Subject: African-American. **Application.** Best Way: no unsolicited scripts. Deadline: ongoing.

CTA Crossroads Theatre [CA]

California Theater Arts (CTA), 1277 Boulevard Way, Walnut Creek, CA, 94595
Claire Yarrington, Artistic Dir.
Tel: 925-944-0551
www.ctacrossroads.org

Est. 1984. **Preference.** Subject: children's, family. Production: orchestra limit 8. **Application.** Best Material: full script, audio, submissions not returned. Response: 2 mos.

Cumberland County Playhouse

Box 484, Crossville, TN, 38557
Jim Crabtree, Producing Dir.
Tel: 931-484-4324, Fax: 931-484-6299
www.ccplayhouse.com

Est. 1965. **Preference.** Length: full length (over 90 min). Subject: children's, Tenn., South, rural, family audience. **Application.** Best Material: query, synopsis. Best Time: Aug-Dec. Response: 2 wks query, 1 yr script.

Curan Repertory Company

561 Hudson St., #88, New York, NY, 10014
Ken Terrell, Artistic Dir.
Tel: 212-479-0821
kenatcuran@hotmail.com; www.curan.org

Est. 1990. Non-Equity. 5 original full-length plays and one-act fest each season. **Preference.** Length: all length. Style: adaptation, comedy, drama, translation. Subject: all subjects, gay, multi-ethnic. Production: cast of 2-15, small set. **Application.** Best Way: unsolicited, agent. Best Material: query, 10-pg sample, SASE. Best Time: Jan-Mar. Response: 4 mos.

Cyrano's Theatre Company (CTC)

413 D St., Anchorage, AK, 99501
Sandy Harper, Producing Artistic Dir.
Tel: 907-274-2599, Fax: 907-277-4698
cyrano@ak.net; www.cyranos.org

Est. 1992. Formerly Eccentric Theatre Company. **Preference.** Length: full length (over 90 min), one-act (30-60 min). Style: adaptation, comedy, drama. **Application.** Best Way: professional recommendation. Response: 8 mos.

Dad's Garage Theatre Co.

280 Elizabeth St., #C-101, Atlanta, GA, 30307
Kate Warner, Artistic Dir.
kate@dadsgarage.com; www.dadsgarage.com

Est. 1995. **Consideration.** Remuneration: royalty. **Preference.** Style: adaptation, comedy, musical. **Application.** Best Way: professional recommendation. Best Material: query, synopsis, sample.

Dallas Children's Theater

5938 Skillman St., Dallas, TX, 75231
Artie Olaisen, Artistic Assoc
www.dct.org

Est. 1984. Professional family theater. **Preference.** Length: full length (over 90 min). Subject: children's, family. **Application.** Best Material: query, synopsis, cast/scene list.

Dallas Theater Center
3636 Turtle Creek Blvd., Dallas, TX, 75219
Kevin Moriarty, Artistic Dir
Tel: 214-526-8210, Fax: 214-521-7666
www.dallastheatercenter.org

Est. 1959. **Preference.** Length: full length (over 90 min). **Application.** Best Way: professional recommendation. Best Material: synopsis, 10-pg sample. Response: 1 yr.

Danisarte
PO Box 286146, 1617 Third Ave., New York, NY, 10128
Alicia Kaplan, Producing Artistic Director
Tel: 212-561-0191
Danisarte@aol.com; www.danisarte.org

Est. 1992. **Preference.** Subject: children, latino, senior, women. Production: cast limit 6. Material Must Be: unpublished, unproduced. **Application.** Best Way: invite. Best Material: query, SASE.

Delaware Theatre Company
200 Water St., Wilmington, DE, 19801
David Stradley, Artistic. Assoc.
Tel: 302-594-1104, Fax: 302-594-1107
dstradley@delawaretheatre.org; www.delawaretheatre.org

Est. 1978. Equity LORT D. Opportunities incl. reading and production. Season is usually 5-6 productions. **Preference.** Length: full length (over 90 min), mid-length (60-90 min). Production: cast limit 8, small orchestra, unit set. **Application.** Best Way: agent submission only. Response: 6 mos.

Dell'Arte Company
Box 816, Blue Lake, CA, 95525
Michael Fields, Artistic Dir.
Tel: 707-668-5663, Fax: 707-668-5665
dellarte@aol.com; www.dellarte.com

Est. 1977. Equity LOA. Topical and issue-oriented comedy for touring performers. **Preference.** Length: full length (over 90 min). Style: adaptation. Subject: children's. Production: cast of 3-4, touring set. **Application.** Best Material: query, synopsis. Best Time: Jan-Mar.

Detroit Repertory Theatre/Millan Theatre Company
13103 Woodrow Wilson, Detroit, MI, 48238-3686
Barbara Busby, Literary Mgr.

Preference. Style: comedy, drama. Subject: issue-oriented plays. Production: no children.

Discovery Theater
Smithsonian Institution, Box 23293, Washington, DC, 20026
Roberta Gasbarre, Artistic Dir.
Tel: 202-633-8700, Fax: 202-343-1073
gasbaro@si.edu; www.discoverytheater.org

Commissions 4-5 productions each year. **Preference.** Length: one-act (45 mins.). Style: all styles. Subject: children's. **Application.** Best Way: unsolicited. Best Material: synopsis, full script, cast 26 scene breakdown, submissions returned with SASE. Deadline: ongoing.

District of Columbia Arts Center (DCAC)
2438 18th St., NW, Washington, DC, 20009

Est. 1989. Nonprofit in Adams Morgan neighborhood that supports emerging artists trying to get a foothold in the public arena.

Diversionary Theatre

4545 Park Blvd., #101, San Diego, CA, 92116
Dan Kirsch, Exec/Artistic Dir.
Tel: 619-220-0097, Fax: 619-220-0148
www.diversionary.org

Est. 1986. 3rd oldest LGBT theater in US. 6-show season and new-work readings in 106-seat space. Staff: Bret Young (Managing Dir). **Consideration.** Remuneration: royalty. **Preference.** Subject: LGBT. **Application.** Best Way: online. Best Material: application, synopsis, 15-pg sample. Response: 6 mos.

Dixon Place

258 Bowery, Fl. 2, New York, NY, 10012
Ellie Covan, Exec Dir.

Est. 1986. Nonprofit laboratoty theater for NY- based performing and literary artists to create and develop new works in front of a live audience.

Do Gooder Productions

359 W. 54th St., #4-FS, New York, NY, 10019
Tel: 212-581-8852, Fax: 212-541-7928
dgp@dogooder.org; www.dogooder.org

Dobama Theatre

2490 Lee Blvd., #325, Cleveland Heights, OH, 44118
Joyce Casey, Artistic Dir.
Tel: 216-932-6838, Fax: 216-932-3259
dobama@dobama.org; www.dobama.org

Est. 1959. **Preference.** Length: full length (over 90 min). Production: cast limit 9, no fly. Author Must Be: resident of OH. **Application.** Best Material: query, synopsis, sample.

Double Edge Theatre

948 Conway Rd., Ashfield, MA, 01330
Carlos Uriona, Producing Dir.
Tel: 413-628-0277, Fax: 831-307-6159
office@doubleedgetheatre.org; www.doubleedgetheatre.org

Est. 1982. Opportunities incl. Individual Artist Retreats. **Preference.** Style: solo, performance art. **Application.** Best Material: video. Response: 6 mos.

3/15/08, 8/15/08, 12/01/08. Downstage Left (DSL)

Stage Left Theatre, 3408 North Sheffield, Chicago, IL, 60657
John Sanders, DSL Director
Tel: 773-883-8830 ext. 3
john@stagelefttheatre.com; www.stagelefttheatre.com

Consideration. Assistance:. Remuneration: royalty. **Preference.** Length: full length (over 90 min). **Application.** Best Way: submit application online. Best Material: full script, 1 page synopsis, resume, SASE. Deadline: 3/15/2008, 8/15/2008, 12/1/2008.

Dream Theatre

484 W. 43rd St., #14-Q, New York, NY, 10036
Andrea Leigh, Artistic Dir.
Tel: 212-564-2628
andrealeigh88@hotmail.com

Est. 2001. New works that have not been optioned or produced in NYC. Application. Best Way: e-mail. **Application.** Best Material: synopsis, full script, submissions not returned. Response: 6 mos..

Drilling Company
107 W. 82nd St., #1-A, New York, NY, 10024
Hamilton Clancy, Artistic Dir.
Tel: 212-877-4234, Fax: 212-877-0099
DrillingCompany@aol.com; www.drillingcompany.org

Est. 1999. Commissions for shorts produced in NYC, workshops for full-lengths. Staff: Dave Marantz (Asst Artistic Dir). **Consideration.** Remuneration: $500 . **Preference.** Length: short (under 30 min). Style: comedy, drama, musical. Material Must Be: unoptioned, unpublished, unproduced. **Application.** Best Way: professional recommendation. Best Material: 10-pg sample, submissions not returned. Best Time: Jan. Response: 3 mos.

East West Players
120 N. Judge John Aiso St., Los Angeles, CA, 90012
Jeff Liu, Literary Mgr.
Tel: 213-625-7000 x27, Fax: 213-625-7111
jliu@eastwestplayers.org; www.eastwestplayers.org

Est. 1965. 4 mainstage productions/season in addition to readings. **Preference.** Length: full length (over 90 min). Subject: Asian American. **Application.** Best Material: query, synopsis, full script, resume, SASE. Response: 9 mos.

Egyptian Theatre Company
328 Main St., Box 3119, Park City, UT, 84060
Terence Goodman, Artistic Dir.
Tel: 435-645-0671, Fax: 435-649-0446
terence@parkcityshows.com; www.egyptiantheatrecompany.org

Est. 1981. **Preference.** Length: full length (over 90 min). Style: musical. **Application.** Best Way: professional recommendation. Response: 6 mos.

El Centro Su Teatro
4725 High St., Denver, CO, 80216
Tony Garcia, Artistic Dir.
Tel: 303-296-0219, Fax: 303-296-4614
elcentro@suteotro.org; www.suteatro.org

Est. 1971. **Preference.** Length: full length (over 90 min), one-act (30-60 min). Style: no musical. Subject: children's, Chicano/Latino. Production: cast of 6-8. Material Must Be: bilingual or Spanish. **Application.** Best Material: full script. Best Time: Oct-Jan. Response: 6 mos.

Emelin Theatre for the Performing Arts
153 Library Ln., Mamaroneck, NY, 10543
Michale Bush, Artistic Dir.
Tel: 914-698-3045, Fax: 914-698-1404
emelin98@aol.com; www.emelin.org

Est. 1972. **Preference.** Length: full length (over 90 min). Production: small cast, no fly. **Application.** Best Way: professional recommendation. Response: 6 mos.

Emerging Artists Theatre (EAT)
311 W. 43rd St., Suite 307, New York, NY, 10036-6030
Paul Adams, Artistic Dir
Tel: 212-247-2429
eattheatre@gmail.com; www.eatheatre.org

Est. 1993. Develop and produce new work from shorts to full-lengths. **Preference.** Length: all length. Style: comedy, drama, musical. Subject: Black, disabled, gay, latino, senior, women. Production: 20-70, cast 2-10. Material Must Be: unproduced. **Application.** Best Way: call for scripts thru DG. Best Material: query, synopsis (full-lengths), by email, SASE. Response: 3-6 mos.

Encompass New Opera Theatre

138 S. Oxford St., #1-A, Brooklyn, NY, 11217
Nancy Rhodes, Artistic Dir.
Tel: 718-398-4675, Fax: 718-398-4684
encompassopera@yahoo.com; www.encompassopera.org

Est. 1975. Contemporary opera and music theater. Staff: Lisa E. Harris (Mgr.) **Preference.** Style: musical. **Application.** Best Way: professional recommendation. Best Material: query, synopsis, audio, SASE. Best Time: Jun.

Enrichment Works

5605 Woodman Ave., # 207, Van Nuys, CA, 91401
Abraham Tetenbaum, Exec Dir
Tel: 818-780-1400, Fax: 818-780-0300
atetenbaum@enrichmentworks.org; www.enrichmentworks.org

Est. 1999. Nonprofit presenting tours in L.A. schools and community venues of works to inspire learning. **Consideration.** Remuneration: 10\% royalty. **Preference.** Length: one-act (30-60 min). Style: comedy, drama, musical. Subject: children's. Production: cast limit 3, touring set. **Application.** Best Material: full script, SASE. Best Time: Oct-Feb. Response: 6 mos.

Ensemble Theater [Cleveland, OH]

Box 181309, Cleveland Heights, OH, 44118
Tel: 216-321-2930
ensemble-theater@sbcglobal.net

Ensemble Theatre [TX]

3535 Main St., Houston, TX, 77002
Eileen J. Morris, Artistic Dir.
Tel: 713-520-0055
ejmorris@ensemblehouston.com; www.ensemblehouston.com

Est. 1976. **Preference.** Length: full length (over 90 min) for mainstage productions. Subject: African, African-American, children's, also needed plays for youth ages 8-18 that relte to math and science. Production: cast limit 5, touring set. **Application.** Best Material: query, synopsis, sample, audio, resume, SASE. Best Time: Sep-Jan. Response: 3 mos.

Ensemble Theatre Company of Santa Barbara [CA]

Box 2307, Santa Barbara, CA, 93120
Jonathan Fox, Exec Artistic Dir.
Tel: 805-962-5365, Fax: 805-965-5400
info@ensembletheatre.com; www.ensembletheatre.com

Est. 1979. **Preference.** Length: full length (over 90 min), mid-length (60-90 min.). Production: cast limit 8, unit set. **Application.** Best Way: invite. Best Material: query, synopsis, 10-pg sample, submissions not returned. Response: 9 mos.

Ensemble Theatre of Cincinnati [OH]

1127 Vine St., Cincinnati, OH, 45202
D. Lynn Meyers, Producing Artistic Dir.
Tel: 513-421-3555, Fax: 513-562-4104

Est. 1986. **Preference.** Length: full length (over 90 min). Production: cast limit 10, simple set. **Application.** Best Material: query, synopsis, sample, resume. Response: 2 mo query, 4 mos script.

eta Creative Arts Foundation Inc.

7558 S. Chicago Ave., Chicago, IL, 60619
Runako Jahi, Artistic Dir.
email@etacreativearts.org; www.etacreativearts.org

Est. 1971. Playwrights Speak Reading Series: staged readings followed by discussion, plays considered for mainstage productions. **Preference.** Subject: African-American. **Application.** Best Way: unsolicited. Best Material: synopsis, full script, bio, submissions returned with SASE. Deadline: ongoing.

Express Children's Theatre

Houston Community Coll., 446 Northwest Mall, Houston, TX, 77092
Pat Silver, Exec Dir
Tel: 713-682-5044
expresstheatre@sbcglobal.net; www.expresstheatre.com

Est. 1991. In residence at Houston Community Coll. Central Fine Arts Dept. **Preference.** Length: one-act (30-60 min). Style: multi-ethnic. Subject: children's. Production: cast of 3-4, touring set. Material Must Be: bilingual encouraged. **Application.** Best Material: query, synopsis. Response: 2 wks query, 8 ws script.

11/15/2008. First Light Festival

Theater of the First Amendment (TFA), George Mason Univ., 4400 University Dr., MS 3E6, Fairfax, VA, 22030
Suzanne Maloney, Asst Dramaturg
Tel: 703-993-2195, Fax: 703-993-2191
smaloney@gmu.edu; www.gmu.edu/cfa

Annual fest of new play readings. **Preference.** Length: full length (over 90 min). Style: no musical. Subject: no children's. **Application.** Best Material: query, sample. Deadline: 15-Nov-08. Response: 2 wks query, 6 mos script.

First Stage Children's Theater [WI]

325 W. Walnut St., Milwaukee, WI, 53212
Rob Goodman, Managing Dir.
Tel: 414-267-2929, Fax: 414-267-2930
rgoodman@firststage.org; www.firststage.org

Est. 1987. **Preference.** Style: adaptation, musical, translation. Subject: children's. **Application.** Best Material: query, synopsis, resume. Best Time: spring-summer. Response: 1 mo query, 3 mos script.

Flat Rock Playhouse

Box 310, Flat Rock, NC, 28731
Robin R. Farquhar, Artistic/Exec Dir

Flea Theater

41 White St., New York, NY, 10013
Gary Winter, Literary Mgr.
Tel: 212-226-0051, Fax: 212-965-1808
garyw@theflea.org; www.theflea.org

Est. 1996. Produces 3 original shows/yr plus theater, music, dance, and cross-disciplinary pieces in a second space. Also offers mini-fests and regular ongoing programs, incl. Pataphysics playwriting workshops. **Preference.** Length: full length (over 90 min). Subject: political themes, language-driven plays. Production: ages 20-30. **Application.** Best Way: agent. Best Time: May-Sep. Response: 1 yr.

Florida Repertory Theatre

2267 1st St., Fort Myers, FL, 33901
Bari Newport, Assoc Dir
www.floridarep.org

Est. 1989. Equity LORT D. 8 mainstage plays Sep-Jun. Staff: Robert Cacioppo (Producing Artistic Dir). **Preference.** Length: full length (over 90 min). Style: all styles. Subject: children's, senior, women, Florida. Production: cast limit 10, orchestra of 4-5, sets limit 2. **Application.** Best Way: agent. Best Material: synopsis, full script, SASE. Best Time: Jan-May. Response: 1 yr.

Florida Stage

262 S. Ocean Blvd., Manalapan, FL, 33462
Javier Chacin, Artistic Assoc
Tel: 561-585-3404, Fax: 561-588-4708
javier@floridastage.org; www.floridastage.org

Est. 1987. Equity LORT C. Thought-provoking, issue-oriented material. Opportunities incl New Works Fest. **Preference.** Length: full length (over 90 min). Style: comedy, drama. Subject: contemporary issues and ideas. Production: cast of 2-6, unit set. Material Must Be: unproduced. **Application.** Best Way: email. Best Material: query, synopsis, 10-page sample, playwright bio. Response: 4 mos.

Florida Studio Theatre

1241 N. Palm Ave., Sarasota, FL, 34236
Cristin Kelly, Literary Manager
Tel: 941-366-9017, Fax: 941-955-4137
ckelly@floridastudiotheatre.org; www.floridastudiotheatre.org

Preference. Length: full length (over 90 min). **Application.** Best Material: query, synopsis, 5-pg sample, SASE. Best Time: Aug-Apr. Response: 1 month query, 6 mos script.

Foothill Theatre Company

Box 1812, Nevada City, CA, 95959
Gary Wright, Assoc Artist
Tel: 530-265-9320, Fax: 530-265-9325
gary@foothilltheatre.org; www.foothilltheatre.org

Est. 1977. Opportunities incl New Voices of the West staged readings. **Consideration.** Remuneration: reading. Frequency: annual. **Preference.** Length: full length (over 90 min), mid-length (60-90 min). Subject: rural American West. Production: cast limit 6. Material Must Be: unproduced. **Application.** Best Material: query, synopsis, 10-pg sample, SASE. Response: 1 yr.

Ford's Theatre Society

511 10th St., NW, Washington, DC, 20004
Paul Tetreault, Producing Dir
www.fordstheatre.org

Est. 1968. Equity LORT. 4-5 shows/yr, incl. perhaps 1 original play or musical. Staff: Mark Ramont (Assoc Prod/Artistic Dir). **Consideration.** Remuneration: royalty. **Preference.** Length: full length (over 90 min). Subject: US historical. Production: orchestra limit 7. **Application.** Best Way: professional recommendation. Best Material: query, synopsis, 10-pg sample, SASE. Response: 1 yr.

Fountain Theatre

5060 Fountain Ave., Los Angeles, CA, 90029
Simon Levy, Producing Dir./Dramaturg
Tel: 323-663-2235, Fax: 323-663-1629
www.fountaintheatre.com

Equity 99-seat. **Consideration.** Remuneration: 6\% royalty. **Preference.** Length: full length (over 90 min), mid-length (60-90 min). Style: no translation. Production: cast limit 12, unit set, no fly. **Application.** Best Way: professional recommendation. Best Material: query, synopsis. Response: 3 mos.

Fountainhead Theatre

2003 Columbia Pike, #218, Arlington, VA, 22204
Charlotte Akin, Artistic Director
Tel: 703-920-5923, Fax: 703-920-5923

Est. 1992 as New Theater Company (NTC).

Free Street Programs

1419 W. Blackhawk St., Chicago, IL, 60622
Bryn Magnus, Managing Dir
www.freestreet.org

Est. 1969. Creates experimental work in collaboration with youth, emerging and professional artists. Staff: Ron Bieganski (Artistic Director), Anita Evans (Creative Director) **Application.** Best Way: invite. Submissions not accepted.. Best Material: query with project ideas, submissions not returned. Best Time: summer-fall.

Freed-Hardeman Univ.
Theater Dept., 158 E. Main St., Henderson, TN, 38340
Cliff Thompson, Dir. of Theater
Tel: 731-989-6780
cthompson@fhu.edu

Preference. Length: full-length, one-act. Style: all styles. Subject: children's, religious, women's. **Application.** Best Way: unsolicited. Best Material: synopsis, 30-pg writing sample, submissions returned with SASE. Best Time: after 12/15/03. Deadline: ongoing.

Freedom Repertory Theatre
1346 N. Broad St., Philadelphia, PA, 19121
Walter Dallas, Producing Artistic Dir
Tel: 215-765-2793, Fax: 215-765-4191
www.freedomtheatre.org

Est. 1966. **Preference.** Length: full length (over 90 min). Subject: African-American, contemporary themes. **Application.** Best Way: professional recommendation. Response: 3 mos.

GableStage
1200 Anastasia Ave., Coral Gables, FL, 33134
Joseph Adler, Producing Artistic Dir
Tel: 305-446-1116, Fax: 305-445-8645
jadler@gablestage.org; www.gablestage.org

Est. 1979. Equity SPT-5. 6 productions/yr. **Preference.** Length: full length (over 90 min). **Application.** Best Material: query.

GALA Hispanic Theatre
Box 43209, Washington, DC, 20010
Hugo Medrano, Producing Artistic Dir
www.galatheatre.org

Est. 1976. **Preference.** Length: full length (over 90 min). Subject: Latino. Production: cast of 6-8. Author Must Be: Spanish, Latino or Hispanic. Material Must Be: in Spanish or English only. **Application.** Best Material: query, synopsis. Best Time: Apr-May. Response: 1 mo query, 1 yr script.

Geffen Playhouse
10886 LeConte Ave, Los Angeles, CA, 90024
Amy Levinson Millan, Literary Mgr/Dramaturg
www.geffenplayhouse.com

Est. 1995. **Preference.** Length: full length (over 90 min). **Application.** Best Way: agent. Response: 6 mos.

Genesis Repertory Ensemble
23-23 30th Ave., Fl. 2, Astoria, NY, 11102
J. Michaels, Artistic Dir
Tel: 646-226-0370
genesisnyc@gmail.com; www.genesis-repertory.org

Est. 1999. New works, non-Equity and Equity Showcase. **Application.** Best Material: full script. Response: 2 mos.

George Street Playhouse
9 Livingston Ave., New Brunswick, NJ, 08901
Jeremy Stoller, Literary Apprentice
www.georgestplayhouse.org

Est. 1974. Equity LORT C. Productions, readings, tours of issue-oriented 40-min one-acts for schools, and Next Stage Fest workshops. Prefer fresh perspectives on society, compelling personal and human stories that entertain, challenge, and stretch the imagination. **Preference.** Length: full length (over 90 min), mid-length (60-90 min). Style: no translation. Production: cast limit 7. **Application.** Best Way: professional recommendation. Best Material: query, synopsis, 10-pg sample, cast/scene list, tech needs. Response: 10 mos.

Georgia Shakespeare

4484 Peachtree Rd. NE, Atlanta, GA, 30319

Est. 1985. Staff. Richard Garner (Producing Artistic Dir); Stacy Shaw (Managing Dir).

Germinal Stage Denver

2450 W. 44th Ave., Denver, CO, 80211
Ed Baierlein, Dir/Mgr
Tel: 303-455-7108
gsden@privatei.com; www.germinalstage.com

Est. 1974. **Preference.** Length: full length (over 90 min). Production: cast limit 10. **Application.** Best Material: query, synopsis, 5-pg sample. Response: 2 wks query, 6 mos script.

Geva Theatre Center

75 Woodbury Blvd., Rochester, NY, 14607
Marge Betley, Literary Mgr/Dramaturg
Tel: 585-232-1366, Fax: 585-232-4031
www.gevatheatre.org

Est. 1972. Equity LORT B and D. Produces classics to musicals to new works, incl. readings and workshops. Staff: Jean Gordon Ryon (New Plays Coord.). **Consideration.** Assistance: stipend, room/board, room/board. **Preference.** Length: full length (over 90 min). **Application.** Best Way: professional recommendation. Best Material: query, synopsis, 10-pg sample, SASE. Response: 3 mos query; 6 mos script.

Golden Fleece Ltd.

70-A Greenwhich Ave., #256, New York, NY, 10011
Lou Rodgers, Producing Artists Dir.
Tel: 212-691-6105
info@goldenfleeceltd.org; www.goldenfleeceltd.org

Est. 1974. Golden Fleece Ltd. nurtures, develops and produces new works by emerging American composers as well as playwrights, lyricists and librettists. The Composers Chamber Theatre; annual commissioned opera/music theater production; Square One Series of works by composers, lyricists and librettists in progress; Argonaut Series of new works by poets and playwrights in progress. **Preference.** Length: short (under 30 min.). Style: all styles. Subject: all subjects. Production: all ages, cast limit of 8, orchestra of 4, set varies. Material Must Be: unpublished, unproduced. **Application.** Best Way: unsolicited, professional recommendation. Best Material: synopsis or treatment, resume, submission returned if SASE provided. Best Time: Oct. 1. Deadline: ongoing. Response: varies.

Goodman Theatre

170 N. Dearborn St., Chicago, IL, 60601
Tanya Palmer, Literary Mgr
www.goodmantheatre.org

Est. 1925. Equity LORT B+ and C. 1992 Regional Theater Tony winner. Staff: Robert Falls (Artistic Dir.), Roche Schulfer (Exec. Dir.). **Preference.** Length: full length (over 90 min). **Application.** Best Way: agent. Best Material: 10 pg sample. Response: 6 mos.

Goodspeed Musicals

Box A, East Haddam, CT, 06423
Donna Lynn Cooper Hilton, Line Producer
Tel: 860-873-8664, Fax: 860-873-2329
info@goodspeed.org; www.goodspeed.org

Est. 1959. 1995 Regional Theater Tony winner. Staff: Michael P. Price (Exec. Dir.). **Preference.** Length: full length (over 90 min). Style: musical. **Application.** Best Way: agent.

Great Lakes Theater Festival

1501 Euclid Ave., # 300, Cleveland, OH, 44115
Charles Fee, Producing Artistic Dir.
Tel: 216-241-5490
www.greatlakestheater.org

Est. 1961. **Preference.** Length: full length (over 90 min). Style: adaptation, translation, relevant to classical repertoire. **Application.** Best Way: professional recommendation. Response: 3 mos.

Greenbrier Valley Theatre

113 E. Washington St., Lewisburg, WV, 24901
Cathey Sawyer, Artistic Dir.
Tel: 304-645-3838, Fax: 304-645-3818
www.gvtheatre.org

Est. 1967. Equity LOA. **Preference.** Length: full length (over 90 min), mid-length (60-90 min). Style: adaptation, comedy or variety, drama, musical. Subject: Black, children's, senior, women. Production: age 7 and older, cast of 6-10, orchestra of 1-4, set limit 1. Author Must Be: resident of US. Material Must Be: unoptioned, unproduced. **Application.** Best Way: professional recommendation, agent. Best Material: synopsis, 5-pg sample, submissions not returned. Best Time: Dec-Feb. Response: 6 mos.

Gretna Theatre

Box 578, Mt. Gretna, PA, 17064
Larry Frenock, Producing Dir
Tel: 717-964-3322
www.gretnatheatre.com

Est. 1927. Equity Guest Artists LOA. Opportunities incl. reading. **Preference.** Length: full length (over 90 min). **Application.** Best Material: synopsis, 5-pg sample, audio. Best Time: Nov-Feb. Response: 1 mo query, 3 mos script.

Growing Stage - The Children's Theatre of New Jersey

P.O. Box 36, Netcong, NJ, 07857
Stephen L. Fredericks, Exec Dir
Tel: 973-347-4946, Fax: 973-691-7069
exdir@growingstage.com; www.growingstage.com

Est. 1982. **Preference.** Length: full length (over 90 min). Subject: intelligent theater for the entire family. **Application.** Best Material: full script, audio, SASE. Best Time: Jun-Aug. Response: 4 mos.

Guthrie Theater

818 S. 2nd St., Minneapolis, MN, 55415
Michael Kinghorn, Literary Mgr.
www.guthrietheater.org

Est. 1963. Equity LORT A, B, D. 1982 Regional Theater Tony winner. New Play Program has over 110 commissions, workshops, publications or productions. New 3-theater complex opened 2006, incl. 1100-seat thrust, 700-seat proscenium, and 199-seat studio. **Preference.** Length: full length (over 90 min). **Application.** Best Way: agent only. Best Material: full script. Response: 6 mos.

Hadley Players

207 W. 133rd St., New York, NY, 10030
Tel: 212-368-9314
hadleyplayers@yahoo.com

Preference. Subject: African-American or Hispanic-American. **Application.** Best Material: 10 pg. sample, SASE.

Hangar Theatre KIDDSTUFF
Box 205, Ithaca, NY, 14850
Wendy Dann, Assoc Artistic Dir
wendy@hangartheatre.org; www.hangartheatre.org

Staff: Robert Moss (Interim Artistic Dir). **Consideration.** Remuneration: royalty. **Preference.** Length: one-act (30-60 min). Subject: children's, families. **Application.** Best Material: full script, SASE. Response: 6 mos.

Harlem Stage at The Gatehouse
150 Convent Ave, New York, NY, 10031
Tel: 212-281-9240, Fax: 212-281-9318

Sunday Works reading Series. **Preference.** Subject: new work by artists of color.

Harlequin Productions
Cayuga Community College, 197 Franklin St., Auburn, NY, 13021
Robert Frame, Dir, Theater
framer@cayuga-cc.edu; www.cayuga-cc.edu

Est. 1958. 6 perfs over 2 weekends (fall and spring) with college students in high-quality extracurricular program. **Consideration.** Remuneration: flat fee. **Preference.** Style: adaptation, comedy, drama. Production: age 16-35, cast of 7-14. **Application.** Best Material: full script, SASE. Response: 1 yr.

Hartford Stage
50 Church St., Hartford, CT, 06103
Jeremy B. Cohen, Assoc Artistic Dir/New Play Development
www.hartfordstage.org

Est. 1963. Equity LORT B. 1989 Regional Theater Tony winner. **Preference.** Length: full length (over 90 min). **Application.** Best Way: agent, unsolicited (CT residents only). Best Material: full script.

Harwich Junior Theatre (HJT)
Box 168, 105 Division St., West Harwich, MA, 02671
Nina Schuessler, Artistic Dir.
hjt@capecod.net; www.hjtcapecod.org

Est. 1951. New plays for intergenerational casts and audiences. **Consideration.** Remuneration: royalty. **Preference.** Subject: children's. Production: intergenerational, no fly. **Application.** Best Material: synopsis, SASE. Best Time: Sep. Response: 6 mos.

Hedgerow Theatre
64 Rose Valley Rd., Media, PA, 19063
Penelope Reed, Producing Artistic Dir
www.hedgerowtheatre.org

Est. 1923. Readings of new plays by Delaware Vallex writers in readings and workshops. **Preference.** Length: full length (over 90 min). Style: comedy, mystery. Production: cast of 2-8. Author Must Be: resident of NJ, PA, DE. Material Must Be: unpublished, unproduced. **Application.** Best Material: query, synopsis. Response: 2 mos query, 4 mos script.

Hip Pocket Theatre
Box 136758, Ft. Worth, TX, 76136
Johnny Simons, Artistic Dir.
Tel: 817-246-9775
www.hippocket.org

Est. 1977. **Preference.** Length: full length (over 90 min). Subject: stories with poetic-mythic slant using ritual and ensemble. Production: simple set, outdoor amphitheater. **Application.** Best Material: synopsis, sample, audio. Best Time: Oct-Feb. Response: 2 mos.

Hippodrome State Theatre

25 SE 2nd Pl., Gainesville, FL, 32601
Tamerin Dygert, Dramaturg
Tel: 352-373-5968
thehipp.org

Est. 1973. Equity SPT. **Preference.** Length: full length (over 90 min). Production: cast limit 6, unit set. **Application.** Best Way: agent. Best Time: Oct-Mar. Response: 5 mos.

Honolulu Theatre for Youth

229 Queen Emma Sq., Honolulu, HI, 96813
Eric Johnson, Artistic Dir.
Tel: 808-839-9885, Fax: 808-839-7018
htyeric@gmail.com; www.htyweb.org

Est. 1955. Producing and commissioning new plays, Sep-May. **Preference.** Length: mid-length (60-90 min), one-act (30-60 min). Subject: Asian-Pacific, children's. Production: cast limit 5. **Application.** Best Material: query, submissions not returned. Best Time: Apr-Sep.

Horizon Theatre Rep [NY]

41 E. 67th St., New York, NY, 10021
Rafael DeMussa, Artistic Dir.
Tel: 212-737-3357, Fax: 212-737-5103
info@htronline.org; www.htronline.org

Est. 2000. Equity Showcase. Staff: Andrew Cohen (Managing Dir). **Preference.** Length: full length (over 90 min), mid-length (60-90 min). Style: no musical. Production: ages 16-75, cast size 4-15. Material Must Be: unoptioned, unproduced. **Application.** Best Material: synopsis, submissions not returned. Response: 1 mo.

Horse Trade Theater Group

85 E. 4th St., New York, NY, 10003
Morgan Lindsey Tachlo, Assoc Producer
www.horsetrade.info

Est.1998. Readings, workshops, and productions in 3 OOB venues by resident, co-production and rental companies. Staff: Erez Ziv (Managing Dir). **Application.** Best Way: professional recommendation. Best Material: query, sample, SASE.

Hudson Theatres

6539 Santa Monica Blvd., Los Angeles, CA, 90038
Elizabeth Reilly, Artistic Dir.
Tel: 323-856-4252, Fax: 323-856-4316
ereilly@hudsontheater.com; www.hudsontheatre.com

Est. 1991. Primarily rental house Equity 99-seat. Hollywood Theatre Row complex incl. Mainstage, and Backstage (Comedy Central in residence); 43-seat Guild; and Caffe Bacio. **Application.** Best Material: query, synopsis, sample. Response: 6 mos query, 1 yr script.

Human Race Theatre Company

126 N. Main St., #300, Dayton, OH, 45402
Kevin Moore, Exec Dir
www.humanracetheatre.org

Est. 1986. Opportunities incl. Musical Theatre Workshops. **Preference.** Length: full length (over 90 min), one-act (30-60 min). Subject: children's, contemporary issues. Production: small cast, touring set, no fly. Author Must Be: resident of OH. **Application.** Best Way: professional recommendation. Best Time: Dec-Feb. Response: 6 mos.

Hyde Park Theatre

511 W. 43rd St., Austin, TX, 78751
Peck Phillips, Literary Mgr.
peck@hydeparktheatre.org; www.hydeparktheatre.org

Est. 1992. Southwest premieres of alternative and classic works that challenge modern audiences. Also Frontera Fest, 5-wk unjuried fringe fest. Play Development Reading Series is on hold. **Preference.** Length: full length (over 90 min). Style: no musical. **Application.** Best Material: query, synopsis, SASE. Response: 3 mos query, 6 mos script.

Hypothetical Theatre Company

344 E. 14th St., New York, NY, 10003
Amy Feinberg, Producing Artistic Dir.
htc@hypotheticaltheatre.org; www.hypotheticaltheatre.org

Est. 1986. **Preference.** Length: full length (over 90 min). Style: adaptation, comedy, drama. Material Must Be: unproduced in NYC. **Application.** Best Way: agent. Best Material: full script, SASE. Response: 6 mos.

Idaho Repertory Theater (IRT)

Univ. of Idaho (UI), Box 443074, Moscow, ID, 83844
Jere Hodgin, Artistic Dir
theatre@uidaho.edu; www.uitheatre.com

Consideration. Remuneration: royalty. **Preference.** Production: ages 13-35, cast of 2-10. Author Must Be: new/emerging writer. Material Must Be: unpublished. **Application.** Best Way: email. Best Material: query. Response: 4 mos.

Illinois Theatre Center

Box 397, Park Forest, IL, 60466
Literary Mgr.
Tel: 708-481-3510, Fax: 708-481-3693
ilthctr@bigplanet.com; www.ilthctr.org

Est. 1976. **Preference.** Length: full length (over 90 min). Production: cast limit 9 (play) or 14 (musical). **Application.** Best Material: query, synopsis, SASE. Response: 1 mo query, 2 mos script.

Illusion Theater

528 Hennepin Ave., #704, Minneapolis, MN, 55403
Michael Robins, Exec Producing Dir.
Tel: 612-339-4944, Fax: 612-337-8042
info@illusiontheater.org; www.illusiontheater.org

Est. 1974. **Preference.** Length: full length (over 90 min), one-act (30-60 min). **Application.** Best Way: professional recommendation. Best Time: Sep-Jan. Response: 1 yr.

Imagination Stage

4908 Auburn Ave., Bethesda, MD, 20814
Janet Stanford, Artistic Dir.
Tel: 301-961-6060, Fax: 301-718-9526
kbryereimaginationstage.org; www.imaginationstage.org

Est. 1979 **Preference.** Length: mid-length (60-90 min). Style: drama, musical. Subject: children's. Production: cast of 4-10. **Application.** Best Material: query, sample.

Immigrants' Theatre Project

44 Douglass St., Brooklyn, NY, 11231
Marcy Arlin, Artistic Dir.
Tel: 347-512-5572, Fax: 718-237-4545
immigrantstheat@aol.com; www.immigrantstheat.org

est. 1988 **Consideration.** Assistance: varies. Remuneration: reading, royalties by agreement. **Preference.** Length: all lengths. Style: all styles, no musical. Subject: immigrant and/or multicultural. Production: 18+, up to 12. **Application.** Best Way: unsolicited, email okay. Best Material: query letter (note theme addressed), synopsis, 20-pg writing sample, submissions returned with SASE. Deadline: ongoing. Response: 3-6 months.

Impact Theatre [CA]

Box 12666, Berkeley, CA, 94712
Melissa Hillman, Artistic Director
melissa@impacttheatre.com; www.impacttheatre.com

Est. 1996. **Preference.** Length: full length (over 90 min), mid-length (60-90 min.). Style: all styles. Subject: all subjects. Material Must Be: unoptioned. **Application.** Best Way: unsolicited, professional recommendation, agent. Best Material: synopsis, 20 page sample, full script, SASE. Deadline: ongoing. Response: varies.

Impact Theatre Company [NY]

190 Underhill Ave., Brooklyn , NY, 11238
E. K. Rivera, Theater Mgr
Tel: 718-390-7163
impacttheaternyc@yahoo.com; geocities.com/impacttheaternyc

Staff: Tim Lewis (Exec Producer). **Preference.** Material Must Be: unoptioned. **Application.** Best Material: query, SASE.

Indiana Repertory Theatre

140 W. Washington St., Indianapolis, IN, 46204
Richard J. Roberts, Resident Dramaturg
Tel: 317-635-5277, Fax: 317-236-0767
rroberts@irtlive.com; www.irtlive.com

Est. 1972. Equity LORT, 6-show Signature Series (Sep-May) in 600-seat proscenium mainstage, 2-show Discovery Series for family/youth in 300-seat thrust upperstage. **Preference.** Length: full length (over 90 min) (Signature series), one-act (under 75 min) (Discovery series). Style: adaptation, translation, solo; no musical. Subject: classic lit, cultural-ethnic issues. Production: cast limit 10. Material Must Be: Midwest voice. **Application.** Best Way: email. Best Material: query, synopsis, resume; all via email. Best Time: year-round. Response: 6 mos.

Infamous Commonwealth Theatre

4845 North Harding, Unit 1, Chicago, IL, 60625
Genevieve Thompson, Artistic Director
Tel: 312-458-9780
gthompson@infamouscommonwealth.org; www.infamouscommonwealth.org

est. 2001

InnerAct Productions

138 S. Oxford St., #2-C, Brooklyn, NY, 11217
John Shevin Foster, Artistic Dir.
Tel: 718-230-1323
mail@inneractpd.com; www.inneractpd.com

Est. 1998. Equity. Theater by/for artists of color. **Consideration.** Remuneration: 5\% royalty. **Preference.** Style: no revues. Subject: African American. Production: cast limit 8. Author Must Be: age 18 or older. **Application.** Best Way: email. Best Material: query, synopsis.

INTAR (International Arts Relations) Theatre

Box 756, New York, NY, 10108
Lorenzo Mans, Literary Mgr
Tel: 212-695-6134
submissions@intartheatre.org; www.intartheatre.org

Est. 1966. Equity LOA. Opportunities incl. workshops, productions of works in progress, and mainstage productions. **Preference.** Length: full length (over 90 min). Style: comedy, drama. Subject: Latino. Material Must Be: unproduced. **Application.** Best Material: full script. Response: 3 mos.

InterAct Theatre Company [PA]

2030 Sansom St., Philadelphia, PA, 19103
Peter Bonilla, Literary Manager
Tel: 215-568-8077, Fax: 215-568-8095
pbonilla@interacttheatre.org; www.interacttheatre.org

Est. 1988. Resident company at Adrienne Theatre **Preference.** Length: full length (over 90 min). Subject: political, social or cultural issues. Production: 8-Jan. **Application.** Best Way: unsolicited. Best Material: query, synopsis, bio, SASE. Response: 6-12 months.

Interborough Repertory Theater Inc. (IRT)

154 Christopher St., #3-B, New York, NY, 10014
Jonathan Fluck, Co-Founder
Tel: 212-206-6875, Fax: 212-206-7037
www.irt.dreamhost.com

Est. 1986. Equity Showcase. Provdes accessible theater to schools and families of diverse cultural backgrounds in an atmosphere where theater professionals can grow and develop. **Preference.** Length: full length (over 90 min). Subject: children's, disabled, multi-ethnic. **Application.** Best Material: query, SASE.

International City Theatre

1 World Trade Center, #300, Long Beach, CA, 90831
Shashin Desai, Artistic Dir/Producer
Tel: 562-495-4595, Fax: 562-436-7895
shashinict@earthlink.net; www.ictlongbeach.org

Est. 1985. Equity SPT, Long Beach PAC resident company, 349-seat venue. Staff: Caryn Desai (Gen Mgr). **Consideration.** Remuneration: 7\% royalty. **Preference.** Length: full length (over 90 min). Production: cast limit 9, orchestra limit 6. **Application.** Best Way: professional recommendation. Best Material: synopsis, sample, full script, SASE. Best Time: Nov-Apr. Response: 6 mos.

Interplayers Ensemble Theatre

174 S. Howard St., Spokane, WA, 99210
Esta Rosevear, Business Mgr
Tel: 509-455-7529
businessmanager@interplayers.com; www.interplayers.com

Est. 1981. **Preference.** Length: full length (over 90 min). Production: cast limit 8, unit set, thrust stage. Author Must Be: age 21 or older. Material Must Be: unoptioned. **Application.** Best Material: query, synopsis, 10-pg sample, full script, SASE.

Intiman Theatre

201 Mercer St., Seattle, WA, 98109
Kate Godman, Assoc. Dir.
Tel: 206-269-1901, Fax: 206-269-1928
literary@intiman.org; www.intiman.org

Est. 1972. Equity LORT C. 2006 Regional Theater Tony winner. 6-play season (Apr-Dec) in 450-seat theater. **Preference.** Length: full length (over 90 min). Style: no musical. Subject: complex ideas, unique use of form, language-oriented; no domestic realism. **Application.** Best Way: professional recommendation. Best Material: query, synopsis, SASE. Best Time: Nov-Mar. Response: 8 mos.

Irish Classical Theatre Company (ICTC)

625 Main St., Buffalo, NY, 14203
Fortunato Pezzimenti, Producing Director
Tel: 716-853-1380, Fax: 716-853-0592
vinco@irishclassical.com; www.irishclassicaltheatre.com

Est. 1990. Equity Buffalo-Rochester Special Agreement, 5-play season. **Consideration.** Remuneration: royalties. **Preference.** Length: full length (over 90 min), one-act (30-60 min.). Style: adaptation, comedy, drama. Subject: Irish, Irish-American. Author Must Be: Irish or Irish-American. **Application.** Best Way: professional recommendation. Best Material: synopsis, sample. Best Time: May-July. Response: 3 mos.

Irish Repertory Theatre

132 W. 22nd St., New York, NY, 10011
Kara Manning, Literary Mgr
Tel: 212-255-0270, Fax: 212-255-0281
kara@irishrep.org; www.irishrep.org

Ongoing monthly new works reading series on the Irish and Irish American experience. **Preference.** Length: full length (over 90 min). Subject: Irish, Irish American. Material Must Be: unpublished, unproduced. **Application.** Best Material: synopsis, audio, SASE.

Irondale Ensemble Project

Box 150604, Brooklyn, NY, 11215
Jim Niesen, Artistic Dir.
Tel: 718-488-9233, Fax: 718-488-9185
irondalert@aol.com; www.irondale.org

Est. 1983. Equity LOA. Classic work in unorthodox production and original work combining new and classic styles of performance, music, dance and design. **Preference.** Length: full length (over 90 min). Subject: political or social relevance. Production: cast limit 9. **Application.** Best Material: query. Best Time: Apr-Sep. Response: 10 wks.

Jefferson Performing Arts Society

1118 Clearview Pkwy., Metairie, LA, 70001
Dennis G. Assaf, Executive/Artistic Dir.
Tel: 504-885-2000, Fax: 504-885-3437

Est. 1978.

9/1/2008. Jewish Ensemble Theatre

6600 W. Maple Rd., West Bloomfield, MI, 48322
Evelyn Orbach, Artistic Director
Tel: 248-788-2900
e.orbach@jettheatre.org; www.jettheatre.org

Est. 1989. In addition to a 4-5 production annual subscription season (Equity SPT), JET sponsors an annual fest of new plays, presented for 2 perfs in staged readings. **Preference.** Length: full length (over 90 min). Style: all styles. Subject: Jewish perspective. Material Must Be: unproduced. **Application.** Best Way: unsolicited. Best Material: full script, SASE. Best Time: May-Sep. Deadline: 9/1/2008. Response: 1/31/2009.

Jewish Theater of New York

Box 845, Times Sq. Sta., New York, NY, 10108
Liz Lauren
thejtny@aol.com; www.jewishtheater.org

Est. 1994. Staff: Tuvia Tenenbom (Artistic Dir). **Preference.** Length: full length (over 90 min). Style: comedy, drama, musical. Subject: Jewish. Material Must Be: unoptioned, unpublished, unproduced. **Application.** Best Way: invite. Best Material: synopsis, submissions not returned. Response: 3 mos.

John Capo Productions

PMB 112, 222 Guideboard Rd., Clifton Park, NY, 12065
Jack Dowd, Producing Dir.
Tel: 518-383-0743

est. 2001 **Consideration.** Remuneration: production. **Preference.** Length: full length (over 90 min). Style: all styles. Subject: all subjects. Material Must Be: unpublished, unproduced. **Application.** Best Way: unsolicited. Best Material: query, synopsis, full script, SASE. Deadline: ongoing. Response: 3-6 mos.

Jubilee Theatre

506 Main St., Forth Worth, TX, 76102
Ed Smith, Artistic Dir.
Tel: 817-338-4204, Fax: 817-338-4206
ed.smith@jubileetheatre.org; www.jubileetheatre.org

Preference. Subject: African-American. **Application.** Best Material: query, 10 pg. sample, resume, SASE. Best Time: beginning of each year.

Judith Shakespeare Company

367 Windsor Hwy., #409, New Windsor, NY, 12553
Joanne Zipay, Artistic Dir/Producer
Tel: 212-592-1885
www.judithshakespeare.org

Est. 1995. Offers resurgence concert reading series of new plays with heightened language and significant roles for women.

Kairos Italy Theater (KIT)

50 E. 8th Street, #12B, New York, NY, 10003
Laura Caparrotti, Artistic Dir.
Fax: 801-749-6727
info@kitheater.com; www.kitheater.com

Est. 2002. KIT's mission is to produce plays by and about Italian authors and Italian themes. **Preference.** Length: all length. Style: all styles. Subject: Italy; Italians. Production: 5. **Application.** Best Way: send email with synopsis, sample pages. Best Material: SASE. Best Time: ongoing.

Kansas City Repertory Theatre

4949 Cherry St., Kansas City, MO, 64110
Eric Rosen, Artistic Dir.
Tel: 816-235-2727, Fax: 816-235-5367
www.kcrep.org

Est. 1964. Formerly Missouri Repertory Theatre. Equity LORT B. **Application.** Best Way: invite.

Karamu House Inc.

2355 E. 89th St., Cleveland, OH, 44106
Tel: 216-795-7070
www.karamu.com

Nonprofit community-based arts and educational organization to encourage and support the preservation, celebration and evolution of African-American culture and provide a vehicle for social, economic and educational development.

Kavinoky Theatre

D'Youville Coll., 320 Porter Ave., Buffalo, NY, 14221
David Lamb, Artistic Dir.
Tel: 716-829-7668
www.kavinokytheatre.com

Est. 1981 **Preference.** Length: full length (over 90 min). Production: cast limited 7, no fly, limited wing. **Application.** Best Way: professional recommendation. Best Time: Jun-Aug. Response: 1 mo.

Kentucky Repertory Theatre at Horse Cave

Box 215, 101 E. Main St., Horse Cave, KY, 42749
Robert Brock, Artistic Dir.
Tel: 270-786-1200, Fax: 270-786-5298
rbrock@kentuckyrep.org; www.kentuckyrep.org

Est. 1977. Equity LOA. Formerly Horse Cave Theater. **Preference.** Length: full length (over 90 min). Subject: Kentucky. Production: cast limit 10, unit set. Author Must Be: resident of KY. Material Must Be: unproduced. **Application.** Best Way: professional recommendation. Best Material: query. Best Time: Oct-Apr.

Kidworks Touring Theatre Co.

5215 N. Ravenswood Ave., #307, Chicago, IL, 60640
Andrea Salloum, Artistic Dir.
Tel: 773-907-9932
kidworkstheatre@aol.com; www.kidworkstheatre.org

Est. 1987.

Killing Kompany

21 Turn Ln., Levittown, NY, 11756
Jon Avner, Artistic Dir.
Tel: 212-772-2590, Fax: 212-202-6495
killingkompany@killingkompany.com; www.killingkompany.com

Interactive shows for dinner theater.

Kumu Kahua Theatre

46 Merchant St., Honolulu, HI, 96813
Harry Wong III, Artistic Dir.
Tel: 808-536-4222, Fax: 808-536-4226
kumukahuatheatre@hawaiiantel.net; www.kumukahua.org

Est. 1971. **Preference.** Length: full length (over 90 min), one-act (30-60 min). Style: adaptation, comedy, drama. Subject: Hawaii. **Application.** Best Material: full script, SASE. Response: 4 mos.

Kuntu Repertory Theatre

University of Pittsburgh, Dept. of Africana Studies, 4140 S. Bouquet St., PIttsburgh, PA, 15260
Dr. Vernall A. Lillie, Artistic Director
Tel: 412-624-7298
www.kuntu.org

est. 1974 **Preference.** Subject: African-American 26 relevant social issues. **Application.** Best Material: full script.

Kuumba Ensemble Heritage House Community Theater

1021 Hartmont Road, #755, Baltimore, MD, 21228
www.kuumbaensemble.org; info@kuumbaensemble.org

Preference. Subject: African-American secular and spiritual. **Application.** Best Material: query, synopsis, 10 pg. sample.

L.A. Theatre Works (LATW)

681 Venice Blvd., Venice, CA, 90291
Brendon Fox, Assoc. Producer
Tel: 310-827-0808
www.latw.org

Est. 1974. Live performances and studio recordings for broadcast over public radio. Some published as Plays on Tape, which authors receive a percentage of gross sales. **Preference.** Length: full length (over 90 min). Style: adaptation, comedy, drama. **Application.** Best Way: agent. Response: 6 mos.

La Jolla Playhouse

Box 12039, La Jolla, CA, 92039
Gabriel Green, Literary Mgr.
Tel: 858-550-1070, Fax: 858-550-1075
www.lajollaplayhouse.org

Est. 1947. LORT B, C. 1993 Regional Theater Tony winner. Commissions playwrights and provides developmental support thru Page to Stage readings (est. 2001). **Preference.** Length: full length (over 90 min), mid-length (60-90 min.). Material Must Be: West Coast premiere. **Application.** Best Way: full script agent. Best Material: 10-page sample accepted from Southern California- based playwrights. Include SASE. Response: 2 mos query, 1 yr script.

La MaMa Experimental Theater Club

74-A E. 4th St., New York, NY, 10003
Ellen Stewart, Artistic Dir.
Tel: 212-254-6468
web@lamama.org; www.lamama.org

Est. 1961. **Preference.** Length: full length (over 90 min), one-act (30-60 min). **Application.** Best Way: professional recommendation. Response: 6 mos.

Laguna Playhouse

Box 1747, Laguna Beach, CA, 92652
Donna Inglima, Dir., Youth Theater
www.lagunaplayhouse.com

Est. 1920. Staff: Andrew Barnicle (Artistic Dir). **Application.** Best Way: invite.

Lamb's Players Theatre (LPT)

Box 182229, Coronado, CA, 92178
Robert Smyth, Producing Artistic Dir.
www.lambsplayers.org

NO MORE SUBMISSIONS. Est. 1971. **Preference.** Length: full length (over 90 min), one-act (30-60 min). **Application.** Best Material: query, synopsis, 10-pg sample, audio. Response: 6 wks query, 6 mos script.

LaMicro Theater

Box 20019, London Ter., New York, NY, 10011
Pietro Gonzalez, Artistic Dir.
Tel: 212-979-5744
info@lamicrotheater.org; www.lamicrotheater.org

Est. 2003. Staff: Martin Balmaceda (Exec Dir), Berioska Ipinza (Exec Dir). **Preference.** Style: comedy, drama, translation. Subject: children's, Latino, women. Production: cast of 2-4. Material Must Be: unproduced. **Application.** Best Material: sample, full script, submissions not returned.

Latin American Theater Ensemble (LATE) / El Portn del Barrio

Box 18, Radio City Sta., New York, NY, 10101
Margarita Toirac, Co-Founder/Exec Producer
Tel: 212-397-3262, Fax: 212-397-3262
elportonlatenyc@aol.com; www.lateny.org

Est. 1970. **Preference.** Length: one-act (30-60 min). Style: comedy, drama. Subject: Latino. Production: cast limit 3. **Application.** Best Material: full script.

Lifeline Theatre

6912 N. Glenwood Ave., Chicago, IL, 60626
Dorothy Milne, Artistic Dir.
www.lifelinetheatre.com

Est. 1982. **Preference.** Length: full length (over 90 min), mid-length (60-90 min). Style: adaptation. Production: cast limit 9. Author Must Be: resident of Chicago. **Application.** Best Way: invite. Best Material: query, synopsis, SASE.

Lincoln Center Theater

150 W. 65th St., New York, NY, 10023
Anne Cattaneo, Dramaturg
Tel: 212-362-7600
www.lct.org

Est. 1966. Equity LORT A & B. **Preference.** Length: full length (over 90 min). **Application.** Best Way: agent. Response: 2 mos.

Little Fish Theatre Company (LFTC)

617 Elvira Ave., Redondo Beach, CA, 90277
Lisa Coffi, Producing Artistic Dir
Tel: 310-512-6030, Fax: 310-507-0269
www.littlefishtheatre.org

Est. 2002. Equity 99-seat. Offers full-length plays that are innovative and thought-provoking, socially and culturally relevant, challenging and entertaining. Staff: Mark Piatelli (Assoc Artistic Dir). **Preference.** Length: full length (over 90 min). Production: cast limit 7, minimal set. **Application.** Best Material: query, synopsis, 10-pg sample, SASE. Response: 2 mos query, 6 mos script.

Live Bait Theater
3914 N. Clark St., Chicago, IL, 60613
Literary Dept
Tel: 773-871-1212
info@livebaittheater.org; www.livebaittheater.org

Est. 1987. Opportunities incl. Fresh Bait reading series. **Preference.** Length: full length (over 90 min). Style: no musical. Subject: non-realistic, multimedia works. Production: cast limit 9, unit set, no fly/wing space. Author Must Be: resident of Chicago area. **Application.** Best Material: query, synopsis. Response: 6 wks query, 6 mos script.

Looking Glass Theatre [NY]
422 W. 57th St., New York, NY, 10019
Erica Nilson, Lit. Man.
Tel: 212-307-9467
admin@lookingglasstheatrenyc.com; www.lookingglasstheatrenyc.com

est. 1993. Off-Off Broadway Showcase Theatre. **Preference.** Length: one-act (30-60 min.), short (under 30 min.). Style: all styles. Subject: women. Production: minimal. **Application.** Best Way: unsolicited. Best Material: full script. Deadline: ongoing. Response: 6 mos-1 yr..

Lorraine Hansberry Theater
620 Sutter St., 7th Fl., San Fransisco, CA, 94102
Stanley Williams, Artistic Dir.
Tel: 415-345-3980, Fax: 415-345-3983
stanley@lhtsf.org

Preference. Length: all lengths. Style: all styles. Subject: African-American. **Application.** Best Way: unsolicited. Best Material: synopsis, full script, submissions returned with SASE. Deadline: ongoing. Response: 5/15/2004.

Lost Nation Theater
39 Main St., Montpelier, VT, 05602
Mr. Kim Bent, Founding Artistic Dir
Tel: 802-229-0492
info@lostnationtheater.org; www.lostnationtheater.org

Est. 1977. **Preference.** Length: full length (over 90 min). Subject: children's. Production: cast limit 10, unit set, no fly. **Application.** Best Material: query, synopsis, sample, resume. Best Time: Nov. Response: 1 mo query, 3 mos script.

4/15/08. Luna Stage
695 Bloomfield Ave., Montclair, NJ, 07042
Cheryl Katz, Play Development Dir.
Tel: 973-744-3309, Fax: 973-509-2388
cheryl@lunastage.org; www.lunastage.org

Est. 1992. Equity SPT-2. 3-6 new plays/season. Staff: Jane Mandel (Artistic Dir), Charlotte McKim (Managing Dir). **Consideration.** Remuneration: $1,000 in lieu of royalty. **Preference.** Length: full length (over 90 min), mid-length (60-90 min). **Application.** Best Material: see website for guidelines, SASE. Best Time: after 9/15. Deadline: 15-Apr. Response: 3 - 6mos.

Lyric Stage Company of Boston
140 Clarendon St., Boston, MA, 02116
Rebecca Curtiss, Producing Assoc, New Play Development
www.lyricstage.com

Est. 1974. Opportunities incl. Growing Voices new work development program. **Preference.** Length: full length (over 90 min). Style: comedy, musical. Subject: Boston. Production: cast limit 6 (plays) or 12 (musicals), modest orchestra, unit set. Author Must Be: resident of MA, women and minorities encouraged. **Application.** Best Material: query, 1-pg synopsis, 15-pg sample, audio, cast list, SASE. Best Time: Jun-Jul. Response: 2 mos query, 6 mos script.

Ma-Yi Theatre Company

520 8th Ave, #309, New York, NY, 10018
Ralph Pena, Artistic Dir.
www.ma-yitheatre.org

Est. 1989. **Preference.** Length: full length (over 90 min), mid-length (60-90 min). Subject: Asian-American. Material Must Be: unoptioned, unpublished, unproduced. **Application.** Best Material: query, synopsis, submissions not returned. Best Time: Nov-Feb.

Madison Repertory Theatre

1 S. Pinckney St., #340, Madison, WI, 53703
Richard Corley, Artistic Dir.
Tel: 608-256-0029, Fax: 608-256-7433
www.madisonrep.org

Est. 1969. **Preference.** Length: full length (over 90 min). Production: cast limit 15, no fly. **Application.** Best Way: agent. Best Time: Jun-Aug. Response: 6 mos.

Magic Theatre

Ft. Mason Ctr., Bldg. D, San Fransisco, CA, 94123
Mark Routhier, Literary Mgr.
Tel: 415-441-8001, Fax: 415-771-5505
www.magictheatre.org

Est. 1967. Opportunities incl. reading, workshop, full production, commission, and residency. Staff: Chris Smith (Artistic Dir). **Preference.** Length: full length (over 90 min). Style: comedy, drama. Production: cast limit 8. Material Must Be: unproduced. **Application.** Best Material: query, 1-pg synopsis, 20 pg sample, resume, SASE. Best Time: Sep-May. Response: 6 wks query, 8 mos script.

Main Street Theater

2540 Times Blvd., Houston, TX, 77005
Rebecca Greene Udden, Artistic Dir.
Tel: 713-524-3622, Fax: 713-524-3977
rudden@mainstreettheater.com; www.mainstreettheater.com

Est. 1975. **Consideration.** Remuneration: royalty. **Preference.** Length: full length (over 90 min), mid-length (60-90 min). Production: cast limit 9. **Application.** Best Material: query, synopsis, 20 pg sample.

Manhattan Ensemble Theater (MET)

55 Mercer St., New York, NY, 10013
Shannon Sindelar, Literary Mgr.
Tel: 212-925-1900, Fax: 212-925-1947
shannon@met.com; www.met.com

Est. 1999. Closed 2007. **Preference.** Style: adaptation. Production: cast limit 10. **Application.** Best Way: professional recommendation. Best Material: query, synopsis, resume. Response: 3 mos.

Marin Theater Company (MTC)

397 Miller Ave., Mill Valley, CA, 94941
Maryanne Olson, Literary Manager
Tel: 415-388-5200, Fax: 415-388-1217
maryanne@marintheatre.org; www.marintheatre.org

Est. 1966. Staff: Jason Minadakis (Artistic Dir). **Preference.** Length: full length (over 90 min), mid-length (60-90 min). **Application.** Best Way: agent. Best Material: full script, SASE. Response: 8 mos.

MCC Theater
311 W. 43rd St., #206, New York, NY, 10036
Stephen Willems, Literary Mgr.
Tel: 212-727-7722, Fax: 212-727-7780
literary@mcctheater.org; www.mcctheater.org

Est. 1986. Equity ANTC. Staff: Jaime Green (Asst Lit Mgr). **Preference.** Production: cast limit 10. Material Must Be: unoptioned, unproduced in NYC. **Application.** Best Material: query, synopsis, 10-pg sample, SASE. Response: 2 mos.

McCarter Theater Center
91 University Pl., Princeton, NJ, 08540
Carrie Hughes, Literary Mgr.
Tel: 609-258-6500
www.mccarter.org

Equity LORT B+, C, and experimental. 1994 Regional Theater Tony winner. Staff: Emily Mann (Artistic Dir), Douglas Langworth (Dramaturg). **Preference.** Length: full length (over 90 min). **Application.** Best Way: agent. Best Material: full script, SASE. Response: 6 mos.

Meadow Brook Theatre
Oakland Univ., 207 Wilson Hall, Oakland Univ., Rochester, MI, 48309
David L. Regal, Artistic Dir.
Tel: 248-370-3322
jm@mbtheatre.com; www.mbtheatre.com

Est. 1967. Equity LORT C. 600-seat venue. **Preference.** Length: full length (over 90 min). Production: no fly. **Application.** Best Material: synopsis, SASE. Best Time: Feb-Mar.

Melting Pot Theatre Company
2440 Broadway, #197, New York, NY, 10024
Larry Hirschhorn, Founding Artistic Dir.
larry@meltingpottheatre.com; www.meltingpottheatre.com

Est. 1998. Equity LOA. **Preference.** Length: full length (over 90 min). Style: drama, musical. Subject: multi-ethnic. Production: cast limit 10, orchestra limit 6, sets limit 3. **Application.** Best Way: professional recommendation. Best Material: query, synopsis, full script, SASE. Response: 6 mos.

Merrimack Repertory Theatre
132 Warren St., Lowell, MA, 01852
Adam Scarano, Artistic Admin.
Tel: 978-654-7550, Fax: 978-654-7575
info@merrimackrep.org; www.merrimackrep.org

Est. 1979. Equity LORT D. **Preference.** Length: full length (over 90 min). Style: no musical. Subject: contemporary US. Production: cast limit 7. **Application.** Best Way: agent only. Best Material: full script, SASE. Best Time: summer. Response: 13 mos.

Merry-Go-Round Playhouse
17 Williams St., Fl. 2, Auburn, NY, 13021
Amy Simolo, Education Theater Coord.
Tel: 315-255-1305, Fax: 315-252-3815
youthinfo@merry-go-round.com; www.merry-go-round.com

Est. 1958. **Consideration.** Remuneration: royalty. **Preference.** Length: mid-length (60-90 min), one-act (30-60 min). Subject: children's. Production: cast of 2-4, unit set. **Application.** Best Material: synopsis, full script, submissions not returned.

Metro Theater Company

8308 Olive Blvd., St. Louis, MO, 63132
Carol North, Artistic Dir.
Tel: 314-997-6777, Fax: 314-997-1811
carol@metrotheatercompany.org; www.metrotheatercompany.org

Est. 1973. Mainstage shows, tours and commissions of theater for children and family audiences. **Consideration.** Remuneration: 6\% royalty. **Preference.** Length: mid-length (60-90 min), one-act (30-60 min). Subject: children's. Production: cast limit 10. **Application.** Best Way: professional recommendation. Best Material: synopsis, sample, SASE. Best Time: summer-early fall. Response: 3 mos.

MetroStage

1201 N. Royal St., Alexandria, VA, 22314
Carolyn Griffin, Producing Artistic Dir.
Tel: 703-548-9044, Fax: 703-548-9089
info@metrostage.org; www.metrostage.org

Est. 1984. Equity SPT. **Consideration.** Remuneration: royalty. **Preference.** Length: full length (over 90 min), mid-length (60-90 min). Style: drama, musical. Production: cast limit 6, orchestra limit 5, unit set. **Application.** Best Way: agent. Best Material: synopsis, 10-pg sample, SASE.

Milk Can Theatre Company

Michael Weller Theatre, 311 W. 43rd St., #602, New York, NY, 10036
Julie Fei Fan Balzer, Artistic Dir.
www.milkcantheatre.org

Est. 2003. Staff: Julie Fei-Fan Balzer (Artistic Dir.).

Mill Mountain Theatre

1 Market Sq., Fl. 2, Roanoke, VA, 24011
Patrick Benton, Producing Artistic Dir.
Tel: 540-342-5730, Fax: 540-342-5745
www.millmountain.org

Est. 1964. Equity LOA. Center Piece program offers monthly lunchtime staged readings of one-acts. Submission to other programs by invitation. **Consideration.** Remuneration: reading. **Preference.** Length: one-act (20-45 min). Style: all styles. Subject: all subjects. Production: small cast favored. Material Must Be: unpublished. **Application.** Best Way: unsolicited, invitation (all other programs). Best Material: full script, submissions returned with SASE. Best Time: October-May. Deadline: rotating. Response: 6 months.

Milwaukee Chamber Theatre

158 N. Broadway, Milwaukee, WI, 53202
Jacque Troy, Literary Mgr
Tel: 414-276-8842, Fax: 414-277-4477
jacque@chamber-theatre.com; www.chamber-theatre.com

Est. 1975. Equity SPT. **Preference.** Length: full length (over 75 min). Style: no musical. Production: small cast, unit set. **Application.** Best Way: professional recommendation. Best Material: query, synopsis, 10-pg sample, SASE. Best Time: summer. Response: 6 mos.

Milwaukee Repertory Theater

108 E. Wells St., Milwaukee, WI, 53202
Literary Dir.
Tel: 414-224-1761, Fax: 414-224-9097
www.milwaukeerep.com

Est. 1954. **Preference.** Length: full length (over 90 min), mid-length (60-90 min). Style: no musical. **Application.** Best Way: professional recommendation. Response: 4 mos.

Miracle Theatre Group
425 SE 6th Ave., Portland, OR, 97214
Olga Sanchez, Artistic Dir
Tel: 503-236-7253
www.milagro.org

Est. 1985. **Preference.** Length: full length (over 90 min). Style: no musical. Subject: Hispanic. Production: cast limit 10, no fly. Author Must Be: Hispanic. **Application.** Best Material: full script. Response: 5 mos.

Mixed Blood Theatre Company
1501 S. 4th St., Minneapolis, MN, 55454
Aditi Kapil, Resident Artist
Tel: 612-338-0937
literary@mixedblood.com; www.mixedblood.com

Est. 1976. **Preference.** Length: full length (over 90 min), mid-length (60-90 min). Subject: disabled, gay, multicultural. **Application.** Best Material: query, synopsis, 10-pg sample, SASE. Response: 4 mos.

Montana Repertory Theater
Univ. of Montana, Dept. of Drama & Dance, Missoula, MT, 59812
Salina Chatlain, Asst to the Artistic Dir.
Tel: 406-243-6809, Fax: 406-243-5726
salina.chatlain@mso.umt.edu; www.montanarep.org

Est. 1967. **Preference.** Length: full length (over 90 min), mid-length (60-90 min). Subject: Native American themes. Production: touring set. **Application.** Best Material: query, synopsis, resume. Best Time: summer. Response: 3 mos query, 6 mos script.

Moving Arts
Box 481145, Los Angeles, CA, 90048
Trey Nichols, Literary Dir.
www.movingarts.org

Est. 1992. 99-seat. **Preference.** Length: full length (over 90 min). Style: no musical. Material Must Be: unproduced in L.A.. **Application.** Best Material: query, synopsis, 20-pg sample, resume, SASE. Response: 3 mos query, 5 mos script.

Mu Performing Arts
2700 NE Winter St., #4, Minneapolis, MN, 55413
Rick Shiomi, Artistic Dir.
Tel: 612-824-4804, Fax: 612-824-3396
info@muperformingarts.org; www.muperformingarts.org

Est. 1992. Formerly Theater Mu. Equity and non-Equity. **Preference.** Length: full length (over 90 min). Style: no translation. Subject: Asian, Asian-American, children's. Production: cast limit 15, simple set. **Application.** Best Material: query, full script. Response: 2 mos query, 3 mos script.

NaCl Theatre (North American Cultural Laboratory)
Box 2201, Times Sq. Sta., New York, NY, 10108
Brad Krumholz, Director
nacl@nacl.org; www.nacl.org

Est. 1997. **Preference.** Style: no musical. Subject: experimental, multidisciplinary performance works. Production: cast of 4-8, minimal set. **Application.** Best Way: professional recommendation. Response: 10 wks.

National Theatre of the Deaf
139 N. Main St., West Hartford, CT, 06107
Paul L. Winters, Exec Dir.
pwinters@ntd.org; www.ntd.org

Est. 1967. **Preference.** Length: full length (over 90 min). Style: adaptation, comedy, drama. Subject: children's, deaf, culturally diverse. Production: cast limit 10, touring set. Material Must Be: unproduced professionally. **Application.** Best Material: query, synopsis, sample, SASE. Response: 1 mo query, 6 mos script.

Near West Theatre (NWT)

6514 Detroit Avenue, Cleveland, OH, 44102
Bob Navis Jr., Artistic Dir.
Tel: 216-961-9750, Fax: 216-961-6381
nearwesttheatre.org

Nebraska Repertory Theatre

Univ. of Nebraska, 215 Temple Bldg., Lincoln, NE, 68588
Paul Steger, Executive Dir.
Tel: 402-472-2072, Fax: 402-472-9055
psteger@unl.edu

ON HOLD. Equity URTA. **Consideration.** Remuneration: possible future production. **Preference.** Length: full-length. Style: comedy, drama. Subject: all subjects. Material Must Be: unpublished, unproduced. **Application.** Best Way: agent submission. Best Material: full script, submissions returned with SASE. Best Time: after 12/15/03. Response: 5/15/2004.

Nebraska Theatre Caravan

Omaha Community Playhouse, 6915 Cass St., Omaha, NE, 68132
Lara Marsh, Artistic Coord
Tel: 402-553-4890 x135, Fax: 402-553-6288
caravan@omahaplayhouse.com; www.nebraskatheatrecaravan.com

Est. 1975. Seasonal touring theater. **Preference.** Length: full length (over 90 min). Style: adaptation. Production: age 8 and older, cast limit 25, touring set. **Application.** Best Way: professional recommendation. Best Material: video.

Negro Ensemble Company

303 West 42nd St, #501, New York, NY, 10036
Charles Weldon, Artistic Dir.
Tel: 212-582-5862, Fax: 212-582-9639
info@necinc.org; www.negroensemblecomany.org

Preference. Subject: African-American. **Application.** Best Way: unsolicited.

New Conservatory Theatre Center

25 Van Ness Ave., Lower Lobby, San Fransisco, CA, 94102
Ed Decker, Artistic Dir.
Tel: 415-861-4914, Fax: 415-861-6988
www.nctcsf.org

Est. 1981. **Consideration.** Remuneration: 6\%-8 \% royalty. **Preference.** Length: full length (over 90 min), mid-length (60-90 min). Style: no translation. Subject: children's, gay-lesbian. Author Must Be: resident of US. Material Must Be: unoptioned. **Application.** Best Way: visit website for submission policy. Best Material: query, synopsis, SASE. Response: 6 mos.

New Federal Theatre

292 Henry St., New York, NY, 10002
Woodie King Jr., Producing Dir.
Tel: 212-353-1176, Fax: 212-353-1088
newfederal@aol.com; www.newfederaltheatre.org

Est. 1970. Equity Showcase. **Consideration.** Remuneration: $500 option fee. **Preference.** Length: full length (over 90 min). Style: drama. Subject: Black. Production: cast limti 5, unit set. Material Must Be: unoptioned, unpublished, unproduced. **Application.** Best Way: professional recommendation. Best Material: full script, SASE. Response: 6 mos.

New Georges

109 W. 27th St., #9-A, New York, NY, 10001
Kara-Lynn Vaeni, Literary Mgr.
info@newgeorges.org; www.newgeorges.org

Est. 1992. Equity Tiered Showcase. Staff: Susan Bernfield (Artistic Dir). **Consideration.** Remuneration: royalty. **Preference.** Length: full length (over 90 min), mid-length (60-90 min). Style: comedy, drama. Author Must Be: female. **Application.** Best Material: full script, SASE. Response: 1 yr.

New Ground Theatre

2822 Eastern Ave., Davenport, IA, 52803
Chris Jansen, Artistic Dir.
Tel: 563-326-7529
www.newgroundtheatre.org

Est. 2001. **Preference.** Production: cast limit 6, unit set, no fly. Author Must Be: resident of Midwest. **Application.** Best Material: full script. Best Time: Apr-Jun. Response: 6 mos.

New Group

410 W. 42nd St., New York, NY, 10036
Ian Morgan, Assoc Artistic Dir
Tel: 212-244-3380, Fax: 212-244-3438
info@thenewgroup.org; www.thenewgroup.org

Est. 1991. Opportunities incl. workshops and readings. We do not respond to electronic submissions. **Preference.** Length: full length (over 90 min), mid-length (60-90 min). **Application.** Best Material: query, synopsis, 10-pg sample, resume, SASE. Response: 9 mos.

New Jersey Repertory Company

179 Broadway, Long Branch, NJ, 07740
Suzanne Barabas, Artistic Dir
Tel: 732-229-3166, Fax: 732-229-3167
info@njrep.org; www.njrep.org

Est. 1997. Equity SPT-2. **Consideration.** Remuneration: royalty. **Preference.** Length: full length (over 90 min), mid-length (60-90 min). Style: comedy, drama. Production: cast limit 5, unit set. Material Must Be: unproduced. **Application.** Best Material: full script, SASE.

New Jomandi Productions, Inc.

675 Ponce de Leon Ave., Fl. 8, Atlanta, GA, 30308
Carol Mitchell-Leon, Artistic Dir
Tel: 404-784-1587
jomandiproductions@yahoo.com; www.jomandi.org

Est. 1978. Formerly Jomandi Prods. **Preference.** Length: full length (over 90 min). Subject: African-American. Production: small cast, unit set. **Application.** Best Material: query, synopsis, sample, resume. Best Time: spring-summer. Response: only if interested.

New Perspectives Theatre Company

456 W. 37th St., New York, NY, 10018
Melody Brooks, Artistic Dir.
Tel: 212-630-9945
www.newperspectivestheatre.org

Est. 1992. Staged reading workshops and full productions provided to new scripts in development. **Preference.** Length: full length (over 90 min), mid-length (60-90 min). Style: comedy, drama, translation. Subject: women, multi-ethnic. Material Must Be: unoptioned, unpublished, unproduced. **Application.** Best Material: synopsis, 15-pg sample, SASE. Response: 3 mos.

New Playwrights Program

Detroit Repertory Theatre, 13103 Woodrow Wilson St., Detroit, MI, 48238
Literary Mgr.
Tel: 313-868-1347, Fax: 313-868-1705
detrepth@aol.com; www.detroitreptheatre.com

Est. 1957. Equity SPT-3. **Consideration.** Remuneration: 8\% royalty. **Preference.** Length: full length (over 90 min). Production: age 18-65, cast of 5-7, non-traditional casting. Material Must Be: unproduced. **Application.** Best Material: full script, SASE. Best Time: Sep-Jun. Response: 6 mos.

New Repertory Theatre
200 Dexter Ave., Watertown, MA, 02472
Rick Lombardo, Producing Artistic Dir.
artistic@newrep.org; www.newrep.org

Est. 1984. Equity. **Consideration.** Remuneration: 5\%-10\% royalty. **Preference.** Length: full length (over 90 min), mid-length (60-90 min), one-act (30-60 min). Production: cast limit 12. Material Must Be: unoptioned. **Application.** Best Way: professional recommendation. Best Material: synopsis, 10-pg sample. Best Time: Sep-Oct.

New Stage Theatre
1100 Carlisle St., Jackson, MS, 39202
Francine Thomas Reynolds, Interim Artistic Dir
Tel: 601-948-3533, Fax: 601-948-3538
mail@newstagetheatre.com; www.newstagetheatre.com

Est. 1965. **Preference.** Length: full length (over 90 min), mid-length (60-90 min). Style: comedy, drama. Production: cast limit 8. **Application.** Best Material: query, synopsis. Best Time: summer-fall. Response: 1 mo query, 3 mos script.

New Theatre
4120 Laguna St., Coral Gables, FL, 33146
Ricky J. Martinez, Artistic Dir.
Tel: 305-443-5373, Fax: 305-443-1642
rjmartinez@new-theatre.org; www.new-theatre.org

Est. 1986. Equity SPT-4. **Consideration.** Remuneration: 5-7 percent royalty. **Preference.** Length: full length (80 min). Style: all styles, piano musicals accepted. Production: cast limit 6, minimal set. Material Must Be: unpublished, unproduced, second and third productions are also welcome. **Application.** Best Material: query, synopsis, sample pages, SASE. Best Time: June- Dec. Response: 2-3 mos.

New Village Productions
145 E. 27th St., #1-A, New York, NY, 10016
Kevin Brofsky, Dir.
shoesinthehall@yahoo.com; newvillageproductions.org

Est. 1989. Readings and Showcase productions of plays with non-mainstream characters or situations. **Preference.** Author Must Be: women and minorities encouraged. Material Must Be: unoptioned. **Application.** Best Way: email. Best Material: query, SASE. Response: 3 mos.

New WORLD Theater (NWT)
Univ. of Massachusetts, Amherst, 100 Hicks Way, #16 Curry Hicks, Amherst, MA, 01003
Andrea Assaf, Artistic Dir.
Tel: 413-545-1972, Fax: 413-545-4414
nwt@admin.umass.edu; www.newworldtheater.org

We host New WORKS for a New WORLD every summer & invite 4 artists for a development residency. See website for details. **Application.** Best Way: professional recommendation. Best Material: query.

New York Stage and Film (NYSAF)
315 W. 36th St., #1006, New York, NY, 10018
Johanna Pfaelzea, Artistic Dir.
Tel: 212-736-4240, Fax: 212-736-4241
info@newyorkstageandfilm.org; www.newyorkstageandfilm.org

Est. 1985. Summer season (Jun-Aug) in residence as part of Powerhouse program at Vasser Coll. **Consideration.** Assistance: $100 stipend. Remuneration: $550 . **Preference.** Length: full length (over 90 min). Style: comedy, drama, musical. Material Must Be: unpublished, unproduced. **Application.** Best Way: no unsolicited scripts; unsolicited queries and synopsis, agent. Best Material: full script, SASE. Best Time: Sep. Response: 6 mos.

New York State Theatre Institute (NYSTI)

37 1st St., Troy, NY, 12180
Patricia Di Benedetto Snyder, Producing Artistic Dir.
Tel: 518-274-3200
www.nysti.org

Est. 1974. Equity TYA. **Consideration.** Assistance: room/board, room/board. **Preference.** Length: full length (over 90 min), mid-length (60-90 min). Subject: family. Material Must Be: unproduced. **Application.** Best Way: agent. Best Material: full script, SASE. Best Time: Jan. Response: 6 mos.

New York Theatre Workshop (NYTW)

83 E. 4th St., New York, NY, 10003
Literary Office
Tel: 212-780-9037, Fax: 212-460-8996
info@nytw.org; www.nytw.org

Est. 1979. Works of innovative form & language about socially relevant issues. **Preference.** Subject: political and historical themes. **Application.** Best Material: query, synopsis, 10-pg sample, resume, SASE. Response: 3 mos query, 8 mos script.

4/1/2008. Next Act Theatre

342 N. Water St., Fl. 2, Milwaukee, WI, 53202
David Cecsarini, Producing Artistic Dir
Tel: 414-278-7780, Fax: 414-278-5930
cez@nextact.org; www.nextact.org

Est. 1990. Equity SPT-8. **Preference.** Length: full length (over 90 min). Style: contemporary, no musical. Production: cast limit 8. **Application.** Best Material: query, synopsis, 10-pg sample, email ok. Deadline: 1-Apr-08. Response: 1 yr.

Next Theater Company

927 Noyes St., Evanston, IL, 60201
Jason Loewith, Artistic Dir.
Tel: 847-475-1875, Fax: 847-475-6767
info@nexttheatre.org; www.nexttheatre.org

Est. 1981. Equity CAT 1/2. Commissions 1 world premiere per season. **Preference.** Length: full length (over 90 min), mid-length (60-90 min). Subject: socially provocative. Production: cast limit 10. **Application.** Best Material: query, synopsis, 10-pg sample, SASE.

North Shore Music Theatre (NSMT)

Box 62, Beverly, MA, 01915
Barry Ivan, Artistic Dir.
Fax: 978-921-7874
www.nsmt.org

Est. 1955. Equity COST. 1,500-seat arena, 100-seat studio. Readings, workshops, commisssions and productions. **Consideration.** Assistance: per diem, room/board, room/board. Remuneration: Royalty: negotiable. **Preference.** Length: full length (over 90 min). Production: cast of 5 or more, orchestra of 2 or more. Material Must Be: unoptioned. **Application.** Best Way: professional recommendation. Best Material: query, synopsis, 25-pg sample, audio, SASE. Best Time: Nov-Apr. Response: 6 mos.

Northeast Theatre (TNT)

Box 854, Scranton, PA, 18501
David Zarko, Producing Artistic Dir
Tel: 570-558-1520
dzarko@thenortheasttheatre.us; www.thenortheasttheatre.us

Est. 1992. **Preference.** Length: full length (over 90 min). Style: comedy, drama. Production: cast limit 6. **Application.** Best Material: query, synopsis. Best Time: May-Aug. Response: 3 mos.

Northern Stage

Box 4287, White River Junction, VT, 05001
Brooke Ciardelli, Artistic Dir.
www.northernstage.org

Est. 1997. Equity LORT-D. **Application.** Best Way: professional recommendation. Best Material: query, SASE.

Northlight Theatre

9501 N. Skokie Blvd., Skokie, IL, 60077
Meghan Beals McCarthy, Lit. Manager
www.northlight.org

Est. 1975. Equity LORT C. **Preference.** Length: full length (over 90 min), mid-length (60-90 min). **Application.** Best Material: query, 10-pg sample, SASE. Response: 1 mo query, 8 mos script.

Northside Theatre Company

848 E. William St., San Jose, CA, 95116
Richard Orlando, Managing Artistic Dir.
www.northsidetheatre.com

Equity BAPP. **Preference.** Length: full length (over 90 min). Style: no musical. Subject: no children's. Production: thrust stage, no fly. **Application.** Best Material: synopsis, sample, SASE.

Not Merely Players

173 14th St., NE, Atlanta, GA, 30309
Gene-Gabriel Moore, Artistic Dir.
Tel: 404-872-8940, Fax: 404-522-1903
ggmnmp@bellsouth.net

Est. 1998. Nonprofit professional theater of inclusion. **Consideration.** Assistance:. Remuneration: royalty. **Preference.** Style: no musical. Subject: disabled, women, multi-ethnic. Production: cast limit 8. Material Must Be: unoptioned, unproduced. **Application.** Best Way: professional recommendation. Best Material: query, synopsis, SASE.

Obsidian Theatre Company

943 Queen St. East, Toronto, Ontario, M4M 1J6 Canada
Philip Akin, Aristic Dir.
Tel: 416-463-8444
obsidiantheatre@bellnet.ca; www.obsidian-theatre.com

Check website for submission details. **Preference.** Length: full length (over 90 min). Subject: primarily African Diaspora.

Odyssey Theatre Ensemble [CA]

2055 S. Sepulveda Blvd., Los Angeles, CA, 90025
Sally Essex-Lopresti, Literary Mgr
Tel: 310-477-2055
www.odysseytheatre.com

Est. 1969. Equity 99-seat. **Preference.** Length: full length (over 90 min). Subject: culturally diverse, provocative. **Application.** Best Material: query, synopsis, 10-pg sample, SASE. Response: 2 wks query, 6 mos script.

Old Globe

Box 122171, San Diego, CA, 92112
Kim Montelibano Heil, Literary Assoc
www.theoldglobe.org

Est. 1935. Equity LORT B, C. 1984 Regional Theater Tony winner. **Preference.** Length: full length (over 90 min). **Application.** Best Way: agent. Best Material: query, synopsis, 10-pg sample, SASE. Response: 3 mos quiery, 6 mos script.

Old Log Theater

Box 250, Excelsior, MN, 55331
Don Stolz, Producer
Tel: 952-474-5951, Fax: 952-474-1290
info@oldlog.com; www.oldlog.com

Est. 1940. Equity theater. **Consideration.** Remuneration: royalty. **Preference.** Length: full length (over 90 min). Style: comedy, drama. Production: cast limit 8. **Application.** Best Material: full script, SASE. Response: 2 wks.

Oldcastle Theatre Company

Box 1555, Bennington, VT, 05201
Eric Peterson, Producing Artistic Dir.
Tel: 802-447-1267, Fax: 802-442-3704
vtpeterson@adelphia.net; www.oldcastletheatreco.org

Est. 1972. Equity LOA. Productions and workshops. **Preference.** Length: full length (over 90 min). **Application.** Best Material: full script, SASE. Best Time: fall-winter.

Olney Theatre Center for the Arts

2001 Olney-Sandy Spring Rd, Olney, MD, 20832
Jim Petosa, Artistic Dir.
Tel: 301-924-4485, Fax: 301-924-2654
www.olneytheatre.org

Est. 1937. **Preference.** Length: full length (over 90 min). Style: no musical. Production: cast limit 8. **Application.** Best Way: professional recommendation. Response: 6 mos.

Omaha Theater Company

Rose Theater, 2001 Farnam St., Omaha, NE, 68102
James Larson, Artistic Dir.
Tel: 402-502-4618
www.otcyp.org

Est. 1949. **Preference.** Length: one-act (60 min). Style: adaptation, comedy, drama. Subject: children's. Production: cast limti 10, unit set. **Application.** Best Way: professional recommendation. Response: 6 mos.

Open Circle Theater (OCT)

429 Boren Ave. N., Seattle, WA, 98109
Ron Sandahl, Artistic Dir.
Tel: 206-382-4250
www.octheater.com

Est. 1992. **Preference.** Length: full length (over 90 min). Subject: fantasy and myth speaking to the human condition, no naturalism. **Application.** Best Way: local professional recommendation. Best Material: query, synopsis, 10-pg sample, resume. Response: 3 mos query, 6 mos script.

Open Eye Theater

Box 959, Margaretville, NY, 12455
Amie Brockway, Producing Artistic Dir.
Tel: 845-586-1660, Fax: 845-586-1660
openeye@catskill.net; www.theopeneye.org

Est. 1972. Readings and productions for a multigenerational audience. **Preference.** Length: mid-length (60-90 min.). Subject: all subjects. Production: small cast, modest set. Material Must Be: unproduced or looking for a second production. **Application.** Best Way: professional recommendation. Best Material: query, synopsis. Best Time: Jan-Apr. Response: 6 mos.

OpenStage Theatre & Company

Box 617, Fort Collins, CO, 80522
Denise Burson Freestone, Artistic Dir.
Tel: 970-484-5237, Fax: 970-482-4858
denisef@openstagetheatre.org; www.openstagetheatre.org

Est. 1973. **Preference.** Length: full length (over 90 min), one-act (30-60 min). Style: no musical. **Application.** Best Material: query, resume. Response: 1 mo query, 6 mos script.

Opera Cleveland

1422 Euclid Ave, #1052, Cleveland, OH, 44115
Dean Williamson, Artistic Dir.
Tel: 216-575-0903
www.operacleveland.org

Est. 2006 (merger of Lyric Opera Cleveland, Cleveland Opera). Spring-fall season and summer fest of 5 full-length operas. **Consideration.** Assistance: room/board, room/board. **Preference.** Length: full length (over 90 min). Style: opera. **Application.** Best Way: agent. Best Material: query, synopsis, full script, audio, SASE. Best Time: after 12/15/03. Response: 1 mo.

Oregon Shakespeare Festival

Box 158, Ashland, OR, 97520
Lue Morgan Douthit, Dir, Literary Development/Dramaturgy
Tel: 541-482-2111, Fax: 541-482-0446
www.osfashland.org

Est. 1935. Equity LORT B+. 1983 Regional Theater Tony winner. Staff: Bill Rauch (Artistic Dir). **Preference.** Length: full length (over 90 min). Subject: idea/language-oriented plays. Author Must Be: women/minorities encouraged. **Application.** Best Way: agent. Best Material: query. Best Time: fall. Response: 6 mos.

Organic Theater Company

Box 578189, Chicago, IL, 60657
Dorian Hadley
Tel: 312-634-0199
dhadley@organictheater.org; www.organictheater.org

Equity CAT-2. **Preference.** Length: all lengths. Style: all styles. Subject: all subjects. **Application.** Best Way: agent submission. Best Material: query letter (note theme addressed), 10-pg writing sample, submissions returned with SASE. Best Time: after 12/15/03. Deadline: ongoing. Response: 5/15/2004.

Pan Asian Repertory Theatre

520 8th Ave., #314, New York, NY, 10018
Tisa Chang, Artistic/Producing Dir.
Tel: 212-868-4030, Fax: 212-868-4033
panasian@aol.com; www.panasianrep.org

Est. 1977. Equity LOA. **Preference.** Length: full length (over 90 min). Style: comedy, drama. Subject: Asian, Asian-American. Production: cast limit 5, unit set. **Application.** Best Material: query, synopsis, 10-pg sample, bio, SASE. Best Time: summer. Response: 6 mos query, 9 mos script.

Pangea World Theater

711 W. Lake St., #101, Minneapolis, MN, 55408
Meena Natarajan, Exec/Literary Dir.
Tel: 612-822-0486, Fax: 612-821-1070
pangea@pangeaworldtheater.org; www.pangeaworldtheater.org

Est. 1995. **Preference.** Length: full length (over 90 min). Style: no musical. Subject: multi-ethnic. **Application.** Best Material: query. Response: 6 mos.

Pasadena Playhouse
39 S. El Molino Ave., Pasadena, CA, 91101
Literary Dept.
Tel: 626-792-8672
www.pasadenaplayhouse.org

Est. 1917. Equity LORT B. Year-round season in 670-seat and 99-seat theaters. **Preference.** Length: full length (over 90 min), mid-length (60-90 min). **Application.** Best Material: query, 10-pg sample, SASE.

Passage Theatre
Box 967, Trenton, NJ, 08605
Literary Consultant
Tel: 609-392-0766, Fax: 609-392-0318
info@passagetheatre.org; www.passagetheatre.org

Est. 1985. **Preference.** Length: full length (over 90 min). Style: comedy, drama. Subject: African-American, Jewish. Production: small cast, no fly. **Application.** Best Way: professional recommendation. Best Time: summer. Response: 3 mos.

PCPA Theatrefest
800 S. College Dr., Santa Maria, CA, 93454
Patricia M. Troxel, Literary Mgr
Tel: 805-928-7731, Fax: 805-928-7506
literary@pcpa.org; www.pcpa.org

Est. 1964. **Preference.** Length: full length (over 90 min). **Application.** Best Material: query, synopsis. Response: 3 mos query, 6 mos script.

Pegasus Players
Truman Coll., 1145 W. Wilson Ave., Chicago, IL, 60640
Alex Levy, Artistic Dir
Tel: 773-878-9761, Fax: 773-271-8057
info@pegasusplayers.org; www.pegasusplayers.org

Est. 1978. **Preference.** Length: full length (over 90 min). **Application.** Best Material: query, synopsis. Response: 1 mo query, 6 mos script.

Pegasus Theater Company
Box 942, Monte Rio, CA, 95462
www.pegasustheater.com

Est. 1998.

Pendragon Theatre
15 Brandy Brook Ave., Saranac Lake, NY, 12983
Molly Pietz-Walsh, Literary Mgr.
www.pendragontheatre.com

Est. 1980. **Preference.** Material Must Be: unpublished, unproduced. **Application.** Best Material: query, 10-pg sample, SASE.

Penguin Repertory Company
Box 91, Stony Point, NY, 10980
Staci Swedeen, Literary Mgr.
www.penguinrep.org

Est. 1977. Equity Guest Artist. Staff: Joe Brancato (Artistic Dir), Andrew Horn (Exec Dir). **Preference.** Length: full length (over 90 min). **Application.** Best Material: full script, submissions not returned. Response: 6 mos.

Penumbra Theatre Company
270 N. Kent St., St. Paul, MN, 55102
Sarah Bellamy, Assoc Producer
Tel: 651-288-6790, Fax: 651-288-6789
sarah.bellamy@penumbratheatre.org; www.penumbratheatre.org

Est. 1976. **Preference.** Length: full length (over 90 min), one-act (30-60 min). Subject: African-American or African diaspora, children's. **Application.** Best Material: query, full script, resume. Best Time: after 6/1/07. Response: 9 mos.

People's Light and Theatre Company
39 Conestoga Rd., Malvern, PA, 19355
Alda Cortese, Literary Mgr.
cortese@peopleslight.org; www.peopleslight.org

Est. 1974. Equity LORT. **Consideration.** Remuneration: royalty. **Preference.** Length: full length (over 90 min). Style: adaptation, comedy, drama. **Application.** Best Material: query, synopsis, 10-pg sample.

Performance Network Theatre
120 E. Huron St., Ann Arbor, MI, 48104
Carla Milarch, Artistic Dir.
Tel: 734-663-0696, Fax: 734-663-7367
info@performancenetwork.org; www.performancenetwork.org

Est. 1981. **Preference.** Length: full length (over 90 min). Production: cast limit 10, no fly. **Application.** Best Material: synopsis, 10-pg sample, SASE. Response: 6 mos.

Perseverance Theatre (PT)
914 3rd St, Douglas, AK, 99824
Tel: 907-364-2421, Fax: 907-364-2603
info@perseverancetheatre.org; www.perseverancetheatre.org

Est. 1979. Staff: PJ Paparelli (Artistic Dir), Jeffrey Herrmann (Producing Dir). **Preference.** Length: full length (over 90 min), one-act (30-60 min). Subject: gay and lesbian, Native American, sociopolitical themes. Author Must Be: resident of AK, women encouraged. **Application.** Best Material: query, synopsis, sample. Response: 1 mo query, 3 mos script.

Philadelphia Theatre Company (PTC)
230 S. 15th St., Fl. 4, Philadelphia, PA, 19102
Warren Hoffman, Literary Mgr
Tel: 215-985-1400, Fax: 215-985-5800
www.phillytheatreco.com

Est. 1974. Equity LORT D. 4 contemporary US plays/season (Sep-July). **Preference.** Length: full length (over 90 min). Style: comedy, drama, musical, family shows. Subject: contemporary US, social/humanistic themes, no children's or mysteries. Production: cast limit 10. **Application.** Best Way: agent or local writers only. Best Material: full script. Response: 6 mos.

Phoenix Arts Association Theatre [CA]
414 Mason St., #601, San Francisco, CA, 94103
Linda Ayres-Frederick, Artistic Dir
Tel: 415-759-7696, Fax: 415-664-5001
Lbaf23@aol.com; www.phoenixtheatresf.org

Est. 1985. **Preference.** Length: full length (over 90 min), one-act (30-60 min). Style: no musical. Subject: women (especially mature women), public figures. Production: cast limit 7, unit set. Material Must Be: bilingual French-English encouraged. **Application.** Best Material: query, synopsis. Response: 6 wks query, 6 mos script.

1/15/2008. Phoenix Theatre [AZ]
100 E. McDowell Rd., Phoenix, AZ, 85004
Daniel Schay, Managing Director
Tel: 602-258-1974, Fax: 602-899-5297
www.phoenixtheatre.net

Est. 1920. **Consideration.** Assistance: $200 . **Preference.** Length: full length (over 90 min). Subject: suitable for general audience. Material Must Be: unproduced. **Application.** Best Material: query, full script. Best Time: Nov.. Deadline: 1/15/2008. Response: 6 mos.

Phoenix Theatre [IN]
749 N. Park Ave., Indianapolis, IN, 46202
Tony McDonald, Literary Mgr
Tel: 317-635-7529, Fax: 317-635-0010
tmcdonald@phoenixtheatre.org; www.phoenixtheatre.org

Est. 1983. Staff: Bryan Foseca (Producing Dir). **Preference.** Length: full length (over 90 min), mid-length (60-90 min). Subject: African-American, GLBT, Latino, senior, women. Production: cast limit 6. **Application.** Best Way: professional recommendation. Best Material: query, synopsis, 10-pg sample, SASE. Response: 6 mos.

Pier One Theatre
Box 894, Homer, AK, 99603
Lance Petersen, Artistic Dir.
lance@xyz.net; www.pieronetheatre.org

Est. 1973. Non-Equity community theater. **Consideration.** Remuneration: 4\% royalty. **Application.** Best Material: full script, SASE. Best Time: winter. Response: 6 mos.

Pillsbury House Theatre
3501 Chicago Ave. S., Minneapolis, MN, 55407
Tel: 612-825-0459, Fax: 612-827-5818
www.puc-mn.org/theatre.html

Est. 1992. **Preference.** Length: full length (over 90 min), one-act (30-60 min). Style: no musical. Production: cast limit 10. **Application.** Best Way: agent. Best Material: Invitation only. Response: 5 mos query, 6 mos script.

Pioneer Theatre Company
Univ. of Utah, 300 South 1400 East, #205, Salt Lake City, UT, 84112
Charles Morey, Artistic Dir.
Tel: 801-581-6356, Fax: 801-581-5472
www.pioneertheatre.org

Est. 1962. Equity LORT B. **Preference.** Length: full length (over 90 min). **Application.** Best Way: agent submissions only at this time. Best Time: fall. Response: 1 mo query, 6 mos script.

Pittsburgh Public Theater
621 Penn Ave., Pittsburgh, PA, 15222
Kristen Link, Exec Asst
klink@ppt.org; www.ppt.org

Est. 1975. Equity LORT B. **Preference.** Length: full length (over 90 min). Style: comedy, drama. **Application.** Best Way: professional recommendation. Best Material: query, synopsis, 10-pg sample, SASE. Response: 6 mos.

Plan-B Theatre Company

138 W. 300 S., Salt Lake City, UT, 84101
Jerry Rapier, Producing Dir.
Tel: 801-297-4200, Fax: 801-466-3840
jerry@planbtheatre.org; www.planbtheatre.org

Est. 1995. Equity Special Appearance. **Consideration.** Remuneration: royalty. **Preference.** Length: mid-length (60-90 min). Style: drama. Subject: gay and/or socially conscious. Production: cast limit 5, minimal set. Material Must Be: unoptioned, unpublished, unproduced. **Application.** Best Way: email (PDF). Best Material: full script, SASE. Response: 3 mos.

Playhouse on the Square

51 S. Cooper St., Memphis, TN, 38104
Jackie Nichols, Exec Dir
Tel: 901-725-0776, Fax: 901-726-4498
www.playhouseonthesquare.org

Est. 1968. **Preference.** Length: full length (over 90 min). **Application.** Best Material: full script. Response: 5 mos.

PlayMakers Repertory Company

Univ. of North Carolina (UNC), Chapel Hilll, CB-3235, Center for Dramatic Art, Chapel Hill, NC, 27516
Adam Versenyi, Resident Dramaturg
www.playmakersrep.org

Est. 1976. Equity LORT D. Staff: Joseph Haj (Producing Artistic Dir). **Preference.** Length: full length (over 90 min). Style: no musical. **Application.** Best Way: agent. Best Material: submissions not returned. Best Time: Aug-May. Response: 6 mos.

Playwrights' Forum [TN]

Box 11265, Memphis, TN, 38111
Billy Pullen, Reading Chair
Tel: 901-725-2040
www.playwrights-forum.org

Est. 1991. 3-weekend run in 100-seat theater. **Consideration.** Assistance:. Frequency: semiannual. **Preference.** Length: full length (over 90 min), mid-length (60-90 min). Style: adaptation, comedy, drama. Subject: African-American, gay, Latino, senior, Women. Production: ages 18-90, cast of 2-6. Material Must Be: unpublished. **Application.** Best Way: professional recommendation. Best Material: query, 10-pg sample. Best Time: Feb. Response: 8 mos.

Playwrights Horizons

416 W. 42nd St., New York, NY, 10036
Adam Greenfield (plays), Christie Evangelisto (musicals)
Tel: 212-564-1235, Fax: 212-594-0296
literary@playwrightshorizons.org; www.playwrightshorizons.org

Est. 1971. Equity Off-Broadway nonprofit dedicated to new American voices, offering 6 productions/season and numerous readings. **Preference.** Length: full length (over 90 min). Style: no adaptation, no jukebox musical. Subject: no children's. Production: cast limit 10. Author Must Be: citizen of US. Material Must Be: unpublished, unproduced in NYC. **Application.** Best Way: professional recommendation, open submission policy. Best Material: full script, audio, bio, SASE. Response: 6-7 mos.

Porchlight Music Theatre Chicago

2814 N. Lincoln Ave., Chicago, IL, 60657
L. Walter Stearns, Artistic Dir.
Tel: 773-325-9884
porchlighttheatre@yahoo.com; www.porchlighttheatre.com

Est. 1994. **Preference.** Style: musical. Material Must Be: unoptioned. **Application.** Best Material: synopsis, audio, bio, SASE. Response: 6 mos.

Portland Center Stage [OR]
128 NW 11th Ave., Portland, OR, 97209
Mead Hunter, Literary Dir.
Tel: 503-445-3792, Fax: 503-445-3721
www.pcs.org

Est. 1988. **Preference.** Length: full length (over 90 min). Style: comedy, drama. Production: cast limit 12. **Application.** Best Material: query, 10-pg sample, resume. Response: 3 mos query, 6 mos script.

Portland Stage Company [ME]
Box 1458, Portland, ME, 04104
Daniel Burson, Literary Mgr.
Tel: 207-774-1043, Fax: 207-774-0576
dburson@portlandstage.com; www.portlandstage.com

Est. 1970. **Preference.** Length: full length (over 90 min). Style: comedy, drama. **Application.** Best Way: agent. Response: 3 mos query, 6 mos script.

Primary Stages
307 W. 38th St, #1510, New York, NY, 10018
Tessa LaNeve, Literary Mgr
info@primarystages.com; www.primarystages.com

Est. 1984. Equity Off-Broadway, ANTC. In residence at 59E59 Theaters. Founded to produce new plays and develop playwrights. Staff: Andrew Leynse (Artistic Dir.) **Preference.** Length: full length (over 90 min). Material Must Be: unproduced. **Application.** Best Way: we no longer accept unsolicited scripts, agent. Response: 1 yr.

Prime Stage Theatre
Box 1849, Pittsburgh, PA, 15230
Wayne Brinda, Artistic Dir.
Tel: 412-771-7373, Fax: 412-771-8585
wbrinda@primestage.com; www.primestage.com

Literature based youth and adult theatre **Preference.** Style: adaptation. Production: age 12 throughsenior citizen. **Application.** Best Way: unsolicited. Best Material: query, synopsis, 30-pg sample, submissions returned with SASE.

Prince Music Theater
100 S. Broad St., #650, Philadelphia, PA, 19110
Tel: 215-972-1000
info@princemusictheater.org; www.princemusictheater.org

Est. 1984. Formerly American Music Theater Festival. **Preference.** Style: musical. Production: cast of 2-12. Material Must Be: unproduced. **Application.** Best Way: professional recommendation. Best Material: query, synopsis, 30-pg sample, audio, SASE. Response: 8 mos.

Prop Thtr
3502-4 N. Elston Ave., Chicago, IL, 60618
Diane M. Honeyman, Executive Dir.
www.propthtr.org

Est. 1981

Prospect Theater Company (PTC)
520 8th Ave., #307, New York, NY, 10018
Cara Reichel, Producing Artistic Dir.
Tel: 212-594-4476, Fax: 212-594-4478
www.prospecttheater.org

Est. 1998. Small company of emerging artists, producing a 3-show season OOB under Equity Showcase. **Consideration.** Remuneration: royalty. **Application.** Best Way: professional recommendation. Best Material: full script, SASE.

Providence Black Repertory Company
276 Westminster St., Providence, RI, 02903
Donald W. King, Artistic Dir.
Tel: 401-351-0353, Fax: 401-621-7136
elephant@blackrep.org; www.blackrep.org

See mission and submission details on website before submitting.

Public Theater [NY]
425 Lafayette St., New York, NY, 10003
Liz Frankel, Literary Assoc
Tel: 212-539-8530, Fax: 212-539-8505
www.publictheater.org

Est. 1954. **Preference.** Length: full length (over 90 min). **Application.** Best Way: agent. Best Material: query, synopsis, 10-pg sample. Response: 6 mos.

Puerto Rican Traveling Theatre
141 W. 94th St., New York, NY, 10025
Allen Davis, Dir., Playwrights Unit
Tel: 212-354-1293, Fax: 212-307-6769

est. 1997. Workshops for beginning and professional playwrights.

Purple Rose Theatre Company
137 Park St., Chelsea, MI, 48118
Guy Sanville, Artistic Dir.
Tel: 734-433-7782, Fax: 734-475-0802
www.purplerosetheatre.org

Est. 1991. Equity SPT-7. **Consideration.** Remuneration: 6\%-8\% royalty. **Preference.** Length: full length (over 90 min), mid-length (60-90 min). Production: ages 18-80, cast of 2-10. Author Must Be: age 18 or older. Material Must Be: unoptioned, unpublished, unproduced. **Application.** Best Way: agent. Best Material: synopsis, 15-pg sample, SASE. Response: 6 mos.

Queens Theatre in the Park
Box 520069, Flushing, NY, 11352
Rob Urbinati, Dir, New Play Development
Tel: 718-760-0064
urbinati@aol.com; www.queenstheatre.org

Est. 2001. New play development series incl. Immigrant Voices Project and Plays a Mother Would Love. Check our website, www.queenstheatre.org for submission policies. **Preference.** Length: full length (over 90 min). Style: comedy, drama, musical. Subject: senior, multiethnic. Production: cast limit 6. **Application.** Response: 6 mos.

Rainbow Dinner Theatre
Box 56, Paradise, PA, 17562
David DiSavino, Exec Prod
david@rainbowdinnertheatre.com; www.rainbowdinnertheatre.com

Est. 1984. Professional non-Equity dinner theater. **Consideration.** Remuneration: 3\% royalty. **Preference.** Length: full length (over 90 min). Style: mainstream comedy. Production: ages 18 and older, cast of 2-12, set limit 2. **Application.** Best Way: agent. Best Material: synopsis, sample, SASE. Response: 6 mos.

Red Barn Theatre
319 Duval St., Rear, Key West, FL, 33040
Mimi McDonald, Managing Dir.
Tel: 305-296-9911, Fax: 305-293-3035
www.redbarntheatre.org

Est. 1981. **Preference.** Length: full length (over 90 min). Production: cast limit 8, small band, no fly. **Application.** Best Way: professional recommendation. Best Material: query, synopsis. Best Time: Mar-Jul. Response: only if interested.

Red Bull Theater
Box 250863, New York, NY, 10025
Jesse Berger, Artistic Dir.
Tel: 212-414-5168
info@redbulltheater.com; www.redbulltheater.com

Est. 2003. Produces reading series and new play workshop. **Preference.** Style: adaptation, translation, classically inspired. **Application.** Best Material: synopsis, sample, SASE.

Red Orchid Theatre
1531 N. Wells St., Chicago, IL, 60610
Nick Minas, Literary Dir.
Tel: 312-943-8722
arot@aredorchidtheatre.org; www.aredorchidtheatre.org

Est. 1993.

Repertory Theatre of St. Louis
130 Edgar Rd., #191730, St. Louis, MO, 63119
Susan Gregg, Assoc Artistic Dir.
Tel: 314-968-7340
sgregg@repstl.org; www.repstl.org

Est. 1966. Equity LORT B, D. **Preference.** Length: full length (over 90 min). Style: comedy, drama. Subject: non-naturalistic, sociopolitical themes. Production: small cast. **Application.** Best Material: query, synopsis. Response: 4 mos query, 2 yrs script.

Riant Theatre
The Black Experimental Theatre, Box 1902, New York, NY, 10013
Tel: 646-623-3488
TheRiantTheatre@aol.com; www.theriantheatre.com

Opportunities incl. semiannual Strawberry One-Act Fest, Core Project workshop. Staff: Van Dirk Fisher (Artistic Dir.), Richard Mover (Assoc. Dir.) **Preference.** Subject: African-American; multi-cultural.

Riverlight and Company
75 Wendell St., Battle Creek, MI, 49017
J. Kline Hobbs, Project Dir.
Tel: 269-962-2453
riverlightbc@yahoo.com; www.willard.lib.mi.us/npa/rlight

Est. 1981. School tours (grades 7-12). **Consideration.** Assistance: room/board, room/board. **Preference.** Length: mid-length (60-90 min). Style: documentary. Subject: US history, literature, social issues. Production: ages 21-85, cast limit 5, piano only, touring set. Author Must Be: age 21 or older, citizen of US, resident of MI preferred. Material Must Be: unoptioned, unpublished, unproduced. **Application.** Best Way: invite. Best Material: query, resume, reviews, SASE. Response: 2 mos.

Riverside Theatre [FL]
3250 Riverside Park Dr., Vero Beach, FL, 32963
Allen D. Cornell, Artistic Dir
Tel: 772-231-5860
backstage@riversidetheatre.com; www.riversidetheatre.com

Est. 1985. **Preference.** Length: full length (over 90 min). Subject: children's. Production: cast limit 10. **Application.** Best Material: query, synopsis. Best Time: spring. Response: 3 mos query, 5 mos script.

Riverside Theatre [IA]
213 N. Gilbert St., Iowa City, IA, 52245
Jody Hovland, Managing Artistic Dir.
Tel: 319-887-1360, Fax: 319-887-1362
artistic@riversidetheatre.org; www.riversidetheatre.org

Est. 1981. **Preference.** Length: full length (over 90 min). Style: all styles. Production: small cast, simple set. **Application.** Best Material: query, synopsis, first 10 pages. Response: only if interested.

Roadside Theater

Box 771, Norton, VA, 24273
Dudley Cocke, Dir.
Tel: 276-679-3116, Fax: 276-679-3116
roadsidetheater@verizon.net; www.appalshop.org/rst

Est. 1975. **Preference.** Length: full length (over 90 min). Style: comedy, drama. Subject: Appalachia. Production: cast of 2-6, touring set. **Application.** Best Material: query, synopsis, sample. Response: 3 wks query, 2 mos script.

Roots & Branches Theater

315 Hudson St., New York, NY, 10013
Arthur Strimling, Artistic Dir.
Tel: 212-366-8032, Fax: 212-366-8033
roots&branches@fegs.org

Ross Valley Players

Box 437, Ross, CA, 94957
raw@rossvalleyplayers.com; www.rossvalleyplayers.org

Opportunities incl. RAW (Ross Alternative Works) staged readings. **Preference.** Author Must Be: Greater San Francisco Bay Area Playwrights showcased.

Round House Theatre

Box 30688, Bethesda, MD, 20824
Tel: 240-644-1099, Fax: 240-644-1090
www.roundhousetheatre.org

Est. 1978. Literary Works Project in Bethesda, and New Works Series in Silver Spring. **Preference.** Length: full length (over 90 min). Subject: children's, contemporary issues, lesser-known classics, experimental works. Production: cast limit 8, piano only, unit set. **Application.** Best Material: synopsis, 10-pg sample. Response: 2 mos query, 1 yr script.

Roxbury Crossroads Theatre

37 Vine St., Roxbury, MA, 02119
Ed Bullins, Artistic Dir.
Tel: 617-442-6627
rct9@verizon.net; http://www.roxburycrossroadstheatre.com

Roxy Regional Theatre

100 Franklin St., Clarksville, TN, 37040
Tom Thayer, Managing Dir.
Tel: 931-645-7699
www.roxyregionaltheatre.org

Est. 1983. **Preference.** Length: full length (over 90 min). Subject: children's. Production: small cast. **Application.** Best Material: full script, audio. Best Time: Jan-Feb.

Royal Court Theatre

Sloane Sq., London, SW1W 8AS England
Literary Dept.
www.royalcourttheatre.com

Est. 1956. Opportunities incl. production and development for both international writers (international@royalcourttheatre.com) and young writers (ywp@royalcourttheatre.com). **Application.** Best Way: by snail mail only. Best Material: 1/2-page synopsis, SASE (intl. reply coupon).

Ryan Repertory Company Inc.

Harry Warren Theatre, 2445 Bath Ave., Brooklyn, NY, 11214
Barbara Parisi, Exec Dir
Tel: 718-996-4800
ryanrep@juno.com

Est. 1972. Staff: John Sannuto, Artistic Dir. **Application.** Best Material: full script, audio, submissions not returned.

Sacramento Theatre Company
1419 H St., Sacramento, CA, 95814
Peggy Shannon, Artistic Dir.
Tel: 916-446-7501, Fax: 916-446-4066
www.sactheatre.org

Est. 1942. Equity LORT D. **Preference.** Length: full length (over 90 min). Style: adaptation, comedy, drama, revue. Subject: contemporary sociopolitical themes. Production: cast limit 10. **Application.** Best Way: agent. Best Time: Jun-Dec. Response: 6 mos.

Salt Lake Acting Company
168 West 500 North, Salt Lake City, UT, 84103
David Mong, Literary Mgr.
Tel: 801-363-0526, Fax: 801-532-8513
mong@saltlakeactingcompany.org; www.saltlakeactingcompany.org

Est. 1970. Four staged readings/year of new plays and some commissions. **Preference.** Length: full length (over 90 min). Material Must Be: unproduced. **Application.** Best Way: professional recommendation. Best Material: query, SASE. Response: 6 mos.

San Diego Repertory Theatre
79 Horton Plz., San Diego, CA, 92101
Steve Morgan-MacKay, Artistic Assoc
Tel: 619-231-3586, Fax: 619-235-0939
www.sandiegorep.com

Est. 1976. **Preference.** Length: full length (over 90 min), mid-length (60-90 min). Subject: multi-ethnic, intercultural, sociopolitical themes. **Application.** Best Material: full script.

San Jose Repertory Theatre
101 Paseo de San Antonio, San Jose, CA, 95113
Kirsten Beandt, Associate Artistic Dir.
Tel: 408-367-7206, Fax: 408-367-7237
www.sjrep.com

Est. 1980. Equity LORT C. Works begin in New America Playwrights Fest of mid-career playwrights. Interested in ethnic plays, plays by women, and plays with music. Staff: Nick Nichols (Managing Dir). **Preference.** Length: full length (over 90 min). **Application.** Best Way: professional recommendation. Best Time: Jun-Oct. Response: 6-9 mos.

Sanctuary: Playwrights Theatre [NY]
616 E. 19th St., Brooklyn, NY, 11230
Bob Jude Ferrante, Co-Artistic Dir.
Tel: 718-859-6625, Fax: 718-421-4178
jude@pipeline.com; sanctuarytheatre.org

Est. 1997. **Preference.** Length: full length (over 90 min). Style: comedy, drama. Subject: unusual, radical/epic work; no kitchen-sink or sitcom. Author Must Be: professionally produced. **Application.** Best Material: query, full script, resume, SASE. Response: 6 mos.

Santa Monica Playhouse
1211 4th St., Santa Monica, CA, 90401
Cydne Moore, Dramaturg
Tel: 310-394-9779, Fax: 310-393-5573
theatre@SantaMonicaPlayhouse.com; www.santamonicaplayhouse.com

Est. 1962. **Preference.** Length: full length (over 90 min). Style: no musical. Subject: no children's. Production: cast limit 10. **Application.** Best Material: query, 1-pg synopsis, 10-pg sample, resume, submissions not returned. Response: 6 mos query, 9 mos script.

Seacoast Repertory Theatre

125 Bow St., Portsmouth, NH, 03801
John McCluggage, Artistic Dir.
Tel: 603-433-4793 x128, Fax: 603-431-7818
www.seacoastrep.org

Est. 1986. Offers 8 mainstage and 6 youth works each year. **Preference.** Length: full length (over 90 min), mid-length (60-90 min.). Style: all styles. Subject: all subjects. Material Must Be: unoptioned. **Application.** Best Way: agent. Best Material: 1-pg synopsis, 10 page sample, SASE. Response: 6 mos.

Seaside Music Theater (SMT)

Box 2835, Daytona Beach, FL, 32120
Lester Malizia, Artistic Dir.
Tel: 386-252-3394, Fax: 386-252-8991
www.seasidemusictheater.org

Est. 1977. **Preference.** Style: musical (youth; adult), revue. Production: cast limit 10 (youth) or 30 (adult), small combo (youth) or orchestra limit 25 (adult). **Application.** Best Material: query, synopsis, audio. Best Time: Sep-Nov. Response: 3 mos query, 6 mos script.

Seattle Children's Theatre

201 Thomas St., Seattle, WA, 98109
Torrie McDonald, Literary/Publications Mgr.
Tel: 206-443-0807, Fax: 206-443-0442
torriem@sct.org; www.sct.org

Est. 1975. Innovative and professional theater for family and school audiences, Sep-Jun. **Preference.** Length: full length (over 90 min), mid-length (60-90 min), one-act (30-60 min). Subject: children's. **Application.** Best Way: professional recommendation only. Best Material: synopsis, 10-pg sample, SASE. Response: 4 mos.

Seattle Repertory Theatre

155 Mercer St., Box 900923, Seattle, WA, 98109
Braden Abraham, Literary Mgr.
Tel: 206-443-2210, Fax: 206-443-2379
bradena@seattlerep.org; www.seattlerep.org

Est. 1963. Equity LORT B+, C. 1990 Regional Theater Tony winner. 8-9 plays/yr on 2 proscenium stages: 850-seat Bagley Wright; 300-seat Leo K. Staff: David Esbjornson (Artistic Dir). **Consideration.** Assistance: room/board, room/board. Remuneration: royalty. **Preference.** Length: full length (over 90 min), mid-length (60-90 min). Style: adaptation, comedy, drama. **Application.** Best Way: agent. Best Material: full script, SASE. Response: 6 mos.

Second Stage Theatre

307 W. 43rd St., New York, NY, 10036
Sarah Bagley, Literary Mgr
Tel: 212-787-8302, Fax: 212-397-7066
sbagley@secondstagetheatre.com; www.secondstagetheatre.com

Est. 1979. Equity LOA. Plays and musicals of heightened realism and sociopolitical issues, particularly by women and minority writers. Staff: Carole Rothman (Artistic Dir), Ellen Richard (Exec Dir). **Preference.** Length: full length (over 90 min). **Application.** Best Material: query, synopsis, 10 pg sample. Response: 1 mo query, 6 mos script.

Seem-To-Be-Players

Lawrence Arts Center, 940 New Hampshire St., Lawrence, KS, 66044
Ric Averill, Artistic Dir.
Tel: 785-843-2787, Fax: 785-843-6629
raverill@sunflower.com; www.lawrenceartscenter.com

Est. 1973. **Preference.** Subject: children's. Production: cast limit 6 adults or 30 youth. Material Must Be: original. **Application.** Best Material: full script. Best Time: Mar-May. Response: 6 wks query, 3 mos script.

Serendipity Theatre Company

2936 N. Southport Ave., Chicago, IL, 60657
Literary Mgr.
Tel: 773-296-0163, Fax: 773-296-0165
Literary@serendipitytheatre.com; www.serendipitytheatre.org

Est. 1999. **Preference.** Length: full length (over 90 min), one-act (30-60 min). Style: adaptation, comedy, drama. Author Must Be: early-career or lesser-known writer. **Application.** Best Material: query, synopsis, sample, SASE. Response: 6 mos.

Seven Angels Theatre

Box 3358, Waterbury, CT, 06705
Semina DeLaurentis, Artistic Dir.
Tel: 203-591-8223, Fax: 203-757-1807
www.sevenangelstheatre.org

Est. 1990. **Preference.** Length: full length (over 90 min). Production: cast limit 10, unit set, no fly. **Application.** Best Way: professional recommendation. Response: only if interested.

ShadowBox: The Sketch Comedy Rock 'n' Roll Club

164 Easton Town Center, Columbus, OH, 41071
Jimmy Mak, Dramaturg
Tel: 614-416-7625, Fax: 614-416-76300
jmak@shadowboxcabaret.com; www.shadowboxcabaret.com

Est. 1989 **Preference.** Length: short (under 30 min.). Style: comedy. Subject: all subjects. Production: age 15-50, cast of up to 5, minimal set. **Application.** Best Way: unsolicited. Best Material: full script. Response: 10 months.

Shadowlight Productions

22 Chattanooga St., San Francisco, CA, 94114
Larry Reed, Artistic Dir.
Tel: 415-648-4461, Fax: 415-641-9734
info@shadowlight.org; www.shadowlight.org

Est. 1972. **Preference.** Length: full length (over 90 min), one-act (30-60 min). Subject: children's, figures from myth or history. Production: cast limit 15. Material Must Be: suitable for shadow theater (puppets and live actors). **Application.** Best Way: professional recommendation. Response: 1 mo.

Shakespeare & Company

70 Kemble St., Lenox, MA, 01240
Michael Hammond, Associate Artistic Dir
Tel: 413-637-1199
mhammond@shakespeare.org; www.shakespeare.org

Est. 1978. **Preference.** Length: full length (over 90 min). Style: no musical. Production: cast of 2-8. **Application.** Best Material: query, synopsis, 10-pg sample, by post only, SASE. Response: 3 mos.

Shakespeare Festival at Tulane

Tulane Univ., 215 McWilliams Hall, New Orleans, LA, 70118
Ron Gural, Artistic Dir.
Tel: 504-865-5105, Fax: 504-865-5205
www.neworleansshakespeare.com

Est. 1993. **Preference.** Length: full length (over 90 min), one-act (30-60 min). Style: adaptation, comedy, drama. Production: unit set, no fly. Author Must Be: resident of LA. **Application.** Best Material: query, synopsis, sample, resume, SASE. Best Time: Aug-Nov. Response: 2 mos query, 3 mos script.

Shakespeare Theatre Company

8th St. SE, Washington, DC, 20003
Akiva Fox, Lit Assoc.
Tel: 202-547-3230, Fax: 202-547-0226
afox@shakespearetheatre.org; www.shakespearetheatre.org

Est. 1986. Classical theatre dedicated to works of Shakespeare and other classical writers in new translations and adaptations. **Consideration.** Fees: royalty. **Preference.** Length: full length (over 90 min). Style: adaptation, translation. **Application.** Best Way: agent. Best Material: query, SASE.

Shotgun Productions Inc.

165 E. 35 St., #7-J, New York, NY, 10016
Linda Nelson, Co-Artist/Producing Dir.
Tel: 212-689-2322, Fax: 718-291-9354
literary@shotgun-productions.org; www.shotgun-productions.org

Est. 1989. Equity. 3-step development, incl. New Playwrights Reading Series (NPRS), workshops and full productions. **Preference.** Length: full length (over 90 min), mid-length (60-90 min). Material Must Be: unoptioned, unproduced. **Application.** Best Way: professional recommendation. Best Material: query, synopsis. Response: 1 yr.

Signature Theatre [VA]

4200 Campbell Ave., Arlington, VA, 22206
Marcia Gardner, Education Dir
Tel: 703-820-9771
www.signature-theatre.org

Est. 1990. **Preference.** Length: full length (over 90 min). Style: musical. Subject: social issues. Production: cast limit 10, no fly. Material Must Be: professionally unproduced. **Application.** Best Way: agent. Best Time: Feb-Jul. Response: 4 mos.

Signature Theatre Company [NY]

630 9th Ave., #1106, New York, NY, 10036
James Houghton, Founding Artistic Dir.
Tel: 212-967-1913, Fax: 212-967-2957
www.signaturetheatre.org

Est. 1991. Season of work by one playwright in residence.

Simpatico Theatre Project

Box 2277, Philadelphia, PA, 19103
Angela S. Zuck, Literary Mgr

Preference. Length: full length (over 90 min), mid-length (60-90 min.), one-act (30-60 min.). Style: comedy, drama. Subject: all subjects. Production: cast size 1-10. Material Must Be: unproduced. **Application.** Best Material: synopsis, SASE. Best Time: Dec-Feb; May-Jul. Response: varies.

SITI Company

520 8th Ave., #310, New York, NY, 10018
Megan Szalla, Managing Dir.

Est. 1992. Staff: Anne Bogart (Artistic Dir).

Skylight

158 N. Broadway, Milwaukee, WI, 53202
Diana Carl, Company Mgr.
Tel: 414-291-7811, Fax: 414-291-7815
dianac@skylightopera.com; www.skylightopera.com

Est. 1959. Formerly Skylight Opera Theatre. **Preference.** Style: musical, revue. Production: cast limit 22, orchestra limit 18. **Application.** Best Material: query, synopsis, audio. Best Time: summer. Response: 2 mos query, 1 yr script.

Society Hill Playhouse

507 S. 8th St., Philadelphia, PA, 19147
Tel: 215-923-0210, Fax: 215-923-1789
www.societyhillplayhouse.com

Preference. Length: full-length. Style: no adaptation, no translation. Subject: all subjects. Production: cast of up to 8. **Application.** Best Material: query letter (note theme addressed), submissions returned with SASE. Deadline: ongoing. Response: 3 months.

SoHo Repertory Theater Inc.

86 Franklin St, Fl. 4, New York, NY, 10013
Sarah Benson, Artistic Dir.
Tel: 212-941-8632, Fax: 212-941-7148
sohorep@sohorep.org; www.sohorep.org

Est. 1975. Apply thru Writer/Director Lab. Staff: Alexandra Conley (Exec Dir). **Preference.** Length: full length (over 90 min), one-act (30-60 min.). Style: drama. **Application.** Best Way: invitation only.

Sonoma County Repertory Theater

104 N. Main St., Sebastopol, CA, 95472

Est. 1993. Staff: Jennifer King (Exec./Art. Dir.), Scott Phillips (Prod./Art. Dir), Jack Weaver (Dev./Marketing Mang.) **Application.** Best Material: 1-pg synopsis, full script, cast list, SASE.

South Camden Theatre Company

318 Hudson St., Gloucester City, NJ, 08030
Joseph M. Paprzycki, Artistic Dir
camdentheatre@aol.com; www.southcamdentheatre.org

Est. 2004. Non-Equity. Opportunities incl. one-act fest. **Consideration.** Remuneration: honorarium. **Preference.** Length: full length (over 90 min), short (under 30 min). Style: drama. Subject: political. **Application.** Best Way: invite. Best Material: synopsis, SASE.

South Coast Repertory

Box 2197, Costa Mesa, CA, 92628
Megan Monaghan, Literary Mgr.
Tel: 714-708-5500
www.scr.org

Est. 1964. 1988 Regional Theater Tony winner. Mainstage series in 507-seat Segerstrom, family series in 335-seat Argyres. Also NewSCRipts reading series and Pacific Playwrights Fest (PPF) of new work. **Consideration.** Remuneration: royalty. **Preference.** Length: full length (over 90 min). **Application.** Best Material: query, synopsis, 10-pg sample, SASE. Response: 2 mos query; 6 mos script.

Springer Opera House

103 10th St., Columbus, GA, 31901
Paul Pierce, Producing Artistic Dir.
Tel: 706-324-5714, Fax: 706-324-4461
ppierce@springeroperahouse.org; www.springeroperahouse.org

Est. 1871. **Preference.** Length: full length (over 90 min). Style: comedy, musical. Subject: children's. Production: small cast, unit set. **Application.** Best Material: query, synopsis. Best Time: Nov-Feb. Response: 2 mos query, 6 mos script.

St. Louis Black Repertory Company

1717 Olive St., Fl. 4, St. Louis, MO, 63103
Ronald J. Himes, Producing Dir.
Tel: 314-534-3807, Fax: 314-534-4035
ronh@theblackrep.org; www.theblackrep.org

Est. 1976. **Preference.** Length: full length (over 90 min). Style: comedy, drama, musical. Subject: children's. **Application.** Best Material: query, synopsis, 5-pg sample, resume. Best Time: Jun-Aug. Response: 2 mos.

Stage One: The Louisville Children's Theater
501 W. Main, Louisville, KY, 40202
J. Daniel Herring, Artistic Dir.
Tel: 502-589-5946, Fax: 502-588-5910
stageone@stageone.org; www.stageone.org

Est. 1946. Equity TYA. Classic and contemporary tales of childhood with strong social and emotional content. **Preference.** Style: adaptation, comedy, drama. Subject: children's. Production: cast limit 12, touring set. **Application.** Best Material: query, sample. Best Time: Oct-Dec. Response: 3 mos.

Stages Repertory Theatre [TX]
3201 Allen Pkwy., #101, Houston, TX, 77019
Kenn McLaughlin, Producing Artistic Dir.
Tel: 713-527-0220, Fax: 713-527-8669
www.stagestheatre.com

Est. 1978. **Preference.** Length: full length plays (over 90 min), one-act children's (30-60 min). Style: comedy, drama. Subject: children's, non-realistic, edgy. Production: cast limit 6. **Application.** Best Material: full script. Response: 9 mos.

Stages Theatre Center [CA]
1540 N. McCadden Pl., Hollywood, CA, 90028
Paul Verdier, Artistic Dir.
Tel: 323-463-5356, Fax: 323-463-3904
ask@stageshollywood.com; www.stagestheatrecenter.com

Est. 1982. **Preference.** Length: full length (over 90 min), one-act (30-60 min). Subject: children's, experimental text, movement-based non-text. Material Must Be: Spanish and French texts encouraged. **Application.** Best Material: full script. Response: 1 yr.

Stages Theatre Company [MN]
1111 Main St., Hopkins, MN, 55343
Bruce Rowan, Mgr, New Play Development
Tel: 952-979-1120, Fax: 952-979-1124
brow@stagestheatre.org; www.stagestheatre.org

Est. 1984. **Preference.** Length: mid-length (75 min). Subject: children's. Production: ages 10-21. Material Must Be: with children in primary roles. **Application.** Best Material: query, synopsis, full script, SASE. Response: 3 mos.

Stageworks/Hudson [NY]
41-A Cross St., Hudson, NY, 12534
Laura Margolis, Exec Artistic Dir
Tel: 518-828-7843, Fax: 518-828-4026
contact@stageworkstheater.org; www.stageworkstheater.org

Est. 1993. Equity SPT, spring-fall season. **Preference.** Length: full length (over 90 min). Style: adaptation, comedy, drama. Subject: contemporary US. Production: cast limit 8, unit set, no fly. **Application.** Best Material: query, synopsis, submissions not returned. Response: 8 mos.

Stamford Theatre Works (STW)
307 Atlantic St., Stamford, CT, 06901
Steve Karp, Producing Dir.
Tel: 203-359-4414, Fax: 203-353-8018
www.stamfordtheatreworks.org

Est. 1988. **Preference.** Length: full length (over 90 min). Subject: contemporary, challenging, social themes. Production: small cast, unit set. **Application.** Best Way: professional recommendation. Response: 2 mos query, 6 mos script.

Steppenwolf Theatre Company
758 W. North Ave., 4th Fl. , Chicago, IL, 60610
Edward Sobel, Dir, New Play Dev.
Tel: 312-335-1888
www.steppenwolf.org

Est. 1976. 1985 Regional Theater Tony winner. Formed by an actors collective, Steppenwolf is now an ensemble of 41, performing in 3 spaces: 515-seat Downstairs (CAT-6); 299-seat Upstairs (CAT-3, CAT-5); 88-seat Garage (CAT-3). **Preference.** Length: full length (over 90 min). Style: adaptation, drama. Production: cast limit 10. Material Must Be: unproduced. **Application.** Best Material: query, synopsis, 10-pg sample, resume. Response: 1 mo query, 6 mos script.

Stepping Stone Theatre for Youth Development
55 Victoria St. N, St. Paul, MN, 55104
Richard Hitchler, Artistic Dir.
Tel: 651-225-9265, Fax: 651-225-1225
www.steppingstonetheatre.org

Est. 1987. **Preference.** Length: mid-length (60-90 min). Production: youth cast of 10-20. Material Must Be: unoptioned, unproduced. **Application.** Best Material: full script, audio. Response: 6 mos.

Stoneham Theatre
125 Main St., Ste. F, Stoneham, MA, 02180
Weylin Symes, Artistic Dir.
weylin@stonehamtheatre.org; www.stonehamtheatre.org

Est. 2000. Equity theatre located 8 miles North of Boston. NEAT contract. **Preference.** Length: full length (over 90 min). Production: cast limit 12 (play) or 18 (musical), orchestra limit 7. **Application.** Best Material: query, synopsis, 20-pg sample, audio, submissions not returned. Response: 4 mos.

Stray Dog Theatre (SDT)
2348 Tennessee Ave., St. Louis, MO, 63104
Gary F. Bell, Artistic Dir.
Tel: 314-865-1995, Fax: 314-865-1995
straydogtheatre@aol.com; www.straydogtheatre.org

Est. 2003. **Preference.** Length: full length (over 90 min), one-act (30-60 min). Production: cast limti 15, no fly. **Application.** Best Material: query, synopsis, 20-pg sample, audio, resume, SASE. Response: 2 mos query, 6 mos script.

StreetSigns Center for Literature and Performance
204 Harland's Creek Dr., Pittsboro, NC, 27312

Est. 1992. Founded in Chicago, Street Signs now works with Georgetown Univ. in Washington and UNC Chapel Hill to develop and present new literary adaptations, company-created works, new plays, and re-imaginings of classics. Staff: Derek Goldman (Artistic Dir), Joseph Megel (Assoc Artistic Dir).

Studio Arena Theatre
710 Main St., Buffalo, NY, 14202
Kathleen Gaffney, Artistic Dir.
Tel: 716-856-8025, Fax: 716-856-3415
www.studioarena.org

Est. 1965. Equity LORT B. **Preference.** Length: full length (over 90 min). Style: adaptation, comedy, drama. Subject: local interest, US history, ethnic cultures. Production: cast limit 6, no fly. **Application.** Best Way: agent. Best Material: 1-pg synopsis. Response: 6 mos.

Studio Theatre
1501 14th St. NW, Washington, DC, 20005
Danielle Amato, Dramaturg/Assoc Lit Mgr
literary@studiotheatre.org; www.studiotheatre.org

Est. 1978. Equity SPT. Rarely produces world premieres. **Consideration.** Remuneration: royalty. **Preference.** Length: full length (over 90 min). **Application.** Best Way: professional recommendation. Best Material: full script, SASE. Response: 6 mos.

SummerNITE

Northern Illinois Univ., NIU School of Theater, DeKalb, IL, 60115
Lit. Management, SummerNite
Tel: 815-753-1334, Fax: 815-753-8415
cmarkle@niu.edu; www.niu.edu/theatre/summernite/playwrights.htm

Premieres (US or Chicago) of innovative and intellectually stimulating stage works. **Application.** Best Way: agent.

Sundog Theatre

Box 10183, Staten Island, NY, 10301
Susan Fenley, Artistic Dir.
sfenley@sundogtheatre.org; www.SundogTheatre.org

Preference. Length: full length (over 90 min), mid-length (60-90 min). Production: cast of 2-10, orchestra limit 4, minimal set. Author Must Be: resident or citizen of US. Material Must Be: unoptioned. **Application.** Best Way: professional recommendation.

Synchronicity Performance Group

Box 6012, Atlanta, GA, 31107
Rachel May, Producing Artistic Dir
Tel: 404-523-1009
info@sychrotheatre.com; www.synchrotheatre.com

Est. 1997. Dedicated to strong women characters, scripts with depth, meaning and social content, and powerful stories. **Preference.** Length: full length (over 90 min). Style: no musical. Subject: children's, women, social issues. Production: cast limit 12, no fly. **Application.** Best Material: query, synopsis, 5-pg sample, SASE. Best Time: May-Sept.. Response: only if interested.

Syracuse Stage

820 E. Genesee St., Syracuse, NY, 13210
Nichole Gantshar, Assoc Literary Mgr
ngantshar@aol.com; www.syracusestage.org

Est. 1974. **Preference.** Length: full length (over 90 min). Production: small cast. **Application.** Best Way: professional recommendation, agent. Best Material: query, synopsis, 10-pg sample, resume, list of characters, SASE.

Teatro Dallas

1331 Record Crossing Rd., Dallas, TX, 75235
Abigail Self, Managing Dir
teatro@airmail.net; www.teatrodallas.org

Est. 1985. Classical and contemporary Latino playwrights. **Preference.** Style: no musical. Subject: children's, Latino. Production: cast limit 8, unit set. **Application.** Best Way: professional recommendation. Best Material: query, synopsis, SASE.

Teatro Vision

1700 Alum Rock Ave., San Jose, CA, 95116
Elisa Marina Alvarado, Artistic Dir
Tel: 408-928-5582, Fax: 408-928-5589
elisamarina@teatrovision.org; www.teatrovision.org

Est. 1984. Equity BAT-2. 3-play season in 500-seat theater. Staff: Raul Lozano (Exec Dir). **Consideration.** Remuneration: royalty. **Preference.** Subject: Latino. Production: age 18 and older, cast limit 12, orchestra limit 4, flexible set. Author Must Be: age 18 or older. **Application.** Best Material: query, synopsis, SASE. Best Time: May-Oct. Response: 1 mo.

Tectonic Theater Project
204 W 84th St, New York, NY, 10024
Beth Whitaker, Literary Mgr
Tel: 212-579-6111, Fax: 212-579-6112
literary@tectonictheaterproject.org; www.tectonictheaterproject.org

Est. 1992. Lab led by Moises Kaufman. **Preference.** Length: full length (over 90 min). Style: all styles, daring/experimental in form/structure. **Application.** Best Way: agent. Best Material: synopsis, full script, SASE. Response: 8 mos.

Ten Grand Productions
532 LaGuardia Pl., #498, New York, NY, 10012
Jason Hewitt, Managing Dir
Tel: 212-696-7344
jhewitt@tengrand.org; www.tengrand.org

Est. 2003. **Preference.** Style: drama. **Application.** Best Material: 20-pg sample, SASE.

Tennessee Repertory Theatre
161 Rains Ave., Nashville, TN, 37203
Rene D. Copeland, Prod. Artistic Dir.
Tel: 615-244-4878
www.tennesseerep.org

Est. 1985. **Preference.** Length: full length (over 90 min). Production: small cast, small orchestra. **Application.** Best Material: query, synopsis, dialogue sample, audio, SASE. Best Time: Jun-Sep. Response: 1 yr.

Thalia Spanish Theatre
41-17 Greenpoint Ave., Sunnyside, NY, 11104
Angel Gil Orrios, Artistic/Exec Dir.
Tel: 718-729-3880, Fax: 718-729-3388
info@thaliatheatre.org; www.thaliatheatre.org

Est. 1977. **Preference.** Length: full length (over 90 min). Style: no musical. Subject: Hispanic. **Application.** Best Material: full script. Response: 3 mos.

Theater at Monmouth
The Shakespeare Theater of Maine, Box 385, Monmouth, ME, 04259
David Greenham, Producing Dir.
www.theateratmonmouth.org

Est. 1970. Only adaptations of popular classics for adults and children. **Preference.** Length: full length (over 90 min), one-act (30-60 min). Style: adaptation. **Application.** Best Material: query, synopsis, SASE. Best Time: Aug-Sep. Response: 2 mos.

Theater by the Blind
306 W. 18th St., New York, NY, 10011
Ike Schambelan, Co-Artistic Dir.
Tel: 212-243-4337, Fax: 212-243-4337
lschambelan@nyc.rr.com; www.tbtb.org

Est. 1979. Equity Tier LOA. Staff: George Ashiotis (Co-Artistic Dir). **Consideration.** Remuneration: $1,000 honorarium. **Preference.** Subject: blind. Production: cast of 1-6. **Application.** Best Material: full script, SASE. Response: 2 mos..

Theater Catalyst [PA]
2030 Sansom St., Philadelphia, PA, 19103
Joe Koroly, Managing Artistic Dir.
Tel: 215-563-4330, Fax: 215-563-4843
tcatalyst@hotmail.com; www.theatercatalyst.org

Est. 1998. Supports diverse and underserved theater artists in the Philadelphia area. **Preference.** Length: mid-length (60-90 min), one-act (30-60 min). Production: cast limit 6. **Application.** Best Material: synopsis, SASE. Response: 6 mos.

Theater for the New City (TFNC)
155 1st Ave., New York, NY, 10003
Crystal Field, Exec. Artistic Dir.
Tel: 212-254-1109, Fax: 212-979-6570
www.theaterforthenewcity.net

Est. 1970. Equity Showcase. Experimental new works. **Preference.** Length: full length (over 90 min). Material Must Be: unproduced. **Application.** Best Material: synopsis, 10-pg sample, SASE.

Theater IV
114 W. Broad St., Richmond, VA, 23220
Janine Serresseque
Tel: 804-783-1688, Fax: 804-775-2325
www.theatreiv.org

Est. 1975. **Preference.** Length: full length (over 90 min). Style: no musical. Subject: children's. Production: cast of 3-5, touring set. **Application.** Best Material: query, synopsis. Response: 2 mos query, 2 yrs script.

Theater J
1529 16th St. NW, Washington, DC, 20036
Ari Roth, Artistic Dir.
Tel: 202-777-3233, Fax: 202-518-9421
www.theaterj.org

Est. 1991. Offers readings, workshops, and productions. **Preference.** Length: full length (over 90 min). Subject: Jewish, multicultural, political. **Application.** Best Material: synopsis, full script, SASE. Response: 6 mos.

Theater of the Seventh Sister
Box 276, Lancaster, PA, 17608
Lydia Brubaker, Assoc. Artistic Director
Tel: 717-396-7764, Fax: 717-509-4662
lydia@seventhsister.com; www.seventhsister.com

Opportunities incl. Project Genesis reading series. **Consideration.** Remuneration: production, reading. Frequency: semiannual. **Preference.** Length: all length. Style: all styles. Subject: all subjects. Material Must Be: unproduced. **Application.** Best Way: unsolicited. Best Material: synopsis, full script.

Theater Ten Ten
1010 Park Ave., New York, NY, 10028
Judith Jarosz, Producing Artistic Dir.
www.TheaterTenTen.com

Est. 1955. **Preference.** Production: small cast. **Application.** Best Way: invite. Best Material: synopsis, 10-pg sample. Response: 1 yr.

Theatre Ariel
Box 0334, Merion, PA, 19066
Deborah Baer Mozes, Artistic Dir.
Tel: 215-735-9481
theatreariel@netreach.net; www.wjt.ca/mem/ariel.htm

Est. 1990. **Preference.** Length: full length (over 90 min), one-act (30-60 min). Style: adaptation, comedy, drama. Subject: children's, Jewish. Production: cast limit 5, touring set. **Application.** Best Material: query, synopsis, 10-pg sample, resume. Best Time: May-Oct. Response: 1 mo query, 9 mos script.

Theatre at Boston Court

Box 60187, Pasadena, CA, 91116
Bryan Davidson, Literary Mgr
Tel: 626-683-6883, Fax: 626-683-6886
bryand@bostoncourt.com; www.bostoncourttheatre.com

Est. 2003. Equity 99-seat. **Preference.** Length: full length (over 90 min). Subject: textually rich and visually arresting. Production: cast limit 12. Author Must Be: Southern California writers only. We are unable to accept unsolicited queries from non-local writers.. **Application.** Best Way: professional recommendation. Best Material: query, synopsis, 10-pg sample, audio, SASE. Response: 6 wks query, 6 mos script.

Theatre Company

Univ. of Detroit Mercy, 4001 W. McNichols, Detroit, MI, 48208
Melinda Pacha, Chair
Tel: 313-993-1130, Fax: 313-993-6465
pachamj@udmercy.edu; libarts.udmercy.edu/dep/thr

Est. 1972. **Preference.** Length: all lengths. **Application.** Best Way: unsolicited. Best Material: synopsis, 30-pg writing sample, SASE. Deadline: ongoing.

Theatre de la Jeune Lune

105 N. 1st St., Minneapolis, MN, 55401
Dominique Serrand, Artistic Dir.
Tel: 612-332-3968, Fax: 612-332-0048
www.jeunelune.org

Est. 1979. 2005 Regional Theater Tony winner. **Preference.** Length: full length (over 90 min). Style: no musical. **Application.** Best Material: query, synopsis.

Theatre in the Square

11 Whitlock Ave., Marietta, GA, 30064
Jessica West, Artistic Assoc
Tel: 770-422-8369, Fax: 770-422-7436
www.theatreinthesquare.com

Est. 1982. Equity SPT. **Preference.** Length: full length (over 90 min). Production: cast limit 5, unit set, no fly. Material Must Be: unproduced in Southeast. **Application.** Best Material: query, synopsis, 10-pg sample, resume, submissions not returned. Response: 6 mos.

Theatre of Yugen

2840 Mariposa St., San Francisco, CA, 94110
Libby Zilber, Co-Artistic Dir.
Tel: 415-621-0507, Fax: 415-621-0223
www.theatreofyugen.org

Est. 1978. Non-Equity. Traditional and new works of East-West fusion primarily based on Noh forms. **Preference.** Length: one-act (30-90 min). Style: translation. **Application.** Best Material: query, SASE.

Theatre Outlet

Box 715, Allentown, PA, 18105
George Miller, Artistic Dir.
Tel: 610-820-9270, Fax: 610-820-9130
theatero@aol.com; www.theatreoutlet.org

Est. 1988. **Preference.** Length: full length (over 90 min), one-act (30-60 min). Style: no musical. Subject: eastern PA history, Celtic experience, social themes. **Application.** Best Material: query, synopsis. Best Time: summer. Response: 1 mo query, 2 mos script.

Theatre Previews
Duke Univ., Box 90680, 209 Bivins Build., Durham, NC, 27708
Miriam Sauls, Director of Theater
Tel: 919-660-3346, Fax: 919-684-8906
mmsauls@duke.edu; www.duke.edu/web/theaterstudies

Est. 1986. **Preference.** Length: full length (over 90 min). **Application.** Best Way: agent. Best Time: spring. Response: 3 mos query, 6 mos script.

Theatre Rhinoceros
2926 16th St., San Francisco, CA, 94103
John Fisher, Exec Dir
Tel: 415-552-4100, Fax: 415-558-9044
www.therhino.org

Est. 1977. **Preference.** Length: full length (over 90 min), one-act (30-60 min). Subject: gay-lesbian. **Application.** Best Way: agent. Response: 6 mos.

Theatre Three, Inc. [TX]
2800 Routh St., Dallas, TX, 75201
Jac Alder, Exec Producer/Dir
admin@theatre3dallas.com; www.theatre3dallas.com

Est. 1961. Equity SPT. 14 shows/yr in 2 spaces. **Preference.** Length: full length (over 90 min). Production: cast limit 20, small orchestra. **Application.** Best Way: professional recommendation. Best Material: query, sample, SASE. Best Time: Sep. Response: 3 mos.

TheatreWorks [CA]
Box 50458, Palo Alto, CA, 94303
Kent Nicholson, New Works Dir.
Fax: 650-463-1963
kent@theatreworks.org; www.theatreworks.org

Est. 1970. LORT C, LOA. Staff: Robert Kelley (Artistic Dir.). **Preference.** Length: full length (over 90 min). Material Must Be: unoptioned. **Application.** Best Way: agent. Best Material: query, synopsis, 10-pg sample, audio, SASE. Response: 8 wks query, 8 mos script.

Theatrical Outfit
Box 1555, Atlanta, GA, 30301
Jill Jane Clements, Artistic Assoc.
Tel: 678-528-1490, Fax: 404-577-5259
www.theatricaloutfit.org

Est. 1976. **Application.** Best Way: not accepting unsolicited manuscripts at this time.

This Women's Work Theatre Co. (TWWTC)
Box 20290, Greeley Sq. Sta., New York, NY, 10001
www.newperspectivestheatre.org

Specializes in original plays by emerging female writers, emphasizing works that liberate characters from outdated stereotypes. For specific requirements see website

Touchstone Theatre
321 E. 4th St., Bethlehem, PA, 18015
Mark McKenna, Artistic Dir.
Tel: 610-867-1689, Fax: 610-867-0561
touchstone@nni.com; www.touchstone.org

Est. 1981. Only accepts proposals for collaborative work with company ensemble. **Application.** Best Material: query. Response: 8 mos.

Town Hall Theatre Company (THT)

3535 School St., Lafayette, CA, 94549
Kevin T. Morales, Artistic Dir.
Fax: 925-283-3481
thtmanager@comcast.net; www.thtc.org

Est. 1944. Formerly Dramateurs (1944-92). Equity BAT. **Consideration.** Assistance: room/board, room/board. Remuneration: 8\% royalty. **Preference.** Length: full length (over 90 min). Style: comedy, drama, musical. Subject: suburban. Production: teen cast of 2-8, orchestra limit 3, unit set. Author Must Be: resident of CA preferred. Material Must Be: unpublished. **Application.** Best Material: query, submissions not returned. Best Time: Sep. Response: 3 mos.

Towne Street Theatre (TST)

4101 Budlong Ave., #4, Los Angeles, CA, 90037
Nancy Cheryll Davis, Exec. Producing-Artistic Dir.

Est. 1992. The premiere African-American theater in L.A., producing and developing original works by local playwrights on the African-American experience. **Application.** Best Material: query, 5-pg sample, resume.

Transport Group

265 Riverside Dr. #3f, New York, NY, 10025
Jack Cummings III, Artistic Dirs.
Tel: 212-560-4372, Fax: 212-678-9594
info@transportgroup.org; www.transportgroup.org

Triangle Productions!

3430 SE Belmont St., Portland, OR, 97214
Donald L. Horn, Artistic Dir.
Tel: 503-230-9404, Fax: 503-230-9303
trianglepro@juno.com; www.tripro.org

Est. 1989. **Preference.** Length: full length (over 90 min). Style: comedy, musical. Subject: children's, gay-lesbian. Production: cast limit 4, touring set. **Application.** Best Way: email. Best Material: query. Response: 1 mo query, 7 mos.

TriArts at the Sharon Playhouse

Box 1187, Sharon, CT, 06069
Michael Berkeley, Artistic Dir.
Tel: 860-364-7469, Fax: 860-364-8043
info@triarts.net; www.triarts.net

Est. 1989. Bryan L. Knapp New Works series. **Preference.** Style: comedy, drama, musical. Subject: children's. Production: no fly. **Application.** Best Material: query, synopsis, audio. Best Time: Jul-Aug. Response: 2 mos query, 6 mos.

Trinity Repertory Company

201 Washington St., Providence, RI, 02903
Craig Watson, Literary Mgr.
cwatson@trinityrep.com; www.trinityrep.com

Est. 1964. Equity LORT. 1981 Regional Theater Tony winner. Staff: Curt Columbus (Artistic Dir), Milchael Gennaro (Exec Dir). **Preference.** Length: full length (over 90 min). **Application.** Best Material: query, synopsis, 10-pg sample. Best Time: Sep-May. Response: 4 mos.

Trustus Theatre

Box 11721, Columbia, SC, 29211
Jon Tuttle, Literary Mgr.
Tel: 803-254-9732, Fax: 803-771-9153
trustus@trustus.org; www.trustus.org

Est. 1985. Late-night series for open-minded audiences. **Preference.** Length: one-act (45-75 min). Style: comedy. Subject: experimental, hard-hitting, off-the-wall. Production: cast limit 6, unit set. **Application.** Best Material: full script, SASE. Best Time: Aug-Dec.

Two River Theatre Company (TRTC)

21 Bridge Ave., Red Bank, NJ, 07701
Aaron Posner, Artistic Dir.
Tel: 732-345-1400, Fax: 732-345-1414
info@trtc.org; www.trtc.org

Est. 1994. **Preference.** Length: full length (over 90 min). Style: adaptation, comedy, drama. Production: cast limit 10. **Application.** Best Way: agent. Best Material: synopsis, 10-pg sample, SASE. Response: 10 mos.

Unicorn Theatre

3828 Main St., Kansas City, MO, 64111
Herman Wilson, Literary Asst.
Tel: 816-531-7529 x 15, Fax: 816-531-0421
www.unicorntheatre.org

Est. 1974. One new play each year is developed and produced in the Unicorn's regular season. **Consideration.** Fees: 2\% subsidiary rights for 5 yrs. Remuneration: $1,000 in lieu of royalty. **Preference.** Length: full length (over 90 min). Style: comedy, drama. Subject: contemporary (post-1950). Production: cast limit 10. Material Must Be: unpublished, professionally unproduced. **Application.** Best Material: query, synopsis, 10-pg sample, bio, cast list, submissions not returned. Response: 8 mos.

Unity Theatre Ensemble

P.O. Box 2466, St. Louis, MO, 63031
Ralph E. Green, Producing Artistic Dir.
Tel: 314-355-3586
www.utensemble.org

Check website for details.

Utah Shakespearean Festival

351 W. Center St., Cedar City, UT, 84720

Accepts scripts through its New American Playwrights Project (NAPP).

Valley Youth Theatre (VYT)

807 N. 3rd St., Phoenix, AZ, 85004
Bobb Cooper, Producing Artistic Dir.
Tel: 602-253-8188, Fax: 602-253-8282
bobb@vyt.com; www.vyt.com

Est. 1989. **Preference.** Style: comedy, drama, musical. Subject: children's, suitable for family audience. **Application.** Best Material: query, audio. Best Time: Aug-Dec. Response: 2 wks query, 2 mos script.

Victory Gardens Theater

2257 N. Lincoln Ave., Chicago, IL, 60614
Andrea J. Dymond, Literary Mgr.
Tel: 773-549-5788, Fax: 773-549-2779
adymond@victorygardens.org; www.victorygardens.org

Est. 1974. Equity CAT-4. 2001 Regional Theater Tony winner. 5 mainstage and 1 second stage productions/season. Staff: Dennis Zacek (Artistic Dir.). **Preference.** Length: full length (over 90 min), mid-length (60-90 min). Author Must Be: resident of Chicago area. Material Must Be: original, not produced more than once. **Application.** Best Way: professional recommendation. Best Material: query, synopsis, 10-pg sample, SASE. Response: 6 mos.

Victory Theatre Center

3326 W. Victory Blvd., Burbank, CA, 91505
Maria Gobetti, Artistic Dir.
Tel: 818-841-4404, Fax: 818-841-6328
victory@thevictorytheatrecenter.org; www.thevictorytheatrecenter.org

Est. 1979. Incl. 99-seat Big Victory and 50-seat Little Victory theaters. **Consideration.** Remuneration: royalty. **Preference.** Production: unit set. **Application.** Best Material: full script, SASE. Response: 1 yr.

Village Theatre

303 Front St. N., Issaquah, WA, 98027
Robb Hunt, Exec Producer
Tel: 425-392-9942, Fax: 425-391-3242
www.villagetheatre.org

Est. 1979. Equity LOA. Readings, workshops, and productions of new musicals. Staff: Steve Tomkins (Artistic Dir). **Consideration.** Remuneration: royalty. **Preference.** Length: full length (over 90 min), mid-length (60-90 min). Style: musical. Subject: all subjects. Production: cast limit 30, limit 20. **Application.** Best Way: professional recommendation, agent. Best Material: full script, audio, SASE. Best Time: year round. Response: 6 mos.

Vineyard Theatre

108 E. 15th St., New York, NY, 10003
Sarah Stern, Assoc Artistic Dir
Tel: 212-353-3366 x215, Fax: 212-353-3803
literary@vineyardtheatre.org; www.vineyardtheatre.org

Est. 1981. **Preference.** Length: full length (over 90 min). **Application.** Best Material: query, synopsis, 10-pg sample, audio, resume, submissions not returned. Response: 1 yr query.

Virginia Stage Company (VSC)

Box 3770, Norfolk, VA, 23514
Patrick Mullins, Artistic Assoc
Tel: 757-627-6988 x309, Fax: 757-628-5958
pmullins@vastage.com; www.vastage.com

Est. 1979. Equity LORT C. **Preference.** Length: full length (over 90 min). Subject: youth culture, issue-oriented. Production: cast limit 8. Author Must Be: resident of VA. Material Must Be: unproduced. **Application.** Best Material: query, synopsis. Response: 1 mo query, 6 mos script.

VS. Theatre Company

Box 2293, Los Angeles, CA, 91610
Johnny Clark, Artistic Dir.
Tel: 323-816-2471
info@vstheatre.org; www.vstheatre.org

Est. 2003. **Preference.** Length: full length (over 90 min), one-act (30-60 min). Style: no musical. Production: cast limit 6. **Application.** Best Way: online. Best Material: application, full script, SASE. Response: 6 mos.

Walnut Street Theatre

825 Walnut St., Philadelphia, PA, 19103
Beverly Elliott, Literary Mgr.
Tel: 215-574-3550, Fax: 215-574-3598
www.walnutstreettheatre.org

Est. 1809. Equity LORT A, D. **Preference.** Length: full length (over 90 min). Subject: socially relevant. Production: cast limit 4 (studio), 14 (play) or 20 (musical). **Application.** Best Material: query, synopsis, 20-pg sample, audio, SASE. Response: 3 mos query, 6 mos script.

Watertower Theatre, Inc.

15650 Addison Rd., Addison, TX, 75001
Terry Martin, Artistic Dir.
Tel: 972-450-6230, Fax: 972-450-6244
www.watertowertheatre.org

Est. 1976. **Preference.** Length: full length (over 90 min). Style: comedy, musical. Production: medium cast. **Application.** Best Way: agent only. Best Material: query, synopsis, SASE. Best Time: Aug-Dec only. Response: 4 mos query, 6 mos script.

Wellfleet Harbor Actors Theater

Box 797, Wellfleet, MA, 02667
Daniel Lombardo, Literary Mgr
Tel: 508-349-3011, Fax: 508-349-9082
djlombardo@juno.com; www.what.org

Est. 1985. **Preference.** Length: full length (over 90 min). Style: no musical. **Application.** Best Way: professional recommendation. Response: 3 mos query, 6 mos script.

West Coast Ensemble

Box 38728, Los Angeles, CA, 90038
Les Hanson, Artistic Dir.
Tel: 323-876-9337, Fax: 323-876-8916
www.wcensemble.org

Est 1982. 99-seat. **Application.** Best Material: full script, SASE. Response: 9 mos.

Western Stage (TWS)

156 Homestead Ave., Salinas, CA, 93901
Jon Selover, Artistic Dir.
Tel: 831-755-6987, Fax: 831-755-6954
www.westernstage.org

Est. 1974. **Preference.** Length: full length (over 90 min). Style: adaptation, musical. Production: large cast. Material Must Be: plays for young performers or with strong roles for women. **Application.** Best Material: query, synopsis, audio. Response: 6 mos query, 3 mos script.

Weston Playhouse

703 Main St., Weston, VT, 05161
www.westonplayhouse.org

Est. 1935. Staff: Malcolm Ewen, Tim Fort, Steve Stettler (Producing Dirs).

Westport Arts Center

51 Riverside Ave., Westport, CT, 06880

Programs in visual and performing arts. Ongoing exhibits. Chamber music, jazz and folk concerts, literary and film events performed in area venues.

Westport Country Playhouse

25 Powers Ct., Westport, CT, 06880
Tazewell Thompson, Artistic Dir.
Tel: 203-227-5137
www.westportplayhouse.org

Est. 1931. 578-seat year-round Equity theater with 75-yr summer program. Staff: Jodi Schoenbrun Carter (Managing Dir). **Consideration.** Remuneration: royalty. **Preference.** Length: full length (over 90 min), mid-length (60-90 min). Production: ages 12 and older, cast of 2-10, orchestra of 4-8. **Application.** Best Way: professional recommendation. Best Material: full script, SASE. Response: 9 mos.

White Horse Theater Company

205 3rd Ave., #6-N, New York, NY, 10003
Cyndy A. Marion, Prod. Artistic Dir.
www.whitehorsetheater.com

Est. 2002. Equity Showcase or staged reading. **Preference.** Length: full length (over 90 min), mid-length (60-90 min). Style: adaptation, comedy, drama. Subject: US. Author Must Be: resident of US. Material Must Be: unproduced. **Application.** Best Way: see website for procedure. Best Material: SASE. Response: 4 mos.

Will Geer Theatricum Botanicum

Box 1222, Topanga, CA, 90290
Ellen Geer, Artistic Dir.
Tel: 310-455-2322, Fax: 310-455-3724
info@theatricum.com; www.theatricum.com

Est. 1973. **Preference.** Length: full length (over 90 min). Production: cast limit 10, simple set. Material Must Be: suitable for outdoor space. **Application.** Best Material: query, synopsis, 10-pg sample, full script, audio. Best Time: Sep-Mar. Response: 1 mo query, 6 mos script.

Williamstown Theatre Festival

229 W. 42nd St. #801, New York, NY, 10036
Suzanne Agins, Artistic Assoc, New Plays
Tel: 212-395-9090, Fax: 212-395-9099
sagins@wtfestival.org; www.wtfestival.org

Est. 1955. 2002 Regional Theater Tony winner. New Play Staged Reading Series offers 7 works/season. **Consideration.** Remuneration: reading. Frequency: annual. **Preference.** Length: full length (over 90 min). **Application.** Best Way: agent. Best Material: query, SASE. Best Time: Oct-Feb.

Willows Theatre Company

1425 Gasoline Alley, Concord, CA, 94520
Alexandra Elliott, Artistic Assoc.
Tel: 925-798-1824
alex@willowstheatre.org; www.willowstheatre.org

Est. 1974. Equity LORT D, LOA. **Consideration.** Frequency: annual. **Preference.** Length: all length. Style: comedy, drama. Subject: all subjects. Production: less than 15. Material Must Be: unproduced. **Application.** Best Way: unsolicited. Best Material: full script. Best Time: Oct - Jan. Deadline: 8-May. Response: 3 mos.

Wilma Theater

265 S. Broad St., Philadelphia, PA, 19107
Walter Bilderback, Dramaturg/Literary Mgr.
Tel: 215-893-9456, Fax: 215-893-0895
wcb@wilmatheater.org; www.wilmatheater.org

Est. 1979. Equity LORT C. **Preference.** Length: full length (over 90 min). Subject: works with poetic dimension, small musicals, comedies with bite. Particular interest in plays dealing with social issues, impact of science on our lives.. Production: cast limit 8. **Application.** Best Way: agent, otherwise, professional reccomendation, query, and 10-pg. sample. Best Material: please check our website for past seasons and Artistic Statement. Response: 1 yr.

Wings Theatre Company, Inc.

154 Christopher St., New York, NY, 10014
Jeffery Corrick, Artistic Dir
Tel: 212-627-2960, Fax: 212-462-0024
jcorrick@wingstheatre.com; www.wingstheatre.com

Est. 1986. Equity Tier III. Gay Play Series (major gay characters & themes) and New Musical Series (any theme). **Preference.** Length: full length (over 90 min). Material Must Be: unproduced. **Application.** Best Material: full script, audio.

Women's Project & Productions

55 West End Ave., New York, NY, 10023
Megan Carter, Assoc. Artistic Dir.
www.womensproject.org

Est. 1978. Equity ANTC contract. Oldest and largest US theater dedicated to producing and promoting theater created by women. **Preference.** Length: full length (over 90 min). Material Must Be: unproduced in NYC. **Application.** Best Way: professional recommendation, agent. Response: 1 yr.

Woolly Mammoth Theatre Company

641 D St. NW, Washington, DC, 20004
Elissa Goetschius, Literary Assoc.
Tel: 202-349-1281, Fax: 202-289-2446
elissa@woollymammoth.net; www.woollymammoth.net

Est. 1980. Equity SPT. **Preference.** Length: full length (over 90 min). Style: no musical. Production: cast limit 6. **Application.** Best Way: professional recommendation. Best Time: Jun. Response: 1 yr.

Working Theater

Box 892, New York, NY, 10002
Connie Grappo, Artistic Dir
Tel: 212-539-5675
www.theworkingtheater.org

Est. 1985. Equity LOA. New plays that appeal to the diverse communities of working people in NYC. **Consideration.** Frequency: semiannual. **Preference.** Length: full length (over 90 min), mid-length (60-90 min). Style: all styles. Subject: Asian, Black, disabled, gay, latino, senior, women. Production: 6 max. Material Must Be: unproduced. **Application.** Best Way: unsolicited, professional recommendation, agent. Best Material: synopsis, sample, full script, SASE. Best Time: June-Oct.. Response: 6 mos.

Writers' Theatre

376 Park Ave., Glencoe, IL, 60022
Jimmy McDermott, Artistic Asst
Tel: 847-242-6001, Fax: 847-242-6011
info@writerstheatre.org; www.writerstheatre.org

Est. 1992. **Preference.** Length: full length (over 90 min). Style: all styles, no musical. Subject: highly literary, writers and writing. **Application.** Best Way: professional recommendation. Best Material: synopsis, 10-pg sample, SASE. Response: 6 mos.

Xoregos Performing Company

496 9th Ave., #4-A, New York, NY, 10018
Shela Xoregos, Artistic Dir.
Tel: 212-239-8405
xoregos.com

Est. 2001. Equity Showcase and non-Equity. **Preference.** Subject: no kitchen-sink. **Application.** Best Way: professional recommendation. Best Material: query, submissions not returned.

Yale Repertory Theatre

Box 208244, New Haven, CT, 06520
Catherine Sheehy, Resident Dramaturg
Tel: 203-432-1591
catherine.sheehy@yale.edu; www.yale.edu/yalerep

Est. 1965. 1991 Regional Theater Tony winner. **Preference.** Length: full length (over 90 min). Style: no musical. **Application.** Best Way: agent. Best Material: query, SASE. Response: 2 mos query, 3 mos script.

Yangtze Repertory Theatre of America

22 Howard St., #3-B, New York, NY, 10013
Dr. Joanna Chan, Artistic Dir.
Tel: 914-941-7575, Fax: 914-923-0733
joanawychan@juno.com; www.yangtze-rep-theatre.org

York Shakespeare Company

Box 720, JAF Sta., New York, NY, 10116
Seth Duerr, Artistic Dir.
Tel: 646-623-7117
sduerr@yorkshakespeare.org; www.yorkshakespeare.org

Est. 2001. **Preference.** Length: full length (over 90 min). Material Must Be: unoptioned. **Application.** Best Way: professional recommendation. Best Material: full script.

York Theatre Company

619 Lexington Ave., New York, NY, 10022
Literary Dept.
Tel: 212-935-5824, Fax: 212-832-0037
mail@yorktheatre.org; www.yorktheatre.org

Est. 1985. Equity Off-Broadway. Opportunities incl. developmental reading series. **Preference.** Length: full length (over 90 min). Style: musical. Production: cast of 3-6, piano only. Material Must Be: unproduced. **Application.** Best Material: full script, audio, SASE. Response: 6 mos.

Z Space Studio

131 10th St., Fl. 3, San Francisco, CA, 94103
Lisa Steindler, Artistic Dir, Z Plays
Tel: 415-626-0453, Fax: 415-626-1138
zspace@zspace.org; www.zspace.org

Est. 1993. Develops new works, new voices, and new opportunities for stage. **Consideration.** Assistance:. Remuneration: 5\% royalty. **Preference.** Material Must Be: unoptioned, unproduced. **Application.** Best Material: synopsis, SASE.

THEATERS (Fee Charged)

Two Chairs Theater Company
Box 3390, Grand Junction, CO, 81502
James Garland, Assoc. Artistic Dir.
Tel: 970-263-7920
submit@twochairs.org; www.twochairs.org

Acts of Brevity Short Play Fest **Consideration.** Fees: $10: $5 for admin, $5 for production. **Preference.** Length: short (10 min.). Production: cast limit 5. **Application.** Best Way: email (pdf, doc, fdr). Best Material: synopsis, full script, production history. Please see website for submission details..

Educational Opportunities

MFA PROGRAMS

Arizona State University
Ms. Karla Elling, Program Manager
Arizona State University - Virginia G. Piper Creative Writing
MFA Creative Writing
Box 875002
Tempe, Arizona 85387
Phone: (602) 965-6018
Email: karla.elling@asu.edu
Website: http://www.asu.edu/graduate/
Degrees Offered: MFA in Creative Writing with Playwriting emphasis
Program Length: 3 years
Students per Class: Not Specified
Represented Faculty: Christopher Danowski, Gus Edwards, Pamela Sterling
Production Opportunities: Staged Readings to Full Student
Other highlights: KCACTF, New Works Festival (internal)

Arkansas at Fayetteville, University of
Dr. Andrew Gibbs, Chair
University of Arkansas at Fayetteville
Department of Drama
619 Kimpel Hall
Fayetteville, Arkansas 72701
Phone: (479) 575-2953
Email: drama@cavern.uark.edu
Website: http://www.uark.edu/%7Edrama/
Degrees Offered: BA, MFA in Playwriting
Program Length: 60 hours
Students per Class: 25 max
Represented Faculty: Roger Gross, Chuck Gorden

Brooklyn College
Mr. Mac Wellman, Coordinator of Playwriting MFA
Brooklyn College CUNY
English Department
2900 Bedford Ave.
Brooklyn, New York 11210
Phone: (718) 951-5000
Website: http://depthome.brooklyn.cuny.edu/english/graduate/mfa/geninfo.htm
Degrees Offered: BA, BFA, MFA in Playwriting
Program Length: 2 years
Students per Class:
Represented Faculty: Erin Courtney, Alison Solomon

Brown University
Mr. Brian Evenson, Director
Brown University
Literary Arts Program
Box 1923
Providence, Rhode Island 2912
Phone: (401) 863-3260, (401) 863-9408
Email: Brian_Evenson@brown.edu
Website: http://www.brown.edu/Departments/Literary_Arts/
Degrees Offered: BA, MA, MFA in Literary Arts: Playwriting; AB English/Creative Writing
Program Length: 2 years
Students per Class: ~3
Represented Faculty: Paula Vogel, Aishah Rahman, Guests

University of California - Riverside
Mr. Eric Barr, Chair
University of California at Riverside
Department of Theatre - 093
Riverside, California 92521
Phone: (951) 827-6488
Email: eric.barr@ucr.edu
Website: www.performingarts.ucr.edu
Degrees Offered: BA, MFA in Creative Writing and Writing for the Performing Arts
Program Length: 6 Quarters/ 48 hours
Students per Class: ~4
Represented Faculty: Eric Barr, Rickerby Hinds, Robin Russin, Guests
Production Opportunities: Various Production Opportunities
Other highlights: Playworks (internal)

University of California - San Diego
Ms. Naomi Iizuka, Head of Playwriting
University of California at San Diego
Department of Theatre and Dance
9500 Gilman Drive MCO344
La Jolla, California 92093
Phone: (858) 534-3791
Website: http://theatre.ucsd.edu/academics/graduatePrograms/playwriting.html
Degrees Offered: MFA Playwriting
Program Length: 3 years
Represented Faculty: Naomi Iizuka, Allan Havis
Other highlights: Baldwin New Play Festival

California State University - Long Beach
Ms. Joanne Gordon, Chair
California State University - Long Beach
Department of Theatre Arts
1250 Bellflower Boulevard
Long Beach, California 90840
Phone: (562) 985-7891
Email: jgordan@csulb.edu
Website: http://www.csulb.edu/depts/theatre/
Degrees Offered: MFA in Theatre Arts with option in Dramatic Writing
Program Length: 2 years
Students per Class: 6
Other highlights: Cal Rep

Carnegie Mellon University School of Drama
Mr. Milan Stitt, Coordinator
Carnegie Mellon University School of Drama
Dramatic Writing, Purnell Center for the Arts
5000 Forbes Avenue
Pittsburgh, Pennsylvania 15213
Phone: (412) 268-2398
Email: Milan@andrew.cmu.edu
Website: www.cmu.edu/cfa/drama
Degrees Offered: MFA Dramatic Writing
Program Length: 2 years
Students per Class: ~5
Represented Faculty: Milan Stitt, Guests
Production Opportunities: Staged Readings to Experimental
Other highlights: KCACTF, Winter/Summer New Play Festival (sponsor), Playground (internal)

Columbia University
Mr. Steven Chaikelson, Chair
Columbia University
School of the Arts, Theatre Division
601 Dodge Hall
2960 Broadway
New York, New York 10027
Phone: (212) 854-3408
Email: theatre@columbia.edu
Website: http://www.columbia.edu/cu/arts/theatre
Degrees Offered: BA, MA, MFA in Playwriting, PhD
Program Length: 3 years
Represented Faculty: Charles Mee, Kelly Stuart, Tina Landau, Guests
Production Opportunities: Staged Readings to Limited Student

Florida State University
Mr. Timothy Long, Head of Writing Area
Florida State University
Film School
University Center 3100A
PO Box 3062350
Tallahassee, Florida 32306
Phone: (850) 644-2907
Email: tlong@film.fsu.edu
Website: http://film.fsu.edu/film_school/programs/mfa_in_writing_for_the_stage_screen
Degrees Offered: MFA in Writing for the Stage & Screen
Program Length: 2 years and 2 Summers
Students per Class: 6
Represented Faculty: Timothy Long, Victoria Meyer
Production Opportunities: Full Production
Other highlights: KCACTF

University of Hawaii - Manoa,
Mr. Gregg Lizenbery, Chair
University of Hawaii at Manoa
Department of Theatre and Dance
Kennedy Theatre
1770 East-West Road
Honolulu, Hawaii 96822
Phone: (808) 956-2464
Email: lgreg@hawaii.edu
Website: www.hawaii.edu/theatre
Degrees Offered: BA, MA, MFA in Playwriting, PhD
Program Length: 60 hours
Students per Class: ~2

Hollins University
Mr. Todd Ristau, Program Director
Hollins University
Graduate Center
PO Box 9603
Roanoke, Virginia 24020
Phone: (540) 362-6386
Email: tristau@hollins.edu
Website: http://www.hollins.edu/grad/playwriting/index.html
Degrees Offered: MFA in Playwriting
Program Length: 4-5 Summers, 60 hours
Represented Faculty: Todd Ristau, Jonathan Dorf, Ruth Margraff, Stephen Sossaman
Other highlights: Mill Mountain Theatre, No Shame Theatre

Iowa, University of
Mr. Art Borreca, Head of Playwrights Workshop
University of Iowa
Department of Theatre Arts
200 North Riverside Drive 107 TB
Iowa City, Iowa 52242
Phone: (319) 353-2401
Email: art-borreca@uiowa.edu
Website: http://www.uiowa.edu/~theatre/programs/playwrighting/playwritinginfo.htm
Degrees Offered: BA, MFA in Playwriting
Program Length: 3 years
Students per Class: 11
Represented Faculty: Art Borreca, Dare Clubb, Artist in Residence, Kate Aspengren, Sydne Mahone, Guests
Other highlights: Iowa New Play Festival (internal)

Juilliard School
Mr. Christopher Durang, Co-Director, American Playwrights
The Julliard School
Drama Division,
60 Lincoln Ctr. Plaza
New York, New York 10023
Phone: (212) 799-5000 x251
Website: http://www.juilliard.edu/college/drama/programs_playwrights.html
Degrees Offered: Non-degree program in Playwriting (1yr. Fellowship, 2nd year invite), MFA equivilant
Program Length: 1 to 2 years
Represented Faculty: Christopher Durang, Marsha Norman

University of Nevada - Las Vegas (UNLV)
Mr. KC Davis, Graduate Coordinator, Playwriting
University of Las Vegas at Nevada
Department of Theatre
4505 S. Maryland Parkway
Box 455036
Las Vegas, Nevada 89154
Phone: (702) 895-3666
Email: kc.davis@unlv.edu
Website: http://theatre.unlv.edu/mfaplaywriting.html
Degrees Offered: BA, MFA in Playwriting
Students per Class: ~8
Represented Faculty: KC Davis

University of New Mexico,
Ms. Judith Bennahum, Chair
University of New Mexico
Theatre Arts
Fine Arts Center, Rm. 1412
Albuquerque, New Mexico 87131
Phone: (505) 277-4332
Email: theatre@unm.edu
Website: www.unm.edu/~theatre
Degrees Offered: BA, MFA in Dramatic Writing
Program Length: 3 years
Represented Faculty: James Linnell
Production Opportunities: Staged Readings to Full Student
Other highlights: Words Afire Festival (internal)

New School University
Mr. Pippin Parker, Chair, Playwriting MFA
The New School University
The New School for Drama
151 Bank Street
New York, New York 10014
Phone: (212) 229-5859
Website: http://www.newschool.edu/academic/drama/playwriting.aspx?s=1:3
Degrees Offered: MFA in Playwriting
Program Length: 3 yearsRepresented Faculty: Pippin Parker, Nicole Burdette, Laura Maria Censabella, Frank Pugliese, Christopher Shinn, Michael Weller, John Patrick Shanley (in residence)
Production Opportunities: Staged Readings to Full Student

New York University, Tisch School of the Arts
Mr. Richard Wesley, Chair
NYU, Tisch School of the Arts
Goldberg Department of Dramatic Writing
721 Broadway, 7th Floor
New York, New York 10003
Phone: (212) 998-1535
Email: rew3@nyu.edu
Website: www.nyu.edu/tisch/bul-dwp.html
Degrees Offered: BFA in Dramatic Writing, MFA in Dramatic Writing with a Concentration in Playwriting, Screenwriting, or Television Writing.
Program Length: 2 years
Students per Class: ~20
Represented Faculty: Richard Wesley, Walter Bernstein, Sabrina Dhawan, Jeremy Pikser, Charlie Rubin, Marsha Norman, Janet Neipris, Rinne Groff, Guests
Production Opportunities: Student Readings to Full Student
Other highlights: KCACTF, ATHE, UG Ten Minute Play Festival, Ten Minute Play Festival, Festival of New Work

Northwestern University
Mr. David Tolchinsky, Director
Northwestern University
MFA Writing for the Screen and Stage, Dept of Radio-TV-Film
1800 Sherman Avenue, Ste.106
Evanston, Illinois 60201
Phone: (847) 491-2252
Email: write@northwestern.edu
Website: http://www.write.northwestern.edu/
Degrees Offered: BA Creative Writing for the Media, MFA in Writing for the Screen and Stage
Program Length: 2 years
Represented Faculty: Bill Bleich, Jay Bonansinga, Shawn Douglass, Paul Edwards, Kat Falls, Rebecca Gilman, David Kukoff, Penny Penniston, Ana Puga, Anna Shapiro, Dave Tolchinsky, Barbara Wallace and Tom Wolfe, Harvey Young, Mary Zimmerman, Guests
Production Opportunities: Full Support, multi-media, including $5000 Grant
Other highlights: Cinestory, Flicker Festival (film)

Ohio University
Mr. Charles Smith, Head of MFA Playwriting Program
Ohio University
MFA Playwriting Program, School of Theatre
Kantner Hall 307
Athens, Ohio 45701
Phone: (740) 593-4818
Email: ohioplaywriting@gmail.com
Website: http://www.finearts.ohio.edu/theater/
Degrees Offered: BA, BFA, MFA, BFA in Playwriting, MFA Playwriting
Program Length: 3 years
Students per Class: ~2 to 4
Represented Faculty: Charles Smith, Erik Ramsey
Production Opportunities: Staged Readings to Full Student
Other highlights: Annual Playwrights Festival (internal)

Rutgers University - New Brunswick
Mr. Lee Blessing, Head of Playwriting Program
Rutgers University
Mason Gross School of the Arts, Department of Theatre Arts
33 Livingston Ave.
New Brunswick, New Jersey 8901
Phone: (201) 932-1766
Email: contactus@masongross.rutgers.edu
Website: http://www.masongross.rutgers.edu/theater/MFAPlaywriting.html
Degrees Offered: BA, BFA, MFA in Playwriting
Program Length: 3 years
Students per Class: 2
Represented Faculty: Josph Hart, Lee Blessing, Guests
Production Opportunities: Staged Readings to Full Professional

San Francisco State University
Mr. Roy Conboy, Head of Playwriting Program
San Francisco State University
College of Humanities - Department of Creative Writing
1600 Holloway Ave.
San Francisco, California 94132
Phone: (415) 338-1891
Email: rconboy@sfsu.edu or cwriting@sfsu.edu
Website: http://online.sfsu.edu/~rconboy/
Degrees Offered: BA, MA in English: Creative Writing, MFA in Creative Writing - Playwriting
Program Length: 30hours MA, 59 hours MFA
Students per Class: Not Specified
Represented Faculty: Michelle Carter, Roy Conboy, Anne Galjour, Brian Thorstensen
Production Opportunities: Staged Readings to Full Student
Other highlights: KCACTF, GreenHouse Productions, One-Act Festival (internal), One-Act Fringe (internal), Bay Area Playwrights Festival

University of Southern California
Ms. Madeline Puzo, Dean
University of Southern California
School of Theatre
1029 Childs Way
Los Angeles, California 90089
Phone: (213) 821-2744
Email: thtrinfo@usc.edu
Website: http://theatre.usc.edu
Degrees Offered: BA, BFA, MA, MFA in Dramatic Writing
Program Length: 3 years
Students per Class: ~13
Represented Faculty: Velina Hasu Houston, Oliver Mayer, Luis Alfaro, Paula Cizmar Guests

Southern Illinois University - Carbondale
Dr. David A. Rush, Head of Playwriting Program
University of Southern Illinois at Carbondale
Department of Theatre and Dance
Carbondale, Illinois 62901
Phone: (618) 453-4757
Email: darush@siu.edu
Website: http://www.siuc.edu/%7Emcleod/department/courses/index.html

Degrees Offered: BA, MFA in Playwriting, PhDin Playwriting (Doctor of Philosophy in conjunction with Speech Communication)
Program Length: 60 hours
Represented Faculty: Dr. David A. Rush, Guests
Production Opportunities: Staged Readings to Full Student
Other highlights: Various, Script Camp (sponsor)

University of Texas - Austin
Ms. Susan Zeder, Area Head, Playwriting
University of Texas at Austin
Department of Theatre and Dance
1 University Station D3900
Austin, Texas 78712
Phone: (512) 232-5325
Email: suzanz@mail.utexas.edu
Website: http://www.utexas.edu/cofa/theatre
Degrees Offered: BA in Theatre and Dance with Playwriting concentration, MFA in Playwriting
Program Length: 3 years
Students per Class: 2
Represented Faculty: Suzan Zeder, Ruth Margraff
Production Opportunities: Staged Readings to Full Student
Other highlights: KCACTF, Cohen New Works Festival (internal)

University of Texas - El Paso (UTEP)
Dr. Joel K. Murray, Key Contact
University of Texas at El Paso
Theatre, Dance & Film Department
500 W. University Ave.
El Paso, Texas 79968
Phone: (915) 747-7854
Email: jmurray@utep.edu
Website: http://academics.utep.edu/Default.aspx?tabid=12330
Degrees Offered: BA, MA Theatre with a specialization in Playwriting
Represented Faculty: Joel Murray, Guests
Production Opportunities: Experimental no readings
Other highlights: New Voices Play Festival (internal)

Yale School of Drama
Mr. James Bundy, Dean
Yale University
Yale School of Drama
PO Box 208244
New Haven, Connecticut 6520
Phone: (203) 432-1505
Email: james.bundy@yale.edu
Website: www.yale.edu/drama
Degrees Offered: MFA in Playwriting
Program Length: 3 years
Students per Class: ~11
Represented Faculty: John Guare, Michael Korie, Lisa Kron, Tina Landau, Lindsay Law, Richard Nelson, Lynn Nottage, Peter Parnell and Adam Rapp.
Production Opportunities: Staged Readings to Full Student
Other highlights: New Play Festival (internal)

NON-DEGREE PROGRAMS

Adelphi University
Ms. Judith Baumel, Director
English Department
Adelphi University
PO Box 701
Garden City, NY 11530
Phone: (516) 877-4031
Email: BAUMEL@adelphi.edu
Website: http://academics.adelphi.edu/artsci/creativewriting/index.php
Degree Offered: BA, MFA in Creative Writing
Represented Faculty: Anton Dudley, Kermit Frazier

Arizona State University
Mr. Guillermo Reyes, Head of Playwriting
Theatre Department
Arizona State University - Herberger College of the Arts
Box 872002
Tempe, Arizona 85287
Phone: (602) 965-5351, (602) 965 0517
Email: guillermo.reyes@asu.edu
Website: http://theatre.asu.edu
Degree Offered: BA
Represented Faculty: Guillermo Reyes, Jeff McMahon, Pamela Sterling, Phillip Taylor, Guests
Production Opportunities: Staged Readings to Full Student
Other Highlights: KC/ACTF

Bennington College
Ms. Sherry Kramer, Key Contact
Dance/Drama
Bennington College
One College Drive
Bennington, Vermont 5201
Phone: (802) 442-5401
Email: skramer@bennington.edu
Degree Offered: BA
Represented Faculty: Sherry Kramer, Jean Randich, Guests
Production Opportunities:

Chapman University
Mr. Thomas Bradac, Chair
Department of Theatre
Chapman University
One University Drive
Orange, California 92866
Phone: (714) 744-7016
Email: bradac@chapman.edu
Website: http://www.chapman.edu/theatre/
Degree Offered: BA

College of Charleston
Mr. Todd McNerny, Chair
Theatre Department, School of the Arts
College of Charleston
66 George Street
Charleston, South Carolina 29424
Phone: (843) 953-6306
Email: olcksiakm@cofc.edu
Website: http://www.cofc.edu/theatre/
Degree Offered: BA
Represented Faculty: Dr. Franklin Ashley, Guests
Production Opportunities: Staged Readings to Experimental
Other Highlights: KC/ACTF, ATHE

Chicago State University
Songodina Ifatunji, Key Contact
Breakey Theater
Chicago State University
9501 South King Drive
Chicago, Illinois 60628
Phone: (773) 995-2419
Email: s-ifatunji@csu.edu
Website: http://www.csu.edu/speech/theatre/index.htm
Degree Offered: BA

Dartmouth College
Mr. Dan Kotlowitz, Director
Department of Theatre
Dartmouth College
Box 6204 Hopkins Center
Hanover, New Hampshire 3755
Phone: (603) 646-3104
Email: Department.of.Theater@Dartmouth.EDU
Website: www.dartmouth.edu/~theater
Degree Offered: BA
Represented Faculty: Joe Sutton, Guests

Duke University
Mr. John M. Clum, Chair
Department of Theatre Studies
Duke University
206 Bivins Building
Box 90680
Durham, North Carolina 27708
Phone: (919) 660-3343
Email: jclum@duke.edu
Website: www.duke.edu/web/theaterstudies
Degree Offered: BA
Represented Faculty: John Clum, Neal C. Bell, Elisabeth Benfey, Guests

George Mason University
Ms. Heather McDonald, Instructor
Department of Theatre, College of Visual and Performing Arts
George Mason University
4400 University Drive
MSN 3E6
Fairfax, Virginia 22030
Phone: (703) 993-1120
Email: dulcinae@earthlink.net
Website: http://www.gmu.edu/departments/theatre/
Degree Offered: BA
Represented Faculty: Heather McDonald

Georgetown University
Dr. Derek Goldman, Artistic Director
Program in Performing Arts
Georgetown University
Davis Performing Arts Center
Box 571063
Washington, D.C. 20057
Phone: (202) 687-3838
Email: dag45@georgetown.edu
Website: http://performingarts.georgetown.edu/theater.html
Degree Offered: BA, MFA

Houston, University of
Dr. Steven W. Wallace, Director
School of Theatre and Dance
University of Houston
133 CWM
Houston, Texas 77204
Phone: (713) 743-3003
Email: swwallace@UH.edu
Website: http://www.theatre.uh.edu/default.html
Degree Offered: BA, MA, MFA
Represented Faculty: Steven W. Wallace, Dr. Syndey Berger
Other Highlights: Edward Albee Playwrights Workshop, Ostrow Musical Theatre Lab

Howard University
Mr. Joe Selmon, Chair
Department of Theatre Arts
Howard University
Room 2101 Childers Hall
Washington, D.C. 20059
Phone: (202) 806-7050
Email: jselmon@howard.edu
Website: http://www.howard.edu/collegefinearts/Theatre/index.html
Degree Offered: BA, MFA

Livingstone College
Dr. Eddie P. Bradley,
Theatre Arts Department
Livingstone College
Salisbury, North Carolina 28144
Phone: (704) 216-1849
Website: www.livingstone.edu
Degree Offered: BA, BFA
Represented Faculty: Dr. Eddie P. Bradley

Louisiana - Monroe, University of
Dr. Roger Held, Chair
TheatreWorks, ULM
University of Louisiana at Monroe
400 University Avenue
Monroe, Louisiana 71209
Phone: (318) 342-1413
Email: spheld@ulm.edu
Degree Offered: BA, MA
Represented Faculty: Dr. Roger Held, Guests
Production Opportunities: Staged Readings to Full Student
Other Highlights: KCACTF

Louisiana State University
Mr. Michael S. Tick, Chair
Department of Theatre
Louisiana State University
217- Dramatic Arts Building
Baton Rouge, Louisiana 70803
Phone: (225) 578-3531
Email: mtickl@lsu.edu
Website: www.theatre.lsu.edu
Degree Offered: BA
Represented Faculty: Femi Euba

Metropolitain State University
Ms. Suzanne Walfoort, Chair
Communication, Writing, and the Arts Department
Metropolitain State University
Suite 205, Energy Park Place
1380 Energy Lane
St. Paul, Minnesota 55108
Phone: (651) 999-5947
Email: suzanne.walfoort@metrostate.edu
Website: http://www.metrostate.edu/cas/cwa/index.html
Degree Offered: BA Theatre

Miami University of Ohio
Dr. Howard A. Blanning, Key Contact
Department of Theatre
Miami University of Ohio
212 Hiestand Hall
Oxford, Ohio 45056
Phone: (513) 529-1270
Email: blanniha@muohio.edu
Website: http://www.fna.muohio.edu/theweb/index.html
Degree Offered: BA, MA
Represented Faculty: Dr. Howard Blanning, Guests
Production Opportunities: Staged Readings to Experimental
Other Highlights: KCACTF

Michigan - University of
Mr. Gregory Poggi, Chair
Department of Theatre and Drama
University of Michigan
1226 Murfin Avenue
Walgreen Drama Center
Ann Arbor, Michigan 48109
Phone: (734) 764-5350
Email: theatre.info@umich.edu
Website: http://www.music.umich.edu/departments/theatre/programs/bach_theatre_arts.htm
Degree Offered: BA
Represented Faculty: OyamO
Production Opportunities: Limited Productions

Northern Kentucky University
Mr. Ken Jones, Key Contact
Department of Theatre and Dance
Northern Kentucky University
Fine Arts- 205
Nunn Drive
Highland Heights, Kentucky 41099
Phone: (859) 572-6362
Email: jonesk@nku.edu
Website: http://www.nku.edu/~theatre
Degree Offered: BA, BFA
Represented Faculty: Ken Jones, Guests
Production Opportunities: Staged Readings to Limited Productions
Other Highlights: KC/ACTF, KTA, Y.E.S. Festival (sponsor, contact Sandra Forman)

Occidental College
Ms. Susan Gratch, Chair
Theater Department
Occidental College
1600 Campus Road
Los Angeles, California 90041
Phone: (323) 259-2771
Email: beatrice@oxy.edu
Website: http://departments.oxy.edu/theater/
Degree Offered: BA
Represented Faculty: Laurel Meade
Production Opportunities: Limited Productions
Other Highlights: New Play Festival (internal)

San Diego, University of
Dr. David Hay, Director
Department of Theatre Arts
University of San Diego
Camino Hall, C130
5998 Alcala Park
San Diego, California 92110
Phone: (619) 260-7763
Email: dhay@sandiego.edu
Website: http://www.sandiego.edu/theatre/
Degree Offered: BA, MFA
Represented Faculty: Evelyn Diaz Cruz,
Production Opportunities: Staged Readings to Experimental
Other Highlights: Student Lab

Texas A&M University - Commerce
Mr. Jim Tyler Anderson, Key Contact
Theatre
Texas A&M University at Commerce
Performing Arts Center 103
Commerce, Texas 75429
Phone: (903) 886-5338
Email: jim_anderson@tamu-commerce.edu
Website: www.tamu-commerce.edu
Degree Offered: BA, MA
Represented Faculty: Jim Tyler Anderson, Dr. John Hanners
Production Opportunities: Staged Readings to Full Student
Other Highlights: KCACTF, Texas Institute for Educational Parnerships (sponsor)

Tulsa, University of
Mr. Michael Wright, Dirctor of the Interdisciplinary Program in Creative Writing
Department of Theatre and Musical Theatre, Kendall Hall
University of Tulsa
600 S. College Avenue
Tulsa, Okhlahoma 74104
Phone: (918) 631-3174
Email: michael-wright@utulsa.edu
Website: http://www.cas.utulsa.edu/theatre/newsite/tutheatre1.htm
Degree Offered: BA Theatre
Represented Faculty: Michael Wright
Production Opportunities: Staged Readings, Film, to Full Student
Other Highlights: KCACTF

Washington University
Mr. Robert Henke, Chair
Performing Arts Department
Washington University
Campus Box 1108
St. Louis, Missouri 63130
Phone: (314) 935-4473
Email: rhenke@artsci.wustl.edu
Website: www.artsci.wustl.edu/~pad
Degree Offered: BA
Represented Faculty: Carter W. Lewis
Other Highlights: A.E. Hotchner Playwriting Competition (internal)

Western Washington University
Mr. Gregory Lawrence Pulver, Chair
Theatre Arts Department
Western Washington University
Bellingham, Washington 98225
Phone: (360) 650-6862
Email: Gregory.Pulver@wwu.edu
Website: http://www.wwu.edu/depts/theatre/
Represented Faculty: Bryan Willis

Wichita State University
Dr. Steve Peters, Director
School of Performing Arts
Wichita State University
1845 Fairmount
Wichita, Kansas 67260
Phone: (316) 978-3360
Email: steve.peters@wichita.edu
Website: http://webs.wichita.edu/?u=FA_PERFORMINGARTS
Degree Offered: BA, BFA, MFA
Production Opportunities: Staged Readings to Experimental
Other Highlights: KC/ACTF, National Playwrting Contest (Open, Host)

William and Mary, College of
Mr. Steve Holliday, Chair
Department of Theatre, speech and Dance
College of William and Mary
PO Box 8795
Williamsburg, Virginia 23187
Phone: (757) 221-2664

Email: seholl@wm.edu
Website: http://www.wm.edu/theatre/theatrehome.html
Degree Offered: BA
Represented Faculty: M. Fonkijom Fusi, Francis Tanglao-Aguas, Laurie Wolf

OTHER PROGRAMS

Agnes Scott College
Mr. David S. Thompson, Chair
Department of Theatre and Dance
Agnes Scott College
141 E. College Avenue
Decatur, Georgia 30030
Phone: (800) 868-8602
Website: http://www.agnesscott.edu/academics/undergraduate/theatre.aspx
Degree Offered: BA Theatre, emphasis in dramatic writiing

Bard College
Ms. JoAnne Akalaitis, Director
Theatre Department
Bard College
PO Box 5000
Annandale-on-Hudson, New York 12504
Phone: (845) 758-7936
Email: akalaiti@bard.edu
Website: http://www.bard.edu/academics/programs/arts/
Degree Offered: BA Theatre, emphasis in playwriting

Brigham Young University
Mr. Eric Samuelsen, Key Contact
Theatre & Media Arts
Bringham Young University
D-581B HFAC
Provo, Utah 84602
Phone: (801) 422-3305
Email: eric_samuelsen@byu.edu
Website: http://tma.byu.edu/index.php?id=21
Degree Offered: BA in Theatre Arts with an area of interest in playwriting, MFA
Represented Faculty: Eric Samuelson

California - Santa Barbara, University of
Mr. Simon Williams, Chair
Department of Theatre and Dance
University of California at Santa Barbara
Mail Code 7060
552 University Road
Santa Barbara, California 93106
Phone: (805) 893-5515
Email: williams@theaterdance.ucsb.edu
Website: www.dramadance.ucsb.edu
Degree Offered: BA Emphasis in Playwriting, MA, PhD
Program Length: 2 years
Students per class: <20
Represented Faculty: Naomi Iizuka, Dr. Carlos Martin, Robert Potter
Production Opportunities: Staged Readings to Experimental
Other Highlights: KCACTF, ATHE, New Play Festival (internal)

Campbell University
Mr. Stephen J. Larson, Chair
Department of Theatre Arts
Campbell University
PO Box 776
Buies Creek, North Carolina 27506
Phone: (910) 893-1507
Website: http://www.campbell.edu/coas/theatre
Degree Offered: BA in Playwriting
Represented Faculty: Herald Heno
Production Opportunities: Full Student no readings
Other Highlights: no

Case Western Reserve
Ms. Catherine Albers, Academic Representative
Department of Theatre and Dance
Case Western Reserve
10900 Euclid Ave.
Cleveland, Ohio 44106
Phone: (216) 368-4868
Email: catherine.albers@case.edu
Website: http://www.case.edu/artsci/thtr/index.html
Degree Offered: BA in Dramatic Writing
Represented Faculty: Jon Orlock

Columbia College Chicago
Mr. Randall Albers, Chair
Fiction Writing Department
Columbia College Chicago
600 South Michigan Avenue
Chicago, Illinois 60605
Phone: (312) 344-7616
Email: ralbers@colum.edu
Website: http://fiction.colum.edu/program/index.html
Degree Offered: BA Playwriting, BFA Playwriting
Represented Faculty: Randy Albers, Joe Meno, Lisa Schlesinger
Other Highlights: Hair Trigger - anthology (internal publication)

DePaul University
Mr. Dean Corrin, Head of Playwriting
The Theatre School
DePaul University
2135 N. Kenmore
Chicago, Illinois 60614
Phone: (773) 325-7932, (773) 325-7999
Email: dcorrin@depaul.edu
Website: http://theatreschool.depaul.edu/undergraduate_application_playwriting.php
Degree Offered: BFA in Playwriting
Program Length: 4 years
Represented Faculty: Dean Corrin, Reginald Lawrence, Carlos Murillo, Guests
Production Opportunities: Staged Readings to Full Students

Drexel University
Ms. Sharon Walker, Key Contact
Antoinette Westphal College of Media Arts and Design
Drexel University
Nesbitt Hall
33rd and Market Streets
Philadelphia, Pennsylvania 19104
Phone: (215) 895-2408
Email: cinetv@drexel.edu
Website: http://www.drexel.edu/westphal/academics/undergraduate/screenwriting/
Degree Offered: BS in Screenwriting & Playwriting
Represented Faculty: Bruce Graham, Joseph Stinson
Other Highlights: High School Ten-minute Play Contest

Emerson College
Dr. Daniel Tobin, Chair
Department of Writing, Literature & Publishing
Emerson College
120 Boylston Street
Boston, Massachusettes 2116
Phone: (617) 824-8750
Website: http://www.emerson.edu/writing_lit_publishing/graduate/Creative-Writing.cfm
Degree Offered: MFA in Creative Writing (focus in min. 2 areas can include playwriting)
Program Length: 52 hours
Represented Faculty: Andrew Clarke

Fordham University
Mr. Matthew Maguire, Head of Playwriting Program
Fordham Univ. Theatre Program
Fordham University
Lincoln Center Campus
113 W. 60th St. Room 423
New York, New York 10023
Phone: (212) 636-6306
Email: mmaguire@fordham.edu
Website: www.fordham.edu/theatre
Degree Offered: BA in Playwriting
Represented Faculty: Matthew Maguire, Michael John Garces, Guests

Georgia, University of
Dr. David Saltz, Department Head
Department of Theatre and Film Studies
University of Georgia
203B Fine Arts,
Athens, Georgia 30602
Phone: (706) 542-2836
Email: saltz@uga.edu
Website: www.drama.uga.edu
Degree Offered: BA Drama with a concentration in writing
Represented Faculty: Dr. Antje Ascheild, George Contini, Dr. Phillip Auslander
Production Opportunities: Staged Readings to Full Student
Other Highlights: various student related

Independence Community College
Mr. Peter Ellenstein, Director
William Inge Center for the Arts
Independence Community College
PO BOX 708
1057 W. College Avenue
Independence, Kansas 67301
Phone: (800) 842-6063 ext.5490
Email: pellenstein@ingecenter.org
Website: http://www.ingefestival.org/education/playwritingprogram.htm
Degree Offered: Professional Playwriting Certificate Program, AA
Represented Faculty: Various Playwrights in Residence
Production Opportunities:
Other Highlights: William Inge Theatre Festival

Kansas State University
Ms. Kate Anderson, Director of Theatre
Department of Speech Communication, Theatre and Dance
Kansas State University
Nichols Hall 129
Manhattan, Kansas 66506
Phone: (785) 532-6769
Email: Katjef@k-state.edu
Website: http://www.k-state.edu/sctd/theatre/playwriting.html
Degree Offered: BA Theatre, Concentration in Playwriting
Represented Faculty: Charlotte MacFarland, Sally Bailey

Production Opportunities: Staged Readings to Full Student
Other Highlights: KCACTF

Marymount Manhattan College
Ms. Mary Fleischer, Chair
Fine and Performing Arts
Marymount Manhattan College
221 East 71st Street
New York, New York 10021
Phone: (212) 774-0761
Email: mfleischer@mmm.edu
Website: http://marymount.mmm.edu/cgi-bin/MySQLdb?MYSQL_VIEW=/study/programs/view.txt&currentdept=1015
Degree Offered: BA inTheatre Arts concentration in Writing for the Stage

University of Missouri - Kansas City
Dr. Felicia Hardison Londre`, Curators' Professor of Theatre
UMKC Theatre
University of Missouri at Kansas City
5100 Rockhill Road
Kansas City, Missouri 64110
Phone: (816) 235-2781
Email: LondreF@umkc.edu
Website: www.umkc.edu/theatre
Degree Offered: BA, MA in Theatre History, Lit. or Playwriting
Program Length:
Students per class: ~8

State University of New York - Purchase
Ms. Kathleen Tolan, Chair
Dramatic Writing Program
SUNY Purchase
735 Anderson Hill Rd.
Purchase, New York 10577
Phone: (914) 251-6830
http://www.purchase.edu/departments/AcademicPrograms/Arts/taf/DramaticWriting.aspx
Degree Offered: BFA in Dramatic Writing
Program Length: 4 years
Students per class: ~20
Represented Faculty: Kathleen Tolan, A. Dean Bell, Iris Cahn, Madeleine George, Part-time and Guests

Roosevelt Universtity
Ms. Janet Wondra, Coordinator of Creative Writing
Department of Literature and Languages
Roosevelt University
430 S. Michigan Avenue
Chicago, Illinois 60605
Phone: (312) 341-3770
Email: jwondra@roosevelt.edu
Website: http://www.roosevelt.edu/cas/lit/writing/default.htm
Degree Offered: MFA in Creative Writing

Sarah Lawrence College
Ms. Shirley Kaplan, Director
Sarah Lawrence College
One Mead Way
Bronxville, New York 10708
Phone: (914) 395-2430
Email: slcadmit@mail.sic.edu
Website: http://www.slc.edu/theatre/index.php
Degree Offered: BFA, MFA (self-designed, can focus on playwriting)
Program Length: 2 years
Represented Faculty: Allan Baker, Cassandra Medley, Earnest H. Abuba, Amlin Gray, Stuart Spencer
Production Opportunities: Staged Readings to Full Student
Other Highlights: Theatre Outreach

University of Virginia
Mr. L. Douglas Grissom, Playwriting
Department of Drama
University of Virginia
PO Box 400128
Charlottesville, Virginia 22904
Phone: (804) 924-1447
Email: ldg2h@virginia.edu
Website: http://www.virginia.edu/drama
Degree Offered: BA in Drama (Playwriting), MFA
Represented Faculty: Doug Grissom, Guests
Production Opportunities: Staged Readings to Full Student
Other Highlights: KCACTF

Western Washington University
Mr. Gregory Lawrence Pulver, Chair
Theatre Arts Department
Western Washington University
519 High Street/ PA 395B
Bellingham, Washington 98225
Phone: (360) 650-6862
Email: Gregory.Pulver@www.edu
Website: http://www.wwu.edu/depts/theatre/
Degree Offered: BA in Theatre with a concentration in Dramatic Writing
Represented Faculty: Bryan Willis
Other Highlights: KCACTF

Wyoming, University of
Mr. William M. Downs, Professor
Department of Theatre and Dance
University of Wyoming
1000 E. University Avenue
Dept. 3951
Laramie, Wyoming 82071
Phone: (307) 766-2198
Email: downs@uwyo.edu
Website: http://www.uwyo.edu/th&d
Degree Offered: BA, BFA Theatre with Playwriting Concentration
Represented Faculty: William Downs
Production Opportunities: Staged Readings
Other Highlights: KCACTF, RMTF, URTA

WORKSHOPS

$75-$895. Academy for New Musical Theatre (ANMT)

5628 Vineland Ave., N. Hollywood, CA, 91601
Scott Guy, Exec Dir
Tel: 818-506-8500
academy@anmt.org; www.anmt.org

Est. 1981. Supports wide array of programs to further artistic creation of new musical stage works, incl. workshops (Lehman Engel curriculum), readings, and commercial development. Staff: John Sparks (Artistic Dir), Elise Dewsberry (Assoc Artistic Dir). **Consideration.** Fees: $895 (Intro Workshop), $695 (Lab), $395 (Fast Track Lab), $75 (Cabaret Workshop). **Application.** Best Material: query, SASE. Best Time: spring-summer.

11/1/2008. Afterschool Playwriting Workshop (APW)

Young Playwrights Inc (YPI), Box 5134, New York, NY, 10185
Sheri Goldhirsch, Artistic Dir.
Tel: 212-594-5440, Fax: 212-684-4902
admin@youngplaywrights.org; www.youngplaywrights.org

Students from Write a Play! can apply for APW, which meets in midtown Manhattan every Tue, 4:30-7:00pm, Dec-Jun. Exercises help members develop and revise new plays. Members also attend Broadway and Off-Broadway productions, with post-show discussions with playwrights, directors, and actors. **Preference.** Style: comedy, drama. Author Must Be: age 18 or younger. Material Must Be: original. **Application.** Best Material: application, sample, teacher/mentor recommendation, submissions not returned. Deadline: 1-Nov-08.

Around the Block Urban Playwriting Workgroup

Around the Block, 5 E. 22nd St., #9-K, New York, NY, 10010
Carlos Jerome, Leader
Tel: 212-673-9187
info@aroundtheblock.org; www.aroundtheblock.org

Est. 2001. Focusing on (but not restricted to) the life & aspirations of urban communities, particularly NYC. Group meets every 2 wks. No fee. Membership in ATB not required. Staff: Gloria Zelaya, Louis (Co-dir, Theater Arts). **Consideration.** Remuneration: reading. **Preference.** Subject: NYC, urban. **Application.** Best Way: contact us to arrange participation. Response: 2 wks.

3/30/2008. ASCAP Musical Theatre Workshop [NY]

1 Lincoln Plaza, Fl. 7, New York, NY, 10023
Michael A. Kerker, Dir., Musical Theatre
Tel: 212-621-6234, Fax: 212-621-6558
www.ascap.com

Directed by Stephen Schwartz, program of 50-min from works-in-progress before a panel of professional directors, musical directors, producers, critics and fellow writers. All sessions begin 7pm, May-Jun. **Application.** Best Material: synopsis, audio (4 songs), bios, song descriptions.

12/27/2008. ASCAP/Disney Musical Theatre Workshop [CA]

7920 W. Sunset Blvd., Fl. 3, Los Angeles, CA, 90046
Tel: 323-883-1000, Fax: 323-883-1049
www.ascap.com

Directed by Stephen Schwartz, 50-min presentation of works-in-development before a professional panel. All sessions begin 7pm, Jan-Feb. **Application.** Best Material: synopsis, audio (4 songs), bios, song descriptions. Deadline: 27-Dec-08.

Broadway Tomorrow Musical Theatre
191 Claremont Ave., #53, New York, NY, 10027
Elyse Curtis, Artistic Dir.
Tel: 212-531-2447
solministry@juno.com; www.solministry.com

Est. 1983. New musicals on new age, transformative or spiritual themes with redeeming value given self-contained concert readings with writer/composer involvement. Staff: Norman Curtis (Musical Dir). **Preference.** Length: all length. Style: adaptation, musical, translation. Subject: religious, new age, historical. Author Must Be: resident of NYC area. **Application.** Best Material: synopsis, audio (3 songs), SASE. Response: 6 mos.

2/1/2008. Cape Cod Theatre Project
Box 410, Falmouth, MA, 02541
Andrew Polk, Artistic Dir.
Tel: 508-457-4242
andrew@capecodtheatreproject.org; www.capecodtheatreproject.org

Est. 1995. Equity LOA. **Preference.** Length: full length (over 90 min). Style: others. Subject: contemporary US. Author Must Be: resident or citizen of US. Material Must Be: unpublished, unproduced. **Application.** Best Material: query, synopsis, submissions not returned. Best Time: Oct. to Feb.. Deadline: 1-Feb-08.

$250/sem. Charles Maryan's Playwrights/Directors Workshop
777 West End Ave., #6-C, New York, NY, 10025
Charles Maryan, Founder
Tel: 212-864-0542
cmaryan@pace.edu

Est. 1982. **Consideration.** Fees: $250/sem. **Application.** Response: 2 wks.

Cherry Lane Theatre Mentor Project
38 Commerce St., New York, NY, 10014
James King, Managing Dir.
Tel: 212-989-2020
company@cherrylanetheatre.org; www.cherrylanetheatre.org

Est. 1997. Pairs young writers with master to work on scripts for full season, ending with Equity Showcase. Staff: Angelina Fiordellis (Artistic Director), Michael Weller (Supervising Mentor) **Consideration.** Frequency: annual. **Preference.** Length: full length (over 90 min). Production: medium cast size, no orchestra. Material Must Be: unoptioned, unproduced. **Application.** Best Way: professional recommendation. Best Material: submissions not returned.

Colorado New Play Summit
Denver Center Theatre Company (DCTC), 1101 13th St., Denver, CO, 80204
Douglas Langworthy, Literary Mgr
Tel: 303-893-4000, Fax: 303-825-2117
www.dcpa.org

DCTC (est. 1979; 1998 Regional Theater Tony winner) presents the Colorado New Play Summit (est. 2005), which offers rehearsed reading of new work for industry and general audience. **Consideration.** Assistance: room/board, room/board. Frequency: annual. **Preference.** Length: full length (over 90 min). Subject: no children's. Material Must Be: unoptioned, unproduced. **Application.** Best Way: unsolicited (AZ, CO, MT, NM, UT, WY residents only), agent. Best Material: full script, SASE. Response: 6 mos.

8/1/2008. Composers & Lyricists Workshop
BMI (Broadcast Music Inc), 320 W. 57th St., New York, NY, 10019
Jean Banks, Sr. Dir., Musical Theater
Fax: 212-262-2508
jbanks@bmi.com; www.bmi.com

Weekly 2-hr sessions (Sep-May). **Consideration.** Frequency: annual. **Preference.** Style: musical. **Application.** Best Material: application, sample, audio. Best Time: Jan-Jul. Deadline: 1-Aug-08.

$375 . David Henry Hwang Writers Institute

East West Players, 120 N. Judge John Aiso St., Los Angeles, CA, 90012
Jeff Liu, Literary Mgr.
Tel: 213-625-7000, Fax: 213-625-7111
jliu@eastwestplayers.org; www.eastwestplayers.org

Est. 1991. 2 workshops/yr (fall, spring). **Consideration.** Fees: $375 . **Application.** Best Material: query.

$90.00 . Fieldwork

The Field, 161 6th Ave, Fl. 14, New York, NY, 10013
Pele Bauch, Mgr, Programs & Outreach
Tel: 212-691-6969, Fax: 212-255-2053
pele@thefield.org; www.thefield.org

Est. 1986. 10-wk workshop to create original material, share work, and receive peer feedback. **Consideration.** Fees: $90, $65 (Field members). Assistance: work-study option. Frequency: quarterly. **Preference.** Length: short (under 30 min).

Frank Silvera Writers' Workshop

Box 1791, Manhattanville Sta., New York, NY, 10027
Garland Lee Thompson, Founding Exec Dir
Tel: 212-281-8832, Fax: 212-281-8839
playrite@earthlink.net; www.fsww.org

Est. 1973. Equity Showcase. Playwright development program. **Consideration.** Remuneration: 6\% royalty. **Preference.** Author Must Be: age 18 or older, resident or citizen of US. Material Must Be: unoptioned, unpublished, unproduced. **Application.** Best Material: full script, SASE. Best Time: Sep-Jun.

3/15/08. Hangar Theatre Lab Company Playwriting Residencies

Box 205, Ithaca, NY, 14851
Wendy Dann, Assoc Artistic Dir
literary@hangartheatre.org; www.hangartheatre.org

Est. 1991. 4 playwrights offered 2-3 wk residency in Jul-Aug. **Consideration.** Assistance: $300 . Frequency: annual. **Preference.** Length: one-act (30-60 min). Material Must Be: unproduced. **Application.** Best Way: online. Best Material: full script, resume/bio, submissions not returned. Deadline: 15-Mar-08. Response: by 5/30/08.

$400.00 . Harbor Theatre Workshop

160 W. 71st St., #PH-A, New York, NY, 10023
Stuart Warmflash, Artistic Dir.
Tel: 212-787-1945, Fax: 212-712-2378
swarmflash@harbortheatre.org; www.harbortheatre.org

Est. 1994. Equity productions. Staff: Julie Carpenter (Producing Dir). **Consideration.** Fees: $400 . **Preference.** Length: full length (over 90 min), mid-length (60-90 min). Style: comedy, drama, musical. Material Must Be: unoptioned, unpublished, unproduced. **Application.** Best Material: query, synopsis, SASE. Response: 6 wks.

$20/class. Improv for Playwrights

Artistic New Directions, 250 W. 90th St., #15-G, New York, NY, 10024
Kristine Niven, Artistic/Producing Dir
Tel: 212-875-1857
artnewdir@aol.com; www.artisticnewdirections.org

Est. 1986. Jeffrey Sweet teaches technique for setting up scenes to improvise toward first drafts of one-acts, plus revising, introducing characters, and using improv for full-lengths. Monthly sessions, Wed nights. **Consideration.** Fees: $20/class.

Know Theatre of Cincinnati

1120 Jackson St, Cincinnati, OH, 45202
Jason Buffy, Artistic Director
Tel: 513-300-5669
artistic@knowtheatre.com; www.knowtheatre.com

est. 1997. The Know Theatre workshops for future mainstage. **Preference.** Length: full length (over 90 min), mid-length (60-90 min.), one-act (30-60 min.). **Application.** Best Way: unsolicited. Best Material: query, synopsis, 20 page sample.

5/1/2008. Librettists Workshop

BMI (Broadcast Music Inc), 320 W. 57th St., New York, NY, 10019
Jean Banks, Sr. Dir., Musical Theater
Tel: 212-830-2508, Fax: 212-262-2508
jbanks@bmi.com; www.bmi.com

Weekly 2-hr sessions (Sep-May) in NYC. **Consideration.** Frequency: annual. **Preference.** Style: musical. **Application.** Best Material: application, sample. Deadline: 1-May-08.

Manhattan Playwrights Unit (MPU)

338 W 19th St., #6-B, New York, NY, 10011
Saul Zachary, Artistic Dir.
Tel: 212-989-0948

Est. 1979. Ongoing biweekly inhouse workshop for professional-level playwrights and screenwriters. Informal and intense. Staff: Stacie Linardos. **Preference.** Style: all styles. **Application.** Best Way: unsolicited. Best Material: query, resume, submissions not returned.

Missouri Playwrights Workshop (MPW)

Univ. of Missouri, Columbia, 129 Fine Arts Bldg., Columbia, MO, 65211
David Crespy, Artistic Dir
Tel: 573-882-0535
crespyd@missouri.edu; theatre.missouri.edu/mpw/index.htm

Est. 1998. Weekly salon for developing work by Missouri playwrights. **Preference.** Author Must Be: resident of MO, and attend workshop. **Application.** Best Material: query, synopsis, submissions not returned.

Musical Theatre Lab

Univ. of Houston School of Theatre, 133 Wortham, Houston, TX, 77204
Stuart Ostrow
Tel: 713-743-2912

Est. 1973. Each fall, 3 works performed by Lab students at Hobby Center. Recent works incl. 'Twas, Doll, Coyote Goes Salmon Fishing, and 1040. **Preference.** Length: full length (over 90 min). Style: musical. Material Must Be: unoptioned, original. **Application.** Best Material: full script, audio, score, SASE. Response: 1 mo.

$25 + $1,000/yr. 9/1/08. Musical Theatre Writers' Workshop

Theatre Building Chicago (TBC), 1225 W. Belmont Ave., Chicago, IL, 60657
John Sparks, Artistic Dir.
Tel: 773-929-7367 x222, Fax: 773-327-1404
jsparks@theatrebuildingchicago.org; www.theatrebuildingchicago.org

Est. 1984. Formerly New Tuners Workshop. 3-tiered workshop: Intro (1st yr), Intermediate (2nd yr), Advanced (ongoing). **Consideration.** Fees: $25 application, $1,000/yr (Intro/Intermediate), $400/yr (Advanced). **Preference.** Style: musical. **Application.** Best Material: application, 5-pg sample, audio, SASE. Deadline: 1-Sep-08.

$10.00 . National Theatre Workshop of the Handicapped

535 Greenwich St., New York, NY, 10013
Rick Curry S.J., Founder/Artistic Dir
Tel: 212-206-7789, Fax: 212-206-0200
admissions@ntwh.org; www.ntwh.org

Est. 1977. 2-wk summer program at Crosby School in Belfast, Maine, brinigng together disabled and able-bodied playwrights and actors to create pieces on themes of disability. **Consideration.** Fees: $10 application. **Application.** Best Material: application.

2/1/2008. New Directors/New Works (ND/NW)

The Drama League, 520 8th Ave., #320, New York, NY, 10018
Roger Danforth, Artistic Dir.
Tel: 212-244-9494, Fax: 212-244-9191
directorsproject@dramaleague.org; www.dramaleague.org

Directors Project program to support new works by directors and collaborating artists. Application must be submitted by the director. Each team works with a professional mentor. **Consideration.** Assistance: $1,000 stipend. Frequency: annual. **Preference.** Length: full length (over 90 min), mid-length (60-90 min). Author Must Be: resident of US. **Application.** Best Material: application, sample, production budget, two letters of recommendation, SASE. Deadline: 1-Feb-08.

10/1/08. New Harmony Project

Box 441062, Indianapolis, IN, 46244
Joel Grynheim, Project Dir.
Tel: 317-464-1103
jgrynheim@newharmonyproject.org; www.newharmonyproject.org

Est. 1986. Development thru rehearsals and readings in 2-wk conference of scripts that explore the human journey by offering hope and showing respect for the positive values of life. **Consideration.** Assistance: $1,000 stipend, room/board, room/board. Remuneration: reading. Frequency: annual. **Application.** Best Material: 2-pg proposal, 10-pg sample, full script, audio, resume. Deadline: 1-Oct-08.

New Play Development Workshop

ATHE Playwrights Program, Box 1290, Boulder, CO, 80306
Tel: 303-530-2167
playwrightsprogram@athe.org

Playwrights Program develops 7-10 new scripts/yr at the ATHE conference. **Preference.** Length: other (4-10 min.).

8/1/08. New Visions/New Voices (NVNV)

Kennedy Center Education Dept., Box 101510, Arlington, VA, 22210
Kim Peter Kovac, Dir., TYA
Tel: 202-416-8830, Fax: 202-416-8297
kctya@kennedy-center.org; www.kennedy-center.org/education/nvnv.html

Est. 1991. Biennial (even yrs) weeklong residency in Apr to encourage and support creation of new plays and musicals for young people and families. **Consideration.** Assistance: stipend. Frequency: biennial. **Preference.** Length: mid-length (60-90 min). Subject: young audiences. Material Must Be: unproduced. **Application.** Best Way: thru sponsoring theater. Best Material: application, synopsis, sample, full script (3 copies), audio, submissions not returned. Best Time: May. Deadline: 1-Aug-08.

6/15/08. $350/10 sessions. NYC Playwrights Lab

Box 171, Peck Slip Sta., New York, NY, 10272
Dina von Zweck, Dir, New Plays
www.writerightnyc.com

Small group of professional playwrights meeting weekly to make good scripts great, aiming to produce plays with significant impact in contemporary theater. **Consideration.** Fees: $350/10 sessions. **Preference.** Style: adaptation, comedy, drama, opera, experimental. **Application.** Best Material: application, synopsis, 10-pg sample, submissions not returned. Deadline: 30-May-08. Response: 3 mos.

Pataphysics
Flea Theater, 41 White St., New York, NY, 10013
Gary Winter, Literary Mgr.
Tel: 212-226-0051, Fax: 212-965-1808
garyw@theflea.org; www.theflea.org

Pataphysics workshops are scheduled sporadically and occur unexpectedly. **Application.** Best Material: query, 10-pg sample (4 copies), resume, SASE.

Penumbra Theatre Company
Penumbra Theatre Company, 270 N Kent St., St. Paul, MN, 55102
Dominic Taylor, Assoc. Artistic Dir.
Tel: 651-288-6795
www.penumbratheatre.org

Preference. Length: full length (over 90 min). Style: all styles. Subject: Black.

$150.00 . PlayCrafters Group
11 Golf View Rd., Doylestown, PA, 18901
James Breckenridge, Creative Writing Consultant
Tel: 888-399-2506
hbcraft@att.net

Professional play script and screenplay evaluations and consultations for the creative dramatic writer. **Consideration.** Fees: $150 and up. **Application.** Best Material: query.

PlayGround
New Perspectives Theatre, 456 W. 37th St., New York, NY, 10018
Melody Brooks, Artistic Dir
Tel: 212-630-9945
www.newperspectivestheatre.org

Est. 2004. **Preference.** Subject: new work with American themes. **Application.** Best Material: application, synopsis, sample.

PlayLabs
The Playwrights' Center, 2301 Franklin Ave., Minneapolis, MN, 55406
Steve Moulds, Membership/Lit Assoc.
Tel: 612-332-7481, Fax: 612-332-6037
info@pwcenter.org; www.pwcenter.org

30-hr Jul development workshop with distinguished professionals, followed by public reading. **Consideration.** Assistance: honorarium, room/board, room/board. Frequency: annual. **Preference.** Length: full length (over 90 min). Author Must Be: citizen or resident of US. Material Must Be: unpublished, unproduced. **Application.** Best Way: online. Best Material: application. Deadline: Oct. 26, 2008.

Playwrights' Lab
Pulse Ensemble Theatre, 266 W. 37th St., Fl. 22, New York, NY, 10018
Lezley Steele, Dir, New Play Development
Tel: 212-695-1596
www.pulseensembletheatre.org

Develops 1 work of each playwright in 4-mo workshop. Group (limit 10) meets 3 hrs/wk to read scenes, with discussion afterward. Presents two showcases of 3 works/year. Some plays selected for further development. $100/month **Consideration.** Fees: $400 .

$35/yr. Playwrights' Platform
Box 267, State House PO, Boston, MA, 02133
Pat Brennan, Artistic Dir.
membership@playwrightsplatform.org; www.playwrightsplatform.org

Est. 1976. Monthly readings and summer fest at Hovey Theater, Waltham, Mass. **Consideration.** Fees: $35/yr. **Preference.** Author Must Be: resident of MA. **Application.** Best Way: online. Best Time: Sep-May. Response: 3 mos.

1/15/08, 8/1/08. Playwrights Gallery

119 W. 72nd St., #2700, New York, NY, 10023
Deborah Savadge, Coord.
www.playwrightsgallery.com

Est. 1989. Compnay of professional actors reads new work twice monthly. Public readings 2-3 times/yr. Meet Sep-Jun, alt Wed, noon-2pm. **Preference.** Style: comedy, drama. **Application.** Best Way: professional recommendation. Best Material: 20-pg sample, SASE. Deadline: 15-Jan-08, 1-Aug-08. Response: 9 mos.

$450.00 . Primary Stages Playwriting Workshops

307 W. 38th St., #1510, New York, NY, 10018
Michelle Bossy, Assoc Artistic Dir
Tel: 212-840-9705, Fax: 212-840-9725
michelle@primarystages.com; www.primarystages.com

Est. 2002. Each wk, 8 writers bring 10-15 pgs for instructor feedback and group discussion, completing first draft of new full-length in 8 wks. **Consideration.** Fees: $450 . **Preference.** Length: full length (over 90 min). **Application.** Best Material: let of interest, resume. Best Time: July, Dec.

$150.00 . PRTT Playwrights Unit

Puerto Rican Traveling Theatre, 304 W. 47th St., New York, NY, 10036
Allen Davis III, Dir.
Tel: 212-354-1293, Fax: 212-307-6769
allen@prtt.org; www.prtt.org

Est. 1977. Developmental workshops for beginners and for professionals (Oct-Apr), with readings and staged productions. **Consideration.** Fees: $150 . Remuneration: production, reading. Frequency: annual. **Preference.** Author Must Be: resident of NYC area, Latino/minorities preferred. **Application.** Best Material: query, full script (professional unit), SASE. Best Time: Sep. Response: 1 mo.

Sage Theater

235 W. 48th St., #26B, New York, NY, 10036
Diana Blake
Tel: 212-302-6665, Fax: 212-302-4661
info@sagetheater.us; sagetheater.us

Preference. Length: mid-length (60-90 min), short (under 30 min). Style: sketch/musical comedy only. **Application.** Best Material: full script, SASE. Response: 4 mos.

Scripteasers

3404 Hawk St., San Diego, CA, 92103
Jonathan Dunn-Rankin, Corresponding Secy
Tel: 619-295-4040
thescripteasers@msn.com; www.scripteasers.org

Est. 1948. Writers' development group with biweekly readings of original plays and facilitated discussion. Staff: Michal Conley (Pres). **Preference.** Author Must Be: resident of SoCal. Material Must Be: unoptioned, unpublished, unproduced. **Application.** Best Material: full script, SASE.

Scripts Up!

355 South End Ave., #5-N, New York, NY, 10280
David Spaulding
Tel: 212-946-1155

Est. 1999. Nonprofit play development org specializing in professional workshop stagings of full-length plays. **Preference.** Length: full length (over 90 min). Material Must Be: unoptioned, unpublished, unproduced. **Application.** Best Material: synopsis, 15-pg sample, resume.

$35 + $225-$450. Simon Studio

Box 231469, Ansonia Sta., New York, NY, 10023
Roger Simon, Dir.
Tel: 212-841-0204, Fax: 212-543-0286
rhsstudio@hotmail.com; www.simonstudio.com

Development through long distance consultation and/or residency of 5-10 weeks or short term intensive (1-5) days in NYC and/or Poughkeepsie/NY. Writers develop and showcase new work for stage, TV/Film, radio. Consideration for Samuel French National Short Play Fest, Simon Studio/Drama Book Shop Cinema & Theatre Fest. and Time Warner TV's Simon Studio Presents. *Service includes ongoing readings and critiques in workshops for in house, public and invited industry. **Consideration.** Fees: $15 aplication fee, $225-$450 program fee. **Preference.** Length: all lengths. Style: all styles. **Application.** Best Way: unsolicited. Best Material: query letter (note theme addressed), synopsis, 30-pg writing sample, audio, submissions returned with SASE. Deadline: ongoing.

Southern Writers Project (SWP)

Alabama Shakespeare Festival (ASF), 1 Festival Dr., Montgomery, AL, 36117
Nancy Rominger, Artistic Assoc
Fax: 334-271-5348
webswp@asf.net; www.southernwritersproject.net

ASF accepts scripts through its Southern Writers' Project (est. 1991). Up to 6 scripts each year are developed in weeklong workshop, with some chosen for production next season. **Consideration.** Assistance: room/board, room/board. **Preference.** Length: full length (over 90 min). Subject: African-American, South. Material Must Be: unproduced. **Application.** Best Material: full script, SASE. Response: 6 mos.

3/1, 8/15, 12/1. Stage Left Theatre Company

3408 N. Sheffield Ave., Chicago, IL, 60657
John Sanders, Dir, DSL
Tel: 773-883-8830 x3
scripts@stagelefttheatre.com; www.stagelefttheatre.com

Est. 1982. Storefront theatre for plays that raise debate on sociopolticial issues, incl. Downstage Left (or DSL) development program. Staff: LaRonkia Thomas (Literary Mgr). **Consideration.** Assistance:. Remuneration: royalty. **Preference.** Length: full-length (over 90 min). **Application.** Best Material: application, 1-pg synopsis, full script, resume, SASE. Deadline: Mar 1, 2008(Jun-Sep), Aug 15, 2008 (Oct-Jan), Dec 1, 2008(Feb-May). Response: 1 yr.

12/15/08. $30. Sundance Institute Theatre

8530 Wilshire Blvd., Fl. 3, Beverly Hills, CA, 90211
Christopher Hibma, Associate Dir.
Tel: 310-360-1981, Fax: 310-360-1975
theatre@sundance.org; www.sundance.org

Est. 1981. Equity Special Agreement. Developmental Jul workshops for directors and playwrights in Sundance, UT. **Consideration.** Fees: $30 application. Assistance: $500 , room/board, room/board. Frequency: annual. **Preference.** Length: full length (over 90 min), mid-length (60-90 min). Material Must Be: unproduced. **Application.** Best Material: application, full script, audio, video, SASE. Deadline: 15-Dec-08. Response: 4 mos.

Sundance Institute Theatre at White Oak

8530 Wilshire Blvd., Fl. 3, Beverly Hills, CA, 90211
Christopher Hibma, Associate Dir.
Tel: 310-360-1981, Fax: 310-360-1975
theatre@sundance.org; www.sundance.org

Est. 2003. Equity Special Agreement. 2-wk developmental workshop focusing on musical theater and ensemble-created work. **Consideration.** Assistance: stipend, room/board, room/board. Frequency: annual. **Preference.** Material Must Be: unproduced. **Application.** Best Way: invite. Best Material: synopsis, submissions not returned. Best Time: Dec.

$1,650. 4/9/08. Urban Retreat

Young Playwrights Inc (YPI), Box 5134, New York, NY, 10185
Sheri Goldhirsch, Artistic Dir.
Tel: 212-594-5440, Fax: 212-684-4902
admin@youngplaywrights.org; www.youngplaywrights.org

1-wk Jul intensive of 2-3 workshops/day in NYC. Participants then collaborate with professional dramaturgs, directors, and actors on production of a new play. **Consideration.** Fees: $1,650 . Assistance: room/board, room/board, theater tickets. **Preference.** Style: comedy, drama. Author Must Be: age 14-21. Material Must Be: original. **Application.** Best Material: application, sample, submissions not returned. Deadline: 9-Apr-08.

5/15/08. Writer/Director Lab

SoHo Repertory Theater, 86 Franklin St., Fl. 5, New York, NY, 10013
Sarah Benson, Co-Chair
Tel: 212-941-8632, Fax: 212-941-7148
writerdirector@sohorep.org; www.sohorep.org

Est. 1998. Writers and directors apply separately, then are paired for the workshop. Meet bimonthly Oct-April to read plays aloud and discuss. Each writers brings work in 3 times during workshop. **Application.** Best Material: query, application, full script, resume, SASE. Deadline: 15-May-08.

Writer Resources

Affordable Hotel Index, New York City

Discount Manhattan Hotels

Hotel Newton
Rating: ★½
2528 Broadway
212-687-6500, 800-643-5553
Price Range: 95-160
Location: Upper West Side

Milburn Hotel
Rating: ★★★½
242 W 76th St
800-833-9622, 212-362-1006
Price Range: 129-245
Location: Upper West Side

The Pod Hotel
Rating: ★★
230 E 51st St
212-355-0300, 800-742-5945
Price Range: 129-694
Location: Turtle Bay

Hotel Alexander
Rating: ★★½
306 W 94 St
800-372-2496
Price Range: 79-169
Location: Upper West Side

Latham Hotel
Rating: ★★
4 E 28 St
212-685-8300
Price Range: 99-169
Location: Gramercy

Hotel St. James
Rating: ★★
109 W 45 St
212-730-9444, 212-869-7329
Price Range: 99-250
Location: Midtown

Days Hotel
Rating: ★★
215 W 94 St
212-581-7000
Price Range: 116-269
Location: Upper West Side

Hotel Riverside Studios
Rating: ★★½
342 W 17 St
800-372-2496
Price Range: 100-367
Location: Upper West Side

Hotel 31
Rating: ★★½
120 E 31 St
212-685-3060
Price Range: 120-214
Location: Murray Hill

Hotel 17
Rating: ★★½
225 E 17 St
212-475-2845
Price Range: 120-180
Location: Gramercy

Chelsea Savoy Hotel
Rating: ★★
204 W 23rd St.
866-929-9353, 212-929-9353
Price Range: 99-425
Location: Chelsea

Colonial House Inn
Rating: ★★½
318 W 22nd St
800-689-3779, 212-243-9669
Price Range: 80(single)-140(deluxe)
Location: Chelsea

Cosmopolitan Hotel-Tribeca
Rating: ★★★
95 W Broadway
888-895-9400, 212-566-1900
Price Range: 129-159
Location: Financial District

The Gershwin
Rating: ★★★
7 E 27th St
212-545-8000
Price Range: 99 and up
Location: Flatiron District

Larchmont Hotel
Rating: ★★★
27 W 11th St
212-989-9333
Price Range: 70-125
Location: Greenwich Village

The Marcel
Rating: ★★★
201 E 24th St
212-696-3800
Price Range: 125 and up
Location: Flatiron

New Yorker Hotel
Rating: ★★★
481 Eighth Avenue (at 34th Street)
212-971-0101
Price Range: 99 and up
Location: Garment District

Red Roof Inn
Rating: ★★★
6 W 32nd St
800-567-7720, 212-643-7100
Price Range: 89-329
Location: Murray Hill

Super 8 Hotel Times Square
Rating: ★★★
59 W 46th St.
800-848-0020, 212-719-2300
Price Range: 89-329
Location: Midtown

Second Home on Second Avenue
Rating: ★★★½
221 Second Ave
212-677-3161
Price Range: 80-195
Location: East Village

Howard Johnson Express Inn
Rating: ★★
135 E Houston St
212-358-8844
Price Range: 109 and up
Location: Lower East Side

Union Square Inn
Rating: ★★
209 E 14th St
212-614-0500
Price Range: 109 and up
Location: Union Square

SoHotel
Rating: ★★
341 Broome St
212-226-1482
Price Range: 94 and up
Location: SoHo

Chelsea Inn
Rating: ★★★
46 W 17th St
212-645-8989
Price Range: 99-259
Location: Chelsea

Chelsea Lodge
Rating: ★★
318 W 20th St
212-243-4499
Price Range: 95 and up
Location: Chelsea

Murray Hill Inn
Rating:★★
143 E 30th St
212-683-6900
Price Range: 89 and up
Location: Murray Hill

Bentley Hotel
Rating: ★★
500 E 62nd St
212-644-6000
Price Range: 135 and up
Location: Lenox Hill

Ten City Guide for Dramatists

ATLANTA

Theatres

Academy Theatre
119 Center Street, Avondale Estates
Atlanta, GA 30002
404-474-8332
Lorenne Fe, Managing Director
academytheatre@mindspring.com
www.academytheatre.org
*season focuses on new work and offers new play development program

Actor's Express
887 West Marietta Street NW
Suite J-107
Atlanta, GA 30318
404-875-1606
Fax: 404-875-2791
Freddie Ashley, Artistic Director
www.actors-express.com
*season focuses on new work and offers new play development program

Alliance Theatre
Literary Department
1280 Peachtree Street NE
Atlanta, GA 30309
404-733-4650
Fax: 404-733-4625
Susan V. Booth, Artistic Director
www.alliancetheatre.org
susan.booth@woodruffcenter.org
*offers new play development program

Art Within
1080 Holcomb Bridge Road
Building 200, Suite 140
Roswell, GA 30076
770-558-8185
Fax: 770-558-8198
Bryan Coley, Artistic Director
www.artwithin.org
artwithin@artwithin.org
*season features some new work and offers new play development program

Atlanta Coalition of Performing Arts
65 Upper Alabama Street
Atlanta, GA 30303
404-588-9890
Fax: 404-586-0054
Kim Patrick Bitz, Executive Director
info@atlantaperforms.com
www.atlantaperforms.com
*season features some new work

Atlanta Radio Theatre Company
3577-A Chamblee Tucker Road, #189
Atlanta, GA 30341-4409
770-923-4043
William Alan Ritch, President
info@artc.org
www.artc.org
*broadcasts and distributes new radio plays

Aurora Theatre
128 Pike Street
Lawrenceville, GA, 30045
770-476-7926
Anthony P. Rodriguez, Producing Artistic Director
www.auroratheatre.com
Anthony@auroratheatre.com
*season features some new work

Dad's Garage Theatre
280 Elizabeth Street, Suite C-101
Atlanta, GA 30307
404-523-3141
Fax: 404-688-6644
Kate Warner, Artistic Director
www.dadsgarage.com
kate@dadsgarage.com
*offers new play development program

Dorsey Theatre
Dorsey Studios for the Performing Arts
3593 Clairmont Road
Atlanta, GA 30319
404-633-3256
www.dorseystudios.com/theatre.htm
*season features some new work

The Essential Theatre
PO Box 8172
Atlanta, GA 30306
Stacy Hyken Edelstein, Director
www.essentialtheatre.com
pmhardy@aol.com
*season focuses on new work
*offers new play development program

Fly-By Theatre
471 Bartram Street SE, Unit B
Atlanta, GA 30316-6808
404-683-7350
Pam Joyce, Artistic Director
www.flybytheatre.org
pjoyce@flybytheatre.org
*season features new work

Horizon Theatre Company
PO Box 5376
Atlanta, GA 31107
404-523-1477 X 117
Lisa Adler, Co-Artistic/Producing Director
www.horizontheatre.com
boxoffice@horizontheatre.com
*season focuses on new work
*offers new play development program

Jewish Theatre of the South
Marcus Jewish Community Center of Atlanta
5342 Tilly Mill Road
770-395-2613
Fax: 770-396-2474
Mira Hirsch, Artistic Director
www.jplay.org
Mira.hirsch@atlantajcc.org
*season features some new work

New Jomandi Productions, Inc.
675 Ponce de Leon Avenue, Floor 8
Atlanta, GA 30308
404-784-1587
Carol Mitchell-Leon, Artistic Director
www.jomandi.org
jomandiproductions@yahoo.com
*season features some new work

Not Merely Players
1105 Euclid Avenue
Atlanta, GA 30307
404-614-0099
Fax: 404-5221903
Gene-Gabriel Moore, Artistic Director
ggmnmp@bellsouth.net
Atlanta, GA

Offshoot Productions
PO Box 2462
Peachtree City, GA 30269
770-631-2362
Susan S. Steadman, Ph.D., Artistic Director
www.offshoot.org
offshootpr@aol.com
*season features some new work

Process Theatre Company
404-245-4205
DeWayne Morgan, Artistic Director
www.theprocesstheatre.org
theprocesstheatreco@yahoo.com
*season features some new work
*offers new play development program

PushPush Theater
121 New Street, #4
Decatur Station, Atlanta, GA 30030
404-377-6332
Elisa M. Fay, Board Chair
www.pushpushtheater.com
pushpushtheater@gmail.com
efay@kpmg.com
*offers new play development

Theatre Decatur
430 West Trinity Place
Decatur, GA 30030
404-373-3904
Sonny Goff, Managing Artistic Director
www.theatredecatur.com
sonny@theatredecatur.com
*season focuses on new work

Theatre on Main
Cobb Playhouse and Studio
4857 North Main Street, Suite 240
Acworth, GA 30101
770-565-3995
Fax: 770-565-3583
Bill Jury, Artistic Director
www.cobbplayhouse.com
bill@theatreonmain.net
*season features some new work

Theatre in the Square
11 Whitlock Ave
Marietta, GA 30064
770-422-8369
Fax: 770-422-7436
Jessica West, Artistic Associate
www.theatreinthesquare.com
Jessica@theatreinthesquare.com
*season features some new work
*offers play development program

Membership Organizations and Workshops for Writers

Working Title Playwrights
PO Box 585
Decatur, Georgia 30031-0585
404-474-8332
Jill Patrick, Managing Artistic Director
www.workingtitleplaywrights.com
managing@workingtitleplaywrights.com

Original Play and Musical Contests and Festivals

Annual New South Play Festival
Horizon Theatre Company
PO Box 5376
Atlanta, GA 31107
404-523-1477 X 117
Lisa Adler, Co-Artistic/Producing Director
www.horizontheatre.com
http://www.horizontheatre.com/contact.htm

Essential Theatre Playwriting Award
Box 1872
Atlanta, GA 30306
404-212-0815
Peter Hardy, Producing Artistic Director
www.essentialtheatre.com
pmhardy@aol.com
New South Play Festival
Horizon Theatre Company
Box 5376
Atlanta, GA 31107
404-523-1477 x 113
J. Caleb Boyd, Literary Manager
www.horizontheatre.com
literary@horizontheatre.com

Power Play Festival
The Essential Theatre
PO Box 8172
Atlanta, GA 30306
Stacy Hyken Edelstein, Director
www.essentialtheatre.com
pmhardy@aol.com

Percolating Playreading Series (PPS)
Theatre in the Square
11 Whitlock Avenue
Marietta, GA 30064
770-422-8369
Fax: 770-424-2637
Jessica West, Artistic Associate
www.theatreinthesquare.com
Jessica@theatreinthesquare.com

Theatre Gael – Marki Shalloe Theatre Festival
Writing Workshops
PO Box 77156,
Atlanta, GA 30357
1401 Peachtree Street, Suite 100
Atlanta, GA 30309
404.876.1138
TheatreGael@mindspring.com

Southeastern Theatre Conference (SETC) High School New Play Award
C/o Walker School
700 Cobb Parkway
Marietta, GA 30062
Katie Watts
www.setc.org/scholarship
wattsk@thewalkerschool.org

Opportunities and Resources for Dramatists

Alternate ROOTS Inc.
1083 Austin Avenue
Atlanta, GA 30307
404-577-1079
Fax: 404-577-7991
Carolyn Morris, Executive Director
www.alternateroots.org
info@alternateroots.org

Atlanta Coalition of Performing Arts
65 Upper Alabama Street
Atlanta, GA 30303
404-588-9890
Fax: 404-586-0054
www.atlantaperforms.com

Colleges And Universities For Dramatic Writers

Agnes Scott College
Department of Theatre and Dance
141 East College Avenue
Decatur, GA 30030
404-471-6000
800-868-8602
David S. Thompson, Chair
www.agnesscott.edu
dthompson@agnesscott.edu
*offers undergraduate courses in Playwriting

Emory University
201 Dowman Drive
Atlanta, GA 30322
404-727-6751
John Ward, Head of Theatre Arts
www.theater.emory.edu
Jward03@emory.edu
*offers undergraduate courses in Playwriting

LaGrange College
Department of Theatre Arts
601 Broad Street
LaGrange, GA 30240
706-880-8324
800-593-2885

Kim Barber Knoll, Chair of Theatre Arts
www.lagrange.edu
kbarber@lagrange.edu
*offers undergraduate courses in Playwriting/ Screenwriting

State University of West Georgia
Theatre Arts
1601 Maple Street
Carrollton, GA 30118
678-839-4700
Shelly Elman, Director of Theatre
http://www.westga.edu/~theatre/
kmcgehee@westga.edu
*offers undergraduate courses in Playwriting

University of Georgia
UGA Creative Writing Program
Park Hall 111-A
Atlanta, GA 30602
706-542-2659
706-542-1739
Stanley Longman, Professor of Playwriting
J. Rich, Program Coordinator
www.uga.edu
jrich@room343.english.uga.edu
*offers an MFA program in Creative Writing

BOSTON

Theatres

Algonkuin Theatre Company
1231 Pulaski Blvd.
Bellingham, MA 02019
508-883-1808
Marty BlackEagle-Carl, Artistic Director
http://members.aol.com/algonkuin/index.html
blackeagle@algonkuin.org
*season features new work

American Repertory Theatre (ART)
64 Brattle Street
Cambridge, MA 02138
617-495-2668
Chris DeCamillis, Artistic Coordinator of New Play Development
www.amrep.org
information@amrep.org
*season features new work

Barrington Stage Company
30 Union Street
Pittsfield, MA 01201
413-499-5446
Fax: 413-499-5447
Julianne Boyd, Artistic Director
www.barringtonstageco.org
jboyd@barringtonstageco.org
*season features new work

Berkshire Theatre
Box 797
Stockbridge, MA 01262
413-298-5576
Kate Maguire, Executive Director
www.berkshiretheatre.org
info@berkshiretheatre.org
*offers play development program for new writers

Boston Playwrights' Theatre
Boston University,
949 Commonwealth Ave.
Boston, MA 02215
617-353-5443
Fax: 617-353-6196
Kate Snodgrass, Artistic Director
www.bu.edu/bpt
newplays@bu.edu
*season focuses primarily on new work

Boston Theatre Works
31 St. James Ave., #360
Boston, MA 02116
617-728-4321
Fax: 617-262-8633
Bridget Frey, Literary Manager
www.bostontheatreworks.com
bridget@bostontheatreworks.com
*offers play development program for new writers

Double Edge Theatre
948 Conway Road
Ashfield, MA 01330
413-628-0277
Fax: 831-307-6159
Carlos Uriona, Producing Director
www.doubleedgetheatre.org
office@doubleedgetheatre.org
*season focuses primarily on new work

Harwich Junior Theatre (HJT)
105 Division Street
Box 168
West Harwich, MA 02671
508-432-2002
Fax: 508-432-0726
Nina Schuessler, Artistic Director
www.hjtcapecod.org
hjt@capecod.net
*season focuses primarily on new work

Lyric Stage Company of Boston
140 Clarendon Street
Boston, MA 02116
617-585-5680
Rebecca Curtiss, Producing Associate of New Play Development
www.lyricstage.com
Rebecca_Curtiss@lyricstage.com
*offers play development program for new writers

Merrimack Repertory Theatre
132 Warren Street
Lowell, MA 01852
978-654-7550
Fax: 978-654-7575
Charles Towers, Artistic Director
www.merrimackrep.org
artdir@merrimackrep.org

New Repertory Theatre
200 Dexter Avenue
Watertown, MA 02472
617-923-7060
Fax: 617-923-7625
Rick Lombardo, Producing Artistic Director
www.newrep.org
artistic@newrep.org
*season features new work

NewWORLD Theatre (NWT)
University of Massachusetts, Amherst,
100 Hicks Way, 16 Curry Hicks
Amherst, MA 01003
413-545-1972
Fax: 413-545-4414
Andrea Assaf, Artistic Director
www.umass.edu/fac/nwt/
andrea@theater.umass.edu
*offers play development programs for new writers

Stoneham Theatre
125 Main Street, Suite F
Stoneham, MA 02180
781-279-7885
Weylin Symes, Artistic Director
www.stonehamtheatre.org
weylin@stonehamtheatre.org
*season features new work

Wellfleet Harbor Actors Theatre (WHAT)
Box 797
Boston, MA
Wellfleet, MA 02667
508-349-3011
Daniel Lombardo, Literary Manager
www.what.org
djlombardo@juno.com
*season features new work

Williamstown Theatre Festival
P.O. Box 517
Williamstown, MA 01267-0517
413-458-3200
Fax: 413-458-3147
Suzanne Agins, Artistic Associate, New Plays
www.wtfestival.org
sagins@wtfestival.org
*season features new work

Membership Organizations and Workshops

Playwright's Platform
Box 267, State House
Boston, MA 02133-0267
Kelly DuMar, Interim President and Membership Director
www.playwrightsplatform.org
diarydoor@aol.com

Stage Source
88 Tremont Street Suite 714
Boston, MA 02108
617-720-6066
Fax: 617-720-4275
Jeremy Johnson, Member Services
www.stagesource.org
info@stagesource.org
Fund For Women Artists
1236 Northampton, MA 01061
413-585-5968
Fax: 413-586-1303
www.womenarts.org
info@womenarts.org

Original Play Contests and Festivals

Boston Theatre Marathon
Boston Playwrights Theatre
949 Commonwealth Avenue
Boston, MA 02215
617-353-5443
Kate Snodgrass, Artistic Director
www.bu.edu/btm/
newplays@bu.edu

Boston Theatre Works Unbound
31 St. James Avenue, #360
Boston, MA 02116
617-728-4321
Fax: 617-262-8633
Bridget Frey, Literary Manager
www.bostontheatreworks.com
bridget@bostontheatreworks.com

Baker's Plays High School Playwriting Contest
Box 699222
Quincy, MA 02269
617-745-0805
Fax: 617-745-9891
www.bakesplays.com

Breaking Ground Festival
Huntington Theatre Company
281 Huntington Avenue
Boston, MA 02474
617-266-7900
Fax: 617-353-8300
Ilana Brownstein, Literary Manager
www.huntingtontheatre.org
ibrownstein@huntingtontheatre.bu.edu

Opportunities and Resources for Dramatists

American Antiquarian Society Fellowships
185 Salisbury Street
Worcester, MA 01609-1634
508-755-5221
Fax: 508-753-3311
Cheryl McRell, Outreach Assistant
www.americanantiquarian.org
cmcrell@mwa.org

Radcliffe Institute Fellowships
Harvard University,
34 Concord Avenue
Cambridge, MA 02138
617-495-8212
Fax: 617-495-8136
Judith Vichniac, Director
www.radcliffe.edu/fellowships
fellowships@radcliffe.edu
Boston, MA

Colleges and Universities for Dramatic Writers

Amherst College
PO Box 5000
Amherst, MA 01002-5000
413-542-2000
Constance Congdon, Playwright in Residence
www.amherst.edu
cscongdon@amherst.edu
[413-542-8130]
*offers undergraduate courses in Playwriting

College of the Holy Cross
1 College Street
Worcester, MA 01610
508-793-2011
Edward Isser, Theatre Department Chair
www.holycross.edu
webmaster@holycross.edu
*offers undergraduate courses in Playwriting

Boston College
140 Commonwealth Avenue
Chestnut Hill, MA 02467
617-552-0823
John Houchin, Chair, Theatre Department
www.bc.edu
houchijo@bc.edu
*offers a BA in Dramatic Writing

Boston University
Office of Admissions
121 Bay State Road
Boston, Massachusetts 02215
617-353-2300
www.bu.edu
askus@bu.edu
Lydia Diamond, Teacher of Playwriting
617-353-3390
ldiamond@bu.edu
*offers BFA in Theatre Arts- Playwriting

Brandeis University
415 South Street
PO Box 549110
Waltham, MA 02454-9110
781-736-3340
Fax: 781-736-3408
Ryan McKittrick, Teacher of Playwriting
www.brandeis.edu
mckittr@brandeis.edu
*offers undergraduate courses in Playwriting

Emerson College
120 Boylston Street
Boston, MA 02116-4624
617-824-8500
Maureen Shea, Chair, Theatre Department
www.emerson.edu
auditions@emerson.edu
*offers undergraduate courses in Playwriting

Hampshire College
893 West Street
Amherst, MA 01002
877-937-4600
www.hampshire.edu
admissions@hampshire.edu
*offers undergraduate courses in Playwriting

Harvard University
American Repertory Theater, Harvard University
64 Brattle Street
Cambridge, MA 02138
617-496-2000 ext 8890
Scott Zigler, Program Director
www.harvard.edu
institute@amrep.org
*offers MFA in Dramaturgy with an emphasis in Playwriting

Mount Holyoke College
50 College Street
South Hadley, MA 01075
413-538-2832
Vanessa James, Chair of Theatre
www.mtholyoke.edu
* Offers undergraduate courses in Playwriting

Northeastern University
360 Huntington Avenue
Department of Theatre
Room 180, Ryder Hall
Boston, MA 02115
617-373-2244
Fax: 617-373-4149
Ed Bullins, Playwriting
www.neu.edu
cnajarian@neu.edu
* Offers undergraduate courses in Playwriting

Salem State College
352 Lafayette Street
Salem, MA 01970
978-542-6464
William Cunningham, Chair
www.salemstate.edu
William.cunningham@salemstate.edu
* Offers undergraduate courses in Playwriting

Smith College
Northhampton, MA 01063
413-585-3206
Leonard Berkman, Advisor
www.smith.edu
lberkman@email.smith.edu
*offers undergraduate courses in Playwriting
*offers an MFA in Playwriting

University of Massachusetts-Amherst
Department of Theater, Fine Arts Center
151 Presidents Drive
Amherst, MA 01003-9331
413-545-6812
Fax: 413-577-0025
Harley Erdman, Department Chair
www.umass.edu
harley@theater.umass.edu
*offers undergraduate courses in Playwriting
*offers graduate courses in Playwriting

Wellesley College
106 Central Street
Wellesley, MA 02481
781-283-1000
Box Office: 781-283-2000
www.wellesley.edu
Nora Hussey, Program Director
nhussey@wellesley.edu
*offers undergraduate courses in Playwriting

Williams College
880 Main Street
Williamstown, MA 01267
413-597-2014
Robert-Baker White, Department Chair
www.williams.edu
Robert.E.Baker-White@williams.edu
*offers undergraduate courses in Playwriting

CHICAGO

Theatres

A Red Orchid Theatre
1531 N Wells Street
Chicago, IL 60610
312-943-8722
Nick Minas, Literary Director
www.aredorchidtheatre.org
arot@aredorchidtheatre.org
*partial season devoted to new work

About Face Theatre
1222 W Wilson Avenue, 2nd Floor
Chicago, IL, 60640
773-784-8565
Fax: 773-784-8557
Eric Rosen, Artistic Director
www.aboutfacetheatre.com
heather@aboutfacetheatre.com
*season primarily focuses on new work

American Theater Company
1909 W Byron Street
Chicago, IL 60613
773-929-5009
Fax: 773-929-5171
Damon Kiely, Artistic Director
www.atcweb.org
http://www.atcweb.org/getinvolved/contactus.php
*partial season devoted to new work

Bailiwick Repertory
1229 West Belmont Avenue
Chicago, IL 60657
773-883-2090
David Zak, Artistic Director
http://www.bailiwick.org
david@balliwick.org
*season primarily focuses on new work

Black Ensemble Theatre
4520 N Beacon
Chicago, IL 60640
773-769-4451
773-769-4533
Jackie Taylor, Artistic Director
www.blackensembletheater.org
blackensemble@aol.com
*season primarily focuses on new work

Chicago's Children's Theatre
1464 North Milwaukee Avenue, 2nd Floor
Chicago, IL 60622
773-227-0180
Attn: Artistic Department
www.chicagochildrenstheatre.org
jabelson@chicagochildrenstheatre.org
*season features some new work

Circle Theatre
7300 West Madison St.
Forest Park, IL 60130
Kevin Bellie, Artistic Director
www.circle-theatre.org
info@circle-theatre.org
*season features some new work

Citadel Theatre
P.O. Box 763
Lake Forest, IL 60045
Madelyn Sergel
www.citadeltheatre.org
msergel@citadeltheatre.org
*season features some new work
*offers play development program

City Lit Theater Company
1020 Bryn Mawr
Chicago, IL 60660
773-293-3682
Fax: 773-293-3682
Terry McCabe, Artistic Director
www.citylit.org
citlittheatre@aol.com
*offers new adaptation development program

CollaborAction Theatre
437 North Wolcott
Chicago, IL 60622
312-226-9633
Fax: 312-226-6107
Anthony Moseley, Artistic Director
www.collaboraction.org
anthony@collaboraction.org
*season features new work
*offers play development program

Congo Square Theatre Company
2936 N Southport, #210
Chicago, IL 60657
Aaron Todd Douglas, Associate Artistic Director
www.congosquaretheatre.org/augustwilson.asp#
atdouglas125@congosquaretheatre.org
*season features new work

Court Theatre
University of Chicago
5535 South Ellis Avenue
Chicago, IL 60637
773-702-7005

Charles Newell, Artistic Director
www.courttheatre.org
info@courttheatre.org

Curious Theatre Branch
3502-4 N Elston Avenue
Chicago, IL 60618
773-267-6660
Beau O'Reilly, Artistic Director
http://curioustheatrebranch.com
*season focuses on new work and offers new play development program

Diamante Productions
2303 Mohawk Lane
Glenview, IL 60026
312-305-2850
Tony Fiorentino
www.diamanteproductions.com
info@diamanteproductions.com
*season focuses on new work

Dog & Pony Theatre Company
PO Box 13105
Chicago, IL 60613
773-235-0492
Krissy Vanderwarker, Artistic Director
http://dogandponychicago.org
dogandponytheatre@gmail.com
*season focuses on new work

ETA Creative Arts
7558 South Chicago Avenue
Chicago, IL 60619
773-752-3955
Chicago, IL
Fax: 773-752-8727
Runako Jahi, Artistic Director
www.etacreativearts.org
http://www.etacreativearts.org/contact_us.html
*offers play development program

Free Street Programs
1419 W Blackhawk Street
Chicago, IL 60622
Ron Beiganski
www.freestreet.org
ron@freestreet.org
*offers play development program

Goodman Theatre
170 N Dearborn Street
Chicago, IL 60601
312-443-3811
Tanya Palmer, Literary Manager
www.goodman-theatre.org
artistic@goodman-theatre.org
*season features some new work

GroundUp Theatre
3324 West Belden Avenue, #1
Chicago, IL 60647
Sabrina Lloyd, Artistic Director
www.grounduptheatre.com
grounduptheatre@hotmail.com
*season features some new work

Hypatia Theatre Company
1335 W Roscoe St. #3
Chicago, IL 60657
312-714-0571
Erica L Weiss, Artistic Director
http://www.hypatiatheatre.org
erica@hypatiatheatre.org
*season devoted to new work

In the Works...Theatre Company
6222 S Meade Avenue
Chicago, IL 60638
773-788-1035
Jenniffer J. Thusing, Artistic Director
www.intheworks.us
Intheworks@comcast.net
*season focuses on new work

InFusion Theatre Company
2214 N Lakewood Avenue
Chicago, IL 60614
773-525-8981
773-525-8061
Mitch Golob, Artistic Director
www.infusiontheatre.com
Info@infusiontheatre.com
*season focuses on new work

The Journeyman Theater Company
3915 N Janssen
Chicago, IL 60613
Attn: Literary Dept.
www.thejourneymen.org
info@thejourneymen.org
*season features some new wor

Keyhole Theatre
1536 W North Avenue, #2F
Chicago, IL 60622
773-805-5055
Frank Merle, Artistic Director
www.keyholetheatre.com
keyholetheatre@comcast.net
*season focuses on new work

Lifeline Theatre
6912 N Glenwood Avenue
Chicago, IL 60626
773-761-4477
Fax: 773-761-4582
Dorothy Milne, Artistic Director
www.lifelinetheatre.com
Dorothy@lifelinetheatre.com
*season features some new work

Live Bait Theater
3914 N Clark Street
Chicago, IL 60613
773-871-1212
Sharon Evans, Artistic Director
http://www.livebaittheater.org/
Sharon@livebaittheater.org
*season focuses on new work

LiveWire Chicago Theatre
PO Box 11226
Chicago, IL 60611-0226
Glenn Proud, Artistic Director
Chicago, IL
www.livewirechicago.com
glenn@livewirechicago.com
*season features some new work

Lookingglass Theatre
2936 North Southport
Chicago, IL 60657
773-477-9257
Ms. Heidi Stillman, Artistic Director of New Work
Margaret Bordelon, Literary Associate and Board Coordinator
www.lookingglasstheatre.org
hstillman@lookingglasstheatre.org
mbordelon@lookingglasstheatre.org
*season features new work

Mary-Arrchie Theatre
735 West Sheridan Road
Chicago, IL 60613
773-871-0442
Richard Cotovski, Artistic Director
www.maryarrchie.com
rich@maryarrchie.com
*season features some new work

Next Theatre Company
Noyes Cultural Arts Center
927 Noyes Street
Evanston, IL 60201
Jason Loewith, Artistic Director
www.nexttheatre.org
Jason@nexttheatre.org
*season features some new work

Northlight Theatre
InterPlay
9501 Skokie Blvd
Skokie, IL 60076
847-679-9501
B.J. Jones, Artistic Director
www.northlight.org
*season features new work

Pegasus Players
1145 W Wilson Avenue
Chicago, IL 60640
773-878-9761
Fax: 773-271-8057
Alex Levy, Artistic Director
www.pegasusplayers.org
info@pegasusplayers.org
*features some new work

Piven Theatre Workshop
927 Noyes Street
Evanston, IL 60201
847-866-6597
Joyce Piven, Artistic Director
http://piventheatre.org
*season focuses on new work

Porchlight Music Theatre Chicago
2814 N Lincoln Avenue
Chicago, IL 60657
773-325-9884
L. Walter Stearns, Artistic Director
www.porchlighttheatre.com
porchlighttheatre@yahoo.com

Prop Theatre
3502-4 N Elston
Chicago, IL 60618
Scott Vehill, Artistic Director
www.propthtr.org
info@propthtr.org
*offers a play development program

Rasaka Theatre Company (South Asian Artists)
2936 N Southport Avenue
Chicago, IL 60657
312-777-1070
www.rasakatheatre.org
info@rasakatheatre.org
*season features some new work

Raven Theatre
6157 North Clark Street
Chicago, IL 60660
773-338-2177
Michael Menendian, Artistic Director
www.raventheatre.com

raventheatre@aol.com
*season features some new work
Rivendell Theatre
1711 W Belle Plaine
Chicago, IL 60613
773-472-1169
Tara Mallen, Artistic Director
www.rivendelltheatre.net
Chicago, IL
info@rivendelltheatre.net
*season focuses on new work

Seanachai Theatre Company
2206 N Tripp
Chicago, IL 60639
773-878-3727
Jacqueline Flaherty, Artistic Director
www.seanachai.org
info@seanachai.org
*season features some new work

Serendipity Theatre Company
2936 N Southport Avenue
Chicago, IL 60657
773-296-0163
Adam Belcuore, Director of Artistic Development
www.serendipitytheatre.org
adam@seredipitytheatre.org
*season features new work

The Side Project
1439 W Jarvis Ave.
Chicago, IL 60626
773-973-2150
Adam Webster, Artistic Director
www.thesideproject.net
http://www.thesideproject.net/contact.php
*offers new play development program

Silk Road Theatre Project
The Historic Chicago Temple Building
77 W. Washington St., Pierce Hall
Chicago, IL 60602
Jamil Khoury, Artistic Director
www.srtp.org
jamil@srtp.org
*season focuses on new work

Smoke & Mirror Productions
1020 W Foster, #2
Chicago, IL 60640
315-724-1685
www.smokeandmirrorpro.com
info@smokeandmirrorpro.com
Nick Jones, Artistic Director
*season focuses on new work

Stockyards Theatre Project
6167 N. Broadway #357
Chicago, IL 60660
Lori Howard, Executive Director
http://stockyardstheatre.tripod.com/index.html
stockyardstheatre@lycos.com
*season focuses on new work and offers new play development program

Stage Left Theatre Company
3408 N Sheffield Avenue
Chicago, IL 60657
773-883-8830 x3
John Sanders, Director of New Play Development
www.stagelefttheatre.com
john@stagelefttheatre.com
*season focuses on new work

Steep Theatre Company
3902 North Sheridan Road
Chicago, IL 60613
Brad Atkin, Literary Manager
www.steeptheatre.com
brad@steeptheatre.com
*season features some new work

Steppenwolf Theatre Company
1650 North Halsted St
Chicago, IL 60614
312-335-1605
Edward Sobel, Director of New Play Development
www.steppenwolf.org
*offers play development program

Teatro Luna
5215 N Ravenswood, #210
Chicago, IL 60640
Tanya Seracho, Co-Artistic Director
www.teatroluna.org
teatroluna@aol.com
*season features new work
*offers new play development program

Teatro Vista
3712 North Broadway
Suite 275
Edward F. Torres, Artistic Director/Founder
www.teatrovista.org
diana@teatrovista.org
Chicago, IL 60613
312-494-5767

TimeLine Theatre Company
615 West Wellington
Chicago, IL 60657
www.timelinetheatre.com
info@timelinetheatre.com
Ben Thiem, Literary Manager
*season features some new work

Victory Gardens Theater
2257 North Lincoln Avenue
Chicago, IL 60614
773-549-5788
Fax: 773-549-2779
Andrea J. Dymond, Literary Manager/Resident Director
www.victorygardens.org
adymond@victorygardens.org
*season features some new work

Vittum Theater
1012 N Noble Street
Chicago, IL 60622
Tel (773) 278-7471
Fax (773) 278-2621
Tom Arvetis, Producing Artistic Director
www.vittumtheater.org
tom@vittumtheater.org
*season features some new work

Writer's Theatre
376 Park Avenue
Glencoe, IL 60022
Michael Halberstam, Artistic Director
www.writerstheatre.org
http://www.writerstheatre.org/contact.asp
*season features some new work

Membership Organizations and Workshops

Chicago Alliance for Playwrights
C/o Joanne Koch
343 Dodge Avenue
Evanston, IL 60202
847-864-5357
Fax: 847-864-2312
Joanne Koch, President
www.chicagoallianceforplaywrights.org
info@chicagoallianceforplaywrights.org

Chicago Dramatists
1105 West Chicago Avenue
Chicago, IL 60622
312-633-0630
Russ Tutterow, Artistic Director
www.chicagodramatists.org
info@chicagoallianceforplaywrights.org

Chicago Writers Bloc
junediana@earthlink.net

Cunningham Commision for Youth Theatre
DePaul University
2135 North Kenmore Avenue
Chicago, IL 60614
773-325-7938
Anna Ables, Director of Marketing/PR
Theatreschool.depaul.edu
aables@depaul.edu

Downstage Left (DSL)
Stage Left Theatre Company
3408 North Sheffield Avenue
Chicago, IL 60657
773-883-8830 x3
John Sanders, Director
www.stagelefttheatre.com
john@stagelefttheatre.com

Musical Theatre Writers' Workshop
1225 W Belmont Avenue
Chicago, IL 60657
773-929-7367
Fax: 773-327-1404
John Sparks, Artistic Director
www.theatrebuildingchicago.org

Women's Theatre Alliance
2936 N Southport Avenue
Chicago, IL 60657
Katie Carey Govier, President
www.wtachicago.org
womenstheatre@lycos.com

Contests and Festivals

DCA Theater
(Chicago-themed plays only)
C/o Chicago Blueprints on Stage
78 East Washington Street
Chicago, IL 60602
312-744-7085
Chicago, IL
Amanda Friedberg, Literary Manager

Harvest Festival of New Works
1439 West Jarvis Ave.
Chicago, IL 60626
(773) 973-2150
Attn: Literary
www.thesideproject.net
tsp@thesideproject.net

Stages
1225 W Belmont Avenue
Chicago, IL 60657
773-929-7367
Fax: 773327-1404
John Sparks, Artistic Director
www.theatrebuildingchicago.org
joan@theatrebuildingchicago.org

Theodore Ward Prize
Columbia College Chicago Theatre Center
72 East 11th Street, #413
Chicago, IL 60605
Chuck Smith, Facilitator
312-344-6136
www.colum.edu
csmith@colum.edu

Vitality Festival
Speaking Ring Theatre Company
3105 North Ashland Avenue
Chicago, IL 60657
Info@speakingringtheatre.org
www.speakingringtheatre.org

Opportunities and Resources

Cunningham Commission for Youth Theatre
2135 N Kenmore Avenue
Chicago, IL 60614
773-325-7939
Anna Ables, Director of Marketing/PR
Theatreschool.depaul.edu
theatreadmissions@depaul.edu
aables@depaul.edu

Illinois Arts Council
100 W Randolph Street, #10-500
Chicago, IL 60601
312-814-6750
Fax: 312-814-1471
www.state.il.us/agency/iac
iac.info@illinois.gov
Chicago Artists Resource
Chicago Department of Cultural Affairs
Barbara Keonen, Director
http://www.chicagoartistsresource.org
Barbarakeonen@cityofchicago.org

Theater Building Chicago
1225 West Belmont Avenue
Chicago, IL 60657
773-929-7367
http://www.theatrebuildingchicago.org/
www.theatrebuildingchicago.org

Colleges and Universities

Bradley University
Dept. of Theatre Arts
1501 West Bradley Avenue
Peoria, IL 61625
309-676-7611
Jim Langley, Chair
www.bradley.edu
*offers undergrad course in Playwriting

Chicago State University
9501 S King Drive
Chicago, IL 60628
773-995-2000
Arthur Reese, Program Coordinator
www.csu.edu
Areese20@csu.edu
*offers undergrad course in Playwriting

Columbia College
600 S Michigan
Chicago, IL 60605
312-663-1600
Sheldon Patinkin, Chair, Theatre/Music Department
www.colum.edu
spatinkin@popmail.colum
*offers BA and BFA program in Playwriting

Southern Illinois University, Carbondale
425 Clocktower Drive
Carbondale, IL 62901
618-453-5741
Mark Varns, Chair, Department of Theatre
www.siuc.edu
varns@siu.edu
*offers undergrad course in Playwriting and MFA program in Playwriting

DePaul University
Theatre School
2135 N Kenmore Avenue
Chicago, IL 60614
773-325-7929
Dean Corrin, Head of Playwriting, Assoc. Dean
http://theatreschool.depaul.edu
theatreadmissions@depaul.edu
*offers BFA program in playwriting

Elmhurst College
190 Prospect Avenue
Elmhurst, IL 60126
630-617-3500
Alan W. Weiger, Director of Theatre
http://public.elmhurst.edu/
alanw@elmhurst.edu
*offers undergrad course in Playwriting

Illinois State University
Dept. of Theatre Campus
Box 5600
Normal, IL 61761
309-438-8321
Don Lacasse, Chair
www.ilstu.edu
delacas@ilstu.edu
*offers graduate course in Playwriting

Illinois Wesleyan University
School of Theatre Arts
PO Box 2900
Bloomington, IL 61702
309-556-3944
Curtis C. Trout, Professor/Director
http://www2.iwu.edu/home.shtml
*offers undergrad course in Playwriting

Loyola University of Chicago
6525 N Sheridan
Road Sky Bldg, Room 807
Chicago, IL 60626
773-508-3830
Sarah Gabel, Chair
http://www.luc.edu/
jwilsol@luc.edu
*offers undergrad course in Playwriting

Millikin University
Department of Theatre and Dance
1184 W Main Street
Decatur, IL 62522
800-373-7733
Barry Pearson, Dean, College of Fine Arts
http://www.millikin.edu/
*offers BFA in Creative Writing

Northwestern University
Department of Theatre
1949 Campus Drive
Evanston, IL 60208-2430
847-491-3170
Rives Collins, Chair
http://www.communication.northwestern.edu/theatre
r-collins@northwestern.edu
*offers undgrad course in Playwriting and MFA program in Writing for the Stage and Screen

University of Illinois, Chicago
Dept. of Performing Arts
M/C 255/1040 W Harrison Street
Chicago, IL 60607
312-986-2977
Michael J Anderson, Chair
www.uic.edu
mja@uic.edu
*offers undergrad course in Playwriting

University of Illinois
Dept. of Theatre
4-122 Krannert, 500 S Goodwin
Urbana, IL 61801
217-333-1000
Robert Graves, Art Head
http://www.uiuc.edu/
rbgraves@ad.uiuc.edu
*offers undergrad course in Playwriting

Western Illinois University
Dept of Theatre
Brown Hall 101
Macomb, IL 61455
309-298-1543
JeanieWoods, Chair
www.wiu.edu
*offers graduate course in pPlaywriting

DENVER

Theatres

Avenue Theater
417 East 17th Street
Denver, CO 80203
303-321-5925
Bob Wells, Owner/Executive Director
info@avenuetheater.com
www.avenuetheater.com
*season features some new work

The Bug Theatre
3654 Navajo Street
Denver, CO 80211
303-477-9984
Donna Morrison, Executive Artistic Director
www.bugtheatre.org
info@bugtheatre.org
*season features some new work
*offers new play development program

Colorado Stage Company
10153 South Knoll Circle
Highlands Ranch, CO 80130
303-471-8171
Constance Cawlfield, Director
www.coloradostage.com
coloradostage@comcast.net
*season features new work

Creede Repertory Theatre
124 N. Main Street
PO Box 269
Creede, CO 81130
719-658-2540
Maurice LaMee, Executive/Artistic Director
www.creederep.org
mo@creederep.com
*season features new work

Curious Theatre Company
1080 Acoma Street
Denver, CO 80204
303-623-2349
Bonnie Metzgar, Associate Artistic Director
www.curioustheatre.org
bonnie@curioustheatre.org
*season features new work

El Centro Su Teatro
4725 High Street
Denver, CO 80216
303-296-0219
Fax: 303-296-4614
Anthony J. Garcia, Artistic Director
www.suteatro.org
elcentro@suteatro.org

Germinal Stage Theatre
2450 West 44th Avenue
Denver, CO, 80211
303-455-7108
Ed Baierlein, Director/Manager
www.germinalstage.com
gsden@privatei.com
*partial season devoted to new work

Paragon Theatre
PO Box 18896
1124 Santa Fe Dr.
Denver, CO 80218
The Trench Play Submissions
9883 Quay Way
Westminster, CO 80021
303-300-2210
Michael Stricker, Executive Director/Co-Founder
thetrench@paragontheatre.org
www.paragontheatre.com
info@paragontheatre.org
*partial season devoted to new work
*offers reading series for new plays

The Theatre Group
1124 Santa Fe Drive
Denver, CO 80240
303-777-3292
Steven Tangedal, Executive Artistic Director
www.theatregroup.org
TGcontact@theatregroup.org
*partial season devoted to new work

Membership Organizations and Workshops for Dramatists

Chameleon Stage
PO Box 22420
Denver, CO 80222
Attn: Tami Canaday
www.chameleonstage.com
info@chameleonstage.com

Colorado Dramatists
PO Box 40516
Denver, CO 80204
303-629-9306
Melanie Tem, President
www.coloradodramatists.org

Colorado New Play Summit
Denver Center Theatre Company (DCTC)
1101 13th Street
Denver, CO 80204
303-893-4000
303-825-2117
Chad Henry, Literary Associate
www.dcpa.org

Colorado Theatre Guild
PO Box 8625
Denver, CO 80201-8625
303-778-7724
Gloria Shanstrom, General Manager
shanstrom@comcast.net
www.coloradotheatreguild.org

Original Play and Musical Contests and Festivals

Boulder Fringe
720-563-9950
Alana Eve Burman, Festival Director
Mobile: 303-882-4568
www.boulderfringe.com
info@boulderfringe.com
alanaeve@boulderfringe.com

Cherry Creek Arts Festival
C/o: Skyline Talents & Events, Inc.
915 Santa Fe Drive
Denver, CO 80204
Event Address: 2 Steele Street, Suite B-100
Denver, CO 80206
303-355-2787
Terry Adams, Executive Director/Performing Arts
management@cherryarts.org
www.cherryarts.org/users/

Colorado New Play Summit
Denver Center for the Performing Arts
13th Street
Denver, CO 80204
303-893-4000
Attn: Chad Henry
www.denvercenter.org/page.cfm?id=9514048
www.denvercenter.org/faq/contact_form.cfm (fill out the form at this website)

Playwrights Showcase
Red Rocks Community College
13300 West Sixth Avenue
Lakewood, CO 80228
303-914-6231
Pamela Jamruszka Mencher, Coordinator
http://www.rrcc.edu/playwrightshowcase/call4plays.html
pamela.mencher@rrcc.edu

Write Angle's Ten Minute Play Award
Ken Crost, Coordinator
http://writeangle.org/contest_info.htm
kcrost@msn.com

Opportunities and Resources for Dramatists

Playwrights Showcase of the Western Region
Red Rocks Community College
13300 West Sixth Avenue
Lakewood, CO 80228
Pamela Jamruszka Mencher, Coordinator
pamela.mencher@rrcc.edu

Boot Camp for Playwrights
Playwrights Showcase
Red Rocks Community College
13300 West Sixth Avenue
Lakewood, CO 80228
303-914-6231
Pamela Jamruszka Mencher, Coordinator
http://www.rrcc.edu/playwrightshowcase/bootcamp.html
pamela.mencher@rrcc.edu

Colorado Council on the Arts
Organization: Colorado Office of Economic Development and International Trade
1625 Broadway, Suite 2700
Denver, CO 80202
303-892-3802—Rachel Cain AIPP Administrative Asst.
303-892-3870—Elaine Mariner Executive Director
http://www.coloarts.state.co.us/contactForm.asp (fill out the form at this website)
www.coloarts.state.co.us/

Colleges and Universities for Dramatic Writers

University of Colorado-Boulder
Boulder, CO 80309
303-492-1411
Bud Coleman, Chair of Theatre and Dance
www.colorado.edu
*offers undergraduate courses in Playwriting

University of Colorado – Denver
Campus Box 162
PO Box 173364
Denver, CO 80217-3364
303-556-2279
Fax: 303-556-2335
Kathryn Maes, Interim Dean
David Dynack, Dean (as of 7/07)
303-352-3868
http://thunder1.cudenver.edu/cam/tfvp/index.html
start@cudenver.edu
Kathy.maes@cudenver.edu

*offers a BFA in Theatre Arts with a Writing/ Directing emphasis

University of Denver
2199 South University Blvd
Denver, CO 80208
303-871-2000
Fax: 303-871-2505
William Temple Davis, Chair, Department of Theatre
303-871-3164
http://www.du.edu/thea
www.du.edu/resources/email.html
wdavis@du.edu
*offers undergraduate courses in Playwriting

University of Northern Colorado
School of Theatre and Dance
Campus Box 49
Greeley, CO 80639
970-351-2515
Fax: 970-351-2699
David Grapes, Director of School of Theatre Arts and Dance
Andrew Jay Svedlow, Dean
http://www.arts.unco.edu/theatredance
davidgrapes@unco.edu
Andrew.svedlow@unco.edu
*offers undergraduate courses in Playwriting

Red Rocks Community College
13300 West Sixth Avenue
Lakewood, CO 80228
Pamela Jamruszka Mencher, Coordinator
www.rrcc.edu
pamela.mencher@rrcc.edu
*offers courses in Playwriting

LOS ANGELES

Theatres

About Productions
145 N. Raymond Ave.
Pasadena, CA 91103
626-396-0920
Fax: 626-449-0139
Theresa Chavez, Artistic Director
www.aboutpd.org
aboutpd.@aol.com
*their season primarily focuses on new work

Actors Art Theatre
6128 Wilshire Blvd. #110
Los Angeles, CA 90048
323-969-4953
Jolene Adams, Artistic Director
www.actorsart.com
info@actorsart.com
*partial season devoted to new work

Actors Co-op
1760 N. Gower Street
Los Angeles, CA 90028
323-969-4953
Paul Stuart Graham, Producing Director
www.Actorsco-op.org
actorsco-op@fpch.org
*offers an original play-reading series

Actor's Forum
10655 Magnolia Blvd.
North Hollywood, CA 91601
818-506-0600
Audrey Marilyn Singer
www.actorsforumtheatre.org
Actors4mtheatre@aol.com
*partial season devoted to new work

Actors Workout Repertory Company
C/o Actors Workout Studio
4735 Lankershim Blvd.
North Hollywood, CA 91602
818-766-2171
Fran Montano, Artistic Director
www.actorsworkout.com
info@actorsworkout.com
*offers a play development program for new writers

Alliance Repertory
3204 W. Magnolia Blvd.
Burbank, CA 91605
818-566-7935
Robert Spuhler
www.alliancerepertory.com
plays@alliancerepertory.com
*partial season devoted to new work

Athena Theatre
11840 Riverside Drive, Suite 23
Valley Village, CA 91607
818-754-1423
Veronique Ory, President and Founder
www.athenatheatre.com
Veronique@athenatheatre.com
*offers an original play reading series

Attic Theatre and Film Center
5429 W. Washington Blvd.
Los Angeles, CA 90016-1112
323-525-0600
Fax: 323-525-0661
James Carey, Producing Artistic Director
Jerry Kernion, Artistic Director
Kacey Camp, Literary Manager
www.attictheatre.org
litmanager@attictheatre.org
*offers a play development program for new writers

Black Dahlia Theatre
5354 West Pico Blvd
Los Angeles, CA 90019
323-525-0070
Matt Shakman, Artistic Director
www.thedahlia.com
info@thedahlia.com
*their season primarily focuses on new work
*offers a play development program for new writers

Blank Theatre Company LRS
Business Office: 1301 Lucile Avenue
Los Angeles, CA 90026
323-662-7734
Main Stage: 6500 Santa Monica Boulevard
Los Angeles, CA 90038
323-601-9827
Daniel Henning, Artistic Director
Noah Wyle, Artistic Producer
www.theblank.com
info@theblank.com
*their season primarily focuses on new work
*offers an play development series

Buffalo Nights Theatre Company
11575 Missouri Ave. Ste. 6
Los Angeles, CA 90025-5478
323-969-4744
Mivra Smith, Literary Manager
www.buffalonights.org
info@buffalonights.org
*their season partially focuses on new work

Celebration Theatre
7985 Santa Monica Boulevard #109-1
Los Angeles, CA 90046
323-957-1884
Fax: 323-957-1826
Michael Matthews, Artistic Director
Allain Rochel, Literary Manager
celebrationthtr@earthlink.net
www.celebrationtheatre.com

The Colony Theatre Company
555 North Third Street
Burbank, CA 91502
818-558-7000
Fax: 818-558-7110
Barbara Beckley, Artistic Director
Trent Steelman, Managing Director
Michael David Wadler, Literary Manager
www.colonytheatre.org
trentsteelman@colonytheatre.org
*partial season devoted to new work

Company of Angels
Mailing Address: PO Box #3480
Hollywood, CA 90078
323-883-1717
Armando Molina, Artistic Director
Dolores Chavez, Executive Producing Director
Yael Prizant, Literary Manager
www.companyofangels.org
amolina@companyofangels.org
dchavez@companyofangles.org
yael@companyofangels.org
*their season primarily focuses on new work

Conejo Players Theatre
351 S. Moorpark Road
Thousand Oaks, CA 91361-1008
805-495-3715
Dick Johnson, Executive Director
www.conejoplayers.org
info@conejoplayers.org
*their season is partially devoted to new children's work

Cornerstone Theatre Company
708 Traction Avenue
Los Angeles, CA 90013
312-613-1700
Fax: 213-613-1714
Michael John Garces, Artistic Director
www.cornerstonetheater.org
mgarces@cornerstonetheater.org

Dramatic Women
111 Skyline Circle
Santa Barbara, CA 93109
805-965-5826
Ellen K. Anderson, Artistic Director
www.dramaticwomen.org

info@dramaticwomen.org
*their season is devoted to new work

Dillon Street Players
802 North Dillon Street,
Los Angeles, CA 90026
Scott Crawford, Artistic Director

East-West Players
120 North Judge John Aiso Street
Los Angeles, CA 90012
213-625-7000 x27
Fax: 213-625-7111
Jeff Liu, Literary Manager
www.eastwestplayers.org
jliu@eastwestplayers.org

Echo Theatre Company
12400 Venture Blvd., #165
Studio City, CA 91604
Chris Fields, Artistic Director
Tara Karsian, Reading Coordinator
www.echotheatrecompany.com
cfields@echotheatrecompany.com
submissions@echotheatrecompany.com
*their season primarily focuses on new work
*offers an original play-reading series
*offers a play development program for new writers

Ensemble Studio Theatre – LA
137 N. Larchmont Blvd., # 134
Los Angeles, CA 90004
213-368-9552
Laura Shane Salvato and Dan Bonnell, Artistic Directors
Liz Rose, Interim Literary Manager
www.ensemblestudiotheatrela.org
info@ensemblestudiotheatrela.org
*their season primarily focuses on new work
*offers a play development program

The Foothill Theatre Company
PO Box 1812
Nevada City, CA 95959
Business Office: 404 Spring Street
Nevada City, CA 95945
530-265-9320
Fax: 530-265-9325
Carolyn Howarth, Assoc. Artistic Director
carloyn@foothilltheatre.org
Scott Gilbert, Artistic Director
scott@foothilltheatre.org
Gary Wright, Literary Manager
gary@foothilltheatre.org
www.foothilltheatre.org
*partial season devoted to new work
*offers a reading series of new plays

The Fountain Theatre
5060 Fountain Avenue
Los Angeles, CA 90020
323-663-2235, Administrative Office
Fax: 323-663-1629
Deborah Lawlor, Artistic Director
323-663-2838
Simon Levy, Producing Director/Dramaturg,
323-663-1542
www.fountaintheatre.com
Ftheatre@aol.com
*partial season devoted to new work

Furious Theatre Company
39 South El Molina Ave.
Pasadena, CA 91101
808-679-8854
Vanessa Martin, Managing Director
Damaso Rodriguez, Producing Director
www.furioustheatre.org
info@furioustheatre.org
*focuses primarily on new work

Geffen Play House
10886 LeConte Avenue
Los Angeles, CA 90024
310-208-6500
Fax: 310-208-0341
Amy Levinson Millan, Literay Manager/Dramaturg
www.geffenplayhouse.com
*partial season devoted to new work

Hudson Theatres
6539 Santa Monica Boulevard
Los Angeles, CA 90038
323-856-4252
Fax: 323-856-4316
Elizabeth Reilly, Artistic Director
www.hudsontheatre.com
ereilly@hudsontheatre.com
*season primarily focuses on new work

Interact Theatre Company
Mailing Address: P.O. Box 349
North Hollywood, CA 91603
818-765-8732
Rob Kahn, President/Artistic Chair
www.interactla.org
rob@interactla.org
info@interactla.org
*offers a reading series for new plays
*partially devoted to new work

Little Fish Theatre Company
617 Elvira Avenue
Redondo Beach, CA 90277
Theatre address:
777 Centre Street
San Pedro, CA 90731
310-512-6030
310-507-0269
Mark Piatelli, Associate Artistic Director
mark@littlefishtheatre.org
Lisa Coffi, Producing Artistic Director
lisa@littlefishtheatre.org
www.littlefishtheatre.org
*partial season devoted to new work

Lodestone Theatre Ensemble
PO Box 1072
Studio City, CA 91614
323-993-7245
Philip W. Chung, Artistic Director
Chil Kong, Artistic Director
www.lodestonetheatre.org
shplodestone@aol.com
*partial season devoted to new work
*offers a reading series of new plays

Los Angeles Theatre Ensemble
619 Rutgers Drive
Davis, CA 95616
Tom Burmester, Artistic Director
www.latensemble.org
*partial season devoted to new work

Los Angeles Theatre Works
681Venice Boulevard
Venice, CA 90291
310-827-0808
Brendon Fox, Associate Producer
www.latw.org
bfox@latw.org
*season focuses primarily on new work

Lucid by Proxy
5714 Craner Avenue
North Hollywood, CA 91601
818-913-0838
Jeanette Scherrer, Literary Manager
jeanette@lucidbyproxy.com
literary@lucidbyproxy.com
www.lucidbyproxy.com
*their season primarily focuses on new work

Matrix Theatre
7657 Melrose Avenue
Los Angeles, CA 90046
323-852-1445
Fax: 323-653-3279
Joseph Stern, Producer
www.matrixtheatre.com
thematrixtheatre@sbcglobal.net
*partial season devoted to new work

Moving Arts
PO Box 481145
Los Angeles, CA 90048
323-666-3259
Fax: 323-666-2841
Trey Nichols, Literary Director
www.movingarts.org
info@movingarts.org
*their season primarily focuses on new work
*offers a play development program for new writers
*offers a reading series of new plays

Musical Theatre Guild
PO Box 2612
Toluca Lake, CA 91610
818-848-6844
www.musicaltheatreguild.com
*partial season devoted to new work
*offers a reading series of new musicals

NeedTheatre
454 S Crescent Drive
Beverly Hills, CA 90212
917-703-0161
Matt B. Wells, Artistic Director
www.needtheater.com
*partial season devoted to new work

Odyssey Theatre Ensemble
2055 S Sepulveda Blvd
Los Angeles, CA 90025
310-477-2055
Fax: 310-444-0455
Ron Sossi, Artistic Director
Sally Essex-Lopresti, Director of Literary Programs
www.odysseytheatre.com
ote2@ix.netcom.com
*partial season devoted to new work

Pacific Resident Theatre Ensemble
PO Box 568
Venice, CA 90294
310-301-3971
Trish Soodik, New Works Committee
www.pacificresidenttheatre.com
prtrequest@pacificresidenttheatre.com
*partial season devoted to new work

Padua Playwrights
213-625-1766
Guy Zimmerman, Artistic Director
www.paduaplaywrights.net
info@paduaplaywrights.net
playwrights@paduaplaywrights.net
*their season primarily focuses on new work

Playwrights' Arena
514 S Spring Street
Los Angeles, CA 90013
213-627-4473
Jon Lawrence Rivera, Artistic Director
Tony Foster, Literary Manager
www.playwrightsarena.org
jrivera923@juno.com
*their season primarily focuses on new work
*offers a play development program for new writers

Playwrights 6
9903 Santa Monica Blvd, Ste# 272
Beverly Hills, CA 90212
323-860-6625
Larry Dean Harris, Co-Founder
www.playwrights6.org
playwrights6@aol.com
*their season primarily focuses on new work
*offers a reading series for new plays

Push to Talk Theatre
PO Box 56823
Sherman Oaks, CA 91413
Emily Weisberg, Artistic Director
www.pushtotalktheatre.com
info@pushtotalktheatre.com
*partial season devoted to new work

Quantum Theatre Company
8550 Cashio, #6
Los Angeles, CA
Ursula Schmidt & Natalie Sofer, Producing Directors
www.quantumtheatre.org
literary@quantumtheatre.org
info@quantumtheatre.org
*their season primarily focuses on new work

The Road Theatre Company
5108 Lankershim Blvd
N Hollywood, CA 91601
818-761-8838
Taylor Gilbert, Artistic Director
www.roadtheatre.org
info@roadtheatre.org
*their season primarily focuses on new work

The Robey Theatre Company
514 S Spring Street
Los Angeles, CA 90013
213-489-7402
Fax: 213-489-4520
Ben Guillory, Artistic Director
www.robeytheatrecompany.com
robeytc@sbcglobal.net
*their season primarily focuses on new work

Rubicon Theatre Company
1006 E Main Street
Ventura, CA 93001
805-667-2900
James O'Neill, Artistic Director
www.rubicontheatre.org
info@rubicontheatre.org
*offers a play development program for new writers

Sacred Fools Theatre Company
660 N Heliotrope
Hollywood, CA 90004
323-666-5067
Stacey Jackson, Literary Manager
www.sacredfools.org
Sfliterary@sacredfools.org
*partial season devoted to new work

Santa Monica Playhouse
1211 4th Street
Santa Monica, CA 90401
310-394-9779
Fax: 310-393-5573
Chris DeCarlo, Co-Artistic Director
www.santamonicaplayhouse.com
theatre@santamonicaplayhouse.com

Sight Unseen Theatre
844 17th Street, #105
Santa Monica, CA 90403
310-315-1477
Clark Freeman, Business Manager
www.sightunseentheatre.com
info@sightunseentheatre.com
*partial season devoted to new work

Son of Semele Ensemble
3301 Beverly Blvd
Los Angeles, CA 90004
213-351-3507
Matthew McCray, Artistic Director
Edgar Landa, Managing Director
Jeremy Gabriel, Literary Manager
www.sonofsemele.org
Jeremy@sonofsemele.org
*offers a reading series for new writers

South Coast Repertory
PO Box 2197
Costa Mesa, CA 92628-2197
714-708-5500
Megan Monaghan, Literary Manager
www.scr.org
*partial season devoted to new work
*offers a play development program for new writers
*offers a reading series for new plays

STAGEStheatre
400 East Commonwealth #4
Fullerton, CA 92832
714-525-4484
Brian Kojac, Managing Artistic Director
www.stagesoc.org
stagesoc@stagesoc.org
bkojac@adelphia.net
*partial season devoted to new work
*offers a play development program for new writers

Stages Theatre Center
1540 North McCadden Place
Hollywood, CA 90028
323-463-5356
Fax: 323-463-3904
Paul Verdier, Artistic Director
www.stagestheatrecenter.com
ask@stageshollywood.com

Syzygy Theatre Group
1125 East Broadway, #67
Glendale, CA 91205
323-254-9328
Los Angeles, CA
Attn: Martin Bedoian, Artistic Director
www.syzygytheatre.org
info@syzygytheatre.org
*their season primarily focuses on new work

Theatre Neo
PO Box 48553
Los Angeles, CA 90048
323-769-5858
David Cheaney, Chairman-Dramaturgy Committee
www.theatreneo.com
theatreneo@hotmail.com
*partial season devoted to new work
*offers a reading series for new writers

Theatre of NOTE
1517 Cahuenga Blvd
Hollywood, CA 90028
323-856-8611
Scott McKinley, Literary Manager
www.theatreofnote.com
mckinleyscott@yahoo.com
*partial season devoted to new work
*offers a reading series for new writers

Towne Street Theatre
4101 Budlong Avenue, #4.
Los Angeles, CA 90037
213-624-4796
Nancy Cheryl Davis
www.townestreet.org
info@townestreet.org
*season primarily focuses on new work
*offers a reading series for new writers
Unknown Theater
1110 North Seward Street
Los Angeles, CA 90038
323-466-7781
Chris Covies, Artistic Director
www.unknowntheater.com
cu@unknowntheater.com
*offers a reading series for new writers

The Vagabond Players Theatre Company
PO Box 10278
Burbank, CA 91510
818-206-4000
www.thevagabondplayers.com
*partial season devoted to new work

Victory Theatre
3326 W Victory Blvd
Burbank, CA 91505
818-841-4404
Maria Gobetti, Artistic Director
www.thevictorytheatrecenter.org
thevictory@mindspring.com
*season primarily focuses on new work

Vox Humana
PO Box 93338
Los Angeles, CA 90093
323-769-5794
Liza Guzman, Company Manager
www.voxhumanaproductions.org
info@voxhumanaproductions.org
*partial season devoted to new work
*offers a reading series for new writers

Like Versus (VS)
PO Box 2293
Los Angeles, CA 91610
323-816-2471
Johnny Clark, Artistic Director
Ron Klier, Literary Director
www.vstheatre.org
info@vstheatre.org
*season primarily focuses on new work
*offers a reading series for new writers

Watts Village Theater Company
1827 East 103rd Street
Los Angeles, CA 90002
818-919-9705
Guillermo Aviles-Rodriguez, Artistic Director
www.wattsvillagetheater.org
slapdrama@yahoo.com
*season primarily focuses on new work

West Coast Ensemble
2106 Hyperion Ave
Los Angeles, CA 90027
Les Hanson, Artistic Director
323-876-9337
www.wcensemble.org
wcensemble@aol.com
*partial season devoted to new work

West Coast Jewish Theater
PO Box 1723
Los Angeles, CA
Studio City, CA 91614-0723
323-860-6620
Herb Isaacs, Artistic Director
www.westcoastjewishtheatre.org
wcjt@sbcglobal.net
*partial season devoted to new work

The Whitefire Theatre
13500 Ventura Blvd
Sherman Oaks, CA 91423
818-990=2324
Bryan Rassmussen, Artistic Director
www.whitefiretheatre.com
info@whitefiretheatre.com
*partial season devoted to new work

Will Geer Theatricum Botanicum "Seedlings"
1419 N. Topanga Cyn Boulevard
Topanga, CA 90290
310-455-2322
Jennie Webb, Playwrights Development Director
www.theatricum.com
info@theatricum.com
*offers a reading series for new writers

Write Act Repertory
6125 Carlos Avenue
Hollywood, CA 90028
323-469-3113
John Lant, Artistic Director
www.writeactrep.org
johnlant@writeactrep.org
*season primarily focuses on new work

Membership Organizations and Workshops for Dramatists

The Alliance of Los Angeles Playwrights (ALAP)
7510 Sunset Blvd, #1050
Los Angeles, CA 90046-3410
323-957-4752
Dan Berkowitz and John Dorf, Co-Chairs
www.laplaywrights.org
info@laplaywrights.org

Academy for New Musical Theatre
5628 Vineland Ave.
North Hollywood, CA 91601
818-506-8500
Scott Guy, Executive Director
www.anmt.org
academy@anmt.org

The All Original Playwright Workshop
PO Box 33081
Granada Hills, CA 91394
818-973-2262
Lisa Soland
www.LisaSoland.com/workshop.htm
LisaSoland@aol.com

ASCAP/Disney Musical Theatre Workshop
7920 West Sunset Boulevard, Floor 3
Los Angeles, CA 90046
323-883-1000
Fax: 323-883-1049
www.ascap.com

Broadway on Sunset
10800 Hesby Street, Unit #9
North Hollywood, CA 91601
818-508-9270
Kevin Kaufman, Executive Director
www.broadwayonsunset.org
Broadwayonsunset@aol.com

East West Players – David Henry Hwang Writers Institute
120 N. Judge John Aiso St.
Los Angeles, CA 90012
213-625-7000 ext. 27
Jeff Liu, Literary Manager
www.eastwestplayers.org
jliu@eastwestplayers.org

FirstStage
Box 38280
Los Angeles, CA 90038
323-850-6271
Fax: 323-850-6295
Dennis Safren, Literary Manager
www.firststagela.org
firststagela@aol.com

LA Stage Alliance
644 S. Figueroa Street
Los Angeles, CA 90017
213-614-0556
Terrence McFarland, Executive Director
www.lastagealliance.com
tmcfarland@lastagealliance.com

LA Writers Bloc
817 N Citrus Avenue
Los Angeles, CA 90038
310-770-6570
Susan Merson, Founding Member
www.writersblockpresents.com
susan@susanmerson.com
sofismom@aol.com

New Playwrights Foundation
608 San Vicente Blvd., #18
Santa Monica, CA 90402
310-393-3682
Jeff Bergquist, Artistic Director
www.newplaywrights.org
dialogue@newplaywrights.org

New Voices Playwrights Workshop
PO Box 53921
Irvine, CA 92619-3921
714-897-2961
John Lane
www.geocities.com/newvoicesplaywrights
born2win@hotmail.com

Orange County Playwrights Alliance
PO Box 6927
Fullerton, CA 92834
714-962-7686
Eric Eberwein, Director
www.ocplaywrights.org
firenbones@aol.com

Playwrights Ink
6230 Wilshire Boulevard, Suite 1776
Los Angeles, CA 90004
213-385-4562
Attn: Tom Jacobson
www.hometown.aol.com/playinkla
tom.Jacobson@sbcglobal.net

Sundance Institute Workshops
8530 Wilshire Blvd., Floor 3
Beverly Hills, CA 90211
310-360-1981
Fax: 310-3601975
Philip Himberg, Producing Artistic Director
www.sundance.org
Christopher_hibma@sundance.org

Ten Minute Musicals Project
Box 461194
West Hollywood, CA 90046
Michael Koppy, Producer
www.tenminutemusicals.org
info@tenminutemusicals.org

Theatre East
6760 Lexington Avenue
Hollywood, CA 90038
323-957-5782
Chris White, President
www.theatreeast.com
contact@theatreeast.com

Theatre West
3333 Cahuenga Boulevard, W.
Hollywood, CA 90036
323-851-4839
Fax: 323-851-5286
John Gallogly, Executive Director
www.theatrewest.org
theatrewest@theatrewest.org

Women in Theatre
11684 Ventura Blvd., #444
Studio City, CA 91604
818-763-5222
Talmadge Ragan, President
www.nohoartsdistrict.com/womenintheatre
witprez05@aol.com

Original Play and Musical Contests and Festivals

Attic Theatre Ensemble-One Act Marathon
5429 W. Washington Blvd.
Los Angeles, CA 90016-1112
323-525-0600
James Carey, Producing Artistic Director
Jerry Kernion, Artistic Director
www.attictheatre.org
info@attictheatre.org

Beverly Hills Theatre Guild Awards
Box 148
Beverly Hills, CA 90213
Candace Coster, Competition Coordinator
www.beverlyhillstheatreguild.org

Blank Theatre Company Young Playwrights Festival
1301 Lucile Avenue
Los Angeles, CA 90036
Stacy Reed, Festival Producer
www.youngplaywrights.com

Bilingual Foundation of the Arts-New Works Festival
421 N. Avenue 19
Los Angeles, CA 90031
323-225-4044
Luisa Cariaga, Ex-Officio
Carmen Zapata, President and Co-Founder
www.bfatheatre.org
ofa99@earthlink.net

Celebration Theatre Playwriting Contest
7051-B Santa Monica Blvd.
West Hollywood, CA 90038
323-957-1884
Michael Matthews, Managing Artistic Director
www.celebrationtheatre.com
celebrationthtr.@earthlink.net

Circus Theatricals – Fall Festival of One-Act Plays
C/o The Hayworth Theatre Center
2511 Wilshire Blvd.
Los Angeles, CA 90057
310-226-6144
Jack Stehlin, Artistic Director
Jeannine W. Stehlin, Managing Director
www.circustheatricals.com
jack@circustheatricals.com
jeannine@circustheatricals.com

EdgeFest
PO Box 931301
Los Angeles, CA 90093-1301
310-281-7920
Ray Simmons, Executive Director
www.edgeoftheworld.org
information@edgeoftheworld.org

Fire Rose Productions-10 Minute Play Contest
11246 Magnolia Blvd.
North Hollywood, CA 91601
818-766-3691
Kaz Matamura, Artistic Director
www.secretrose.com
www.fireroseproductions.com
info@secretrose.com

First Stage Playwrights Express
PO Box 38280
Los Angeles, CA 90038
323-850-6271
Dennis Safren, Literary Manager
www.firststagela.org
firststagela@aol.com

Fremont Centre Theatre- New Playwright Contest
1000 Fremont Avenue
South Pasadena, CA 91030
626-441-5977
Lissa Layng Reynolds & James Reynolds, Artistic Directors
Carol Doehring, Literary Manager
www.fremontcentretheatre.com
info@fremontcentretheatre.com
fct@freemontcentretheatre.com

Grove Theater Center-New Play Initiative
PO Box 2090
Long Beach, CA 90801
714-741-9555
Kevin Cochran, Artistic Director
Sondi Kroeger Foley, Literary Manager
www.gtc.org
Kevin@gtc.org
sondi@gtc.org

The Long Beach Playhouse –New Works Festival
5021 East Anaheim Street
Long Beach, CA 90804
562-494-1014
Gigi Fusco Meese, Executive Director/Producer
Jo Black-Jacob, Literary Manager/New Works Festival Committee
www.lbph.com
longbeachplayhouse@yahoo.com

Los Angeles Women's Theatre Festival
1411 Cumpston Avenue, #204
North Hollywood, CA 91601
818-760-0408
Attn: Adilah Barnes
www.lawtf.com
lawtfspotlight@yahoo.com

The Lyric Theatre-StageWRITE
520 N. La Brea Avenue
Los Angeles, CA 90036
323-939-9270
Daniel O'Brien, Artistic Director
www.lyrictheatrela.com
dan@lyrictheatrela.com
Moving Arts Premiere One-Act Competition
Box 481145
Los Angeles, CA 90048
Trey Nichols, Literary Director
www.movingarts.org

Ojai Playwrights Conference
PO Box 1288
Ojai, CA 93024
805-640-0400
Robert Egan, Artistic Director
Catherine Kimmel, Literary Director
www.ojaiplaywrightsconf.org
info@ojaiplays.org

Pacific Playwrights Festival
South Coast Repertory
PO Box 2197
Costa Mesa, CA 92628-2197
714-708-5500
Megan Monaghan, Literary Manager
www.scr.org

Robert Chesley Award
8282 North Laurel Avenue
Los Angeles, CA 90046
Victor Bumbalo, President
http://www.publishingtriangle.org/awards.asp
awards@publishingtriangle.org

Teatro Leido
Bilingual Foundation of the Arts (BFA)
421 North Avenue 19
Los Angeles, CA 90031
323-255-4044
Fax 323-225-1250
Margarita Galban, Artistic Director
www.bfatheatre.org
bfa99@earthlink.net

The Ten-Minute Musicals Project
PO Box 461194
West Hollywood, CA 90046
415-864-3496
323-841-8025
Michael Koppy, Producer
www.tenminutemusicals.org
info@tenminutemusicals.org

Opportunities and Resources for Dramatists

Audrey Skirball-Kenis (ASK) Unpublished Play Collection
Los Angeles Public Library (LAPL)
213-228-7325
Bette McDonagh, Senior Librarian
www.lapl.org/central/literature.html

No Shame Theatre
C/o Powerhouse Theatre
4075 Sea View Avenue
Los Angeles, CA 90065
323-646-0033
Brian E Rochlin, Executive Producer
www.noshamela.com
Brian@noshamela.com

Colleges and Universities for Dramatic Writers

University of California – Los Angeles (UCLA)
Box 951622
102 E. Melnitz
Los Angeles, CA 90095-1622
310-825-5761
Edith Villareal, Chair, MFA Playwriting Program/Assoc. Dean, Academic Affairs
www.tft.ucla.edu
*offers undergraduate courses in Playwriting
*offers MFA in Playwriting

University of California – Santa Barabara
Department of Dramatic Art
Santa Barbara, CA 93106
805-893-3241
Simon Williams, Chair
www.dramadance.ucsb.edu
*offers a Bachelor of Arts in Dramatic Art–Playwriting

University of Southern California
School of Theatre
1029 Childs Way
Los Angeles, CA 90089-0791
213-821-2744
www.theatre.usc.edu
Velina Hasu Houston, Director of Playwriting
*offers undergraduate courses in playwriting
*offers MFA in Dramatic Writing

California Institute of the Arts
24700 McBean Parkway
Valencia, CA 91355-2397
661-255-1050
Carl Hancock Rux, Head
www.calarts.edu
*offers MFA in Writing for Performance

California State University – Fullerton
Department of Theatre-093
Riverside, CA 92521-0324
951-827-7193
D. Eric Barr, Professor
www.theatre.ucr.edu
*offers BA in Theatre – Playwriting requirement
*offers MFA in Creative Writing and Writing for Performing Arts

University of La Verne
1950 3rd Street
La Verne, CA 91750
909-593-3511

Dr. David Flaten, Department Chair
www.ulv.edu
*offers undergraduate theatre degree with playwriting requirement

California State University, Dominguez Hills
1000 East Victoria Street
Carson, CA 90747
310-243-3696
Bill DeLuca, Professor of Theatre Arts
www.csudh.edu
*offers undergraduate Playwriting courses

California State University- Pomona
Theatre Department
3801 West Temple Ave, Bldg. 25
Pomona, CA 91768
Bernardo Solano, Teacher of Playwriting
www.csupomona.edu
*offers undergraduate Playwriting courses

California State University – Bakersfield
9001 Stockdale Highway
Bakersfield, CA 93311
661-654-CSUB
Mandy Rees, MFA, Chair
www.csubak.edu
*offers undergraduate Playwriting courses

California State University – Northridge
18111 Nordhoff Street
Northridge, CA 91330
818-677-1200
Peter Grego, Chair of Theatre
www.csun.edu
*offers undergraduate Playwriting courses

California State University – Long Beach
1250 Bellflower Blvd
Long Beach, CA 90840
562-985-4111
Joanne Gordon, Chair
www.csulb.edu
*offers undergraduate Playwriting courses
*offers MFA in Dramatic Writing

Loyola Marymount University
1 LMU Drive
Los Angeles, CA 90045
310-338-2700
Beth Henley, Professor of Theatre
www.lmu.edu
*offers undergraduate Playwriting courses

Occidental College
1600 Campus Road
Los Angeles, CA 90041
323-259-2500
Laurel Meade, Teacher of Playwriting
www.oxy.edu
*offers undergraduate Playwriting courses

Pomona College
Department of Theatre and Dance
300 East Bonita Avenue
Claremont, CA 91711
909-621-8186
Art Horowitz, Teacher of Playwriting
www.pomona.edu
*offers undergraduate Playwriting courses

MINNEAPOLIS/ ST. PAUL

Theatres

20% Theatre Company
2530 Dupont Avenue South #204
Minneapolis, MN 55405
612-227-1188
Kari Hammer, Literary Manager
Claire@tctwentypercent.org
submissions@tctwentypercent.org
www.tctwentypercent.org
*partial season devoted to new work

The Children's Theatre Company (CTC)
2400 Third Avenue South
Minneapolis, MN 55404-3597
612-874-0500
info@childrenstheatre.org
www.childrenstheatre.org
*partial season devoted to new children's work

Commonweal Theatre Company
Box 15
Lanesboro, MN 55949
507-467-2905 x203
Fax: 507-467-2468
Hal Cropp, Executive Director
www.commonwealtheatre.org
hal@commonwealtheatre.org

The Guthrie Theater
818 South 2nd Street
Minneapolis, MN 55415
612-225-6159
Attn: Amy Wegener
www.guthrietheater.org
*partial season devoted to new work
*offers a reading series for new plays
*offers a play development program for new writers

Illusion Theater
528 Hennepin Avenue, Suite 704
Minneapolis, MN 55403
612-339-4944
Michael H. Robbins, Executive Producing Director
info@illusiontheater.org
www.illusiontheater.org
*offers a play development program for new writers
*season devoted to new work

The Jungle Theater
2951 South Lyndale Avenue
Minneapolis, MN 55408
612-822-4002
Buffy Sedlachek, Literary Manager
www.jungletheater.com
buffy@jungletheater.com
*partial season devoted to new work

Minneapolis Musical Theatre
Hennepin Stages, 824 Hennepin Avenue
Minneapolis, MN 55403
Administrative:
8520 West 29th Street
Minneapolis, MN 55403
952-544-1372
Steven J. Meerdink, Artistic Director
http://www.aboutmmt.org/
info@aboutmmt.org
*partial season devoted to new work

Mixed Blood Theatre Company
1501 South 4th Street
Minneapolis, MN 55454
612-338-0937
Jack Reuler, Artistic Director
junior@mixedblood.com
www.mixedblood.com
*partial season devoted to new work

Mu Performing Arts
2700 NE Winter Street, Suite 4
Minneapolis, MN 55413
812-824-4804
Rick Shimoi, Artistic Director
ricks@muperformingarts.org
www.muperformingarts.org
*primarily focuses on new work

Nimbus Theatre
1101 Stinson Blvd. NE # 16
Minnesota, MN 55413
651-229-3122
Cockroach, Artistic Director
Josh Cragun, A.D.
Liz Neerland, A.D.
submissions@nimbustheatre.com
info@nimbustheatre.com
www.nimbustheatre.com
*partial season devoted to new work

Ordway Center For The Performing Arts
345 Washington Street
St. Paul, MN 55102
651-282-3000
James A. Rocco, Producing Artistic Director
www.ordway.org
jrocco@ordway.org

Pangea World
711 West Lake Street, Suite 101
Minneapolis, MN 55408
612-203-1088
Dipankar Mokherjee, Artistic Director
Meena Natarajan, Literary Director
www.pangeaworldtheater.org
dipankar@pangeaworldtheater.org
meena@pangeaworldtheater.org
*offers a play development program for new writers of color
*season devoted to new works

Park Square Theatre
Historic Hamm Building
20 W. 7th Place
St. Paul, MN 55102
651-767-8482
Richard Cook, Artistic Director
www.parksquaretheatre.org
cook@parksquaretheatre.org
*season features some new work

Penumbra Theatre Company
270 North Kent Street
St. Paul, MN 55102
651-288-6790
Fax: 651-288-6789
Lou Bellamy, Founder and Artistic Director
www.penumbratheatre.org
lou.bellamy@penumbratheatre.org

Pillsbury House Theatre
Minneapolis/St. Paul, MN
3501 Chicago Avenue, South
Minneapolis, MN 55407
612-825-0459
Fax: 612-827-5818
Faye Price, Co-Artistic Producing Director of Pillsbury House Theatre
http://www.puc-mn.org/PillsburyHouseTheatre/tabid/231/Default.aspx
pricef@puc-mn.org
*partial season devoted to new work

Plymouth Playhouse
I-494 & Hwy 55
Plymouth, MN
763-553-1600
www.plymouthplayhouse.com
bompp@plymouthplayhouse.com

Ritz Theater
345 13th Ave. NE
Minneapolis, MN 55413
612-623-7660
Fax: 612-623-4523
Jim Bovino, Managing Director
www.ritztheatrefoundation.org
jim@balletofthedolls.org
*season features some new work

Southern Theatre
1420 Washington Avenue South
Minneapolis, MN 55454
612-340-0155
Jeff Bartlett – Artistic Director
www.southerntheatre.org
jeff@southerntheater.org

Stepping Stone Theatre for Youth Development
314 Landmark Center
75 West 5th Street, #314
St. Paul, MN 55102
651-225-9265
Fax: 651-225-1225
Richard Hitchler, Artistic Director
www.steppingstonetheatre.org
Richard@steppingstonetheatre.org
*season focuses primarily on new work

The Red Eye Theater
15 West 14th Street
Minneapolis, MN 55403
612-870-7531
Steve Busa, Artistic Director
www.theredeye.org
redeye@mtn.org
*season primarily focuses on new work
*offers a play development program for new writers

Ten Thousand Things
3153 36th Avenue South
Minneapolis, MN 55406
612-724-4494
Michelle Hensley, Artistic Director
www.tenthousandthings.org
contact@tenthousandthings.org

Theatre de la Jeune Lune
105 North 1st Street
Minneapolis, MN 55401
612-332-3968
Fax: 612-332-0048
Dominique Serrand, Artistic Director
www.jeunelune.org
info@jeunelune.org
*season features some new work

Membership Organizations and Workshops for Dramatists

Intermedia Arts
2822 Lyndale Avenue South
Minneapolis, MN 55408
612-871-4444
Julie Bates, Literary Programs Manager
julie@intermediaarts.org
www.intermediaarts.org
www.intermediaarts.org/Pages/Programs/literary/lit_grants/index.html

PlayLabs
The Playwrights Center
2301 East Franklin Avenue
Minneapolis, MN 55406-1099
612-332-7481
Steve Moulds, Membership and Literary Associate
stevem@pwcenter.org
www.pwcenter.org

Original Play and Musical Contests and Festivals

Mu Performing Arts -New Eyes Festival
2700 NE Winter Street, Suite 4
Minneapolis, MN 55413
612-824-4804
Rick Shiomi, Artistic Director
info@muperformingarts.org
www.muperformingarts.org

Francesca Primus Prize
American Theatre Critics Association (ATCA)
773 Nebraska Avenue West
St. Paul, MN 55117
651-261-7804
Katie Burger
http://www.americantheatrecritics.org/awards.html
atca_admin@msn.com

Jerome Playwright-in-Residence Fellowships
C/o The Playwrights' Center
2301 Franklin Avenue East
Minneapolis, MN 55406-1099
612-332-7481
info@pwcenter.org
www.pwcenter.org/fellowships_Jerome.asp

Jungle Theatre
2951 Lyndale Avenue South
Minneapolis, MN 55408
612-822-4002
Buffy Sedlachek, Literary Manager
www.jungletheater.com
buffy@jungletheater.com

Many Voices Playwriting Residency Awards
C/o The Playwrights' Center
2301 Franklin Avenue East
Minneapolis, MN 55406-1099
612-332-7481
info@pwcenter.org
www.pwcenter.org/fellowships_MV.asp

McKnight Advancement Grants
C/o The Playwrights' Center
2301 Franklin Avenue East
Minneapolis, MN 55406-1099
612-332-7481
info@pwcenter.org
www.pwcenter.org/fellowships_MAG.asp

McKnight National Playwriting Residency and Commission
C/o The Playwrights' Center
2301 Franklin Avenue East
Minneapolis, MN 55406-1099
612-332-7481
www.pwcenter.org/fellowships_MRC.asp
info@pwcenter.org

Minnesota Fringe Festival
528 Hennepin Avenue #503
Minneapolis, MN 55403
612-872-1212
www.fringefestival.org
http://www.fringefestival.org/contact.cfm (fill out the form on this website).

PlayLabs
C/o The Playwrights Center
2301 Franklin Avenue East
Minneapolis, MN 55406-1099
612-332-7481
info@pwcenter.org
www.pwcenter.org/PlayLabs.asp

Colleges and Universities for Dramatic Writers

Minnesota State University-Moorhead
1104 7th Avenue South
Moorhead, MN 56563
800-593-7246
John Early, MFA Coordinator
www.mnstate.edu
*offers an MFA in Creative Writing

PHILADELPHIA

Theatres

1812 Productions
421 N 7th Street, #218
Philadelphia, PA 19123
215-592-9560
Fax: 215-592-9580
Jennifer Childs, Artistic Director
www.1812productions.org
jen@1812productions.org
*partial season devoted to new work

Act II Playhouse
56 East Butler Pike
Ambler, PA 19002
215-654-0200
Fax: 215-654-9050
Steve Blumenthal, Producing Artistic Director
www.act2.org
steve@act2.org
*offers a reading series for new work

Arden Theatre Company
40 N 2nd Street
Philadelphia, PA 19106
215-922-8900
215-922-7011
Dennis Smeal, Literary Manager
www.ardentheatre.org
dsmeal@ardentheatre.org
*partial season devoted to new work

Azuka Theatre
525 S. 4th Street
Suite 362
Philadelphia, PA 19147
Literary Manager
215-733-0255
Fax: 215-733-0257
Kevin Glaccum, Producing Artistic Director
www.azukatheatre.org
Kevin@azukatheatre.org
*partial season devoted to new work

BCKSEET Productions
507 S. 8th Street
Philadelphia, PA 19147
215-923-0211
Fax: 215-923-1789
Gregory G. DeCandia, Founder/Producing Artistic Director
www.bckseet.com
g@bckseet.com
*primarily focuses on new work

Brat Productions
56 South 2nd Street,
Philadelphia, PA 19106
215-627-2577
Fax: 215-627-4304
Michael Alltop, Producing Artistic Director
www.bratproductions.org
brat@bratproductions.org

Flashpoint Theatre Company
PO Box 54453
Philadelphia, PA 19148
215-563-4330
Erin Lucas, Producing Artistic Director
www.flashpointtheatre.org
erin@flashpointtheatre.org
*partial season devoted to new work

Freedom Repertory Theatre
1346 Broad Street
Philadelphia, PA 19121
215-765-2793
Fax: 215-765-4191
Walter Dallas, Producing Artistic Director
www.freedomtheatre.org
http://www.freedomtheatre.org/main.html

Gas and Electric Arts
PO Box 38524
Philadelphia, PA 19104
215-407-0556
Lisa Jo Epstein, Artistic Director
www.gasandelectricarts.org
gas.electric.arts@verizon.net
*partial season devoted to new work

InterAct Theatre Company
2030 Sansom Street
Philadelphia, PA 19103
215-568-8077
Fax: 215-568-8095
Peter Bonilla, Literary Associate
www.interacttheatre.org
interact@interacttheatre.org
*primarily focuses on new work

The Madhouse Theater Company
17 Walnut Street, 1st Floor
Ambler, PA 19002
215-260-4968
madhousetheater@yahoo.com
www.madhousetheater.com
*partial season devoted to new work

The Peoples' Light and Theatre Company
39 Conestoga Road
Malvern, PA 19355-1798
610-647-1900
Fax: 610-640-9521
Abigail Adams, Artistic Director
Alda Cortese, Literary Manager
www.peopleslight.org
adams@peopleslight.org
cortese@peopleslight.org
*partial season devoted to new work

Philadelphia Theatre Company
230 S. 15th Street, 4th Floor
Philadelphia, PA 19102
215-985-1400
Fax: 215-985-5800
Warren Hoffman, Literary Manager
www.phillytheatreco.com
whoffman@philadelphiatheatrecompany.org
*partial season devoted to new work

Players Club of Swarthmore Theatre
P.O. Box 236
Swarthmore, PA 19081
Box Office Phone: 610-328-4271
Greg Miller, Producing Director
www.pcstheatre.org
info@pcstheatre.org
*offers a new play reading series

Prince Music Theatre
100 South Broad Street #650
Philadelphia, PA 19110
215-972-1000
Richard M. Parison Jr., Associate Artistic Director
www.princemusictheater.org
rparison@princemusictheater.org
*partial season devoted to new work

Random Acts of Theater at The Triangle Theater
1220 N. Lawrence Street
Philadelphia, PA 19122
215-760-0230
Fax: 215-922-4028
www.randomactsoftheater.com
jane@randomactsoftheater.com
*partial season devoted to new work
*offers a play development program for new writers

Simpatico Theatre Project
PO Box 2277
Philadelphia, PA 19103
215-423-0254
Angela Zuck, Co-Literary Manager
Daniel Student, Co-Literary Manager
www.simpaticotheatre.org
stp@simpaticotheatre.org
azuck@simpaticotheatre.org
dstudent@simpaticotheatre.org
*partial season devoted to new work

Tapestry Theatre
14 Mansfield Road
Lansdowne, PA 19050
215-888-6873
Karen Getz, Co-Artistic Director
Kelly Jennings, Co-Artistic Director
www.etapestrytheatre.org
tapestry@etapestrytheatre.org
*partial season devoted to new work
*offers a reading series for new work

Theatre Catalyst
2030 Sansom Street
Philadelphia, PA 19103
215-563-4330
Fax: 215-563-4843
Joe Koroly, Managing Artistic Director
www.theatercatalyst.org
tcatalyst@hotmail.com
*season primarily focuses on new work

The Wilma Theater
265 S. Broad Street
Philadelphia, PA 19107
215-893-9456
Fax: 215-893-0895
Walter Bilderback, Literary Manager
www.wilmatheater.org
wcb@wilmatheater.org
*partial season devoted to new work

Walnut Street Theatre
825 Walnut Street
Philadelphia, PA 19103
215-816-3550
Fax: 215-574-3598
Beverly Elliot, Literary Manager
www.wstonline.org
http://www.walnutstreettheatre.org/contact.php

Membership Organizations and Workshops for Dramatists

Philadelphia Dramatists Center (PDC)
C/o CEC, 3500 Lancaster Ave
Philadelphia, PA 19104
Attn: Walt Vail
http://www.pdc1.org/
pdc@usner.org

Philadelphia Young Playwrights
7 Benjamin Franklin Pkwy, 2nd Floor
Philadelphia, PA 19103
215-665-9226
Fax: 215-665-9228
www.phillyyoungplaywrights.org
Glen Knapp, Executive Producing Director
glen@phillyyoungplaywrights.org

Original Play and Musical Contests and Festivals

Philadelphia Live Arts Festival and Philly Fringe
32 N. Front Street
Philadelphia, PA 19106
215-413-9006
Fax: 215-413-9007
Nick Stuccio, Producing Director
215-413-9006 x11
Mathilda McCommon, Fringe Coordinator
215-413-9006 x18
getinfo@livearts-fringe.org
www.livearts-fringe.org
nick@livearts-fringe.org
mathilda@livearts-fringe.org

The Theater Alliance of Greater Philadelphia –New Play Festival
1616 Walnut Street, Ste. 1800
Philadelphia, PA 19103
215-413-7150
Fax: 215-413-7155
www.theateralliance.org
info@theateralliance.org

Play Penn
PO Box 116
2457 Flowing Springs Road
Birchrunville, PA 19421
610-827-2251
Fax: 610-827-9520
Paul Meshejian, Artistic Director
www.playpenn.org
paul@playpenn.org

The Smith Prize
National New Play Network
C/o InterAct Theatre Company
2030 Sansom Street
Philadelphia, PA 19103
215-568-8077
Fax: 215-568-8095
www.nnpn.org
davidg@nnpn.org
tpplay@cox.net

Timothy Smith Prize c/o Borderlands Theater
PO Box 2791
Tucson, AZ 85702
Toni Press-Coffman, Contest Admin
N814, Big Pine Lane
Irma WI, 54442

Opportunities and Resources for Dramatists

Pew Fellowships in the Arts (PFA)
1608 Walnut Street, 18th Floor
Philadelphia, PA 19103
267-350-4920
Fax: 267-350-4997
Melissa Franklin, Director
www.pewarts.org
pfa@pcah.us

Philadelphia Theatre Initiative
Philadelphia Center for Arts and Heritage
1608 Walnut Street, 18th Floor
Philadelphia, PA 19103
267-350-4940
Fax: 260-397-4997
Fran Kumin, Director
www.philadelphiatheatreinitiative.org
pti@pcah.us

The Theater Alliance of Greater Philadelphia –New Play Festival
1616 Walnut Street, Ste. 1800
Philadelphia, PA 19103
215-413-7150
Fax: 215-413-7155
Vincent Marini, Executive Director
www.theateralliance.org
info@theateralliance.org

Colleges and Universities for Dramatic Writers

Arcadia University
450 S Easton Road
Glenside, PA 19038-3295
215-572-2900
1-877-272-2342
Mark Wade, Director of Theatre Arts
www.arcadia.edu
wadem@arcadia.edu
*offers undergraduate classes in Playwriting

Bucknell University
Dept of Theater and Dance
701 Moore Avenue
Lewisburg, PA 17837
570-577-2000
Gary Grant, Department Chair
www.bucknell.edu
grantg@bucknell.edu
*offers undergraduate classes in Playwriting

Drexel University
Antoinette Westphall College
Screenwriting and Playwriting Program
3141 Chestnut Street
51 University Crossings
Philadelphia, PA 19104
215-895-1332
Fax: 954-671-6392
Ian Abrams, Program Director
www.drexel.edu
Abrams@drexel.edu

Franklin and Marshall College
PO Box 3003
Lancaster, PA 17604-3003
717-291-3911
Dorothy Louise, Professor of Theatre
www.fandm.edu
Dorothy.louise@fandm.edu
*offers undergraduate classes in Playwriting

Lafayette College
Easton, PA 18042
Phone: 610-330-5100
Fax: 610-330-5355
Suzanne Westfall, English Chair
P 610-330-5249
www.lafayette.edu
admissions@lafayette.edu
westfals@lafayette.edu
*offers undergraduate classes in Playwriting

Muhlenberg College
Dept of Theatre Arts
2400 Chew Street
Allentown, PA 18104
484-664-3623
Charles Richtor, Director of Theatre
484-664-3330
www.muhlenberg.edu
richter@muhlenberg.edu
*offers undergraduate classes in Playwriting

Temple University
801 North Broad Street
Philadelphia, PA 19122
215-204-7000
Robert Hedley, Professor, Playwriting
215-204-8413
www.temple.edu
rhedley@temple.edu
*offers undergraduate classes in Playwriting

University of the Arts
320 South Broad Street
Philadelphia, PA 19102
800-616-ARTS
Gene Terruso, Director of School of Theater
215-717-6448
www.uarts.edu
gterruso@uarts.edu
*offers undergraduate classes in Playwriting

Villanova University
800 Lancaster Avenue
Villanova, PA 19085-1603
610-519-6000
Michael Hollinger, Teacher of Playwriting
610-519-6886
www.villanova.edu
michael.hollinger@villanova.edu
*offers graduate classes in Playwriting

Swarthmore College
Department of Theatre
500 College Avenue
Swarthmore, PA 19078
610-328-8000
Lizzie Olesker, Teacher of Playwriting
610-957-6065
www.swarthmore.edu
lizzieo@mindspring.com
*offers undergraduate classes in Playwriting

University of Pennsylvania
3451 Walnut Street
Philadelphia, PA 19104
215-898-5000
Bruce Graham, Professor of Playwriting
www.upenn.edu
neighborpr@aol.com
*offers undergraduate classes in Playwriting

SAN FRANCISCO

Theatres

Actors Theatre of San Francisco
855 Bush Street
San Francisco, CA 94108.
415-345-9582
Fax: 415-345-9768
Attn: Kenneth Vandenberg
www.actorstheatresf.org
information@actorstheatresf.org
*season primarily devoted to contemporary plays with a focus on new work

AlterTheater Ensemble
1337 Fourth Street, Suite A
San Rafael, CA 94901
415-454-2787
www.altertheater.org
info@altertheater.org
*offers a development program and reading series for new writers

Asian American Theatre Company (AATC)
690 Fifth Street, #211
San Francisco, CA 94107
415-543-5738
Fax: 415-543-5638
Jeannie Barroga, Artistic Director
www.asianamericantheater.org
info@asianamericantheater.org

Aurora Theatre Company
2081 Addison Street
Berkeley, CA 94704
510-843-4042
Fax: 510-843-4826
Tom Ross, Artistic Director
general@auroratheatre.org
www.auroratheatre.org
*season primarily devoted to new work
*offers development program and annual reading series for new writers

Brava! For Women In The Arts
2781 24th Street
San Francisco, CA 94110
415-641-7657
Fax: 415-641-7684
Ellen Gavin, Artistic Director
www.brava.org
ellen@brava.org

Central Works Theater Ensemble
PO Box 9771
Berkeley, CA 94709
510-558-1381
Gary Graves, Director
www.centralworks.org
http://www.centralworks.org/contact_us.html
*season primarily devoted to new work

Crowded Fire Theater Company
131 Tenth Street, 3rd Floor
San Francisco, CA 94103
415-255-7846
Fax: 415-626-1138
Cassie Beck, Co-Artistic Director
Kent Nicholson, Co-Artistic Director
www.crowdedfire.org
cassie@crowdedfire.org
kent@crowdedfire.org
*season primarily devoted to new work

Impact Theater
PO Box 12666
Berkeley, CA 94712-3666
510-464-4468
Melissa Hillman, Artistic Director
www.impacttheatre.com
info@impacttheatre.com
*partial season devoted to new work

Just Theater
www.justtheater.org
molly@justtheater.org
jonathan@justtheater.org
Molly Aaronson-Gelb, Co-Artistic Director
Jonathan Spector, Co-Artistic Director
*season primarily focuses on new work
*offers a play development program for new writers

Magic Theatre
Fort Mason Center, Bldg D, 3rd Floor
San Francisco, CA 94123
415- 441-8001
Fax: 415-771-5505
Chris Smith, Artistic Director
www.magictheatre.org
chriss@magictheatre.org
*season primarily focuses on new work
*offers a reading series for new plays

The Marsh
1062 Valencia Street
San Francisco, CA 94110-2427
415-641-0235
Fax: 415-643-9070
Stephanie Weisman, Artistic Director and Founder
www.themarsh.org
marsh@themarsh.org
*offers a new play development program for new writers
*offers a reading series for new work

New Conservatory Theatre Center (NCTC)
25 Van Ness Avenue
San Francisco, CA 94102
415-861-4914
Fax: 415-861-6988
Ed Decker, Artistic Director
www.nctcsf.org
ed@nctcsf.org

The Pear Avenue Theatre
1220 Pear Avenue, Unit K
Mountain View, CA 94043
650-254-1148
www.thepear.org
info@thepear.org
*partial season devoted to new work
*offers a reading series for new plays

Phoenix Arts Association Theatre
414 Mason Street, #601
San Francisco, CA 94103
415-759-7696
Fax: 415-664-5001
Linda Ayres-Frederick, Artistic Director
www.phoenixtheatresf.org
lbaf23@aol.com
*partial season devoted to new work

Renegade Theatre
1346 The Alameda, Suite7-265
San Jose, CA 95126
408-351-4440
Sean C Murphy, Artistic Director
www.renegadetheatre.com
rte@renegadetheatre.com
*partial season devoted to new work

Shadowlight Productions
22 Chattanooga Street
San Francisco, CA 94114
415-648-4461
Fax: 415-641-9734
Kate Sheehan, Managing Director
www.shadowlight.com
info@shadowlight.com
*season features some new work

Sonoma County Repertory Theater
104 N Main Street
Sebastopol, CA 95472
707-823-0177
Fax: 707-824-1719
Michael Hazen, Literary Coordinator
www.the-rep.com
theater@the-rep.com
*partial season devoted to new work
Theatre Rhinoceros
2926 16th Street
San Francisco, CA 94103
415-552-4100
Fax: 415-558-9044
John Fisher, Executive Director
www.therhino.org
jfisher@therhino.org
*partial season devoted to new work

Theatre of Yugen
2840 Mariposa Street
San Francisco, CA 94110
415-621-0507
Fax: 415-621-0223
Libby Zilber, Joint Artistic Director
www.theatreofyugen.org
libby@theatreofyugen.org

Three Wise Monkeys Theatre Company-Short Leaps
Literary Department
PO Box 640326
San Francisco CA 94164-0326
www.threewisemonkeys.org
Info: info@threewisemonkeys.org
Submissions:scripts@threewisemonkeys.org
Scott McMorrow, Literary Manager
*season primarily focuses on new work
*offers a reading series for new plays

Membership Organizations and Workshops for Dramatists

Playwrights' Center of San Francisco
588 Sutter Street, #430
San Francisco, CA 94102
Morgan Ludlow, Producing Director
415-820-3206
www.playwrightscentersf.org
morgan@playwrightscentersf.org

Theatre Bay Area (TBA)
870 Market Street #375
San Francisco, CA 94102
415-430-1140
Fax: 415-430-1145
Brad Erickson, Executive Director
www.theatrebayarea.org
tba@theatrebayarea.org

The Z Space Studio
131 Tenth Street, 3rd Floor
San Francisco, CA 94103
415-626-0453
www.zpace.org
zspace@zspace.org

Original Play and Musical Contests and Festivals

The Actors' Theatre Full Length Play Contest
C/o The Actor's Theatre of Santa Cruz
1001 Center Street
Santa Cruz, CA 95060
831-425-1003
www.sccat.org

The Actors' Theatre Ten-Minute Play Contest
C/o The Actor's Theatre of Santa Cruz
1001 Center Street
Santa Cruz, CA 95060
831-425-1003
www.sccat.org

Bay Area Playwrights Festival
C/o The Playwrights Foundation
131 Tenth Street, 3rd Floor
San Francisco, CA 94103
415-626-0453
Fax: 415-626-1138
Amy L. Mueller, Artistic Director
www.playwrightsfoundation.org
info@playwrightsfoundation.org
amy@playwrightsfoundation.org

BASH- Bay Area Shorts
C/o The Playwrights Foundation
131 Tenth Street, 3rd Floor
San Francisco, CA 94103
415-626-0453
Fax: 415-626-1138
www.playwrightsfoundation.org
info@playwrightsfoundation.org

Bay One-Acts Festival
Three Wise Monkeys Theatre Company
Literary Department
PO Box 640326
San Francisco CA 94164-0326
www.threewisemonkeys.org
newplays@threewisemonkeys.org
Submissions: scripts@threewisemonkeys.org

James D. Phelan Literary Award
Intersection For The Arts
446 Valencia Street
San Francisco, CA 94103
415-626-2787
Awards Coordinator
www.theintersection.org/resource_awards.php

Global Age Project (GAP)
Aurora Theatre Company
2081 Addison Street
Berkely, CA 94704
510-843-4042
Fax: 510-843-4826
www.auroratheatre.org
tbentley@auroratheatre.org

PlayGround
268 Bush Street, #2912
San Francisco, CA 94104
415-704-3177
Fax: 415-704-3177
James A Kleinmann, Artistic Director
www.playground-sf.org
info@playground-sf.org
jim@playground-sf.org

ReOrient
Golden Thread Productions
131 10th Street
San Francisco, CA 94103
415-626-4061
Fax 415-626-1138
Torange Yeghiazarian, Artistic Director
www.goldenthread.org
torange@goldenthread.org

Risk is this….The Cutting Ball New Plays Festival
131 Tenth Street, 3rd Floor
San Francisco, CA 94102
415-419-3584
Bill Selig, Literary Manager
www.cuttingball.com
bill@cuttingball.com

Opportunities and Resources for Dramatists

Play Café
980 Middlefield Road
Berkeley, CA 94708
510-704-8855
Steve Lyons, Playwright/Facilator
www.playcafe.org
salyons@playcafe.org

The Playwrights Foundation
131 Tenth Street, 3rd Floor
San Francisco, CA 94103
415-626-0453
Fax: 415-626-1138
www.playwrightsfoundation.org
info@playwrightsfoundation.org

Theatre Bay Area
870 Market Street, #375
San Francisco, CA 94102
415-430-1140
Fax: 415-430-1145
Brad Erickson, Executive Director
www.theatrebayarea.org
tba@theatrebayarea.org
executivedirector@theatrebayarea.org

Colleges and Universities for Dramatic Writers

San Francisco State University
Department of Creative Writing Playwriting Program
College of Humanities
1600 Holloway Avenue
San Francisco, CA 94132
www.sfsu.edu
415-338-1111
415-338-1891
Roy Conboy, Professor
http://online.sfsu.edu/~rconboy/contact.html
cwriting@sfsu.edu
rconboy@sfsu.edu
*offers undergraduate courses in Playwriting
*offers MFA in Creative Writing-Playwriting

SEATTLE

Theatres

ACT Theatre
Kreielsheimer Place
700 Union Street
Seattle, WA 98101
206-292-7660
Kort Beattie, Artistic Director
www.acttheatre.org
artistic@acttheatre.org
*partial season devoted to new work
*New play development program

Annex Theatre
PMB 1440
1122 East Pike Street
Seattle, WA 98122
206-728-0933
Fax: 206-774-6083
Gillian Jorgensen, Artistic Director
Jennifer Pratt, Literary Manager
www.annextheatre.org
Gillian.Jorgensen@annextheatre.org
Jennifer.pratt@annextheatre.org
*season devoted to new work

Driftwood Players at
James Wade Memorial Theatre
950 Main Street
Edmonds, WA 98020
www.driftwoodplayers.com
*season features new work

Fifth Avenue Theatre
1308 5th Avenue
Seattle, WA 98101
206-625-1418
Fax: 206-292-9610
David Armstrong, Producing Artistic Director
www.5thavenuetheatre.org
admin@5thavenuetheatre.org

Intiman Theatre
201 Mercer Street
Seattle, WA 98109
206-269-1901
Fax: 206-269-1928
www.intiman.org
bart@intiman.org
Bartlett Sher, Artistic Director
*season features new work

Key City Playhouse
1128 Lawrence Street
Port Townsend, WA 98368
360-379-0195
Denise Winter, Artistic Director
info@keycityplayers.org
www.keycityplayers.org
*offers play development program

Open Circle Theatre (OCT)
429 Boren Avenue North
Seattle, WA 98109
206-383-4250
Ron Sandahl, Artistic Director
www.octheater.com
*partial season devoted to new work

Seattle Children's Theatre
201 Thomas Street
Seattle, WA 98109
206-443-0807
Fax: 206-443-0442
Torrie McDonald, Literary/Publications Manager
www.sct.org
torriem@sct.org
*partial season devoted to new work

Seattle Repertory Theatre
155 Mercer Street
Seattle WA 98109
206-443-2210.
Braden Abraham, Literary Manager
www.seattlerep.org
braden@seattlerep.org
*season features new work
*offers play development program

Theatre Schmeater
1500 Summit Avenue
Seattle, WA 98122
206-324-5801
David Gassner, Artistic Director
www.schmeater.org
david.gassner@gmail.com
*offers plays development program

Membership Organizations and Workshops for Dramatists

Driftwood Players Education
PO Box 385
Edmonds, WA 98020
425-774-9600
www.Driftwoodplayers.com

Hugo Writing Classes
J.B. Walters Scholarship Fund
Richard Hugo House
1634 Eleventh Avenue
Seattle, WA 98122
206-322-7030
206-320-8767
Brian McGuigan, Registrar and Development Associate
www.hugohouse.org
registrar@hugohouse.org

Seattle Dramatists
1634 Eleventh Avenue
Seattle, WA 98122
206-720-0083
Fax: 206-720-0080
Becky Hellyer, Executive Director
info@seattledramatists.org

Seattle Playwrights Studio
ArtsWest
4711 California Avenue SW
Seattle, WA 98116
206-938-0963 x163
Marvis Lamb, SPS Director
www.artswest.org

Original Play and Musical Contests and Festivals

Annual Playwrights Festival
Key City Playhouse
1128 Lawrence Street
Port Townsend, WA 98368
360- 379-0195
Denise Winter, Artistic Director
www.keycityplayers.org
Seattle, WA

Avalanche: A Festival of New Plays
Seattle Dramatists
1634 Eleventh Avenue
Seattle, WA 98122
206-720-0083
Fax: 206-720-0080
Becky Hellyer, Executive Director
info@seattledramatists.org
Hedgebrook Writers-In-Residence
Hedgebrook Hochstadt Award
2197 Millman Road
Langley, WA 98260
360-321-4786
Fax: 360-321-2171
Amy Wheeler, Executive Director
Contact: Gitana Garofalo
www.hedgebrook.org
gitanag@hedgebrook.org

In Preparation 10-Page Play Festival
St. Genesius Society
15 Roy Street
Seattle, WA 98109
206-286-2952
Julie Newberry, Director

Insatiable! Asian American Playwrights Festival
North West Actors Studio
1100 East Pike Street, 2nd Floor
Seattle, WA 98122
www.sis-production.org/insatiable
info@saintgenesius.org

Mae West Festival
Submissions
Attn: Mae West 2008 Submittals
Mae West Fest
320 Summit Ave. E #1
Seattle, WA 98102
206-498-3126
Heidi Heimark, Executive Director
Ellen Graham, Artistic Director
www.maewestfest.org
heidi@maewestfest.org

New Works Competition
Richard Hugo House
1634 Eleventh Avenue
Seattle, WA 98122
206-322-7030
Fax: 206-320-8767
www.hugohouse.org/programs/newworks

Northwest Playwrights Competition
Theatre Schmeater
1500 Summit Avenue
Seattle, WA 98122
206-324-5801
David Gassner, Artistic Director
www.schmeater.org
david.gassner@gmail.com

Seattle Fringe Festival
1123 East John Street
Seattle, WA 98102
206-342-9172
fringe@seattlefringe.org
www.seattlefringe.org

The Female Protagonist Project
Mae West Fest
Attn: Female Protagonist Project
320 Summit Avenue East, #1
Seattle, WA 98102
Heidi Heimark, Executive Director
www.maewestfest.org/ffp
heidi@maewestfest.org

Women Playwrights Festival
Seattle Repertory Theatre
155 Mercer Street
Seattle, WA 98109
206-443-2222
206-443-2210
Braden Abraham, Literary Manager
www.seattlerep.org/NewWorkWPF.html

Opportunities and Resources For Dramatists

Driftwood Players PlayCafe
The Driftwood Players
PO Box 385
Edmonds, WA 98020
425-774-9600
playcafe@driftwoodplayers.com

Hugo In-Print Series
Richard Hugo House
1634 Eleventh Avenue
Seattle, WA 98122
206-322-7030
206-320-8767
www.hugohouse.org/programs/inprint
welcome@hugohouse.org

Intiman Theatre Facility Rentals
201 Mercer Street
Seattle, WA 98109
206-269-1901
206-269-1928
www.intiman.org/facrentals

Melange on Monday
Richard Hugo House
1634 Eleventh Avenue
Seattle, WA 98122
www.hugohouse.org/programs/melange

Open Box Monthly Open Mike For Playwrights
Jewel Box Theatre
2322 2nd Avenue, Belltown
Seattle, WA 98121
206-441-5823
www.jewelboxtheatre.com

Richard Hugo House Writer's Fund
1634 Eleventh Avenue
Seattle, WA 98122
206-322-7030
206-320-8767
www.hugohouse.org/programs
welcome@hugohouse.org

Seattle Playwrights Studio
Studio Space Rental
ArtsWest
4711 California Avenue SW
Seattle, WA 98116
206-938-0963 x163
Marvis Lamb, SPS Director
206-938-0963 x163
www.artswest.org

Stage Fright Open Mic
Richard Hugo House
1634 Eleventh Avenue
Seattle, WA 98122
206-322-7030
206-320-8767
www.hugohouse.org/programs/stagefright

Colleges and Universities for Dramatic Writers

Central Washington University
Department of Theatre Arts
400 East University Way
Ellensburg, WA 98926
509-973-1760
George Bellah, Coordinator
http://www.cwu.edu/~theatre
*offers undergraduate courses in Playwriting

University of Washington
School of Drama
Box 353950
Seattle, WA 98195
206-543-5140
Sarah Nash Gates, Executive Director
http://depts.washington.edu/uwdrama
*offers undergraduate courses in Playwriting

Whitworth College
Theatre Department
300 West Hawthorne Road
Spokane, WA 99251
509-777-1000
Jennifer Toulouse-Lee, Program Assistant
www.whitworth.edu
*offers undergraduate courses in Playwriting

Western Washington University
Department of Theater Arts
Bellingham, WA 98225-9108
360-650-7905
Kay Reddell, Advisement Coordinator
Gregory Lawrence Pulver, Chair
www.wwu.edu
*offers undergraduate courses in Playwriting

WASHINGTON, D.C.

Theatres

African Continuum Theatre Company
3523 12th Street, NE, 2nd Floor
Washington, DC 20866
202-529-5764 x1
Fax: 202-529-5782
Melvin D. Gerald, Jr., Managing Director
Jennifer Neson, Producing Artistic Director
www.africancontinuumtheatre.com
mgerald@africancontinuumtheatre.com
jnelson@africancontinuumtheatre.com
*partial season devoted to new work
*offers a reading series for new plays

Arena Stage
1101 Sixth Street, SW
Washington, DC 20024
202-554-9066
Mark Bly, Senior Dramaturg
Molly Smith, Artistic Director
www.arenastage.org
info@arenastage.org
*partial season devoted to new work
*offers a play development program for new writers

Charter Theatre
PO Box 3505
Reston, VA 20195
202-333-7009
Richard Washer, Company Dramaturg
Keith Bridges, Artistic Director
rwasher@chartertheatre.org
kbridges@chartertheatre.org
www.chartertheatre.org
*primarily focuses on new work
*offers a reading series for new plays

Ford's Theatre Society
511 10th Street NW
Washington, D.C. 20004
202) 638-2941
Paul Tetreult, Producing Director
www.fordstheatre.org
onstage@fordstheatre.org

GALA Hispanic Theatre
PO Box 43209
Washington, DC 20010
202-234-7174
Hugo Medrano, Producing Artistic Director
info@galatheatre.org
www.galatheatre.org
hugo@galatheatre.org
*primarily focuses on new work

Open Theatre
1725 17th Street, #404 NW
Washington, D.C. 20009
202-234-9816
Fax: 202-234-8816
Joe Martin, Artistic Director
opentheatredc@yahoo.com
www.opentheatre.org
*partial season devoted to new work
*offers a play development program for new writers

Rep Stage
Howard Community College
10901 Little Patuxent Parkway
Columbia, MD 21044
410-772-4942
Lisa A. Wilde, Resident Dramaturg/Literary Manager
Michael Stebbin, Artistic Director
www.repstage.org
lwilde@howardcc.edu
mstebbin@howardcc.edu
*offers a reading series of new plays

Rorschach Theatre
1421 Columbia Road #303
Washington, D.C. 20009
202-452-5538
Randy Baker, Artistic Director
Jenny McConnell Frederick, Artistic Director
info@rorschachtheatre.com

Round House Theatre Bethesda
PO Box 30688
Bethesda, MD 20824-0688
240-644-1099
roundhouse@roundhousetheatre.org
www.roundhousetheatre.org
Blake Robison, Producing Artistic Director
*partial season devoted to new work
*offers a play development program for new writers
*offers a reading series for new plays

Shakespeare Theatre Company
516 8th Street, SE
Washington, D.C. 20003
202-547-3230
Fax: 202-547-0226
Akiva Fox, Literary Associate
www.shakespearetheatre.org
afox@shakespearetheatre.org

Signature Theatre
2800 South Stafford Street
Arlington, VA 22206
571-527-1860
703-845-0236
Eric Schaeffer, Artistic Director
Michael Baron, Associate Director
www.sig-online.org
baronm@signature-theatre.org
schaeffere@signature-theatre.org
*offers a play and musical development program for new writers

Studio Theatre
1501 14th Street NW
Washington, D.C. 20005
Danielle Mages Amato, Dramaturg/Literary Associate
www.studiotheatre.org
literary@studiotheatre.org
*partial season devoted to new work

Theatre J
1529 16th Street, NW
Washington, D.C. 20036
202-777-3233
Fax: 202-518-9421
Ari Roth, Artistic Director
www.theaterj.org
tellari@theaterj.org
*partial season devoted to new work

Venus Theatre
Play Shack, 21 C Street
Laurel, MD 20707
Deborah Randall
www.venustheatre.org
www.venustheatre.org/contactus.html
*partial season devoted to new work
*offers a reading series for new work

Woolly Mammoth Theatre Company
641 D Street NW
Washington, D.C. 20004
202-289-2443
Fax: 202-289-2446
Howard Shalwitz, Artistic Director
Elissa Goetschius, Literary Associate
www.woollymammoth.net
howard@woollymammoth.net
elissa@woollymammoth.net
*primarily devoted to new work
*offers a reading series for new plays

Membership Organizations and Workshops for Dramatists

National League of American Pen Women
1300 17th Street, NW
Washington, D.C. 20036-1973
202-785-1997
Thelma Urich, New Membership
Eugénie R. Rocherolle, New Membership
www.americanpenwomen.org
nlapwl@verizon.net

New Visions/New Voices (NVNV)
Kennedy Center Education Department
Box 101510
Arlington, VA 22210
202-416-8830
Fax: 202-416-8297
Kim Peter Kovac, Director of TYA
www.kennedy-center.org/education/nvnv.html
kctya@kennedy-center.org

Playwrights Forum
Box 5322
Rockville, Maryland 20851
301-816-0569
Ernie Joseviltz, President
www.erols.com/pforum/welcome.html
pforum@erols.com

The Writer's Center
4508 Walsh Street
Bethesda, MD 20815
301-654-8664
Gregory F. Robinson, Executive Director
www.writer.org
postmaster@writer.org

Original Play and Musical Contests and Festivals

American College Theater Festival
The Kennedy Center
2700 F Street NW
Washington, D.C. 20566
202-416-8864
Gregg Henry, Co-Manager, Artistic Director KCACTF
www.kennedy-center.org/education/actf/
ghenry@kennedy-center.org

Capital Fringe
PO Box 50659
Washington, D.C. 20091
202-731-6645
Damien Sinclair, Co-Founder
Julianne Brienza, Co-Founder
www.capfringe.org

Firehouse Theatre Project Festival of New American Plays
1609 Broad Street
Richmond, VA 23220
804-355-2001
Carol Piersol, Artistic Director
www.firehousetheatre.org
carol@firehousetheatre.org

International Festival of Hispanic Theater
Teatro de la Luna
4020 Georgia Ave NW
Washington, D.C. 20011
202-822-6227
info@teatrodelaluna.org
www.teatrodelaluna.org

The John F. Kennedy Center for the Performing Arts-New Visions/New Voices
2700 F Street NW
Washington, D.C. 20566
202-416-8830
www.kennedy-center.org

The Montgomery Playhouse –One-Act Play Festival
PO Box 3490
Gaithersburg, MD 20885
301-977-5751
Jane Bruns, Artistic Director
www.montgomeryplayhouse.org
artisticdirector@montgomeryplayhouse.org

Jane Chambers Playwriting Award
The Women & Theatre Program
Davis Center
Box 571063
Georgetown University
Washington, D.C. 20057-1063
Maya Roth, Coordinator.
www.athe.org/wtp/html/chambers.html

Literature Fellowships: Translation Projects
National Endowment for the Arts
1100 Pennsylvania Avenue NW
Washington, D.C. 20506
202-682-5400
webmgr@arts.endow.gov
www.nea.gov/grants/apply/LitTranslation/index.html

VSA arts Playwright Discovery Award
818 Connecticut Avenue, NW
Suite 600
Washington, D.C. 20006
800-933-8721
info@vsaarts.org
www.vsarts.org/x244.xml

U.S./Japan Creative Artists' Program
Japan-US Friendship Commission
1201 15th Street NW, Suite 330
Washington, D.C. 20005
202-653-9800
jusfc@jusfc.gov
www.jusfc.gov/creativeartists.asp

Opportunities and Resources for Dramatists

District of Columbia (DC) Commission on the Arts and Humanities
Government of the District of Columbia
2901 14th Street N.W., 1st Floor
Washington, D.C. 20010
202-724-5613
www.dcarts.dc.gov/dcarts/site/default.asp?dcartsNav=|31583|

Gaithersburg Arts Barn -Residency
311 Kent Square Road
Gaithersburg, MD 20878
301-258-6394
http://www.gaithersburgmd.gov/
artsbarn@gaithersburgmd.gov

American University
4400 Massachusetts Avenue, NW
Washington, D.C. 20016
202-885-3420
Carl Menninger, Program Director
www.american.edu
*offers undergraduate courses in Playwriting

Catholic University of America
Department of Drama
620 Michigan Avenue NE
Washington, D.C. 20064
202-319-5358
Fax: 202-319-5359
Jon Klein, Head of MFA Playwriting Program
http://drama.cua.edu
*offers undergraduate courses in Playwriting
*offers MFA Program in Playwriting

George Washington University
Department of Theatre and Dance
800 21st Street, NW
Washington, D.C. 20052
202-994-8072
L.B. Jacobson, Chair
www.gwu.edu
*offers undergraduate courses in Playwriting

Georgetown University
PO Box 571063
Washington, D.C. 20057
202-687-3838
Derek Goldman, Program Director
www.georgetown.edu
*offers undergraduate courses in Playwriting

Howard University
2400 Sixth Street, NW
Washington, D.C. 20059
202-806-6100
Joe Selmon, Chairman
www.howard.edu
*offers undergraduate courses in Playwriting

EMERGENCY FUNDS

Authors League Fund

31 E. 32nd St., Fl. 7, New York, NY, 10016
Sarah Heller, Administrator
Fax: 212-564-5363
staff@authorsguild.org; www.authorsleaguefund.org

Interest-free loans for personal emergencies of immediate need (rent, medical, etc.). **Preference.** Author Must Be: produced or published. **Application.** Best Material: application.

Carnegie Fund for Authors

1 Old Country Rd., #113, Carle Place, NY, 11514
Tel: 516-877-2141

Aid to authors (of at least 1 commercially published book) for financial emergency as a result of illness or injury to self, spouse or dependent child, or that has placed author in pressing and substantial verifiable need. **Preference.** Author Must Be: age 18 or older.

Dramatists Guild Fund

1501 Broadway, #701, New York, NY, 10036
Susan Drury, Administrator
Tel: 212-391-8384, Fax: 212-944-0420
sdrury@dramatistsguild.com

Est. 1962. Grants for personal emergencies such as rent, medical, etc. plus grants to nonprofit US theaters producing new works. **Preference.** Author Must Be: produced or published. **Application.** Best Way: Call, e-mail, website. Best Material: application.

Entertainment Industry Assistance Program (EIAP)

The Actors' Fund of America, 729 7th Ave., Fl. 10, New York, NY, 10019
Tel: 212-221-7300 x119
www.actorsfund.org

Helps working entertainment professionals with: counseling; advocacy and referrals to social services; emergency aid for food, rent, medical care. Chicago: 312-372-0989, Los Angeles: 323-933-9244 x15.

Mary Mason Memorial Lemonade Fund

Theatre Bay Area (TBA), 870 Market St, #375, San Francisco, CA, 94102
Tel: 415-430-1140, Fax: 415-430-1145
dale@theatrebayarea.org; www.theatrebayarea.org/programs/lemonade.jsp

PEN Writers Fund

PEN American Center, 588 Broadway, #303, New York, NY, 10012
Andrew Proctor, Coord.
www.pen.org

Est. 1921. Emergency fund for professional writers with serious financial difficulties. **Consideration.** Assistance: $2,000 limit. **Preference.** Length: full length (over 90 min). Author Must Be: resident of US. Material Must Be: produced or published (not self-published). **Application.** Best Material: application. Response: 2 mos.

MEMBERSHIP & SERVICE ORGANIZATIONS

Actors' Fund of America
729 7th Ave., Fl. 10, New York, NY, 10019
Barbara Davis, Chief Program Officer
Tel: 212-221-7300, Fax: 212-764-6404
www.actorsfund.org

Est. 1882. Human services org for all entertainment professionals. Also makes emergency grants for essential needs.

$25.00 . ACTS Institute Inc.
Box 30854, Palm Beach Gardens, FL, 33420
Charlotte Plotsky, Exec Dir
Tel: 561-625-2273

Est. 1981. Nonprofit public foundation and membership group for developing creative artists and projects as a charitable and educational endeavor. Current project is public education (lectures, workshops, etc.) various topics, and publications program. **Application.** Best Material: query.

Alliance for Inclusion in the Arts
1560 Broadway, #1600, New York, NY, 10036
Sharon Jensen, Exec Dir
Tel: 212-730-4750, Fax: 212-730-4820
info@ntcp.org; www.ntcp.org

Est. 1986. Nonprofit advocacy org to address and seek solutions to racism and exclusion in theater, film and TV, working to advance creative participation of US writers of color, female artists, deaf and hard-of-hearing artists, and artists with disabilities. **Preference.** Author Must Be: of color, female or disabled.

Alliance of Artists Communities (AAC)
255 South Main St., Providence, RI, 02903
www.artistcommunities.org

$40/yr. Alliance of Los Angeles Playwrights (ALAP)
7510 Sunset Blvd., #1050, Los Angeles, CA, 90046
Dan Berkowitz, Jon Dorf, Co-Chairs
Tel: 323-957-4752
info@laplaywrights.org; www.laplaywrights.org

Service and support org for professional needs of LA playwrights. Sponsors annual reading series, professional symposia, networking and social events. Also offers phone hotline, email listserv, bimonthly newsletter, resource guide to local theater, model contracts, and annual membership directory. **Consideration.** Fees: $40/yr dues, $20 students, $275 lifetime (tax-deductable). **Application.** Best Way: website. Best Material: application.

$50/yr. Alternate ROOTS Inc.
1083 Austin Ave., NE, Atlanta, GA, 30307
Buseje Crump, Admin Asst
Tel: 888-871-9898, Fax: 404-577-7991
info@alternateroots.org; www.alternateroots.org

Service org for playwrights, directors & choreographers creating original, community-based projects. Services incl. newsletter, bulletin, presenters' subsidy, annual meeting, and professional/artistic training and development. **Consideration.** Fees: $20/yr (intro), $50/yr, $75/yr (voting). **Preference.** Author Must Be: resident of Southeast. **Application.** Best Material: application.

$25-$55/yr. American Assn. of Community Theatre (AACT)
8402 Briar Wood Cir., Lago Vista, TX, 78645
Bill Muchow, Pres.
www.aact.org

Est. 1986.

$25/yr. American Indian Community House
11 Broadway, Fl. 2, New York, NY, 10004
Jim Cyrus, Performing Arts Dir.
Tel: 212-598-0100, Fax: 212-598-4909
jcyrus@aich.org; www.aich.org

Consideration. Fees: $25/yr. **Preference.** Subject: Native American.

$55/yr. American Music Center (AMC)
30 W. 26th St., #1001, New York, NY, 10010
Maritza Norr, Admin Asst
Tel: 212-366-5260, Fax: 212-366-5265
center@amc.net; www.amc.net

Est. 1939. **Consideration.** Fees: $55/yr, $35/yr (student, senior).

$145/yr. American Translators Assn. (ATA)
225 Reinekers Ln., #590, Alexandria, VA, 22314
Walter Bacak Jr., Exec Dir.
Tel: 703-683-6100, Fax: 703-683-6122
ata@atanet.org; www.atanet.org

Est. 1959. Nonprofit to promote, educate and support US translators. Activities incl. conference, 2 awards and several publications. Open to anyone interested in translation and interpretation. **Consideration.** Fees: $145/yr dues (associate). **Application.** Best Material: application.

ASCAP (American Society of Composers, Authors & Publishers)
1 Lincoln Plaza, New York, NY, 10023
Membership Dept.
Tel: 212-621-6234, Fax: 212-621-6558
www.ascap.com

Est. 1914. Membership org for composers, lyricists and publishers of musical works. Programs incl. winter and spring Musical Theater Workshops directed by Stephen Schwartz and Songwriters Showcases in NY and LA. **Preference.** Author Must Be: published, recorded or performed. **Application.** Best Material: application.

Assn. of Authors' Representatives, Inc.
676A 9th Avenue, #312, New York, NY, 10036
Joanne Brownstein

$80/yr. Association for Jewish Theatre (AJT)
Arizona Jewish Theatre, 444 W. Camelback Rd., #208, Phoenix, AZ, 85013
Janet Arnold, Chair, Membership
www.afjt.com

International network of theatres and playwrights to enhance Jewish theatre. Info and increased visibility of Jewish theater, incl. annual newsletter, website with member pages, annual conference, submissions guide, etc. Exec Director- Kayla Gordon **Consideration.** Fees: $80/yr dues (Sep-Aug). **Application.** Best Material: application on website.

$105/yr. Association for Theatre in Higher Education (ATHE)
Box 1290, Boulder, CO, 80306
Tel: 888-284-3737, Fax: 303-530-2168
info@athe.org; www.athe.org

Org of individuals and institutions promoting excellence in theater education thru its publications, conferences, advocacy, projects, and collaborative efforts with other organizations. Membership year runs Jun-May. **Consideration.** Fees: $105/yr (indiv), $80/yr (retiree), $50/yr (student). **Application.** Best Way: online. Best Material: application.

Association of Hispanic Arts (AHA)
Box 1169, New York, NY, 10029
Nicholas L. Arture, Exec Dir.
Tel: 212-876-1242, Fax: 212-876-1285
informacion@latinoarts.org; www.latinoarts.org

Est. 1975. Nonprofit advancing Latino arts as integral to the nation's cultural life. Facilitates projects and programs to foster Latino culture, incl. workshops and seminars for artists and organizations, and a directory of Latino arts.

Audrey Skirball-Kenis (ASK) Unpublished Play Collection
Los Angeles Public Library, 630 W. 5th St., Los Angeles, CA, 90071
Bette McDonough, Sr Librarian
Tel: 213-228-7325
www.lapl.org/central/literature.html

Service org with over 800 unpublished scripts of plays done in L.A. The collection, located in the Lit/Fiction Dept for reference only, incl. reviews and playwright bios. Open Mon-Thu, 10am-8pm; Fri-Sat, 10am-6pm; Sun, 1pm-5pm.

$45/yr. Austin Script Works (ASW)
Box 9787, Austin, TX, 78766
Christina J. Moore, Executive Dir.
Tel: 512-454-9727
info@scriptworks.org; www.scriptworks.org

Est. 1997. Austin Script Works supports playwrights by providing opportunities at all stages of the writing process from inception to production, through a variety of programming. **Consideration.** Fees: $45/yr, $35/yr (student, senior). **Application.** Best Way: online. Best Material: application.

Billy Rose Theatre Division
New York Public Library for the Performing Arts, 40 Lincoln Center Plaza, Fl. 3, New York, NY, 10023
Bob Taylor, Curator
Tel: 212-870-1637
rtaylor@nypl.org; www.nypl.org/research/lpa

Research facility with historical and current docs of performing arts and popular entertainment, incl. books, personal papers, scripts and promptbooks from theater, film, TV and radio. Tape archive incl. Broadway, Off-Broadway and regional productions.

BMI (Broadcast Music Inc)
320 W. 57th St., New York, NY, 10019
Tel: 212-586-2000, Fax: 212-262-2824
www.bmi.com

Est. 1939. Performing rights society that collects royalties from radio, TV, web, restaurants, and other businesses that use music on behalf of songwriters, composers, and music publishers.

$25/yr. Chicago Alliance for Playwrights (CAP)

Theatre Building Chicago (TBC), 1225 W. Belmont Ave., Chicago, IL, 60657
Joanne Koch, President
Tel: 773-929-7367 x60, Fax: 773-327-1404
info@chicagoallianceforplaywrights.org; www.chicagoallianceforplaywrights.org

Networking org for playwrights, theaters and other individuals and groups. Publishes newsletter and annual directory of members and their work. Also sponsors seminars and workshops. **Consideration.** Fees: $25/yr. **Preference.** Author Must Be: current or former resident of Midwest. **Application.** Best Way: email. Best Material: application.

$125/yr. Chicago Dramatists

1105 W. Chicago Ave., Chicago, IL, 60622
Russ Tutterow, Artistic Dir.
Tel: 312-633-0630
newplays@chicagodramatists.org; www.chicagodramatists.org

Est. 1979. Developmental theater and playwright workshop. Programs incl. readings, productions, workshops, panels, marketing services, and referrals to producers, etc. Classes and quarterly 10-min workshop open to all playwrights. Quarterly bulletins and website announce all events and programs. **Consideration.** Fees: $125/year (National Membership), $200/year (Chicago Membership), free (Residency).

$95/yr. Dramatists Guild of America Inc.

1501 Broadway, #701, New York, NY, 10036
Joshua Levine, Dir, Membership
Tel: 212-398-9366, Fax: 212-944-0420
membership@dramatistsguild.com; www.dramatistsguild.com

Est. 1920. Works for the professional rights of writers of stage works and the conditions under which those works are created and produced. Also fights to secure fair royalties and protect subsidiary rights, artistic control, and copyright ownership. Members receive various services and publications, incl The Dramatist magazine, Newsletter, and Resource Directory. **Consideration.** Fees: $95/yr (assoc), $150 (active, estate), $35/yr (student). **Application.** Best Way: online. Best Material: application, full script.

$75/yr. Educational Theatre Association

2343 Auburn Ave., Cincinnati, OH, 45219
David LaFleche, Dir, Membership
Tel: 513-421-3900, Fax: 513-421-7077
dlafleche@edta.org; www.edta.org

Consideration. Fees: $75/yr, $25/yr (student). **Application.** Best Material: application.

$100/yr. Field

161 6th Ave., Fl. 14, New York, NY, 10013
Audra Lang, Manager Sponsored Artists Program, Membership and Fiscal Sponsorship Program
Tel: 212-691-6969, Fax: 212-255-2053
audra@thefield.org; www.thefield.org

Est. 1986. Service org offering space grants for rehearsals/shows, retreat grants, performance showcases, mgmt workshops, fiscal sponsorship, consultations and more. **Consideration.** Fees: $100/$150 a yr.. **Application.** Best Material: application.

$200/yr. FirstStage [CA]

Box 38280, Los Angeles, CA, 90038
Dennis Safren, Literary Mgr.
Tel: 323-850-6271
firststagela@aol.com; www.firststagela.org

Est. 1983. Develops new work for stage and screen. Do not have to be a member for work to be considered. If you wish to joing, dues are $200 per year for local members; $68 per year for non-local members. **Preference.** Material Must Be: unproduced. **Application.** Best Material: full script, SASE. Response: 6 mos.

Foundation Center

79 5th Ave., New York, NY, 10003
Judith Margolin, VP, Public Services
Tel: 212-620-4230, Fax: 212-807-3677
fdonline@fdncenter.org; www.fdncenter.org

Est. 1956. Network of centers with grant info. Doesn't make grants, do research, consult, make referrals, arrange intros, or write/review proposals. HQ in NY. Field offices in Atlanta (50 Hurt Plz, #150), Cleveland (1422 Euclid Ave, #1600), DC (1627 K St NW, Fl 3), and San Francisco (312 Sutter St, #606). Check website for other sites with access to Foundation Center database on CD-ROM or Foundation Directory online.

$75/yr. Fractured Atlas

248 W. 35th St., #1202, New York, NY, 10001
Adam Natale, Dir, Member Services
Tel: 212-277-8020, Fax: 212-277-8025
support@fracturedatlas.org; www.fracturedatlas.org

Est. 2002. Benefits incl. fiscal sponsorship, low-cost healthcare & Liability insurance, press/publicity services, online classes, calendar, forums, grants. Staff: Adam Huttler (Exec Dir), Adam Natale (Dir, Member Services) Maria Ortiz (Dir, Healthcare), Arwen Lowbridge (Mng Dir.), Alexandra Gray (Dir, Development), Dianne Ebicella (Pgm Assoc). **Consideration.** Fees: $75/yr (individual), FREE Associate Membership for Dramatists Guild members.

Fund for Women Artists

Box 1236, Northampton, MA, 01061
Martha Richards, Exec Dir
Tel: 413-585-5968, Fax: 413-586-1303
info@womenarts.org; www.womenarts.org

Founded to ensure women have full access to the resources they need, by challenging stereotypes and increasing opportunities.

$25/yr. Greensboro Playwrights' Forum

200 N. Davie St., #2, Greensboro, NC, 27401
Stephen D. Hyers, Dir.
Tel: 336-335-6426, Fax: 336-373-2659
stephen.hyers@greensboro-nc.gov; www.playwrightsforum.org

Est. 1993. Aids area dramatists in publishling, producing, and learning theater writing. Services incl. monthly meetings, workshops, staged readings, newsletter, and studio space. **Consideration.** Fees: $25/yr. **Application.** Best Material: application.

Hatch-Billops Collection

491 Broadway, Fl. 7, New York, NY, 10012
James V. Hatch, Exec Secy
Tel: 212-966-3231, Fax: 212-966-3231
hatchbillops@yahoo.com; www.hatch-billopscollection.org

Est. 1975. Collection of primary and secondary resource materials in the black cultural arts.

Hispanic Organization of Latin Actors (HOLA)

Clemente Solo Velez Cultural Center, 107 Suffolk St., #302, New York, NY, 10002
Manuel Alfaro, Exec Dir.
Tel: 212-253-1015, Fax: 212-253-9651
holagram@hellohola.org; www.hellohola.org

Inside Broadway

630 9th Ave., #802, New York, NY, 10036
Michael Presser, Exec Dir
Tel: 212-245-0710, Fax: 212-245-3018
mpresser@insidebroadway.org; www.insidebroadway.org

Professional children's theater producing classic musicals in NYC public schools. Also offer hands-on, in-school residencies that enrich core curriculum through drama, dance, and music.

Institute of Outdoor Drama

Univ. of North Carolina (UNC), Chapel Hilll, 1700 MLK Jr. Blvd., CB-3240, Chapel Hill, NC, 27599
Scott J. Parker, Dir.
Tel: 919-962-1328, Fax: 919-962-4212
outdoor@unc.edu; www.unc.edu/depts/outdoor

Public service agency of UNC at Chapel Hill for consultation, info, publicity, employment advice, conferences and symposia, and research material on every phase of planning and producing outdoor theater. **Application.** Best Material: query, SASE.

International Theatre Institute US Center (ITI/US)

Theatre Communications Group (TCG), 520 8th Ave., Fl. 24, New York, NY, 10018
Emilya Cachapero, Dir.
Tel: 212-609-5900, Fax: 212-609-5901
iti@tcg.org; www.tcg.org

TCG is the US center of ITI, a UNESCO network of over 90 centers dedicated to cultural exchange and advocacy. TCG/ITI helps intl. theater professionals and scholars with info about US practice, introductions to US professionals, and planning visits. Similar help is offered to Americans traveling and working abroad. **Consideration.** Fees: $39.95/year.

$45/yr. International Women's Writing Guild (IWWG)

Box 810, Gracie Sta., New York, NY, 10028
Hannelore Hahn, Founder/Exec Dir
Tel: 212-737-7536, Fax: 212-737-9469
www.iwwg.org

Est. 1976. Network for empowering women thru writing, incl. workshops/courses, submission tip sheet, bimonthly newsletter, and dental/vision insurance. **Consideration.** Fees: $45/yr. **Application.** Best Material: application.

$35/yr. LA Stage Alliance

644 S. Figueroa St., Los Angeles, CA, 90017
Trena Pitchford, Membership Mgr
Tel: 213-614-0556, Fax: 213-614-0561
info@lastagealliance.com; www.lastagealliance.com

Est. 1975. Formerly TheatreLA. Nonprofit service org of groups and individuals providing L.A. Stage magazine, networking opportunities, half-price tickets, Ovation Awards, cooperative ads, info and referrals. **Consideration.** Fees: $35/yr (individual), $20/yr (student). **Application.** Best Way: online. Best Material: application.

League of Chicago Theaters/League of Chicago Theaters Foundation

228 South Wabash #200, Chicago, IL, 60604
Tel: 312-554-9800, Fax: 312-922-7202
info@chicagoplays.com; www.chicagoplays.com

Est. 1979.

League of Professional Theatre Women

Lynne Rogers, Box 2292, New York, NY, 10108
Lenore De Karen , VP, Membership
Tel: 212-414-8048, Fax: 212-225-2378
id5columbia.edu; www.theatrewomen.org

Nonprofit advocacy organization promoting visibility and increasing opportunities for women in the professional theater.

League of Washington Theatres (LOWT)

Box 21645, Washington, DC, 20009

Est. 1982. Association of nonprofit professional theaters and related organizations in the greater Washington metropolitan area.

$60/yr. Literary Managers & Dramaturgs of the Americas (LMDA)
Box 728, Village Sta., New York, NY, 10014
Louise McKay, Admin Dir
Tel: 212-561-0315
lmdanyc@hotmail.com; www.lmda.org

Est. 1985. Volunteer membership org w/400 members in US/Canada. Current programs and services incl. annual conference, regional meetings/symposia, LMDA Review quarterly journal, Script Exchange newsletter, outreach program, univ./advocacy caucuses, email network, and dramaturgy prize. Annual memberships is Jun-May. **Consideration.** Fees: $60/yr, $25/yr (student). **Application.** Best Way: online. Best Material: application.

$25/yr. National Audio Theatre Festivals (NATF)
115 Dikeman St., Hempstead, NY, 11550
Sue Zizza, Executive Dir.
Tel: 516-483-8321, Fax: 516-538-7583
www.natf.org

$30/yr. National League of American Pen Women, Inc.
1300 17th St. NW, Washington, DC, 20036
Wanda A. Rider, National President
Tel: 202-785-1997, Fax: 202-452-8868
nlapw1@verizon.com; www.americanpenwomen.org

New members in Letters, contact Thelma Urich, 6143 Tennessee Ave., St. Louis, MO 63111, **Consideration.** Fees: $30/yr.

National Writers Association Foundation (NWAF)
National Writers Association, Box 4187, Parker, CO, 80134
Sandy Whelchel, Acting Director
Tel: 303-841-0246, Fax: 303-841-2607
authorsandy@hotmail.com; www.nationalwriters.com

Est. 1998. 1- $1,000 scholarship and one Conference scholarship which includes an opportunity to speak with four producers. **Consideration.** Remuneration: 1,000. Frequency: annual. **Preference.** Length: all length. Style: all styles. Subject: all subjects. Material Must Be: unoptioned, unpublished, unproduced. **Application.** Best Way: unsolicited. Best Material: application, 10 pg. sample, SASE. Best Time: Begin September. Deadline: 12/31/2008. Response: 4 months.

9/15/2008. New Dramatists
424 W. 44th St., New York, NY, 10036
Emily Morse, Dir, Artistic Development
Tel: 212-757-6960, Fax: 212-265-4738
newdramatists@newdramatists.org; www.newdramatists.org

Est. 1949. Service org offering development programs (reading-workshop; literary services; artistic services) and services (readings; nonperformance workshops w/artistic collaborators; natl Script Share distribution; monthly Member Bulletin; free tickets; intl exchanges; travel grants and other awards). Staff: Todd London (Artistic Dir). **Application.** Best Material: application, full script, SASE. Deadline: 15-Sep-08. Response: 9 mos.

$25/yr. New Playwrights Foundation
608 San Vicente Blvd., #18, Santa Monica, CA, 90402
Jeffrey Bergquist, Artistic Dir.
Tel: 310-393-3682
dialogue@newplaywrights.org; www.newplaywrights.org

Est. 1969. Meets every othe Tursday in Santa Monica. Some members works have been produced by NPF. **Consideration.** Fees: $25/yr. **Preference.** Author Must Be: able to attend workshops in Santa Monica.

$20/yr. North Carolina Playwrights Alliance (NCPA)

Box 10463, Raleigh, NC, 27605
Adrienne Pender, President
www.ncplaywrightsalliance.org

Est. 2001. **Consideration.** Fees: $20/yr. **Preference.** Author Must Be: resident of NC. **Application.** Best Way: online. Best Material: application.

$75/yr. North Carolina Writers' Network (NCWN)

Box 954, Carrboro, NC, 27510
Cynthia Barnett, Exec Dir
Tel: 919-967-9540, Fax: 919-929-0535
mail@ncwriters.org; www.ncwriters.org

Nonprofit to connect, promote and lead NC writers thru conferences, contests, newsletter, website, member pages, member book catalog, critique and consultation, etc. (some services require addl. fees). **Consideration.** Fees: $75/yr, $65/yr (senior), $55/yr (student). **Application.** Best Way: online. Best Material: application.

$55/6 mos. NYC Playwrights

2 12th St., #1013, Hoboken, NJ, 07030
Nancy McClernan
info@nycplaywrights.org; www.nycplaywrights.org

Est. 2000. Writers and actors meet each Wed., 7-10 PM at Where Eagles Dare (347 W. 36th St., #12-A) for in-hand readings of works in progress, free and open to the public. Member writers may reserve a 30 min. slot, on a first-come, first-served basis, up to 8 wks in advance. **Consideration.** Fees: $55/6 mos. **Application.** Best Material: application, 10-pg sample.

Ollantay Center for the Arts

Box 720636, Jackson Heights, NY, 11372-0636
Pedro Monge-Rafuls, Executive-Artistic Dir.
Tel: 718-699-6772, Fax: 718-699-6773

Each season Ollantay offers playwright workshops with well-known Latin American authors and play-reading programs to help local playwrights. A literature program is dedicated exclusively to the promotion of local writers through conferences and panel disc ussions. Creators of Ollantay magazine, a biannual journal in English and Spanish that publishes at least one play in each issue. Ollantay Press publishes books. **Consideration.** Remuneration: awards, possible future production, publication, reading. Frequency: annual. **Preference.** Length: all lengths. Subject: Latino. **Application.** Best Way: unsolicited. Best Material: synopsis, submissions returned with SASE. Deadline: ongoing. Response: 5/15/2004.

$60/yr. OPERA America

330 7th Ave., Fl. 16, New York, NY, 10001
Tel: 212-796-8620, Fax: 212-796-8631
frontdesk@operaamerica.org; www.operaamerica.org

National service org promoting creation, presentation and enjoyment of opera. Provides professional development resources for composers, librettists, educators, etc. Composers may subscribe to Opera Source job search ($45/yr). **Consideration.** Fees: $60/yr. **Application.** Best Way: online. Best Material: application.

Orange County Playwrights Alliance (OCPA)

412 Emerald Place, Seal Beach, CA, 90740
Eric Eberwein, Dir.
firenbones@aol.com; www.ocplaywrights.org

Est. 1995. Member org. workshop of Orange Co. dramatists. Develops new works, staged readings, occasional productions. **Consideration.** Fees: $80/yr.. **Application.** Best Material: full script.

$40/yr. Philadelphia Dramatists Center (PDC)
c/o CEC, 3500 Lancaster Ave., Philadelphia, PA, 19104
Walt Vail, Treasurer
pdc@usner.org; pdc1.pbwiki.com

Membership org for improving the craft, opportunities and conditions of dramatic writers, incl. newsletter, emails, readings, writers' circles, workshops, free/discounted space rental, guest speakers, reading library, social events, resource books, and copyright forms. Members may also list works on PDC's website. **Consideration.** Fees: $40/yr, $20/yr (student). **Application.** Best Material: application.

$25/quarter. Playformers
20 Waterside Plaza, #11-G, New York, NY, 10010
Lynda Crawford
Tel: 917-825-2663

Est. 1987. Monthy meetings (Sep-May) to read new work by members. **Consideration.** Fees: $25/quarter (covering refreshments for actors). **Application.** Best Material: full script, SASE. Best Time: Sep-May (attend 1-2 mtgs before submitting). Response: 2 mos.

$75/yr. Playwrights' Center
2301 Franklin Ave. E., Minneapolis, MN, 55406
Steve Moulds, Membership/Lit Assoc.
Tel: 612-332-7481, Fax: 612-332-6037
info@pwcenter.org; www.pwcenter.org

Provides services that support playwrights and playwriting. Programs incl. emailed listing of submission opportunities, fellowships, workshops, readings, classes, PlayLabs and national outreach. **Consideration.** Fees: $75/yr (local), $40/yr (national, low-income). **Application.** Best Way: online. Best Material: application.

1/15, 5/15, 9/15. $110/session. Playwrights' Forum [MD]
Box 5322, Rockville, MD, 20851
Ernie Joselovitz, President
Tel: 301-816-0569
pforum@erols.com; www.erols.com/pforum/welcome.htm

Est. 1991. Tiered options: Forum 2 professional member; Forum 1 apprentice member; Associate member. **Consideration.** Fees: $120/session (4 mos). **Preference.** Author Must Be: resident of Mid-Atlantic. **Application.** Best Way: online. Best Material: application. Best Time: Dec, Apr, Aug. Deadline: 15-Jan-08, 15-May-08, 15-Sep-08.

$60/yr. Playwrights Center San Francisco (PCSF)
588 Sutter St., #430, San Francisco, CA, 94102
Laylah Muran, Sec.
Tel: 415-820-3206
layla@playwrightscentersf.org; www.playwrightscentersf.org

Est. 1980. Organization of playwrights, directors and actors developing Bay Area writing, audience development and related arts. Weekly events incl. staged readings, scene workshops, classes and panel discussions. Author provieds scripts for actors. No submission process for scene nights. **Consideration.** Fees: $60/yr (full), $30/yr (student). Frequency: semiannual for staged and developmental readings. **Preference.** Author Must Be: resident of Bay Area. **Application.** Best Material: application. Best Time: Fall (for spring) Spring (for fall). Response: 3 mos..

$150/yr. Playwrights Guild of Canada (PGC)
54 Wolseley St., Fl. 2, Toronto, ON, M5T 1A5 Canada
Dian Marie Bridge, Mgr, Membership
Tel: 416-703-0201, Fax: 416-703-0059
info@playwrightsguild.ca; www.playwrightsguild.ca

Est. 1972. Formerly Playwrights Union of Canada. National nonprofit offering triannual directory of Canadian plays/playwrights, contract negotiation with PACT, amateur/professional production administration, and quarterly magazine. **Consideration.** Fees: $150/yr (full), $65/yr (assoc). **Preference.** Author Must Be: citizen or landed immigrant of Canada. **Application.** Best Material: application, resume. Response: 3 wks.

Purple Circuit

921 N. Naomi St., Burbank, CA, 91505
Bill Kaiser, Co-founder/Editor
Tel: 818-953-5096
purplecir@aol.com; www.buddybuddy.com/pc.html

Service group to promote GLBT performing arts worldwide. Maintains Calif. show listings hotline (818-953-5072), directory of GLBT-friendly venues, and freelisting of playwrights. **Preference.** Subject: GLBT. **Application.** Best Way: email.

Rodgers & Hammerstein Theatre Library

229 W. 28th St, FL 11, New York, NY, 10001

$65/yr. Saskatchewan Writers Guild (SWG)

Box 3986, Regina, SK, S4P 3R9 Canada
Jackie Mehlmann, Admin. Asst.
Tel: 306-757-6310
swg@sasktel.net; www.skwriter.com

Est. 1969. Membership is open to all writers, teachers, librarians, publishers, booksellers, students, and others interested in Saskatchewan writing. **Consideration.** Fees: $65/yr (regular), $45/yr (student, senior).

Shubert Archives

149 W. 45th St., New York, NY, 10036
www.shubertorganization.com/divisionsandaffiliates/shubertarchive.asp

Est. 1976. Repository for over 6m docs related to the Shubert brothers and Shubert Org, incl. costume/set designs, scripts, music, publicity, photos, letters, business records, and architectural plans.

$60/yr. Songwriters Guild of America (SGA)

1560 Broadway, #1306, New York, NY, 10036
George Wurzbach, National Projects Dir.
Tel: 212-768-7902, Fax: 212-768-9048
ny@songwritersguild.com; www.songwritersguild.com

Est. 1931. **Consideration.** Fees: $60/yr (gold), $84/yr (platinum), $108/yr (diamond).

$80/yr. STAGE (Society for Theatrical Artists' Guidance and Enhancement)

1106 Lupo Dr., Dallas, TX, 75207
Jeff Fenter, Operations Mgr.
Tel: 214-630-7722, Fax: 214-630-4468
stage@stage-online.org; www.stage-online.org

Est. 1981. Nonprofit promoting theater, broadcast, and film by serving as info clearinghouse and training center for north central Texas. **Consideration.** Fees: $80 (initial), $65/yr (renewal).

$115.00 . StageSource

88 Tremont St., #714, Boston, MA, 02108
Jeremy Johnson, Member Services
Tel: 617-720-6066, Fax: 617-720-4275
info@stagesource.org; www.stagesource.org

Est. 1985. Alliance of artists and organizations in New England. Benefits incl. e-newsletters, group health insurance, professional development seminars, job expo, free/discount tickets, talent bank, and networking events. **Consideration.** Fees: $115 (initial), $65/yr (renewal).

Theater Instituut Nederland (TIN)

Box 19304, Amsterdam, 1000GH Netherlands
Henk Scholten, Dir.
info@tin.nl; www.tin.nl

Est. 1992. Houses a museum and library, collects current info and documentation and organizes events such as discussions, conferences, workshops, exhibitions and international presentations. It also publishes books, CDs and other materials and participates in various international networks.

$65/yr. Theatre Bay Area (TBA)
870 Market St., #375, San Francisco, CA, 94102
Brad Erickson, Exec Dir
Tel: 415-430-1140, Fax: 415-430-1145
tba@theatrebayarea.org; www.theatrebayarea.org

Nonprofit of Bay Area individuals and theater companies. Services incl. monthly Theatre Bay Area magazine with listing of writer opportunities, grants of $1,500-$5,000 for artists and $10,000 new works fund. Other publications incl. regional theater directory. **Consideration.** Fees: $65/yr, $55/yr (student). **Preference.** Author Must Be: resident of Bay Area. **Application.** Best Material: application.

$39.95/yr. Theatre Communications Group (TCG)
520 8th Ave., Fl. 24, New York, NY, 10018
Teresa Eyring, Exec Dir
Tel: 212-609-5900, Fax: 212-609-5901
tcg@tcg.org; www.tcg.org

National service org for nonprofit US professional theater. Services incl. grants, fellowships and awards to artists and institutions; workshops, roundtables and conferences; advocacy; surveys, research and publications, incl. reference, plays and periodicals; US Center for Intl. Theatre Institue. Membership incl. American Theatre magazine subscription, ticket discounts nationwide, savings on TCG resource materials and book discounts from TCG and other select publishers. **Consideration.** Fees: $39.95/yr, $20/yr (student). **Application.** Best Way: online.

$25/yr. Theatre Development Fund (TDF)
1501 Broadway, Fl. 21, New York, NY, 10036
Tel: 212-221-0885, Fax: 212-768-1563
www.tdf.org/application

Est. 1968. Dedicated to the advancement of profit and nonprofit drama, music and dance productions in NYC. Programs incl. TKTS discount booths, TDF membership, Theater Access Project (TAP), Costume Collection. **Consideration.** Fees: $25/yr. **Application.** Best Way: online. Best Material: application.

$75/yr. Theatre for Young Audiences/ USA
1602 Belle View Blvd., #810, Alexandria, VA, 22307
Tel: 703-403-5820
info@assitej-usa.org; www.assitej-usa.org

National service org promoting professional TYA across cultural and international boundaries. Services incl semiannual journal and frequent bulletins, member directories. **Consideration.** Fees: $75/yr, $40/yr (retiree), $35/yr (student). **Preference.** Subject: TYA. **Application.** Best Material: application.

Theatre Project
45 W. Preston St., Baltimore, MD, 21201
Anne Cantler Fulwiler, Producing Dir.
Tel: 410-539-3091
office@theatreproject.org; www.theatreproject.org

Est. 1971. Introduces Baltimore to those experimenting with new forms, incl. both globally recognized and emerging local artists. **Consideration.** Remuneration: box office percentage. **Preference.** Length: mid-length (60-90 min). Style: avant garde. Production: small cast, unit set. Material Must Be: original. **Application.** Best Way: professional recommendation. Best Material: synopsis, video, SASE. Response: 2 mos.

$50/mo. Theatre West
3333 Cahuenga Blvd. W., Hollywood, CA, 90068
John Gallogly, Exec Dir.
Tel: 323-851-4839, Fax: 323-851-5286
theatrewest@theatrewest.org; www.theatrewest.org

Est. 1962. Member org. Mandatory 6 hrs/mo volunterring in 1st year of membership. **Consideration.** Fees: $100 application (if accepted), $50/mo. Remuneration: reading. **Preference.** Length: full length (over 90 min). Author Must Be: resident of S Calif.. **Application.** Best Material: full script.

$50/yr. TRU (Theater Resources Unlimited)
309 W. 104th St., #1-D, New York, NY, 10025
Bob Ost, President
Tel: 212-714-7628, Fax: 212-864-6301
trunltd@aol.com; www.truonline.org

Est. 1992. Suport and educational services for producers, theater companies, and self-producing artists, emphasizing the business side of the arts. **Consideration.** Fees: $50/yr (individual).

$45.00 . United States Copyright Office
Library of Congress, 101 Independence Ave., SE, Washington, DC, 20559
Tel: 202-707-3000
www.copyright.gov

Though registration isn't required for protection, copyright law provides several advantages to registration. **Consideration.** Fees: $45 (basic claim). **Application.** Best Material: application, full script (2 copies), audio (2 copies).

VUA Theatre Collections Reading Room
23 Blythe Road, Blythe House, London, W14 OQX England
Tel: 44-207-471-2697, Fax: 44-207-471-9864
www.vam.ac.uk/tco

$25/yr. Women's Theatre Alliance (WTA)
2936 N. Southport Ave., Chicago, IL, 60657
Katie Carey Govier, President
womenstheatre@lycos.com; www.wtachicago.org

Est. 1992. **Consideration.** Fees: $25/yr (Jan-Dec).

Write LA
11240 Magnolia Blvd., N. Hollywood, CA, 91601
Kaz Matamura, Artistic Director
writela@yahoo.com; www.writela.com

est. 2006. Write LA offers various services to writers including Writers Lounge.

$90/yr. Writers' Guild of Great Britain
15 Britannia St., London, WC1X 9JN England
Anne Hogben, Asst. General Secy.
Tel: 44-20-7833-0777, Fax: 44-20-7833-4777
anne@writersguild.org.uk; www.writersguild.org.uk

TUC-affiliated union for professional writers living or working in UK. **Consideration.** Fees: 90yr (candidate), 150/yr (full).

Writers Guild of America, West (WGAW)
7000 W. 3rd St., Los Angeles, CA, 90048
Corinne Tippin, Membership Admin.
Tel: 323-782-4532
www.wga.org

Writers Lounge
Write LA, 11240 Magnolia Blvd. # 204, N. Hollywood, CA, 91601
Kaz Matamura, Artistic Director
writela@yahoo.com; writela.com

est. 2006. Writers Lounge is an exclusive membership lounge.

$400/6 mos. Writers Room

740 Broadway, Fl. 12, New York, NY, 10003
Donna Brodie, Exec Dir
Tel: 212-254-6995
writersroom@writersroom.org; www.writersroom.org

Est. 1978. Large loft with 44 work stations, library, storage area, kitchen/lounge and phone room. Open 24/7. 1-yr wait list for full-time membership; no wait list for part-time. **Consideration.** Fees: $75 application, $400/6 mos. (6pm-6am), $500/6 mos. (6pm-11:30am), $600/6 mos. (24 hrs). Remuneration: reading. **Application.** Best Material: application. Response: 1 mo.

Young Playwrights Inc. (YPI)

Box 5134, New York, NY, 10185
Sheri Goldhirsch, Artistic Dir.
Tel: 212-594-5440, Fax: 212-684-4902
admin@youngplaywrights.org; www.youngplaywrights.org

Est. 1981 by Stephen Sondheim and Dramatists Guild members, YPI identifies and develops young US playwrights by involving them as active participants in the highest quality professional productions of their plays. **Preference.** Style: comedy, drama. Author Must Be: age 18 or younger. Material Must Be: original. **Application.** Best Way: Check Website for details. Best Material: submissions not returned.

MEMBERSHIP & SERVICE ORGANIZATIONS (Fee Charged)

$50 1/14/2008. PEN Translation Prize
588 Broadway, #303, New York, NY, 10012
Andrew Proctor, Membership Dir.
www.pen.org

Est. 1921. Submission fees can be downloaded from www.pen.org. A $50 submission fee is required to each entry. Fees will be waived for publishers whose annual net sales do not exceed 4 million dollars. **Preference.** Material Must Be: produced or published. **Application.** Best Way: online. Best Material: application, submissions not returned. Response: 2 mos.

CALENDAR AND INDEX

SUBMISSION CALENDAR

These opportunities accept submissions year-round. Consult the company website for the most up to date information. Also, consult the Dramatists Guild website for new opportunities, changes in rules and deadlines, and for on going opportunities not listed in this year's directory.

14-Feb-08	Penobscot Theatre	53
15-Feb-08	Djerassi Resident Artists Program	39
15-Feb-08	Francesca Primus Prize	76
15-Feb-08	Jane Chambers Playwriting Award	77
15-Feb-08	Jane Chambers Student Playwriting Award	77
15-Feb-08	Marin Arts Council Fund for Artistis, Career Dev. Grants	87
15-Feb-08	North Dakota Council on the Arts	90
15-Feb-08	Theatre Oxford 10-Minute Play Contest, Date is Postmarked by	81
15-Feb-08	Travel & Study Grant Program	92
16-Feb-08	Isle Royale National Park Artist-in-Residence	41
22-Feb-08	Artist Trust	83
28-Feb-08	Marilyn Hall Awards	66
28-Feb-08	McLaren Memorial Comedy Playwriting Competition	78
1-Mar-08	Alabama State Council on the Arts	82
1-Mar-08	Alaska State Council on the Arts (ASCA)	82
1-Mar-08	Arthur W. Stone New Play Award	61
1-Mar-08	Centre Stage South Carolina New Play Festival	48
1-Mar-08	Kimmel Harding Nelson (KHN) Center for the Arts	41
1-Mar-08	Kitchen Dog Theater (KDT) New Works Festival	51
1-Mar-08	ReOrient	54
1-Mar-08	South Dakota Arts Council	92
1-Mar-08	Stage Left Theatre Company (Jun-Sep)	193
1-Mar-08	Ucross Foundation Residency Program (fall)	44
1-Mar-08	William Flanagan Memorial Creative Persons Center	170
3-Mar-08	Anna Zornio Memorial Children's Theatre Playwriting Award	61
3-Mar-08	Byrdcliffe Arts Colony Artist-in-Residence (AIR)	39
3-Mar-08	Louisiana Division of the Arts	87
14-Mar-08	Meet the Composer Grant Programs	88
15-Mar-08	Arts & Letters Prize in Drama	75
15-Mar-08	Backdoor Theatre New Play Project	46
15-Mar-08	Barnstormers Theatre	47
15-Mar-08	Blank Theatre Company Young Playwrights Festival	47
15-Mar-08	Colorado Council on the Arts	84
15-Mar-08	Downstage Left (DSL)	116
15-Mar-08	Hangar Theatre Lab Company Playwriting Residencies	188
15-Mar-08	Juneteenth Jamboree of New Plays	58
15-Mar-08	Lamia Ink! Intl. One-Page Play Competition	58
15-Mar-08	Plays for the 21st Century	79
15-Mar-08	Short Attention Span PlayFEST	54
31-Mar-08	Appalachian Festival of Plays and Playwrights	46
31-Mar-08	Envision Retreat	39
31-Mar-08	Fire Rose Prods. 10-Min. Play Festival	57
31-Mar-08	James D. Phelan Literary Award	65
1-Apr-08	Iowa Arts Council (Jul-Jun)	86
1-Apr-08	National Children's Theatre Festival	78
1-Apr-08	New York Mills Arts Retreat (Jul-Dec)	43
1-Apr-08	Next Act Theatre	141
1-Apr-08	Pittsburgh New Works Festival (PNWF)	59
1-Apr-08	Rhode Island State Council on the Arts (Playwrights)	91
4-Apr-08	Joining Sword and Pen	65
6-Apr-08	Nevada Arts Council	89
9-Apr-08	Urban Retreat	194
11-Apr-08	Write a Play! NYC Contest	74
13-Apr-08	New Hampshire State Council on the Arts	89
15-Apr-08	Hambidge Center	40
15-Apr-08	John Gassner Memorial Playwriting Award	77
15-Apr-08	Luna Stage	133
15-Apr-08	MacDowell Colony	42
15-Apr-08	Montana Artists Residency (American Indians)	43
15-Apr-08	New Rocky Mountain Voices	79

1-Aug-08	New Visions/New Voices (NVNV)	190
1-Aug-08	Pennsylvania Council on the Arts	90
1-Aug-08	Playfest! Harriett Lake Festival of New Plays	53
1-Aug-08	Playwrights Gallery	192
1-Aug-08	Political Theatre Festival	53
1-Aug-08	TRU Voices (Musicals)	60
1-Aug-08	Virginia Commission for the Arts	93
1-Aug-08	Yaddo	45
15-Aug-08	David C. Horn Prize	75
15-Aug-08	Delaware Division of the Arts	85
15-Aug-08	Downstage Left (DSL)	116
15-Aug-08	North Carolina New Play Project (NCNPP)	69
15-Aug-08	Stage Left Theatre Company (Oct-Jan)	193
31-Aug-08	None of the Above Playwriting Contest	68
31-Aug-08	Ten-Minute Musicals Project	72
1-Sep-08	Alaska State Council on the Arts (ASCA)	82
1-Sep-08	Connecticut Commission on Culture & Tourism	84
1-Sep-08	Festival of New Plays	49
1-Sep-08	Jewish Ensemble Theatre	129
1-Sep-08	Kimmel Harding Nelson (KHN) Center for the Arts	41
1-Sep-08	Musical Theatre Writers' Workshop	189
1-Sep-08	New Playwrights Competition	68
1-Sep-08	Ohio Arts Council	90
14-Sep-08	Jerome Playwright-in-Residence Fellowships	86
14-Sep-08	Jonathan Larson Performing Arts Foundation	86
15-Sep-08	Hambidge Center	40
15-Sep-08	John Simon Guggenheim Memorial Foundation	86
15-Sep-08	Kleban Award	87
15-Sep-08	MacDowell Colony	42
15-Sep-08	New Dramatists	249
15-Sep-08	Playwrights' Forum [MD]	251
15-Sep-08	Virginia Center for the Creative Arts (Feb-May)	44
17-Sep-08	Wisconsin Arts Board	93
20-Sep-08	Susan Smith Blackburn Prize	72
30-Sep-08	Baltimore Playwrights Festival	56
30-Sep-08	Hawthornden Castle International Retreat for Writers	40
30-Sep-08	Southern Appalachian Playwrights' Conference	54
30-Sep-08	Theatre Three [NY] One-Act Play Festival	55
1-Oct-08	Actors' Theatre [CA] Full-Length Play Contest	61
1-Oct-08	Cultural Conversations, date is postmarked by	48
1-Oct-08	Iowa Arts Council (Jan-Jun)	86
1-Oct-08	Millay Colony for the Arts	42
1-Oct-08	New Generations Program: Future Collaborations	89
1-Oct-08	New Harmony Project	190
1-Oct-08	New York Mills Arts Retreat (Jan-Jun)	43
1-Oct-08	Rhode Island State Council on the Arts (Composers)	91
1-Oct-08	South Carolina Arts Commission	91
1-Oct-08	Stages	55
1-Oct-08	U.S. Dept. of State Fulbright Program for US Students	92
1-Oct-08	Ucross Foundation Residency Program (spring)	44
1-Oct-08	Vermont Arts Council	92
3-Oct-08	Artists' Fellowships	83
5-Oct-08	American Antiquarian Society Fellowships	82
10-Oct-08	Radcliffe Institute Fellowships	91
15-Oct-08	Hedgebrook	40
15-Oct-08	National Playwrights Conference (OPC)	58
15-Oct-08	Playwrights First Award	70
15-Oct-08	ShowOff! Playwriting Festival	60
15-Oct-08	Valencia Character Company	73
24-Oct-08	City of Los Angeles (COLA) Performing Arts Fellowships (Fourth Friday)	84

31-Dec-08	Dorothy Silver Playwriting Competition	63
31-Dec-08	Genesis Festival	50
31-Dec-08	Goshen College Peace Playwriting Contest	64
31-Dec-08	Harold Morton Landon Translation Award	65
31-Dec-08	Lavender Footlights Festival	51
31-Dec-08	Little Festival of the Unexpected	51
31-Dec-08	Mickey Kaplan New American Play Prize	67
31-Dec-08	Mountain Playhouse Playwriting Contest	67
31-Dec-08	Nathan Miller History Play Contest	67
31-Dec-08	National Latino Playwriting Award	68
31-Dec-08	National Writers Association Foundation (NWAF)	249
31-Dec-08	Ohioana Career Award	69
31-Dec-08	Ohioana Citations	69
31-Dec-08	Ohioana Pegasus Award	69
31-Dec-08	Robert J. Pickering Award for Playwriting Excellence	71
31-Dec-08	Seven Devils Playwrights Conference	59

INDEX